Margaret Allen

THE MONEY BOOK
Your Money and Your Life

revised edition

Pan Books London and Sydney

First published 1977 by Sidgwick and Jackson Ltd
First Pan Books edition published 1978
Revised 1982
This revised edition published 1985 by Pan Books Ltd,
Cavaye Place, London SW10 9PG
© Margaret Allen 1977, 1978, 1982, 1985
ISBN 0 330 28937 3
Photoset by Parker Typesetting Service, Leicester
Printed and bound in Great Britain by
Richard Clay (The Chaucer Press) Ltd, Bungay, Suffolk

Acknowledgements

I would not have been able to write this book without the cooperation of many of my friends and my family. The contribution of my researchers, Gillian Seeley and my daughter, Jacki Davis, was vital. Gillian happily took on all the chores of the usual work, checking and rechecking without complaint and I am very indebted to her. My secretary, Jacqueline Neighbour, proved of invaluable comfort when the task seemed impossible and without her assistance and that of Juliet Walker and Susan Whippey, the manuscript would never have been completed in a form acceptable to the printer. They not only typed out the manuscript but read it carefully and came up with many queries and suggestions which were most helpful.

In a book like this there are many sources and a great number of organizations and people have given their help unstintingly. Here, alphabetically, are some of the organizations without whose assistance I could not have finished the book:

Automobile Association; Australian High Commission; Authorised Home Improvement Centres; Avis; Barclays Bank; British Insurance Association; British United Provident Association; Building Societies Association; Central Office of Information; Commercial Union; Customs and Excise Department; *Daily Mirror*; *Daily Telegraph*; *The Director*; Department of Education; Department of the Environment; Department of Health and Social Security; Department of Inland Revenue; Department for National Savings; Electrical Association for Women; Electricity Council; Equal Opportunities Commission; Extel; Finance Houses Association; *Financial Times*; *The Grocer*; Hatton Garden Gem and Precious Metal Company; HMSO; Ladbrokes; Law Society; Life Offices Association; Littlewoods Pools; Lloyds Bank; Lloyds Insurance Brokers Association; London Assay Office; London Graduate School of Business Studies; Manchester Business School; Martins Bank; *Mother* magazine; Mothercare; National Association of Funeral Directors; National Westminster Bank; Nationwide Building Society; Office of Fair Trading; Phillips Auctioneers; The Post Office; Office of Population Census and Surveys; Quotel; Royal Institution of Chartered Surveyors; St Christopher's Motorists Security Association; Stock Exchange; *The Sun*; *Sunday Telegraph*; The Trustee Savings Bank; *Which?* magazine; Wine Development Board.

I am particularly grateful to Danny O'Shea of M and G Unit Trusts for his invaluable help in the section on the Stock Exchange, and to Dryden Gilling-Smith, an expert on pensions, for his assistance in that area. William Halden of the Automobile Association was equally generous in his

5

help in the motoring field, as was John Gaselee in insurance, Ronald Irving and Marcel Berlins on the law, and Bevis Hillier on the antiques world. Without their help I could not have finished the book. Among newspapers who were generous in allowing me to quote them, I must especially thank *The Times* and the *Financial Times*. *The Times* Business News library found anything I wanted in the financial area in seconds, and Jack Lonsdale, head of the Intelligence department, helped me considerably in the more general areas. Michael Cudlipp very kindly read the manuscript for me, pointing out areas which might not have been absolutely clear to anyone not familiar with the financial world.

To all of them, many thanks.

Margaret Allen 1985

Contents

8

Two: Your money and your job

Three: Family finance

Five: Investing

Author's note

I have written this book to help ordinary people with a wide variety of their everyday financial problems. It is not designed as a technical manual for those in the financial world, but for individuals and families who may have little experience of how our lives can be affected by various financial rules and regulations, and how we can best use them to our advantage. But this is a book, not an encyclopaedia. There may be specific areas which it does not cover, but I hope that the general information given will point readers in the right direction in the solving of any of their financial problems.

One warning: money, and the rules surrounding it, are everchanging. Interest rates change from week to week, sometimes even from day to day. Banks change their rules regarding their account holders. New financial services may be launched, others abandoned; certain tax levels may change without requiring a Budget; building societies, finance houses and insurance companies alter the rates and conditions of both borrowing and lending; credit controls may be varied by the government and its payments under the social security system can change. Bear this in mind when you read this book; *you must be careful to check exact current conditions before you take any action.*

The book takes in all the facts and figures which applied to the best of my knowledge either at the end of 1984, where appropriate, or incorporating the proposals contained in the 19 March 1985 Budget, but not the Finance Act 1985.

Preface to the 1985 edition

There have been remarkable changes in the financial world since the last edition of *The Money Book* in 1982. Most outstanding in the overall picture has been the fall in the rate of inflation, which by the end of 1984 was around 5 per cent, the lowest level for some years. There was a price to pay for that fall, however: the number of unemployed continued to rise and by the end of 1984 was showing no signs of falling significantly, if at all. As a result, preoccupation with rising prices gave way for many people to a deep concern about the long-term future of their trade or profession, and for the financial stability of their families.

There was a sharp change, too, in the government's financial policy. Public spending cuts were the priority, and for the individual this was to mean simpler and lower taxes. There was more success with the former than the latter. MIRAS (mortgage interest relief at source) shifted the burden of allowing the individual tax relief on his mortgage from the Inland Revenue to the building society for all those whose mortgages were less than £30,000. The burden on the Inland Revenue was further reduced by the new policy of 'fiscal neutrality', part of the aim of which was to give no form of saving an unfair advantage over another. From 6 April 1985, all forms of saving, apart from National Savings – fiscal neutrality did not extend that far – have been taxed on a tax-paid basis, which previously applied only to building societies. Where such a system applies, the financial institution does the tax gathering, not the tax inspector, and there is no right to reclaim the tax paid for non-tax payers.

This move has meant that National Savings have taken on a new and attractive significance for savers, particularly those on low incomes. Furthermore, a variety of new schemes have been introduced to attract savers away from private savings media. They, in turn, have also offered new schemes, and the whole savings market has become increasingly competitive, offering some of the highest real rates of interest for some years. The new opportunities also carry with them, of course, new possibilities for making the wrong decisions.

Tax levels were raised, however, when the tax relief on life assurance premiums, which for some years had been held at 15 per cent, was removed completely and without warning in the 1984 Budget. Among indirect taxes, value added tax (VAT) had stayed at 15 per cent, but other indirect taxes have been raised. And, allowing for inflation, the cuts in direct taxes have been more apparent than real.

In the personal financial world, competition has not been confined to savings. The building societies and the National Giro began to provide real

15

competition with the clearing banks by offering new facilities with their interest-bearing accounts which made them, for many people, at least as attractive as current accounts at the banks. In turn, the banks attacked the home mortgage market, claiming at times to have as much as 30 per cent of new business. The building societies responded with new and imaginative home loans schemes, including, for the first time, index-linked mortgages.

And, even though inflation has fallen, some prices have risen rather more than average. In particular, the insurance industry, where charges are based on risk, saw some major increases. The rising level of burglaries in the inner-city areas brought a doubling of the cost of some home insurance contents policies. In contrast, some people in rural areas found themselves paying a little less, allowing for inflation.

Car insurance, too, became more costly for most drivers. But again, not all. Companies at long last recognized that, even if women are not better drivers than men, they are certainly a better insurance risk. They have been courted accordingly with lower premiums, in cases where they agree not to let men drive their cars. In life assurance, it was officially recognized that smoking is a health hazard and causes premature death: by 1985 some companies were offering big discounts on life assurance premiums to non smokers.

If prices have stopped rising as sharply as in the late 1970s and early 1980s, so have the various social security benefits, including pensions. The poor, the unemployed and pensioners have barely, if at all, kept pace with inflation – a trend which in the light of the government's intentions seems likely to continue.

On balance, then, in the past three years, the standard of living of those in employment has improved, but that of the rest has worsened. The government has by no means completed its fiscal revolution. If nothing else, changes seem likely which will reduce the old-age pension to a very basic level and compel people to make most of their financial provision for their later years themselves. I hope that this new edition of *The Money Book* will help them move in the right directions towards that end and enable them to make the most of their money during their working lives.

April 1985

Preface to the 1982 edition

The world of money is fluid and complex. Governments come and go and policies towards all aspects of money change with them. In the five years since this book was first published, in 1977, there have been some remarkable changes in both our economic life and financial security. There are three million unemployed living on the barest minimum. For those of us in work, our rates of pay have never been higher, but our living standards have – because high rates of inflation have eroded the value of our money.

In our homes and personal lives, the price of everything has risen sharply. It costs more than twice as much to get married today as it did in 1977. Our children have become much more expensive to rear and educate. A typical 'shopping basket' each week now costs almost three times as much as it did in 1977. Our fuel bills have soared, as have our travel costs; petrol is twice as expensive as five years ago and train and normal air travel are far more costly. The prices of all our entertainments, including tobacco and drink, are sharply higher. Mortgage interest rates rose during the five-year period to their highest point ever, as did all interest rates; only in the past few months have they begun to come down.

Indirect taxes have risen and the cuts in income tax are more apparent than real, because of inflation. Social security benefits including pensions have increased, but not always enough to cover the fall in the value of money. The long-established 'Bank Rate' which was set each week by the Treasury and the Bank of England has gone and the clearing banks set their own minimum lending rates. Index-linked saving certificates are available to all of us and so are gilt-edged index-linked stock. The banks have come into the home mortgage market in a big way, claiming to get as much as thirty per cent of new business. More help has been given to the self-employed to build up their pensions where they are outside the social security system.

The government has brought in better home-improvement grants, allowed council tenants to buy their homes at a discount on the market price, if they wish, offered financial assistance with removal expenses to people who have had to move away to new areas to find jobs during the recession. It has raised the starting point for stamp duty on house purchases, swept away exchange control, allowed us to bring more duty-free goods into the country and improved the tax terms on 'golden handshakes'. In the private sector, the banks are considering paying interest on current accounts and reopening on Saturdays to meet the competition offered by the new facilities in the building societies.

Nevertheless, in the past five years some things have not changed at all. The cost of insurance or assurance per £100 has remained about the same, though benefits and claims are of course worth less because of the fall in the value of the pound sterling. The top level for mortgage relief has remained at £25,000 and the rules about when it is allowed are unchanged.

Just a few things have actually got cheaper, particularly when allowing for inflation. Long-distance coach fares have actually fallen in price in some cases, as have air fares on which special conditions or restrictions apply. This has meant a fall in real terms at least in the price of package holidays abroad, but this is also partly a reflection of the recession which has faced us in the past few years. With 3,000,000 unemployed, package holidays abroad come well down the list of priorities, if they appear at all, with the result that prices have become keener as competition has increased. The recession has had other effects: one is the decline in the cost of credit and hire purchase. In some cases, it may even be free, as retailers scramble for the available business.

For the most part, however, the financial story of the past five years is one of increasing stringency and hardship – all the more reason than ever before to plan carefully and make the most of all our resources to cope with the difficult economic climate of the 1980s.

Introduction

This book is all about money and how you can make the most of it. Whether you are rich or poor, the chances are that you do not manage your money efficiently. Perhaps you are afraid of the whole subject of money. Throughout history it has been praised and castigated; it has been alleged to be the root of all evil; it has been said to make the world go round; it has been described as like muck, not good unless it is spread.

Money is probably all these things, but if you are to benefit from this book, remember Dr Johnson's maxim, 'There are few ways in which a man can be more innocently employed than in getting money.' You may then actually begin to enjoy taking proper care of your money.

It is all very well to say that, but in a time of inflation money can be a source of constant worry. The rate of inflation has fallen during the past five years, but it remains an ever-present threat to many of us – and although it is lower, it has not gone away altogether.

Very often, government has little control over the way prices move. As a result, many of us have been asking ourselves at least some of the following sorts of questions: Will my salary go round? Will I be able to cope with the next increase in the mortgage rate? Will I be able to live on my pension? Will the telephone have to go? Have I seen the last of steak? Where will the money for my next, even more expensive, season ticket come from? Will I still be able to use my central heating now that gas and electricity prices have gone up again? Can I still afford to educate my children privately? Are my annual holidays a thing of the past? How much will the wedding cost?

Problems like these used to be solved fairly quickly – by getting a rise in salary in one's existing job, by getting promotion and thus a higher salary, or by getting a new job that offers more money. Most of us used to be able to count on at least one of these things happening, so that we were able to maintain our standard of living. This is no longer true. Britain's poor economic performance in comparison with that of other industrialized countries since the end of the 1939–45 war has put paid to all that. Wages and salary increases have not kept pace with inflation; unemployment is high; industry has not been able to develop new opportunities.

Inflation is a financial word for something we all know a great deal about today; it is the term used to describe the rate of the annual fall in the value of money. It is happening all over the world, but here in Britain we have, until quite recently, been suffering it to a greater extent than many other countries.

This is what happens. If the rate of inflation is 10 per cent a year, every £1 sterling at the end of the year will only buy nine tenths of the goods it would have bought at the beginning of the year. If your wages do not keep up with the rate of inflation, your standard of living falls by the amount of the difference. When this happens we must use our available money more efficiently to maintain our standards.

There is nothing new about inflation. It is part of the history of mankind. Ever since commercial activity began – and that goes way back beyond the Greeks and Romans – prices have been rising. But they have risen at different rates from time to time and from country to country. Today, after a period of high inflation, the rate has fallen, but at a price: the number of people registered as unemployed has risen sharply. The official figures may disguise the severity of unemployment, as many people seeking work are thought not to register as unemployed, because they are ineligible for benefits. This chart shows you what has happened to the value of the pound since the end of the First World War.

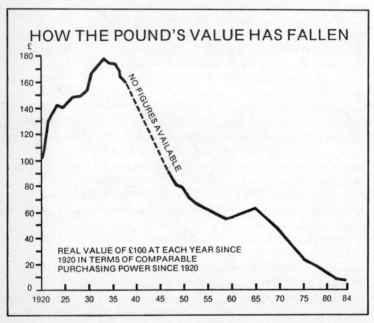

HOW THE POUND'S VALUE HAS FALLEN

REAL VALUE OF £100 AT EACH YEAR SINCE 1920 IN TERMS OF COMPARABLE PURCHASING POWER SINCE 1920

NO FIGURES AVAILABLE

As you can see, the pound today is worth little more than 8p compared with 1920. This means that you need around £12 today to buy what £1 would have bought then. Or put it another way, if you were giving your then seven-year-old daughter £1 a week spending money in 1975, she would need over £2 a week to buy the same amount now.

One thing we must all realize is that there is no way of escaping inflation. No amount of adjusting and adapting of your life style will provide you with enough cuts and savings to match completely the extra money you will have to pay for the goods and services you use. But by thinking about your spending and your saving and changing your financial habits, you can minimize the effects of rising prices and husband your resources in such a way that you can cope without too much strain – and when times get better you will reap the benefits.

Sensible money management can bring savings to everyone, regardless of his income. Money may seem boring when you do not have enough of it, but if you use it like you use any other product, to give you the best possible value you will be able to go through life with money in its right place, and not a dominant worrying factor which can ruin your enjoyment of life.

The first thing to do is work out precisely where your money goes. This in itself can be highly revealing. Maybe your car is too big (and expensive) for your needs; perhaps the children have grown up and you could move to a smaller house to cut costs; perhaps you leave too much in your current account at the bank when it could be put somewhere else to earn interest; or perhaps you are paying too much overdraft interest in order to keep some money on deposit at the bank or post office; perhaps you are over- (or under-) insured. These are just a few of the hundreds of instances of financial mismanagement which can come to light if you just sit down and set out your outgoings.

You must also look at what you really earn. If you are in full-time employment the chances are that you will be paying some tax. Once your tax allowances have been set against your income the government will take away almost a third of the remainder. With sound money management you can at least make sure they don't take more than they are entitled to, and that you are claiming all the allowances you are eligible for.

Always think in terms of your *net* income, not your *gross*. It's no use thinking you are doing well because you earn £10,000 a year or £200 a week gross; that figure is before any deductions. As well as tax, you will have to pay national insurance contributions, and your firm may well take 5 or 7½ per cent in pension contributions – which provide income, it is true, but not until you retire.

This book, then, is a practical guide on how to manage your money; it is not an economic treatise. I do not have any complete solutions to offer to the problems of inflation. This book is designed to help you make the best of your economic and financial situation as it is.

Section one
Basic money management

1 Your personal budget

Why, you may well ask yourself, should you bother to budget? You may feel that you simply don't have enough money, that you scrape by from day to day, and that there is nothing that can be done about it. You may feel that you can leave all that sort of thing to your husband, wife or parents. Or you may, of course, be so rich that you do not need to budget at all. In that case this section is not for you, and you can pass on to Section five, on personal investment, to make sure you stay rich.

A personal budget is important for everyone, and no matter how little money you have it is highly likely that you could use it more efficiently. This is most important for the average family with young children. It doesn't take much experience of life to know that quarrels about money are one of the most upsetting things in married life, and not infrequently a cause of divorce.

The 'average man'

The first step in budgeting is to see how near you are to the national average. Even if your income level is exactly on the average, your own pattern of spending will be quite unique and will depend on your and your family's individual aims and priorities. Only you can answer certain questions about your spending. Do you want to own your home? Do you want a colour television set, a car, or wine with your meals, rather than savings in the bank? If you have spare money, would you prefer it to go on your child's education, on 'educating' them through foreign travel, or on extra-curricular activities like music or sport? These may be substantial items requiring once-and-for-all decisions, but hardly a day goes by when the average family does not have to choose some financial alternative rather than another.

Your budget will change with the composition of your family. Housing

22

costs may rise as a couple has children, then decrease again as the children grow up and leave home, and the mortgage, if there is one, is paid off. Holiday and entertainment costs usually seem to take a very large proportion of the family budget where there are no children, or they have grown up, in comparison with the family with small children, where food and clothes tend to predominate.

In short, there is no one 'budget'. The first rule is to make your budget fit your own requirements. Keeping up with the Joneses is a money-wasting activity; it may not even make you happy.

Even so, a look at the 'average' can be illuminating as regards your own spending.

If you notice that in any one area your spending is way out of line with the average, you would be wise to consider what adjustments you can make. If, for example, you spend a third of your net income on a mortgage or rent, you are probably spending too much. As the table below shows, the 'average' spending on housing is not more than 16 per cent, whatever the income level – though a young couple may prefer to pay rather more on a mortgage at the beginning of their life together. Later on, as their income rises, this proportion goes down, and of course, if they are buying a house on a mortgage, eventually disappears from the budget altogether.

How people spend their money

	low income	middle income	high income
housing	16%	13%	13%
fuel and light	11	8	6
food	35	29	22
alcohol	3	5	6
clothing and footwear	6	8	8
tobacco	4	4	3
consumer durables	3	5	7
transport	6	12	16
miscellaneous	15	17	20

These figures are adapted from the cash spending figures given in the government's annual *Social Trends* for all households. Twenty families in every hundred come into the low income level, twenty into the high, and the rest in the middle. The figures show what percentage of available money goes on various items of spending. Though they are averages, and few people will fit the average exactly, they show quite clearly that the poorer the family the more of its income goes on the basics of food and housing; the better-off the family, the more there is available for non-essentials like consumer durables, entertainment and other services.

What you should aim for is a budget which suits your purposes and income level, and at the same time is flexible enough to meet any changes in your requirements.

Income and outgoings

If you can make your income cover your basic outgoings and have something left over to give you a choice in the rest of your spending and, better still, something to put aside for savings, you are naturally a good manager of money. But most of us are not, and we need to plan carefully to make our money go round. Only young people who have not yet committed their money in definite directions can operate satisfactorily on a simple cash basis.

Many people find it rather horrifying to think of running their own budget like a company or a country in miniature. You should get over such reservations. It may be a bore, but you will certainly find it worthwhile when you see all the trouble it prevents.

Ask yourself these questions:

1 Do you know where your money will be coming from in the next few months, or possibly years?
2 Can you calculate exactly your fixed outgoings?
3 Do you know what you have left over for everyday spending?
4 Do you know what is left after that for luxuries?
5 Have you a realistic idea of what will be left at the end of all this for savings?
6 Can you fit today's spending into the long-term pattern of your spending so that you can achieve financial peace of mind and avoid staggering from one month to the next?

If you can answer yes to all these questions you are very unusual. Most people are hazy in some areas at least. The best way to start to achieve a financial balance is to start on the assumption that you will never have enough money to cater for all your needs and wants. If you get more money, you are likely to raise the level of your expectations – a bigger car or house, for example. Accept that you will probably always have to sort out your priorities and forego some things to get others.

As you go along, always follow three rules, whatever other ones you may make yourself:

1 If you are married, work on a joint budget. You are doomed from the start if you can't agree as a couple on your priorities.
2 Be flexible and always give yourself a personal allowance. You will run into deep trouble, particularly if there are two of you, if you have to account for every minor item of spending.
3 You must keep records. These need not be complicated – in fact, they

should not be complicated. You are the master, not your records. They are there simply to show you how your spending is going and to warn you if spending in any area is getting out of hand. They are to help you, not to put you in a straitjacket.

There are three steps you must now take to ensure that you can answer yes to all these questions I put above. You must:
First: work out exactly how much money you have coming in.
Second: provide for your fixed expenses.
Third: decide your priorities in everyday spending.

First: assess your income

Before you can start managing your money properly, you must first find out how much you have. Draw up a simple chart to show just what you can expect to have coming in during the year. Include everything you can call family income: your basic salary; your husband or wife's; your children's as far as it contributes to the family income; any interest from savings or dividends from investments; any rent from property you own; any cash presents you may expect; any bonuses at work; any profit from selling your house, car or any other possessions; any rebate you may be expecting from the taxman; and anything you may get from freelance activities.

When you fill in your chart:

1 Estimate *exactly* where you can, and if you are not sure put down a *minimum*.
2 Put down *net* amounts after tax and all other payments like national insurance and pension contributions. If you put gross amounts you are only fooling yourself.
3 If you work for yourself and your income is irregular, divide it evenly between months.
4 Don't *revise* your monthly totals *up* because you expect a rise, wait till you get it. But do revise everything downwards if your income suddenly falls.
5 Only put down items that you are sure of.

This should leave you knowing precisely what spending money you will have. Gear your spending to this and not to any estimates which you cannot itemize exactly.

Second: provide for fixed expenses

Your second chart will show those items of expenditure which have to be paid for, and when you can expect to have to pay them. Although they are not fixed in the sense that you can always change your life style to make ends meet – you can sell your house, for example – they are not always avoidable at any particular point in time.

Plan as far as possible to stagger big single payments throughout the year, so that you have more or less the same outgoings each month. Your fixed outgoings will include your rent or mortgage; general and water rates, unless they are included in your rent; ground rent if you own a leasehold property; regular bills like gas, electricity, telephone, TV rental, and so on; any regular payments on hire purchase or insurance policies, holiday or Christmas clubs; once-a-year payments like house and contents insurance, car insurance and road tax; extra tax payments where you can predict them; subscriptions; any transport expenses which you can estimate, like the cost of a season ticket or petrol; any extras like personal allowances for husband and wife and children; education expenses or extra lessons for a member of the family; any medical insurance, like BUPA; any debts you may have.

This list is endless, and every family will have its own particular pattern. As you can see, though these expenses are fixed at any one time, many of them can be flexible to suit changes in circumstances. They will swallow up a large proportion of your income.

Unlike your income, which you estimate at a minimum, put your expenses at a *maximum*.

Ask yourself whether you can include savings as a fixed expense. This may seem odd, but if you can regard any money you put away for the future as a fixed outgoing, you are very sensibly leaving a margin for any unexpected expenses, as well as building up a nest-egg. I will look at the various forms of savings which may suit you in chapter 3 of this section, but it's worth emphasizing at this stage that regular payments into a savings account are relatively painless, if you treat them as a normal part of your outgoings.

Third: decide priorities in everyday spending
Balance up your income and your outgoings. What is left is for day-to-day expenses and any extra saving when you have some money to spare. Now you will know whether you can actually make ends meet. If you can't, you will have to look at the current level of your fixed expenses to see which, if any, can be reduced. If none of them can – and this would be very unusual – look to ways of increasing your income. But on the whole most people have a float, however limited, to live on after dealing with their basic expenses, even though they may have problems in some months. These can often be ironed out by having a 'budget account' at a bank, of which more in chapter 6 of this section. Nevertheless, most of us usually find we have to do some juggling to get the money to go round all the things we feel are vital to our life style. Look at some of the items you may have to cover in your day-to-day expenses, and fill in yet another chart.

1 *Food and related items:* these usually take between 20 and 35 per cent of your total income and more if you include alcohol and tobacco. They may take more than half your floating money.

2 *Household expenses:* repairs, cleaning services, domestic help. Can you afford these? Are they a priority?
3 *Furnishings and consumer durables:* you may already be buying furniture or other items on hire purchase. Have you any money left over for this sort of thing?
4 *Clothes:* a very flexible item, but don't forget to include shoes, accessories, repairs and cleaning, whatever you decide your clothing budget can be.
5 *Transport:* try to estimate your costs over and above anything you have included in your fixed expenses. Don't forget car maintenance.
6 *The hairdresser or barber:* include here anything you need for personal use and care.
7 *Entertainment:* include your holiday spending here; all your sports spending; your reading material; eating out, or your round at the pub; gifts to friends and relatives.
8 *Anything else:* we all have something.

This is the end of the beginning of personal budgeting. If you have followed the steps outlined above you will have a basis for the sensible management of your money. Before I go on to look in detail at the many aspects, here are a few tips:

- **Do** set yourself sensible spending limits. This can't be done immediately, but after a few months or a year's experience you will find it easier.
- **Don't** think you can solve all your problems by cutting down on one item too severely. Your food budget may look high, but don't imagine you can cut it by half.
- **Do** allow yourself some luxuries. If having a holiday abroad is a real need, it would be better to cut down on other forms of entertainment rather than go without it.
- **Don't** forget the unexpected expense. Everyone has these. You may have to buy a new car before you really want to. Your children may suddenly decide to get married. Try to budget for something unforeseen every year. You can always carry anything saved this way forward to the next year.

Bearing these points in mind, work out your planned spending for the year. If you look like spending more than you earn, make the cuts immediately. Don't hope for the best and carry on regardless. Keep records. Once you get used to it, you may actually enjoy it, particularly when you see the result of a nicely balanced budget – and you feel the relief when financial worries are cut down or even eliminated.

Above all when budgeting – *always minimize your income and maximize your expenses.*

2 British banking

Before we go on to look at savings bank accounts, it will help you to know broadly how the British banking system works. Then you will be able to understand just why your bank manager's professional attitude to you may change, even though your own circumstances do not deteriorate, or even improve. Remember that the local bank manager is not his own master. He is subject to the policy decisions of his own head office and also to government instructions which come to the major banks by the government's own banker, the Bank of England. (All the facilities and services offered by the banks are discussed in greater detail in chapter 6 of this section.)

The Bank of England

When the Bank of England was first formed in 1694 it was not the then government's intention to make it the core of all banking in Britain. It was set up simply to raise money to finance Britain and her friends in the Grand Alliance to wage war against France. Like so many institutions, however, it did not disappear with the end of the war, but went on to develop until in 1844 the government decreed that only the Bank of England could issue bank notes in England and Wales. The Banks of Scotland and Northern Ireland are empowered to print their own notes, but though these circulate freely in Scotland and Northern Ireland, they are not in fact legal tender. Before 1844 many banks issued notes and the situation was very confused, with no one knowing just what was 'legal tender'.

Legal tender

What, you may ask, is legal tender? Bank notes and coins currently in use are legal tender; 'legal tender' is the term used to describe the things which can be used for the legal payment of a debt. But payment even in accepted notes and coins does not always amount to legal tender, and if it doesn't the person to whom you owe the money is entitled not to accept it. Legal tender is the only thing which a creditor is required to accept in settlement of a debt. He or she need not accept a cheque, or goods in exchange, or any unusual form of payment.

As far as coins are concerned, they are only legal tender up to certain amounts: 2p or 1p coins up to a value of 20p; and 10p and 5p coins up to £5. This means, for instance, that you cannot make anyone accept £1 in 1p pieces, or £100 in 10p pieces. There have been two new coins in recent years, the 20p and the £1. Old coins, like the half-crown (12½p), are no longer legal tender, and no shopkeeper would accept them. The ½p ceased to be legal tender at the end of 1984.

When it comes to bank notes, only Bank of England notes of current issues are legal tender in England, Wales, Scotland and Northern Ireland. These are Series 'D' green £1 notes, Series 'D' blue £5 notes, Series 'D' brown £10 notes, Series 'D' beige £20 notes and the multi-coloured Series 'D' £50 notes. The Bank of England stopped issuing £1 notes at the end of 1984, but they will remain legal tender at least until the end of 1985. The notes issued by Scottish and Northern Ireland banks, which circulate freely in those areas, are *not* legal tender at all, so if you are visiting and have any left when you leave try to get them exchanged for Bank of England notes before you leave. Many traders today are happy to accept such notes however, and as a general rule, any bank anywhere in the United Kingdom will exchange them for coins or notes issed by the Bank of England. The states of Jersey and Guernsey and the Isle of Man also issue notes, and these *are* legal tender, as well as Bank of England notes, on those islands, but not outside them.

Old notes

If you come across old bank notes which are no longer legal tender, do not despair. You can always get your money back on a Bank of England note, because the Bank undertakes to honour its 'promise to pay the bearer on demand' in perpetuity.

You must apply to the head office of the Bank of England in Thread-needle Street in the City of London. If you cannot go there personally, your bank will do it for you and you will receive whatever is the face value of your notes. It is highly unlikely that you will have to pay a collection fee, unless your bank has to pay an enormous amount in postage and insurance for a large number of notes.

If you do not have a bank account, any local branch of a bank will apply to the Bank of England for you. It may ask for proof of identity to make sure you are reliable and may well charge for any expenses it incurs.

If you have very old notes, they may be worth money as collectors' pieces. I have dealt with this in Section five, chapter 8.

The bankers' bank

The Bank of England, then, is solely responsible for the issue of money, and it is accountable to the government. This means that it must constantly examine and assess the financial climate, and take action when necessary, say in the foreign exchange markets, to support sterling. It also controls the supply of credit to the other banks. It used to fix the commercial banks' rates of interest, but they now do it themselves. One exception to this came in January 1985, when the chancellor of the Exchequer suddenly imposed a minimum lending rate, but for one day only.

The Bank of England helps the government when it wants to borrow money from the public by the issue of its own stock (which I have discussed in Section five, chapter 5). It also takes care of any exchange control regulations, which dictate the movement of sterling in and out of the United Kingdom, if these are in effect at any time. There are, however, no exchange regulations at present.

The Bank of England is also the bankers' bank, that is, the bank for the other banks, and it can, for example, insist that they leave money with it – in what are called special deposits. In this way the money the banks have to play with when they are going about their day-to-day business is controlled by the Bank of England, and through the Bank by the Treasury and, of course, in the end by the government of the day.

The clearing banks

As far as most people are concerned the Bank of England has little direct influence in their daily lives, as it operates from behind the scenes. It is the clearing banks which look after most of the sixty in every hundred of us who have bank accounts. There are eight commercial clearing banks in England and Wales. In order of size in terms of branches at the end of 1984, they were National Westminster, with 3,200, Barclays (2,900), Midland (2,312) and Lloyds (2,176). These are known as the 'big four'. Williams and Glyn's, with 334 branches, and Coutts (14), a subsidiary of National Westminster, are the other two long-established clearing banks. These six were joined by the Central Trustee Savings Bank in 1975. Previously, in February 1974, the existing members of the London Clearing Houses Association had agreed that the Cooperative Bank should have direct access to its clearing services, and in April of that year they offered these clearing agency facilities to other non-clearing institutions. This means that many more people have access to clearing than ever before.

Scotland has its own system. The Bank of Scotland, the Clydesdale Bank and the Royal Bank of Scotland, with their subsidiaries, are the clearing banks. There are some differences in day-to-day practice, but on the whole their services are similar to those offered by English banks, and Scottish banks, just like the English banks, are subject to the Bank of England.

Today, the clearing banks are usually free to fix the minimum rate of interest at which they are prepared to allow customers to borrow and what they will pay to depositors. The rate can change from week to week and sometimes even from day to day. Every bank branch has a notice telling customers what the day's base rate is and also what it is paying out on deposits. It will not always give a loan rate, because that is much more varied. Industrial borrowers pay one rate, there is another one for personal loans, and overdraft interest rates depend on how the bank manager personally assesses your status as a borrower.

Normal banking hours are 9.30 a.m. to 3.30 p.m., Monday to Friday, but Barclays restarted Saturday morning opening at some of its branches in August 1982. The hours are 9.30 a.m. until 12 noon. The other banks did not follow immediately, but by early 1985 most had some branches open, though these were not always offering a full banking service. The Trustee Savings Bank, however, does offer a full service on Saturdays, though it does not open all its branches.

What does the bank do with money it holds?

1 It keeps some cash to meet any demands customers withdrawing money may make.
2 It invests some of its assets, mainly in government stocks.
3 It holds some assets in reserve, usually in Treasury bills.
4 The rest – usually about two-thirds – is available to its customers in the form of loans, overdraft facilities and so on.

Discount houses

The Bank of England and the clearing banks are nothing like the full picture of banking in Britain, but outside the government banking area (see below) they are the parts which most affect our day-to-day lives. There are other institutions in the City of London which exist to aid business. They are just as subject to rules and regulations as the clearing banks. The discount houses, for example, are concerned with the borrowing and investing of short-term money. Ten of them make up the London Discount Market Association. All are public companies with shareholders. They do their business mainly by phone and load mainly in Treasury bills, short-dated government stocks, and local authority loans. By buying and selling these, discount houses can have a considerable influence on the level of interest rates over the short term.

The merchant banks

The business of merchant banks is quite different from that of the clearing banks. They are mainly concerned in financing international trade. They accept bills of exchange to finance the trade of others, and as a result are also called 'accepting houses'. The sixteen members of the Accepting Houses Committee are the only true merchant banks, though in recent years other financial companies have chosen to give themselves the name. All seventeen members are in the City of London, but some have opened regional branches. Some of them have a few current account customers. Today they have expanded into many fields and you are likely to come across one eventually, if you set up a business. They will arrange loans for your company's development (corporate finance), manage your investments, deal with your foreign exchange transactions and gold dealing, and give general financial advice. They are now also involved in hire purchase, equipment leasing, factoring (see Section two, chapter 8), insurance, insurance broking, property development and shipping. They play a vital part in Britain's business life and international trade.

Foreign banks

Hundreds of foreign banks now have branches in the United Kingdom, mainly in London but also outside. Some banks operate through subsidiaries, which means that the bank is registered as a British company, but that it is owned by foreigners. Others simply set up a branch. Some operate as ordinary banks, but others are basically here for business contacts. The Bank of England issues a list of foreign banks from time to time, and they can be useful to you if you are thinking of exporting to their home country, or looking for a foreign partner in your business.

Finance houses

These were originally set up so that people could buy railway wagons on hire purchase. But that was many years ago, and now they will finance the purchase of a great variety of goods and services. I have described the services they offer in detail in chapter 4 of this section. They are subject to government controls similar to those for the clearing banks. Most of the money they have available to borrow comes from the banks and other financial institutions. They do take deposits from the public, but this is only a small part of the total money they have available to lend.

Fringe banks

There is no exact definition of a bank in the United Kingdom. Because of this, all sorts of companies have been able to call themselves banks or banking corporations when they haven't really been banks at all. Many of these companies have been honest, but there have been a few sharks, and although strict rules are applied before these companies are allowed to set up, a few slip through the net nevertheless. The actual use of the name 'Bank' is strictly controlled today, and it is unlikely that any company would be permitted to call itself anything as wide as the European Bank or the British Bank, for instance, but names can and have been found which do not infringe the rules, but impress the potential customer.

Before you invest money with a deposit-paying institution, check its credentials with one of the 'big four'. Many of the 'fringe banks', as they are called, offer very tempting interest rates to depositors, but remember – *the higher the rate of interest to depositors the greater the risk of loss*, because the company may be lending at very high rates to unreliable borrowers. Many people have had their fingers burned this way, and some have even lost all their savings. The rules have been tightened up now, and there are few, if any, unreliable institutions. It is, however, still advisable to check on the company before depositing your money. No interest rate is attractive if you lose all your money.

The government sector

The private sector of banking is supplemented by the National Savings Bank and the National Giro. The National Savings Bank was established in 1861, when a lot of private banks were going bankrupt and its absolute safety was most attractive to depositors. Today it has 21 million active accounts and 20,000 outlets in post offices throughout the country. It is strictly a deposit bank, offering no other services. The National Giro, which was designed to transmit money through the postal system and to provide a cash back-up through the post offices, was formed in 1968. In 1975 its structure was reorganized by legislation and in future it may well become a real competitor to the clearing banks, offering overdraft facilities and credit cards. It already has a cheque guarantee card. At present it offers personal loans, arranged through a finance company. But these are not the same as bank overdrafts. Other services include traveller's cheques and foreign currency, budget accounts and accounts tailored for small businessmen.

The Trustee Savings Banks

These are old-established banking institutions, which have always catered for the less well off. At the end of 1984, the 16 regional Trustee Savings Banks, which all operate autonomously, had more than 1,600 branches and total assets of close on £10 billion. This makes them one of the country's biggest bankers, serving 6 million account customers with 13 million accounts between them.

The Central Trustee Savings Bank, which is owned by the TSB Central Board, operates in the money markets on behalf of all the regional banks. Until 1976 the Treasury exercised control over these banks through the National Debt Office. Now control is exercised by the Registrar of Friendly Societies jointly with the TSB Central Board. At present TSBs are not controlled by the Bank of England in the same way as other banks, but after a transitional period, which ends in 1986, they will be subjected to similar (though not identical) rules to the commercial banks. Today the TSBs make personal loans, grant temporary overdrafts and mortgages, have a cheque guarantee card and issue travellers' cheques. In short, they are becoming more and more like the commercial banks: they even run a unit trust.

In late 1985, it is expected that the TSB will bring its shares to the Stock Market, so that individuals can invest in the bank in the same way as they do in the other commercial banks.

The Co-op Bank

The Co-op Bank, with outlets in many of the Co-op stores, has access to the clearing banks' giro system and offers most of the facilities available through the other banks. It used to have the big advantage of paying interest on current accounts, then abandoned this practice some years ago, but was the first to reintroduce it in December 1981. It is useful for people who cannot get to a bank during normal banking hours, as cheques can be cashed at many Co-op stores six days a week in ordinary shopping hours.

Building societies

Building societies are not strictly speaking part of the British banking system, but today they are operating more and more like banks, offering competing services. Their activities are legally controlled, but there are proposals, which should shortly become law, which will permit them to expand into almost any service connected with home purchase, and even beyond it. Their savings plans are discussed in the next chapter and their other services in chapters 6 and 8 of this section.

The banks' Ombudsman

One complaint customers have had about banks for many years, has been the fact that, if you actually had a complaint about how your bank behaved towards you, there was no higher authority than the head office of the bank to whom you could put your grievance. That changed in February 1985 when seventeen of the high street banks established and funded an independent banking Ombudsman.

The banks were the Bank of Scotland, Barclays, Clydesdale, the Co-op, Coutts, Lloyds, Midland, National Giro, National Westminster, the Royal Bank of Scotland, Trustee Savings Banks, Williams & Glyn's, Yorkshire. Allied Irish, Bank of Ireland, Northern Bank and Ulster Bank.

From now on – you can't dig up an old complaint from the past, unless it is still continuing – the Ombudsman has the power to make an award that is binding on a bank, with an upper limit of £50,000. A customer can choose whether or not to accept the award; if he decides not to, he can still take legal action against the bank involved. The services covered by the Ombudsman include all personal banking services. Do not assume, however, that you will automatically get an award against your bank, if you go to the Ombudsman: he will judge each case on its merits and may well decide that the bank was right to act as it did. The banking Ombudsman followed the insurance Ombudsman, who started operations in 1981.

3 A personal savings programme

Setting out on a programme of sensible saving can be a bewildering business. There is an enormous variety of schemes, and barely a day goes by without something new being offered. The savings market is highly competitive with private institutions vying with one another, and with the highly attractive National Savings schemes offered by the government, usually through the post offices. To add to the confusion, schemes may be described as either *saving* or *investment*. Both have the same objective, that is, to increase your personal wealth, but there are important differences between them. With savings there should be no risk of losing your capital and an income should be assured. With investment, on the other hand, you take a chance as to the level of profit you will make – if any. For this reason the profit is generally greater, but there is a risk that the investment will not pay off to the extent you expected, and sometimes you may even lose part or all of your original stake. This chapter is concerned only with savings. If you have already worked out your savings plans and have money left over, turn to Section five, which sets out the various possibilities for personal investment.

Choosing your account

Many people simply save when they have some money left over from their fixed outgoings. As was suggested in chapter 1 of this section, it is far better to regard your savings as part of your outgoings. In that way you can build up your capital on a regular basis. Of course, savings cannot come before other fixed expenditures, but when you are working out your budget try to fit in something for saving, however little.

If you are at the beginning of your financial life and do not have any capital, you probably do not want to take any risk with money. This means that you must stick to assured savings with interest. The main schemes on offer are:

1 *National savings*. These are offered in various forms. The safety of your capital and interest is guaranteed by the government.

2 *Local authority loans*. Members of the public lend money to various local authorities throughout the country. Every loan raised has to have government approval and is then guaranteed by the Public Works Loans Board.

3 *Savings at the commercial banks and finance houses*. These are private concerns, so the government does not guarantee the safety of your capital and interest. Failings in these are rare, however, and unknown among the leading clearing banks.

4 *Savings in building societies*. These, again, are not guaranteed by the government. There have been some failings in the past, but they are very rare and now covered by the voluntary – soon to be compulsory – compensation scheme.

5 *Savings at the Trustee Savings banks*. These are government guaranteed at the moment, but will cease to be as the status of the TSB changes.

Interest rates are still relatively high in historical terms, even though at the end of 1984 they were rather lower than in the recent past. You will notice this if you go to the bank to borrow money or take out a mortgage. But high interest rates apply both ways. If you are saving money you will benefit from the high interest rates. In times of inflation the interest rate is very important. It is difficult to make your savings keep up with the rate of inflation, and any gap between the two is in effect a loss to you. So think carefully before you decide what to do with your money.

Interest rates are not always what they seem. For example, 10 per cent in one scheme may not be the same as in another which is also offering 10 per cent. It all depends on the rules of the scheme. These may not be stated prominently, or may not be clear, so ask about them. Money may not earn interest as soon as it is deposited: it may have to wait until, say, the beginning of the following month. Similarly, interest may be lost for the whole of the month in which you withdraw money. Then, the way interest is credited has an effect. If you are earning 10 per cent daily (as in banks' deposit accounts), this is worth more than 10 per cent paid monthly or quarterly, as in some forms of saving. Check the small print before you go ahead. I explain in chapter 4 how interest rates work. The calculation is the same whether you are borrowing or getting interest on savings.

If for any reason you are prepared to take a risk with your money, even if you do not have any basic savings, turn to Section five. Most people, however, prefer first to put some money aside for a rainy day, and they will not want to take a risk with any of this money.

Short-term or long-term saving
Next you must ask yourself how long you can afford to have your money tied up in a savings account. This is important because:

1 If you may need money suddenly and urgently you should not put it into

36

a scheme which does not allow you to draw out at short notice. If you do, there may be a severe financial penalty to pay. It usually involves a loss of interest.

2 If you know you can leave your money where it is for some time, you may be able to find a scheme which offers higher rates of interest than many schemes which allow you to draw out immediately or on a week or month's notice. Alternatively, you may be able to get a relatively high rate of interest guaranteed for a long period.

Probably you would like to balance your savings between the two kinds of saving. As I go through, I will indicate with each scheme whether it is suitable for short- or long-term saving

The question of tax

If you look at chapter 1, Section four, you will see that almost all income is subject to tax. This includes not only earnings and any bonuses or fringe benefits from employment, but also any money which comes in from savings and investment, like bank interest or dividends from companies, or rents from any property you own.

Until the 1984–5 tax year, what was called investment income attracted a tax surcharge after certain levels. This is no longer true and investment income is now simply added to the rest of our income in assessing the tax we owe.

There is an anomaly, however, which can mean that married people are taxed at a higher rate than two single people with the same total income. A married woman is allowed to have her earnings taxed separately from her husband, if she wishes (see Section four, chapter 4). For those on high incomes, this can mean a substantial tax saving. But when it comes to her investment income, a wife is required to add that to her husband's income and the total is taxed as if it were all his. As a result, married couples – this applies especially to pensioners who may be getting most of their income from savings – may reach the higher tax levels sooner than two single people. For this reason, and so that they can do some private saving, many married women find some of the tax-free savings I will discuss in this chapter highly attractive compared with other ways of saving.

Additionally, as we shall see, there are also tax-paid savings. It is important that you know whether your savings are liable for tax, tax-paid or tax-free, because each has attractions for different people, depending on whether they do or do not pay tax.

Tax-free savings tend to suit the better off who pay tax at the higher rates; taxable savings should be chosen by non tax-payers, as they benefit from the full gross interest; and tax-paid savings – where the tax paid by the savings institution cannot be reclaimed by the individual – are best for those who pay tax at the standard rate, because the tax charged is only 25.25 per cent, compared with the standard rate of 30 per cent. The

Government permits this lower tax rate to allow for those in such savings schemes who are not tax payers.

National savings

Let's look first at the government sector, which is becoming increasingly attractive for savers, because eventually it will be the only area where interest is paid *gross*, that is, without some tax first being deducted. Gross interest is important for people on low incomes who may not pay tax: they get all the interest immediately it is paid. In certain other cases, they can apply for a rebate from the taxman, but in the case of tax-paid savings (commercial banks, TSBs, building societies, for example), the tax paid cannot be reclaimed. National savings are now also the only means of tax-free saving, which can be very helpful to higher tax payers.

By and large the interest rates paid by the various forms of national savings change much less quickly than other interest rates. It is important to remember this, because it can affect their relative attractiveness in comparison with savings in building societies, banks or finance houses. The movement includes:

1 The National Savings Bank
2 Savings certificates
3 Index-linked saving certificates
4 Income bonds
5 Deposit bonds
6 Premium Bonds

Remember, the safety of your capital and the interest currently offered is guaranteed by the government in all these schemes.

The National Savings Bank

This used to be called the Post Office Savings Bank. The government guarantee it carries was very important when the bank was first set up in the nineteenth century, when many private banks went out of business, but today it is less so. If you take care when choosing your savings account, there is no reason why your capital or interest should be at risk wherever it is.

Nevertheless, there is still a guarantee for those who are at all nervous about their savings. And to encourage people to go into national savings the government offers some concessions on certain national savings which are not available to savers outside this area. The National Savings Bank offers two kinds of account.

1 *The ordinary account.* This account, with a minimum initial deposit of £1 up to a total of £10,000, has a two-tier interest rate structure. In 1984 these rates were 6 per cent for anyone prepared to leave at least £500 in

the account for the whole year. For amounts less than that, the rate was 3 per cent. In both cases, the first £70-worth of interest was tax-free. The 3 per cent, if tax-free, was worth 3.9 per cent gross and the 6 per cent, 7.8 per cent. Anyone paying standard rate income tax of 30 per cent could have a deposit of up to £1,280 in the year before the interest became liable for tax. The interest rates change from time to time, but the two-tier principle seems likely to be maintained for some time.

Would-be savers should note that no interest is paid during the month in which they make their deposit, nor in the month of withdrawal. This means you should deposit money as near to the end of the month as possible and withdraw it immediately after the start.

You should, however (if you are a tax payer), show the amount of interest on your tax return.

This kind of account is simply for saving in, and you are allowed a maximum of £10,000 in one or more accounts. You cannot have a cheque book or an overdraft, though you can get a crossed warrant for a minimum of £1 for some purposes, which can be used like a cheque, and you can also make arrangments for the payment of bills up to £250 to be paid without having to handle cash. Standing orders are paid free of charge from the account.

You can withdraw up to £100 on demand from your account on any one day at any post office. But if you withdraw more than £50 on demand, the bank book will have to be sent to the head office to be checked. If you want more than £100 at any one time, you will have to allow a few days before you get your money, as you must either apply in writing or pay for a telegram to the head office. You can give yourself greater flexibility by having more than one account, or you can arrange to draw up to £250 a day at one chosen post office without having to relinquish your bank book. To qualify, you must have used your account at that particular post office for six months.

2 *The investment account.* This, too, can be opened with a minimum of £1 and carries a higher rate of interest than the ordinary account. Unlike the ordinary account, however, the whole of the interest is taxable, though it is paid gross and so is useful for non-tax payers. At the end of 1984, the interest rate was 11¼ per cent. The account has an upper limit of £50,000, which was set on 4 May 1984. Before that, savers were allowed a deposit up to £200,000. If they were above the £50,000 limit when it was imposed, they were allowed to leave the money in the account, earning interest at the higher amount. This account also differs from the ordinary account in that interest is earned immediately the money is deposited and continues to be earned until the withdrawal warrant is issued. If you want to withdraw money from this account there is no limit, but you must give one month's notice and apply in

writing. Send your bank book and application form (you can get one in any post office) to the National Savings Bank, Glasgow G58 1SB. The investment account's other facilities are the same as the ordinary account. You can open both types of accounts at once and this is a good idea.

Any child over the age of seven can use the account himself. You can deposit or withdraw money at any one of the 20,000 post offices in the United Kingdom which transact National Savings Bank business, as long as you have your bank book with you. This will be supplied when you make your first deposit and all transactions are shown in it, so that you know exactly how much you have in the bank at any time. You cannot operate without your book, so make sure you have it with you.

Both these accounts are for short-term savers, though the ordinary account is rather more short-term than the investment account, at least for small amounts which can be withdrawn without any notice. Either can be joint or in the name of an individual.

Advantages
1 Accessibility. Very few of us live far from a post office and the hours are longer than in the commercial banks.
2 Money on demand, or fairly quickly.
3 Cheapness. There are no bank charges and you earn interest on the money you have deposited in the bank.
4 If you are paying tax above the basic rate, the tax-free element in the ordinary account is attractive.
5 Both accounts are good ways to save for short periods.

Disadvantages
1 There are much better ways of building up your capital than in the ordinary account or even the investment account, though the rate in the investment account is more attractive to non-tax payers than building society interest, which is usually effectively lower as we will see later.
2 The other services are limited compared with some other deposit accounts.
3 The interest offered does not always keep up with inflation and so the real value of your original savings may fall.

Savings certificates
These are a very popular method of saving for the medium term, and all the interest on the certificates is tax-free. So far (in late 1984) there have been 30 different issues, and only one is usually available for sale at any one time. This is because interest rates generally change, so issues are withdrawn when they become too easy or too difficult to sell, because the

interest they offer has become too low or too high compared with other savings. The minimum investment is £25 and the maximum £5,000. The interest rate is 8 per cent on the latest issue.

You can withdraw money at any time with eight days' notice, but interest paid to you is considerably reduced if you do this. Apply to the Director, Savings Certificates and SAYE, Durham DH99 1NS. There are some points to note about savings certificates:

1 They do not carry interest in the usual way. The government simply states what the value of the unit will be, at present £25, and then what it will be on maturity. The current issue will mature after five years and each unit will be worth £38.21, or for every £100 saved, £152.84.

2 Units can be bought outright, or, under a fairly new scheme, the 'Yearly Plan'. In this plan, the saver agrees to make monthly payments for one year. At the end of the year, he receives a Yearly Plan Certificate which states the value of the payments, plus the interest they have received during the year. The maximum guaranteed rate of interest is then earned, if a certificate is held for a full four (not five, which is the life of the issue) years. Lower rates apply if the certificate is cashed before the four years are up. This plan can be continued a year at a time.

3 The value and interest builds up slowly to a maximum in the fifth year like this:

Thirtieth issue

years after purchase	value at end of year £	yield for year* tax-free %
1	26.69	6.76
2	28.69	7.49
3	31.17	8.64
4	34.29	10.01
5	38.21	11.43

*This gives an average tax-free return over the five years of 8.85 per cent

Like other forms of national savings, savings certificates can be bought at post offices, commercial bank branches and Trustees Savings Banks. You will get a holder's card and a registration number, which is printed on all the certificates you can hold. Take care of your card, as this will have your registration number on it and details of all the certificates you hold. As a safeguard, note the registration number down in another place, so that you can always find it. You will need it when buying more certificates or cashing them in.

Advantages
Savings certificates are a very attractive form of long-term saving to anyone who pays tax, as all interest is tax-free.

Disadvantages
Those who do not pay any tax can get better gross rates of interest elsewhere.

Note
Certificates continue to earn interest after maturity, but only on their original, not the final, value. As a general rule, this means that they should be cashed in immediately they mature. There are, however, some exceptions to this rule, so it is advisable to check the position.

Index-linked certificates
The full name for these is index-linked national savings certificates. They were first brought out in June 1975 and represented a new idea in government savings plans. To begin with, they were available only to retired men and women, but now anyone can buy them. Their value is worked out, not on the basis of added interest or an increase in value based on a certain rate of interest, but on the cost of living. As prices rise, so does the value of the units, though anyone cashing their certificates within a year of purchase gets back only the face value of the units, so there is in fact no interest at all unless the units are held for a year or more.

Index-linked certificates are a good form of saving, especially in a period of high inflation. They protect the holder to a great extent from falls in the value of money, offering in addition – if they are kept for a full five years – a 4 per cent tax-free bonus. In a period of a very low inflation, the certificates might lose a lot of their appeal, so the government has added 'sweeteners' in recent years in the form of tax-free supplements, which are also index-linked. For certificates bought before November 1984, and kept at least until 1 November 1985, the supplement is 3 per cent (it was 2.4 per cent in 1982–3 and 1983–4). The government has promised at least three further annual supplements, which will probably mean that, whatever the level of inflation, index-linked certificates will remain competitive with other forms of saving.

The certificates are bought in units of £10, up to a maximum of 1,000 units (£10,000).

The money that you eventually get back on them will be increased in proportion to whatever rise in prices there has been. The government uses the UK General Index of Retail Prices as its measure of the rise in prices.

This index is worked out every month. The government compares the average prices of many goods in day-to-day use, like food, clothing, drink, tobacco, transport and fuel, with the prices paid in the previous month. If prices have risen, the index will rise; if they have fallen, the index will fall. The money you receive when you cash the certificates is calculated by seeing how much the index has changed between your purchase and sale. The national newspapers usually give the values of the certificates bought some years back and they are also listed in post offices. You can easily do the sum to find out what yours are worth:

$$\frac{\text{payment} \times \text{repayment month index}}{\text{payment month index}}$$

Although you get no extra at all unless you hold the certificates for a year, after that their value is calculated from the level at the date of purchase. If prices rise by 20 per cent in a year, for example, you will get £12 for every £10 unit you have bought.

It is clear that these certificates are very attractive when inflation is running at a higher rate than the interest offered on most saving schemes. When that happens, the saver is not getting any 'true' interest at all, after account is taken of the fall in the real value of money saved, because the pound sterling is worth less than it was a year previously. Index-linked certificates always at least maintain their value. All the repayments, too, are free of income tax and capital gains tax, so there is no complication there, either.

Advantages
Index-linked certificates are good for people who pay tax and can make periodic payments:

1 who wish to protect the purchasing power of their savings.
2 who wish to buy in small units of £10.
3 who need a tax-free return.
4 who need the accessibility of the post offices and Trustees Savings Banks for their purchases.

Disadvantages
The only possible disadvantage of index-linked certificates stems from the advantage. If prices generally stopped rising, the adjusted price of the certificates would also stop rising, or even begin to fall. This is something we have not seen for many years, but if the rate of inflation stays at its present level for some time reconsider your position, in case there is something more attractive to be purchased.

Income and Deposit Bonds
When the government abolished British Savings Bonds in December 1979, there were many complaints from people needing a guaranteed income with absolute security. The existing bonds went on earning

interest until December 1983, but in August 1982, in recognition of the need, the government brought in the taxable Income Bond, which paid interest monthly. This demanded a high minimum investment of £5,000 and was clearly not for those with rather limited funds, so it was followed by the taxable Deposit Bond, where the minimum investment was £500. In 1983 the limits were reduced to £2,000 and £250 respectively: clearly the earlier limits had discouraged many people.

Income Bonds

These are sold in units of £1,000, but the minimum purchase is £2,000. They are designed for anyone who needs a regular monthly income, but wishes to maintain his basic level of capital intact. They offer a high rate of interest which is paid gross but is subject to tax and three months notice is required of withdrawal. From 2 January 1985, the interest rate was 12 per cent, giving an annual income of £6,000 gross on the maximum holding of £50,000, or £4,200 after tax at the standard rate of 30 per cent. These would be equivalent to £500 and £3,500 respectively each month.

For taxpayers, the 12 per cent rate of interest was equivalent to 8.4 per cent, after allowing for tax at the standard rate, so the bonds are quite competitive when compared with other forms of saving.

Interest on the Income Bond is calculated on a day-to-day basis and is paid monthly. After a bond has been held for six weeks, income is paid on the fifth of the following month, with the first payment including all the interest which has been earned since the date of purchase.

The main snag for many savers in this scheme at the beginning was the onerous terms for repayment of the bonds, which was set at six months, with no interest being paid in the first year unless such notice was given. Even with full notice, only half the current rate of interest was paid in that first year. This was changed from 1 October 1984 to bring the Income Bond into line with the Deposit Bond, where only three months notice of withdrawal was required. Now full interest is paid during the notice period, if the bond is repaid more than one year after purchase, except that, in the first year, interest on the amount repaid will be at half-rate from the date of purchase. Six weeks notice is always given of a change in the rate of interest, so, if it falls, six weeks is the maximum time one need hold the bonds earning interest at the lower rate before getting them repaid. The only time withdrawal without notice is permitted is upon the death of the holder of the bonds (or sole surviving holder in a joint holding). In such cases, interest is paid in full and no formal notice is required.

How to buy and sell

Apply to the Bonds and Stock Office, Blackpool FY3 9YP. You will probably find a combined application/prospectus form (GS2), along with a pre-paid envelope, at your local post office. If not, you can ring and ask for one on 0272 290871. Repayment forms are also available at most post offices, or direct from the Bonds and Stock Office. The form is number GS3.

Deposit Bonds

National Savings Deposit Bonds were introduced to give the advantages of higher interest rates to those savers who cannot afford a £2,000 minimum investment. The bonds, which come in multiples of £50, require a minimum investment of £250, or five units; after that, any multiple of £50 can be purchased to a maximum of £50,000. Again, like income bonds, interest is taxable but paid gross and is calculated on a daily basis. Deposit bonds are on three months notice and the 12 per cent interest (end of 1984) is the same as on income bonds. If you sell the bonds within a year of their purchase you receive only half the current level of interest, whatever that is. The minimum amount which can be withdrawn is £50 and you can have the bond repaid in full, or take out part of it, as long as you leave in a minimum of £250 (until 2 September 1984, this minimum was £500).

If you are buying bonds for yourself or jointly with someone else, or for your children, you can get them at the post office. Other purchasers, such as clubs, companies, charities or friendly societies, must buy them from the Deposit Bond Office, National Savings, Glasgow G58 1SB. If you want to sell, get a repayment form from the post office, complete it, and send it to the Deposit Bond Office. You will receive the money three months later with interest credited up to the date of repayment. Bonds bought on behalf of children under seven cannot normally be repaid until they reach seven.

Save As You Earn

In 1983 the Government announced that it was bringing to an end the index-linked Save As You Earn scheme. This enabled anyone – earning or not – to make regular savings over a five-year period which were not only index-linked, but also free of tax. Anyone already in a scheme was allowed to continue it and, if you have one, keep it going until it matures. If you can leave the money for a further two years after maturity the whole amount is revalued again in line with the Retail Price Index (in the same way as index-linked National Savings Certificates are valued) and you will also get a bonus equal to twice the monthly payment you were making while the plan was running. This would be a minimum of £4 a month to a maximum of £50.

Premium Bonds

Most forms of saving offered by the government are secure and unexciting. They are meant to help us build our nest-egg for the future. Premium Savings Bonds are the exception. They are in a way a means of gambling with the government. Unlike ordinary gambling (see Section five, chapter

10), however, you never lose your original stake if you do not win a cash prize. Each week and each month, every bond has a chance of winning a prize which ranges from £50 (many thousands of these are won) to £250,000 (one a month). All prizes are tax-free.

You can sell your bonds at any time for the same price as you paid for them – though you have, of course, been losing any interest you could have got on any other form of saving and, because of inflation, your original stake is almost certainly worth less in real terms than it was when you bought the bonds. Of course, you may win a prize, which alters the situation completely.

Do not make Premium Bonds your first expedition into savings, especially if you are trying to project your savings against inflation. But once you have your nest-egg secured they are a good way of having a flutter without losing your initial stake.

When the bonds were first introduced in 1956, the maximum holding allowed was 500 of the £1 units. This has risen steadily over the years and you can now hold 10,000 of them and you must buy in multiples of £5, even though each bond is still for £1. If you hold the maximum holding it is reckoned that you will get at least one prize each year, but that is likely to be only the minimum prize of £50, which is equal to only 1½ per cent tax-free a year, or just under 2 per cent taxable – not much compared with the other savings I have looked at.

Prize winners are selected by means of a rather sophisticated raffle. The main draw is held at the beginning of each month and there is a further smaller draw each Saturday. The winning numbers are selected by ERNIE (Electronic Random Number Indicator Equipment), who is not a man but a computer which selects at random.

The monthly prize money is set by calculating one month's interest at the rate of 7¾ per cent a year on all the bonds which are eligible for the draw in that particular month. You have to hold the bonds for three clear months following the month in which you bought them before you qualify for the draw. Each week there is one prize of £100,000, one prize of £50,000 and one prize of £25,000. There is a main £250,000 prize each month, then smaller prizes from £10,000 (five each month) to £50 (150,000).

The odds on you winning one of these prizes has been calculated at about 11,000 to one bond. The odds vary a little, depending on whether there are four or five weekly draws in a particular month. If you have won one prize in a month, you are not eligible for another one. If the bond number is actually drawn twice, you will receive the higher prize. If you win you will be notified by post, and if the prize is over £100 you will be sent a claim form. A complete list of prize-winning numbers is given every month in the *London Gazette*.

You can claim a prize later if you have failed to do so at the time of the draw. All the numbers of prize-winning bonds won eighteen months or more ago and still unclaimed are listed at the end of the *London Gazette* in January, April, July and October. Copies of this are usually on display at the larger post offices. At the end of 1984, over 40,000 prizes remained unclaimed.

As with all government schemes, the bonds can be bought from all post offices. You must be sixteen to purchase them, though a parent or guardian can buy bonds on behalf of their children and they may be bought as gifts.

Since ERNIE started almost thirty years ago, it has often been claimed that it is biased towards certain numbers, or places in which bonds have been bought. This is not so; every time a check is made over a reasonable length of time it shows that ERNIE is completely impartial.

Advantages and disadvantages
Obviously premium bonds are no use in any plan to build up your capital. You may be lucky and win but that is not the same as having a guaranteed plan. But they are attractive to someone with just a few pounds to spare who likes the idea of a gamble without too much risk.

Trustee Savings Banks

The structure and operations of the Trustee Savings Banks are set out in three Acts of Parliament – the TSB Acts 1969, 1976 and 1978. The 1976 Act was perhaps the most important; it created a federal structure for the TSBs. This is quite unique in British banking and offers an alternative, on the one hand, to the clearing banks and other commercial banks, and on the other to the government national savings and Girobank. By 1986 the government will cease to have any control over the TSBs' operations and they will closely resemble the commercial banks in their relationship with the government. The TSB has several types of saving account at the moment:

1 *The savings account*. These are interest-bearing accounts upon which tax must be paid. The rate at end-1984 was 4 per cent and at any time the current rate is displayed in TSB branches. There is no maximum deposit and withdrawals are on demand.

2 *Deposit accounts*. These normally have a higher rate of interest than savings accounts, but notice may be required before withdrawals can be made. Again, the rate is displayed in TSB branches. It may fluctuate from week to week.Like the clearing banks, the TSB have developed various deposit schemes in recent years, which offer higher rates of interest than that available on a simple deposit. They also have an account linked to the money market (Marketlink) for anyone with savings over £5,000.

These are the basic accounts, but like the commercial banks the TSBs have special accounts at any one time. Larger deposits (usually for a minimum of £1,000) are accepted for minimum terms at fixed rates of interest. These are useful if you think that interest rates will fall and the TSB is offering a higher rate for a relatively long period. At the end of 1984, the TSB was offering 9 per cent on one-year deposits. There is also a scheme, called Moneybuild, which offers a higher interest rate to regulars savers.

Local authority loans

Anyone who pays rates knows that it costs money to run a borough. Local authorities raise the money not only through the rates but also by borrowing money from members of the public and paying them interest (which comes from the rates) on the money. The loans they require are generally advertised on most days in the paper; the Sunday papers are a particularly good vehicle for this kind of advertising.

Though local government is part of the official life of the country, each authority is free to decide what terms it wishes to offer for money lent to it. They all vary, and careful study is worthwhile if you want get the maximum interest on your money. In general, big, powerful authorities can get away with offering lower terms than small authorities, though there is no difference in the security of your investment. Every loan raised is guaranteed by the Public Works Authority after getting government approval.

The first thing to remember about these loans is that they are not designed for short-term saving. As a general rule you will be asked to leave your money for a period from two to ten years – though sometimes you can lend for a year or even less. The length of time will depend to some extent on what the local authorities think is going to happen to interest rates. Say they offer you 10 per cent, but expect that by the end of a year most savings will be offering only 9 per cent, they will encourage you to lend to them for only a year. If, on the other hand, they expect rates to go on rising, they will try to get you to leave your money with them at the 10 per cent rate for as long as possible. This is how you should go about selecting the loan to suit you.

Watch the newspapers carefully. Cut out advertisements which interest you and write for more details. The advertisement will give you the name of the borough, the rate of interest being offered, the minimum period for which you can invest and the minimum amount you can invest. You then apply to the treasurer of the local authority. You will not be likely to be able to invest less than £500, and the minimum may be as high as £1,000. At the end of 1984 rates were between 10.75 per cent and 11.25 per cent before tax, depending on the amount you put in and the length of time you leave it with the authority. On 6 April 1985, the loans moved on to a tax-paid basis.

It is worth considering, however, whether your own local authority would not be more convenient than one a long way off, particularly as that way you can do business personally.

Advantages
Excellent for those who pay little or no tax who can leave their money tied up for a long time.

Disadvantages
1 The interest quoted is always gross, but it will come to you with tax deducted. If you are not a tax payer, you will then have to reclaim the tax. If you would find this a burden, perhaps another form of saving would suit you better.
2 It is hard to get your money back before the loan period is over. Do not leave any money with a local authority which you are likely to need unexpectedly. Remember that it means you will have a relatively large amount of money locked up for a set period. Local authority loans are strictly for medium- to long-term savings.
3 Local authority loans are obviously not for small savers.

Investors in Industry deposits

It is possible to put money on deposit with Investors in Industry (formerly Finance for Industry), a government-sponsored institution which is the parent holding company of the Industrial and Commercial Finance Corporation (ICFC) and Finance Corporation for Industry (FCI), both of which lend money to companies to finance expansion. The deposits are similar to local authority loans and are available at differing rates of interest for periods of from three to ten years. Current rates are published by the *Financial Times* for amounts from £1,000, which is the minimum investment permitted, to £50,000. Rates on larger amounts are given on request. At the end of 1984, interest rates were either 10¼ per cent or 10½ per cent, the bigger rate for loans with a ten-year term.

Send your deposits to, or get further information from, the Chief Cashier, Investors in Industry Limited, 91 Waterloo Road, London SE1 5XP (telephone 01-928 7822). If local authority loans also appeal to you, III deposits are an interesting secure alternative. The advantages and disadvantages are the same.

Savings at the commercial banks and finance houses

Until recently it was relatively easy to decide what kind of saving scheme to choose. That is no longer so. The simple deposit account at the bank has now been joined by a variety of schemes for short- and longer-term saving, for those with limited means and for others with plenty of money. New plans come in with such frequency that what looked good for someone one week can be superceded by something better within days. By that time, of course, the saver can be locked into his existing scheme and unable to switch immediately. It is not surprising that many of us become confused and do not put our money in the most efficient savings to suit our personal circumstances.

The clearing banks

For most people it is the normal *current account* which is important to them in their dealings with the commercial clearing banks. These accounts do not normally earn interest, apart from the Co-op Bank. Current accounts are designed to cope with day-to-day financial transactions. I have described them in chapter 6 of this section. The commercial banks have, however, introduced a number of accounts in recent years which pay interest and allow some cheque transactions. They come in a variety of names, for instance the Prime Account at Barclays or High Interest Cheque Account at Lloyds, but all of them require the holder to put a reasonable amount of money into the account to start off with – £2500 is a typical amount – and the cheques drawn must be for a minimum of £250. Only a certain number of cheques can be drawn free of charge. The interest paid on the account is usually 2–3½ per cent above the rate paid on deposit accounts. The accounts are a bargain for banks, if not particularly for the customer, as they have the guaranteed use of your money in an account which is usually not particularly active and therefore cheap to service.

Banks also offer *deposit accounts*. These are useful places to put money which you may want to transfer quickly to your current account, as it will earn interest until you have to. They are also useful for building up your savings, as regular transfers can easily be made from your current into your deposit account. You can open a deposit account at any bank branch. It need not be the one at which you have your current account, though that would probably be most convenient. And of course you do not need to have a current account at all.

The most important difference between saving with the government and with the commercial banks is that the rate of interest changes far more quickly with the latter. It is based on the particular bank's minimum lending rate at any one time and this can change frequently. The deposit rate is usually between 4½ and 3 per cent points below the lending rate, and the current level is usually posted in bank branches. If the lending rate is 11 per cent, for example, the deposit rate will be 7–8 per cent; if it is 8½ per cent the deposit rate will be 3½–4 per cent. The higher the minimum lending rate, the greater the gap between it and the deposit rate. All commercial bank interest attracts tax. Until 6 April 1985, interest was paid gross: since then it has been tax paid like the building societies.

There are other minor points of difference:

1 You will not usually get a bank book with your deposit account in a clearing bank. You will get a bank statement from time to time, as with your current account. It will show deposits and withdrawals and the interest earned on the account.
2 Interest is paid on a daily, rather than a monthly, basis. The rate is often much higher than in the Post Office, but the fact that the interest is tax paid brings the net rate down whether or not you are a tax payer.
3 There is no minimum or maximum amount which you can have on deposit, though it usually costs £1 to open an account.
4 You can only withdraw money at the branch at which you have an account. With the National Savings Bank account, you can withdraw money at any post office which does bank business.
5 You can draw out as much as you like on demand, though you will usually lose seven days' interest when you do.

A bank deposit account has all sorts of uses, but once you have built up enough money to cover emergencies it is a good idea to look around at the various forms of long-term saving. Even the usually attractive rate of interest is not generally enough to compensate for the fall in the value of money through inflation.

Clearing bank savings schemes
As well as ordinary deposit accounts, the clearing banks offer all kinds of accounts today which can increase your income. Higher amounts over £2,000 pay interest at a higher rate than ordinary deposits and very large sums of money over, say, £25,000 can earn rates of interest close to those quoted in the money market. These extra-large amounts can often be on short notice without any interest penalties. A commitment to regular savings, too, can sometimes get you interest one or two per cent above the normal rate. These special arrangements vary all the time: schemes are introduced and dropped quickly if there is little demand, so there is no point in listing the current ones here. Keep a look out at your local bank branches, or ask your bank manager to help you find the best account for your circumstances. Always ask about the rules on withdrawal of your money. Some managers may not be as eager to tell you how to get your money back as they are to take it off you for the bank's use.

Money market funds
The past two years have seen the introduction of accounts, usually called funds, which offer depositors higher interest than they can get on deposit accounts, by investing their cash in the money markets. These accounts first started in America, where they are very popular, and have not really taken off yet in the United Kingdom. There was not the same need in

Britain, where banking regulations are such that depositors can get quite high interest on short-term deposit, which was not the case in America.

These accounts may or may not offer holders a cheque book and the money may be on very short call – two days is not uncommon – so that you can get at your funds very quickly should you need to. While deposited, your money is earning interest at the top rates available in the money market. The accounts come in two basic forms. The first are the higher interest rate accounts offered by companies which are licensed by the Bank of England to take deposits, or the banks themselves. Such business is simply part of the normal deposit-taking activity of the bank or the company. If the particular institution gets into financial difficulties, higher interest rate depositors are simply creditors just like any depositor. They can claim compensation under the bank deposit scheme which came into operation in 1982. Under this scheme they can claim 75 per cent of their money back on balances up to £10,000 from any one of the 600 recognized banks and licensed deposit-takers in the United Kingdom.

Then there are the simple money market funds run by institutions other than banks and licensed deposit takers. The Bank of England has decided that the ordinary customer will not see the difference between saving in a fund and depositing with a bank, so it has decided that all these institutions must seek a licence. The Bank has also laid down certain rules about the kind of investing which the money market fund managers can do, as it is unlikely that they will come under the bank deposit scheme for compensation. The idea is that, if – most unlikely – all the savers asked for their money back at once the assets could be realized quickly to pay them. The Bank has also ordered the managers to set up internal procedures, which would stop a member of staff making off with the funds. It also requires the managers themselves to put a substantial amount of money into the fund, so that if there is any loss, they will be the first to pay for it.

In this way, it seems that the funds will be secure. And the rewards are an account bearing interest on short notice at an interest rate which may be 2–3 per cent higher than you can get elsewhere.

If you decide to save in this way, look for advertisements in the press and do not forget to ask what the period of notice is and how often interest is paid. When these accounts first started, fund managers were thinking mainly of rather wealthy savers with more than £10,000 to invest. Today, however, amounts as low as £2,500 are permitted.

You may not think these accounts are for you, but they have their uses over the short term for many people. For instance, you might have your hands on a large sum of money between selling one home and buying another. If you have the money for a very short period, you are unlikely to get higher interest than that offered in either a money market fund or a higher interest rate deposit account at the bank.

Currency funds

It is necessary here to mention currency funds, where a British investor can put his money into another currency, like the Swiss franc or the American dollar. And having mentioned them, the ordinary saver without very large funds is well advised to forget about them. They can be highly profitable when the value of a particular currency rises sharply in comparison with the pound sterling, when the money is changed back to sterling or switched into another currency. They can also be very unprofitable and so are not suitable for savers at all. Currency funds are of course managed by experts, who reckon they know the way currencies are moving. Even so, they are not always right. If you do decide you want a flutter, choose one of the funds which invests in a number of currencies. This business is usually done by the merchant banks, though some of the larger unit trust groups also have currency funds.

Finance houses

Finance houses work rather like building societies: they borrow money from the public at one rate of interest and lend it out to people who take out hire purchase contracts at a higher rate. Unlike building societies, however, they are ordinary public companies which exist to make a profit for their shareholders. This generally means that the interest rate they charge and the rate they offer is higher than in many other financial institutions, but the rate on deposits varies enormously, depending on how much you leave with them and the terms on which you leave it.

More than in any other area of banking and finance, take care, through your bank or accountant, to investigate the company thoroughly before putting your money with it. Most of the companies which advertise for deposits today are absolutely reliable, but, in spite of the law, what are called 'fringe banks' have crept into the business from time to time. Some of these have succeeded, but others have gone bankrupt and depositors have lost all or most of their money. You can spot higher-risk companies by the higher-than-average rates of interest they offer. Such schemes may look very attractive, but a promised high return is no use if you lose all your money. Let's look at the reasons why there is some risk with certain of these companies.

Finance houses are primarily a twentieth-century development. They were set up to provide finance as hire purchase and credit sales developed as the ordinary customers began to purchase goods at greater cost than could be paid from a week's or month's wages. It was beyond the reach of most retailers to finance these kinds of sales themselves, and they turned to companies specializing in this work.

But defaults on HP are far more common than defaults on mortgages. These sometimes small periodic payments are often the first thing to be stopped in times of financial stress. Consumer protection for people buying on HP has meant that, more and more, finance companies have had to make proper provision for bad debts. They have either had to go to court to repossess their goods in cases of payment default, or to agree to extended terms for those people in difficulties who have paid more than one third of the total purchase price (see Section six, chapter 4, on the law relating to credit sales). The bigger and older established companies have countered these problems by developing their business away from hire purchase, and today many of them operate in a similar way to banks. More and more they have turned to personal loans rather than HP contracts, because with a loan a defaulter can be taken to court. Many finance houses now have the status of banks. You need have no fears about leaving your money with one of the big established companies, especially if it has bank status, or is associated in one way or another with a clearing bank.

I repeat, this is the most risky area of banking. Do not be led astray by greed. If you want to save with a finance house:

1 Write to the company and ask for details of all its deposit schemes.
2 Or contact your bank manager, who may be prepared to accept money for any finance company which is connected with his bank.
3 Remember that the longer you leave your money and the more there is of it, the better terms you will get.
4 Remember that interest is now tax paid, so these savings are less attractive than they used to be for non-tax payers. Rates vary from company to company, but at the time of writing (end of 1984) you could get around 11 per cent if you are prepared to put your money on three months' notice.

Savings in building societies

A building society is an organization set up to finance house purchase. It does this by lending money to borrowers and charging them interest. It gets the money which it lends on mortgage by a variety of savings schemes, which can be very attractive in certain circumstances. It pays depositors rather less interest than it charges its mortgagees. The Building Societies Association recommends lending and borrowing rates to its members, who usually stick to them, though a few pay a little more to depositors and shareholders. The BSA meets from time to time to consider changes in the rates and it is important to remember that societies are not profit-making organizations – the gap between lending and borrowing rates is simply to allow for running costs and provide a reserve fund should depositors default on their mortgages. There are several good reasons for investing in building societies:

1 There are tax advantages to standard rate tax payers.
2 The schemes on offer usually, though not always, compare well with other forms of saving.

3 People who have put money into a building society often get preferential treatment when it comes to getting a mortgage.

You have plenty of building societies to choose from. There are well over 500 scattered throughout the country, with more than 5,500 branches altogether. Some cover the whole of the United Kingdom and others – generally the smaller ones – are more localized, with only a few branches. You may think that size has something to do with reliability but this is not usually the case. There have been failures in building societies in the past and a few – a very few – cases of fraud. Depositors have not usually lost out, however, as long as the building society in question was a member of the Building Societies Association, and today investors in building societies which are BSA members are protected by the BSA Compensation Scheme. As I write, this is a voluntary scheme, but all members of the BSA belong to it. It is likely to be made compulsory when the next Act of Parliament on building societies is passed, though it may change a little in character. At present, investors in share accounts are guaranteed 90 per cent of their holdings up to a maximum of £30,000, as long as the society is a member of the BSA. For non-members, the level of compensation is 75 per cent.

If the compensation scheme becomes compulsory, it will probably be similar to that which the banks already have. There, compensation is 75 per cent, up to £10,000. In that event, it is expected that the building societies themselves will voluntarily add on the rest to maintain the 90 per cent level.

If you want to be absolutely on the safe side, however, choose a society which has 'trustee status'. This means that it measures up to certain government criteria as being safe for executors dealing with estates to invest in. Your should also check that the society is a member of the Building Societies Association. This has firm rules for its members which protect savers.

Building societies use all sorts of fancy names for their various accounts, but although there are some minor differences between societies they all basically offer the same kind of schemes. The interest rate is often higher the longer you leave your money, and a higher interest rate is generally also paid for regular savings, because the society knows that it can rely on your funds for some time.

	Tax paid %	Taxable equivalent
Ordinary shares	6.75	9.64
shares at 7 days notice	8.00	11.42
28 days notice	8.25	11.78
(or 28 days loss of interest)		
90 days notice	8.50	12.14
(or 90 days loss of interest)		

*Average rates at the end of 1984

These were the average rates offered by building societies at the end of 1984, though higher rates were available with safety for anyone prepared to shop around. The most important thing to look for is any penalty attached to withdrawal at short notice. On 28-day accounts, for instance, some societies impose penalties for early withdrawal, while others do not.

Some societies today, and especially the larger ones, offer cheque books with some of their accounts. Apart from the lack of an overdraft facility, these accounts are to all intents and purposes the same as the bank's current accounts. For anyone of limited resources, who would find the interest paid allied to the cheque book a useful contribution to money management, they may be preferable to a current account (see chapter 6, this section).

Below, as an example, are the types of saving schemes offered by a London-based building society at the end of 1984. You should be able to find something similar either among the country-wide societies, or at your own local one. You will notice that the last column of the table shows a higher interest rate than is actually paid. This shows the interest you would have to earn to get an equivalent amount if you had to pay tax on it at the current standard rate of 30 per cent. If you are paying tax at the higher rates you will have to pay some tax on your account. All forms of tax-paid savings show interest rates in this way now.

type of account	interest paid %	taxable equivalent %
shares	6.75	9.64
shares* with minimum		
£1,000–£2,499	8.15	11.64
£2,500–9,999	8.50	12.14
£10,000–plus	8.65	12.36
7-day notice	8.00	11.43
3-year term	8.90	12.71
regular savings	7.75	11.07
monthly income shares	8.25	11.79
deposits	6.50	9.29

*immediate withdrawal and cheque book facility

Interest rates in building societies change more slowly than in some other parts of the private sector. This means that from time to time saving with a building society may not be as attractive as other forms of saving. Keep an eye on interest rates and switch backwards and forwards if this is financially advantageous to you.

Choosing your savings plan

Everyone will have a different priority when it comes to saving, and we must each work out the scheme which suits us best. This scheme will depend on many things, including

- age
- marital status
- profession
- salary level

1 *Age*. The younger you are the less you will probably need for your nest-egg, but even so try to save £100 or £200 a year. It makes a useful deposit for a car, or can be used to finance a holiday.

2 *Marital status*. As soon as you marry, or indeed think about marrying, your savings should become a more important item in your budget. The more money you can get together before you marry the better. Try, if possible, to save a deposit for a house or flat before you become involved in family budgeting. Once bought, a house is an investment for life. If you are divorced or widowed, try if possible to keep up some saving, however small. More than most, you may find you need your nest-egg.

3 *Profession*. If you are in a steady job with prospects of an increasing salary, tailor your savings to increase as your salary rises. Don't try to save too much at the beginning, but gradually build up. If you are in an uncertain profession, where your earnings may be erratic, it is even more important to make sure you have some money put by for emergencies.

4 *Salary level*. This is most important. It should be a guide to the kind of savings plan you follow. Tax-free, or tax-paid, savings are of less use to those who do not pay tax than to those who do. If you pay tax at the standard rate, or more especially at the higher rates, get as much tax-free saving as you can.

To start with, as I said in chapter 1 of this section, try to think of saving as part of your normal outgoings. Then you must divide your money into:

1 Short-term savings.
2 Long-term savings.

Everyone will need some money for emergencies, and to begin with you may have to concentrate on building up a reserve which you think will cover any sudden payments you may have to make. For short-term saving you should choose from the following:

1 National Savings Bank ordinary account (especially if you are paying tax) or the investment account for non-tax payers.
2 Trustee Savings Bank ordinary account.
3 A deposit account with a clearing bank.
4 A building society deposit or share account (good for those paying tax at the standard rate, less good for those who do not pay tax or who pay at the higher rates).

type of saving	state/ private	interest rate changes	tax status	interest paid
National Savings Bank Ordinary account	State	periodically	tax-free to first £70	monthly
Investment account	State	periodically	taxable	monthly
National Savings Certificates	State	fixed for term	tax-free	When cashing in
Index-linked Savings Certificates	State	Linked to Retail Prices Index	tax-free	When cashing in
Income Bonds	State	periodically	taxable	monthly
Deposit Bonds	State	periodically	taxable	anniversary of purchase
Premium Bonds	State	erratic, now equal to 7¾%	tax-free	as weekly or monthly cash prize
Trustee Savings Bank: Savings account	*Now Private*	periodically	tax-paid†	monthly, but added
Deposit account		periodically	tax-paid†	annually on 20 November
Term deposits		fixed for term	tax-paid†	annually on 20 November
Local authority loans	guaranteed by government	fixed for term	tax-paid†	monthly to yearly
Investors in industry deposits	guaranteed by government	fixed for term	tax-paid†	half-yearly
Clearing Banks Deposit accounts	private	linked directly	tax-paid†	daily
Term deposits		fixed for term	tax-paid†	daily
Building societies	private	periodically	tax paid†	monthly
Finance companies	private	linked to MLR fixed for term	tax-paid†	varies
Money market funds	private	linked to general rates	tax-paid†	varies

*Registrar of Friendly Societies and TSB Central Board.

58

current min/max amount	best long/ short term	withdrawal terms	best for
£1/£10,000	short	£100 on demand, rest in few days	beginners and tax payers
£1/£50,000	either	one month's notice	non-tax payers
£25/£5,000	medium	8 working days, but on penal terms	all tax payers
£10/£10,000	Minimum one year	8 working days, but returned only at purchase price if held less than one year	all tax payers
£2,000/£50,000	medium/long	at least three months or penalties	non or low tax payers
£250/£50,000	medium/long	at least three months or penalties	non or low tax payers
£5/£10,000	a gamble	8 working days	cautious gamblers
none/none	short	£100 on demand, rest in few days	beginners
£1/none	either	one month's notice	non-tax payers
£1,000/none	medium/long	depends on term	tax payers
by negotiation	medium/long	between one and 10 years: difficult to break term	those with ample funds and non-tax payers
£1,000/none	Medium/long	minimum 3 years; maximum 10	as with local authority loans
no limits	short	7 days' notice	non-tax payers
£1,000/£10,000	medium/long	one to 12 months	tax payers
£1/£30,000	depends on scheme	Varies with scheme, from £100 on demand to term	those paying tax at the standard rate
£25/£25,000	depends on scheme	varies; penal terms if contract not fulfilled	those with ample funds and non-tax payers
£2,500/none	short/medium	varies from one day upwards	high interest short-term haven

† At the standard rate
Interest rates change constantly, fill in current rates in the margin.

59

5 A money market account if you have large sums coming in and out of your hands quickly.

In all these you can get your money out quickly without much fuss or loss of interest.

When you have built up your reserves you can turn to longer-term plans. Choose saving schemes where there is a bonus for fulfilling the whole plan, and choose the best terms to suit your circumstances. Choose from:

1 National savings certificates (the interest is free of tax, which makes these very attractive to high tax payers).
2 Income and deposit bonds.
3 Local authority loans (the high rates of interest are good for those who do not pay tax or pay only at the standard rate).
4 The longer-term schemes offered by the building societies (good for standard rate tax payers).
5 The longer-term finance company deposits (high rates of interest, but take care in choosing your company).
6 Index-linked saving certificates (especially good for high tax payers and a hedge against inflation).

Do not buy Premium Bonds as part of either your short- or long-term savings plans. These are quite separate and only for those who like to gamble without losing their original stake.

The table on pages 58–9 will help you to choose sensibly.

When you have built up a good reserve of savings, you may feel you would like to 'diversify' and put some of your money into a wider range of investments. If you have reached the point where you can take some risk with a portion of your savings in the hope of a better return on your money, turn to Section five, where all the possibilities open to you are discussed.

4 When you want to borrow money

Getting credit

Let's clear away right at the start any idea that there is anything wrong with borrowing money to buy things we need. Most people borrow at some time for a particular purpose. Some who quite happily take out a mortgage regard any other form of hire purchase or credit sale as best avoided. This is a mistaken view. It is, of course, wrong to over-extend yourself in your hire purchase commitments, as with any other regular payments, but many people's lives are made more comfortable by the possibility of paying for purchases over a period of time. By borrowing in this way you can have the use of something you need now by committing part of your future income.

To get some idea of the extent of the credit business, look at the figures. Total borrowing by the British public at the end of 1984 had reached the massive figure of £17,400,000,000 in outstanding instalment credit. That is over £300 for every person in the country. Personal loans from the banks now amount to £63,400,000,000 and the building societies are lending £23,800,000,000 a year.

You may think that if you want something it is worth saving for. An admirable idea, but just think of saving up to buy a house. That would take many more years than the period of the average mortgage, and you would be paying tax on interest over the years, rather than getting tax relief on your interest payments on a mortgage. Few people today would not buy a house simply because they disapproved of mortgages, and once you have taken the step of getting a mortgage there is no valid reason for not financing other major purchases – a car, furniture and household fittings, even a holiday or expensive items of clothing – in that way too, though there is no tax relief when you borrow for anything except to buy a home, or improvements to it.

The big development in hire purchase has come about because of a change of attitude towards borrowing not only on the part of the borrowers themselves but also lenders. At first, only people with 'security' were offered loans and the conditions were strict. Borrowers had to have other assets with which to back their application for a loan. Lenders naturally want as much security as they can get to ensure that their money is repaid, particularly following changes in the law, which are very advantageous to anyone buying goods on credit (see Section six, chapter 4, on protection for borrowers).

But lenders have come to realize that it is not only physical assets which represent security. Regular wages or salary can be just as good as actual capital or other assets. In other words, the man or woman (women need no longer provide a male guarantor if they have regular earnings or assets) who is in a steady job, but who does not have sufficient capital or savings to buy, say, a car, can be just as good a risk as the person who owns a house, or has some money in the bank, or a few shares.

As a result, most of us are either borrowers or lenders, and few follow the old adage 'Neither a borrower nor a lender be'. In today's society it is sensible to borrow. Do remember, however, that with credit facilities so widely available there can be a danger of over-reaching yourself if you are not careful. Make sure you know exactly what your total borrowings add up to: a bank overdraft or personal loan, or money outstanding on a credit card, is just as much a debt as the hire purchase you may arrange when buying a car or furniture.

It is important to remember that borrowing is rarely free, unless perhaps you are borrowing from a friend or a member of your family, or sometimes if you are borrowing for no more than six months or a year, for example from some department stores. And interest rates charged on hire purchase are some of the highest that there are.

This fact may not be immediately apparent when you borrow. The stated interest rate may seem quite low, but there is sometimes a great deal of difference between the 'flat rate' and the 'true rate'. In general, you can work out the true rate by using the following formula.

Say you borrow £100 over two years, and you have to pay back a total of £120 in eight quarterly instalments of £15 each. You work out the 'flat' interest rate by taking the difference of £20, which is 20 per cent of £100, and dividing it by two, because the repayment is taking place over two years. This gives an annual 'flat' rate of 10 per cent. This is not the 'true' rate, because you are reducing the debt in quarterly instalments, but the interest is fixed for the period of the full loan and does not decrease as your debt does down. You must multiply the flat rate by 1.8 if you are paying quarterly, by 1.9 if you pay monthly, and by 2 if you pay weekly. This means that the 10 per cent flat rate becomes a true rate of 18, 19 or 20 per cent, and that interest rates are really much higher than they appear. The true rates work out as shown below at different 'flat' rates.

Rates are sometimes given on a monthly basis. In the next chapter, on credit cards, I have set out what they mean on an annual basis.

flat rate %	quarterly %	monthly %	weekly %
5	9.0	9.5	10
6	10.8	11.4	12
7	12.6	13.3	14
8	14.4	15.2	16
9	16.2	17.1	18
10	18.0	19.0	20
11	19.8	20.9	22
12	21.6	22.8	24
13	23.4	24.7	26
14	25.2	26.6	28
15	27.0	28.5	30
16	28.8	30.4	32

It is sensible to shop around when you want to buy on HP to get the cheapest interest rate which is available. In normal economic times, it is difficult to obtain credit at less than the going rate for borrowing, but in the past few years retailers have faced hard times, as sales have been sluggish, and as a result many of them have been offering inducements to buyers in the form of cheap or even interest-free credit in order to keep their sales volume up.

This means that if you want to buy a major item, say, a car or an expensive domestic appliance which is available from a wide variety of retailers, it is worthwhile looking around if you want to buy on hire purchase or credit sale. Even if you have the money to buy cash, why give up interest you could be earning in the bank, if you can get interest-free credit? For many people, the possibility of interest-free credit now can make the difference between deciding to buy something at the present time, or deferring it for twelve months.

Naturally there are rules about when this is available. The schemes vary from store to store, so if you are not eligible in one place, try somewhere else. In many stores, interest-free credit is not allowed on purchases of less than £100 and the repayment period is likely to be a maximum of twelve months, and it may be only six. In that time, conditions may change and stores may find economic conditions so improved that they can go back to the old methods of charging interest. The deposit, too, which you are required to pay may be rather higher than normal, though this is by no means always the case. You may also be required to make the monthly payments by standing order, which of course means that you must have some kind of bank account from which the orders can be made. The reason for this is that shops try to minimize the possibility of default on payments, particularly on interest-free credit. Some shops also only offer interest-free credit for a limited period, perhaps over the sales months of July and January.

If you cannot get interest-free credit, the cheapest way to borrow is probably by bank overdraft, where the true rate interest is the same as the flat rate because interest is charged daily, followed by a bank loan. You may be offered some kind of 'special HP deal', particularly on expensive items; check to make sure that special is not actually more than normal terms. And normal terms may be a real rate of interest which is 10 per cent more than bank borrowing. For most people, the most costly item they buy on hire purchase, after their home, is a car. The AA has put out a set of sensible rules for those buying cars on HP. With modification, they can apply to any HP or credit sale purchase.

1 Make your initial deposit as low as possible. You can lose interest on your money if delivery is delayed for a month or more.
2 Check the true rate of interest before signing any agreement. Look at everything available before making your final choice.
3 Do not raise any money through a finance broker. You may be charged a brokerage fee as well as interest, which will make the loan very expensive.

4 Avoid finance houses which do not have a good reputation: their interest rates may be higher than they should be. Deal only with those which have a reliable record. These are usually associated with one of the clearing banks.

Above all, when you sign a hire purchase contract, or one for a credit sale, read all the small print, and know exactly what you are committing yourself to. Read section six, chapter 4, to make sure you are aware of the legal implications of what you are doing.

Hire purchase rates vary from company to company. If you are very lucky you may manage to get money at a true rate of interest around 15 per cent. The more reputable firms charge interest at about this level. If you are unlucky you may pay more than 40 per cent a year. Avoid this if at all possible, and insist that the lender tells you the true rate of interest he is charging you. Under the Consumer Credit Act you are entitled to be told this *in writing*. There are four other things you must also be told in writing: the amount, number and frequency of payments; the deposit paid; the cash price; and the total price. If you do not get these, do not go ahead with the deal.

You may be required to put down some deposit, unless you are buying what is regarded as an *essential* item like a cooker, fridge or gas fire. If you agree to pay back the money very quickly in any credit sale – that is, within nine months – you may not have to pay a deposit. From time to time the government lays down rules about hire purchase and credit sales – the amount of deposit that must be made, the maximum length of the contract, for example. At the present time, stores and finance houses are free to fix their own terms.

There is an important legal difference between goods bought on hire purchase and those bought on a credit sale. You do not own the former until you have made the final payment, but goods bought on credit sale are yours legally from the moment you buy them. Turn to Section six, chapter 4, where I have set out the legal implications of this difference. Hire purchase and credit sales are the most common ways of borrowing to finance your purchases, but there are many other ways. Let's review the most important of them.

Your bank. I have dealt with this in detail in chapter 6 of this section, on current bank accounts. All you need to know here is that an overdraft, rather than a personal loan, is generally – though not always – the cheaper way to borrow.

Your credit card. Again, this is covered in detail in the next chapter of this section. Do not assume that the money outstanding on your credit card is not a loan. It most certainly is.

Your insurance company. If you have an insurance policy which carries a cash-in (or surrender) value, you may be able to borrow on it. The most common types of policy where this is available are usually a whole-life policy, or an endowment policy with a surrender value. The policy is used as security, and you may be allowed to borrow up to 90 per cent. These are attractive, because you do not need – though you can if you wish – to repay the loan until the policy matures. The interest rate you are charged will be relatively low compared with other forms of borrowing – sometimes only one per cent higher than the bank's current minimum lending rate. You can occasionally sell your policy to raise money. This is *not* a loan and you forfeit your rights under the policy. Auctions of policies take place periodically in London. The longer you have held the policy, the better.

An insurance loan is an excellent way to borrow, but remember that surrender values are low in the early years of a policy (see this section, chapter 13), so you will not be able to borrow for some time after you have taken the policy out. For this reason, it is not a good idea to take out a policy *simply* to provide yourself with a borrowing opportunity.

Personal loan from a finance company. You can use this for whatever purchases you choose. Finance companies prefer this kind of contract to a straight HP loan because it is easier for them to get their money back if the borrower defaults on his repayments, and the minimum loan may be £100 or even £200. Many stores arrange their loans to customers through finance houses and the National Giro Bank, which does not offer over-drafts, also makes loans in this way. As I said earlier, it can be an expensive way to borrow.

Credit accounts with shops. Sometimes these are interest-free, if you are only asking for the credit until the end of the month when you receive the bill. A great deal depends on how the particular store runs its credit accounts. Those that insist on immediate payment monthly generally charge nothing, or very little; those who allow you to pay back over a period in the same way as Barclaycard or Access (see next chapter) may charge a high rate of interest. Some stores allow you the option of paying either way, and you can vary your paying policy as it suits you.

Budget accounts with shops. Each store sets a minimum payment each month and the customer is allowed to buy goods up to twenty times the amount of the monthly payment he has chosen. As each payment is made the credit limit moves up by the same amount.

Such accounts are expensive to run, though the interest may be shown not as a straight payment but as a 'service charge'. This can be anywhere between 1½ and 2½ per cent of the amount outstanding each month. Get an ordinary account if you can, but if you have no security or a low income, a budget account may be all that the store will allow you. After holding it for some time they may be prepared to let you move over to an ordinary account.

Some of the banks have similar accounts today allowing you to borrow up to thirty times your monthly payments. This leaves you free to buy in any store, not just the one where you have an account, but at the end of

1984 the true rate of interest was over 20 per cent a year. Such accounts are usually called revolving credit accounts

Check trading. This form of borrowing is only for those who want small amounts and cannot raise money in any other way. It is a very expensive form of borrowing, with the interest rate going up to 70 per cent overall. It is also expensive for the retailer who accepts the check in payment.

Check trading first developed in the north of England in the mutual clubs in the industrial centres. It works very simply. The check trading company sells checks of values from £1 to £20. These can be used in any shop which accepts them. The repayment is made in twenty weekly instalments, which are usually collected from the borrower by one of the agents of the company. If the borrower pays, say, 5 per cent back on the value of the check the flat rate of interest annually is around 25 per cent. The *true* rate is far more. When the retailer turns the check in, he has to accept a discount of 15 per cent, or 15p in the pound, so the check trading company makes money from both the borrower and the retailer. Retailers, particularly in poor areas, are prepared to accept the high discount because it brings them in business which they would not otherwise get.

Nevertheless, check trading is useful for those with little money. As the collector sells checks as well as calling for the repayments, he or she often gets to know a family well, and in cases of real hardship it is possible to get the repayment deferred.

Mail order. This is probably the most common form of borrowing in the United Kingdom. The companies offering mail order vary enormously in size. Some are one-man businesses serving only their local area, where the customer may also be able to visit the shop and buy over the counter, but usually there is no discount for cash. But the really big area of mail order is the giant companies. These produce very large catalogues which they send to agents, who organize sales for them and take a commission on the value of the goods they sell. The mail order business has a long history, and, as with check trading, the amounts involved are relatively small, as a rule. The business developed from the old shop clubs which grew up in the Victorian era. Mail order firms normally operate on a credit-only basis. Prices are usually 'credit prices', and very often no cash price is given, so you gain nothing by paying cash.

It is rather difficult to work out what interest you pay with mail order. Repayments are generally made in twenty weekly instalments, and if that is the case you are unlikely to be paying more than an annual interest of 20 per cent. Sometimes the period is longer, particularly if expensive items like domestic appliances are involved. But interest is not that important with mail order, because although you pay a high rate you may occasionally find that the 'credit price' is actually lower than the price in shops. This is because mail order companies do not have anything like the overheads which shops and stores have to include in their prices. Mail order companies have few retail outlets, and generally agents are cheaper to run than large department stores.

The real bargains are usually to be found in branded goods. This is a selling ploy, for the customer can then compare prices in the main order catalogue with those in the shops. Non-brand names will usually be a little dearer, though not much, than non-branded goods in the shops.

Small loan societies. There are not many of these, and if you find one you are fortunate, because the rates of interest are comparatively good. They tend to lend small sums of money to their members for fairly short periods. This type of loan is gradually dying out, but you may still find a small loan company, a friendly society, or a non-profit-making credit union, which will lend small amounts

Second mortgage lenders. This type of lending is growing fast. Basically, it works on the principle that if someone has had a first mortgage for some time the value of the mortgaged house has probably risen sharply. This means that the house can be used as security for more borrowing, and that comes from second mortgage companies. They act as go-betweens. After checking the borrower's credentials, they introduce the prospective borrower to the prospective lender, which may be an insurance company, a finance house or some other kind of financial institution.

There are pitfalls, some of which I mention in chapter 8 of this section, on second mortgages, and borrowers should be absolutely certain that they know what they are letting themselves in for. Interest rates are higher than on first mortgages, sometimes much higher, and the borrower may be persuaded to take more money than is actually needed, so that the repayment burden is heavy. If you are seeking a loan for house improvements, try to get one from whoever is lending you the money on your first mortgage. That way you will avoid paying a higher rate of interest. Only get a second mortgage if you can find no other way of getting the money you need.

Where not to borrow

There are some forms of borrowing that you should avoid unless you are desperate, and even then it's wiser to keep on trying rather than resort to them. These are money lenders and pawnbrokers. It is difficult to decide which is the worst bet, but I opt for money lenders: all you lose in pawnbroking is the stuff you have pawned, whereas money lending rates are punitive.

Money lenders. This is an expanding business, despite the pitfalls for borrowers. There are around 3,000 licensed money lenders in Britain, and many more who have tried to avoid being licensed. Obviously, if you must use them, go to a licensed one. As a rule, they lend no more than a few hundred pounds – £100 or £200 are the most popular amounts – and the interest rates are prohibitive. If you have some security for your loan – and if you have, it is unlikely that you would go to a money lender in the first place – you may pay anything between 20 and 40 per cent flat rate of interest.

If you cannot secure the loan – and this is true of most people who go to money lenders – the flat rate will rise to 50 or even 60 or 70 per cent. Try all other possible lenders before resorting to the money lender. He is just for those to whom no one else will lend – for the money lender will consider any loan at all.

Pawnbrokers. These traders make their money from defaulters. The business was dying out in Britain, but there has been a revival as the number of people unemployed has risen. The real cost of a loan may be high, 3p in the pound is typical and there is often an 'arrangement fee' of £1 for each ticket. From May 1985, pawnbrokers, like other lenders, have had to quote the true annual rate of interest they are charging customers. Not that this is likely to put people off when they seek money from pawnbrokers: they are usually very desperate.

The pawnbroker will lend you money on anything which is saleable at a higher price if you default. Jewellery is most often 'pledged' – the term used to describe the security you leave with the pawnbroker – but items like cameras, radios, cassette players, musical instruments or even small antiques might also be acceptable. Remember that if your financial problems are more than very temporary you are quite likely to lose a treasured object.

What kind of borrower are you?

When anyone lends you money, whether for a house or to pay for a holiday, they will want to be as certain as possible that you will be able to pay it back. The lender is likely to want to know whether you are in a steady job, and how long you have held it. If you want a very large loan he will want to know whether you are also buying a house on a mortgage, and what other security you might be able to offer.

So the first thing any prospective lender determines when a loan is being sought is the personal creditworthiness of the borrower. Do not despair if you cannot prove that you are. a good risk because you have only just started working, or for any other reason. Just try to get someone to guarantee your loan. Be clear what this means, however, for *if you default the guarantor will have to pay off any remaining debt*. Minors, that is anyone under eighteen when they take out a loan, must always have a guarantor, because they cannot be sued for debt. Parents will be held responsible for any minor's debt, if there is no guarantor.

Many people take on loans on such terms that they are unable to maintain the payments. The lender does not wish to take court action any more than you will wish it to be taken, so if you run into difficulties inform the lender immediately and he will usually adjust the repayment period.

From time to time, *the rules* about credit sales and hire purchase are changed by the government. Check what the current rules are before you actually start negotiations. Once you have taken on a loan on certain terms these cannot be varied (except in the case of bank overdrafts), even if the rules change. New rules only apply to future contracts.

Finance companies have to obey the same 'credit guidelines' as those set out for the banks. This means that from time to time the money they have available to lend will vary, so even if you have been turned down in the past do not hesitate to go back again, either because your own circumstances are better or because the general economic atmosphere has improved.

Keeping your record clean

If you are in a reasonable financial position you will usually find that you can get a loan, unless you have a record of bad debts, that is, failures to repay previous loans. It is now extremely difficult to keep your bad debts secret. There are private companies who track down the debtor's record for the lender, and if you get a 'thumbs down' from them you are unlikely to get your loan.

Credit reference bureaux like the United Association for the Protection of Trade Ltd and British Debt Services Ltd keep records of all court actions for debt recovery and also seek out any other information which might be useful for a lender to know.

There is also an official organization, the Registry of County Court Judgements, which files all the records of judgements which are unpaid for twenty years, and these are available for public scrutiny for those twenty years. The Registry has been losing an increasing amount of money in recent years and the government from time to time has threatened to abolish it. You may think this would be good news for bad debtors, but this is not so. If companies find that their bad debts increase without the Registry, interest rates will almost certainly rise for all borrowers.

How likely are you to get into too much debt?

Over the years a picture has gradually grown up of the sort of family which is likely to get into more debt than it should. With some adaptation, you can see if you come into this category. If you can see yourself in the following, take extra care before increasing your borrowing.

- You are likely to be young, with more than the average number of children.
- Your total family income is likely to be above average.
- Neither husband nor wife takes financial responsibility for the family's debts (go back to chapter 1 of this section on personal budgeting and

forward to Section three, chapter 2, on setting up a home). Matters can soon get out of control if husband and wife buy what they want without reference to the overall family budget.

- Either husband or wife, or both, is rather happy-go-lucky, preferring to buy anything they need, or think they need, whenever they want to, rather than work out whether they can meet the financial commitment involved.
- As a family, the unit is inclined to blame its financial problems on outside factors which are not really to blame, instead of admitting that it has over-stretched itself.
- You are unlikely to do much reading, so it is certainly a remote chance that you will be reading this, unless you are already desperate. You are far more likely to rely on your TV set when making your financial decisions, rather than reading and looking around at the options open before you buy.
- Your family probably moves around a lot from house to house.
- You may recently be separated or divorced, and find the same money has to keep two homes.
- Finally, but not to be ignored, as it can be as the root of all overspending, a husband may well be happy in his job but his wife unhappy about the level of his income. This can lead to overspending on both sides, the wife through sheer frustration and the husband to prove that he can keep up with his neighbours.

From this list, it is easy to guess which age group tends to be in financial trouble; it is among those aged between eighteen and thirty that the total amount of money owed is way above the level it should be. You can work out more or less the amount of monthly outgoings you can afford; the precise figure will vary in every case. Factors which will influence it are your marital status, the size of your family, your other dependents, your travelling costs, and, of course, your salary and prospects of advancement at work.

In general, try to limit your total borrowing to no more than 15 per cent of the disposable income you have after you have paid your rent or mortgage. Even if you have few other commitments, never go above 20 per cent. Make sure that in any one year you do not owe more than 30 per cent of your annual income after tax and your basic needs. Above all, consider how stable your job is before you get into any debt at all.

Signs of over-borrowing
- You have too many small debts in different places. Your credit card limit may be near. Your overdraft is at its limit. In any revolving credit account your spending is always close to the maximum.
- You find yourself asking for longer and longer term credit and paying as little as possible on deposit.

- You have to stretch the payment of your bills to the point where some of the next instalments fall due before you have paid the current lot.
- You start thinking about putting all your debts into one place in an attempt to keep them under control. You may feel that it is better to have just one creditor, say your bank. This is sometimes a good idea, but there can be a temptation to start building up new debts all over again, unless you are very strong-willed.

The solution to too much debt

1 Sit down and work out the level of your debts and the periods over which you owe the money. If the total is way above the level it should be, look at those debts where the repayment period could be lengthened to ease the burden of your repayments, then contact the creditor and ask whether you can spread the repayment over a longer period.
2 If the excess debt is small, and two or three months of severe budgeting will solve the problem, have these two or three stringent months. It will be well worthwhile in the long run. Look at your future commitments and see which can be avoided altogether or cut down. A smaller car, perhaps? A less expensive holiday? It is likely you will find *something* you can do without.
3 If there really is no way in which you can economize, inform your debtors, and ask for an extension of the loan period, even if you were at the limits when you started. Many of them would prefer to get their money back a little more slowly than not at all.
4 If you decide that you must consolidate your debts, then try to make sure that this overall loan is at the lowest possible interest rate. Check back to earlier in this chapter for what is best for you. In general, it will be your bank if you have an account with one of the clearing banks, or a loan through the National Giro or Trustee Savings Bank if you do not.
5 Above all, *do not panic*. Few of us go bankrupt, but many learn a sharp lesson in avoiding it. If you do reach this stage, turn to Section six, chapter 5, to see what going bankrupt means. Even that is not the end of the world.

5 Using a credit card

Credit cards are possibly the most important development in borrowing since the end of the war – though the wrong use of them has almost bankrupted many people. Used properly, they can be extremely valuable in planning your spending because, to some extent, you can choose the method and timing of repayments. There are now at least fifteen million credit cards in circulation in the United Kingdom.

What a credit card does is to take away the need for a cheque, cash, or a formal hire purchase agreement when you are buying. You can either repay the whole amount at the end of the month, or stagger it over several months.

Bank cards

The two main bank credit cards in Britain are *Barclaycard*, which, as its name suggests, is issued by Barclays Bank, and *Access*, operated by National Westminster, Lloyds and Midland and their subsidiaries, the Clydesdale Bank, the Royal Bank of Scotland, and the Bank of Ireland and Northern Ulster Bank. Barclaycard is the oldest in this country – it was formed in 1963. Today the TSB, the Yorkshire Bank, the Co-op Bank and the Bank of Scotland also issue their own cards.

Credit cards are simple to use. You simply sign a bill when you buy something and keep a copy. The bill is sent each month. Naturally, you have to pay something for this service. At the end of 1984 it was 2.25 per cent a month at both Barclaycard and Access, but this works out at 26.8 per cent a year.

Between them Barclaycard and Access cover most big department stores and many smaller ones, most big garages and hotels and the smarter restaurants. You can also use them abroad. Access is interchangeable with Mastercharge and European Eurocard, Barclaycard with Bank Americard and Ibanco, Carte Bleu and Visa. The frequent traveller may find that they are not sufficient abroad, and not all countries make much use of them.

The Barclaycard, the Yorkshire Bank, the Bank of Scotland, the Co-op Bank and the TSB credit cards all carry the name VISA, the international payment systems group. Access has a similar relationship with Mastercharge, the other large payment systems company. You can use the relevant card where these two names appear.

Snags
- The cost of borrowing. The bank cards are geared to the bank, and therefore to bank interest rates. For this reason, the interest rate will vary from time to time.
- The credit limit. The bank will decide just how much credit it will give you. Students – if they get a card at all – may be limited to £50; £400–£500 is average, though some people get over £1,000.

Independent charge cards

Because of these limitations you may decide to use one of the independent cards for which you pay an annual fee. The main two are *American Express* and *Diners Club*. These can be widely used throughout the world, and there is no limit on how much you can spend. *Clients get generous free credit* – forty-five days from Diners and sixty from Amex. After that they charge around 3 per cent a month, or as much as 39 per cent a year, on the balance. *But*, and it is a big but, they do not like lending money: you are expected to settle the whole of the bill when you receive it. These are *charge*, rather than credit cards. If you make a habit of delaying payments, they will pursue you vigorously and may eventually take away your card. They make their main profit by charging the outlets.

Snags
- Not as useful in the UK as the bank cards, because there are fewer outlets. Do not make either of them your only card.
- They charge you for your card, which the banks do not. At the end of 1984, the cost was £22.50

The Gold Cards

In 1981, American Express, in conjunction with Lloyds Bank, introduced the Gold Card. This costs £50 a year, in addition to the £22.50 on the ordinary card (or £20 joining fee if you do not have a green card), and its added benefits are doubtful. Anyone with a Gold Card is entitled to an unsecured loan with Lloyds for a minimum of £7,500, and more can be negotiated if you are really rich. (The interest rate is never more than 2½ per cent over the Lloyds Bank base rate.) This card, however, is only for those who want to borrow in a major way, repay gradually and who don't mind a high interest charge. The major banks also now offer gold cards, which work in a similar way. They cost £40 a year and, like the Amex card, are charge rather than credit cards. They offer holders special cheque cashing facilities as well as loans.

Department store accounts and others

In many department stores the old monthly accounts are giving way to a system similar to the bank credit cards. If you settle a bill immediately you get it, there is no interest to pay. If you delay or stagger your payments, there will be an interest charge of between 1 and 2 per cent a month (12.7 per cent to 26.8 per cent a year).

Most stores issue a card like the ordinary credit card, either for one store alone (Harrods, for example) or for a group of stores (like Debenhams). Very few charge as much interest as Barclaycard or Access.

You can also have a *budget account*, which has a credit limit. You put in a regular amount each month, and can spend to the limit of your credit. The minimum payment in is usually at least £5 a month and the spending limit at present is 20–30 times the monthly amount. This is called 'revolving credit', because as you put more money in each month so you automatically extend your credit limit by that amount.

There are many other small credit cards, which tend to be for a particular purpose – airlines, hotels and car firms sometimes issue them, for instance. Some offer discounts to card holders. Naturally, they are hard to come by and go only to privileged customers.

Discount cards

A fairly recent development is discount cards. They have been in evidence for a long time, but limited to one particular store or service. Now 'blanket' cards are beginning to be issued. *Countdown*, for instance, allows its customers a discount for paying cash at about 18,000 outlets. The enrolment fee is £3 and the annual charge is £12.95. Students get a special rate, if they are in the National Union of Students. The discount is mostly 10 per cent, but occasionally only 5 per cent.

Even if you do not have this card, you can always ask for a discount if you pay cash, particularly in any establishment which takes cards.

Protecting your credit card

It is possible to insure yourself against the loss of your credit card and the possibility of it being used fraudulently. Insurance companies will insure you to the credit limit you are allowed on Barclaycard or Access, and to an agreed limit on other cards. Many credit card companies offer insurance. Check if their rate is better than the insurance company's.

Remember, you are responsible for any bills, even if you have lost your card, *until you inform the company of the loss*. So phone or telegram immediately you find your card is missing. Confirm this by letter. The company will then inform its outlets and the card will not be able to be used by anyone (even you) if it happens to turn up. You will be supplied with a new card.

Cash and credit card customers

Though there is nothing to stop anyone not using a card and paying cash from asking for a discount, the shops and other traders which accept cards are not allowed to charge a premium to credit card customers. This practice was quite widespread, particularly amongst garages. In September 1980, the Monopolies Commission, a government-appointed body which looks at cases where one business or another may have an unfair advantage over others, proposed that the credit card companies should officially allow traders to make different prices for cash and credit card customers. In December 1981, however, the government announced that this practice would not be permitted. Using a credit card is not the same as buying on credit, because the retailer gets the full amount immediately he puts in the bills, less commission charged by the credit card companies. Some retailers still try to recoup this commission back from the customer. *If it happens to you, refuse to pay and report the trader to your credit card company.*

6 Your current account

Do you need a current account?

Bank advertising always implies that everyone should have a current account at a bank. So far they have managed to convince 60 per cent of us that they are right. Are we correct in assuming then that the other 40 per cent are wrong? Quite simply, no. Not everyone needs a current account.

A current account differs from a deposit account, which I have already discussed, in that you pay in one way or another for the services which you are offered and the degree to which you use them, rather than the bank paying you interest on the money you have in your account.

A current account operates very simply. You can open one with a clearing bank with any sum from a few pounds upwards. In return you will be provided with a cheque book, which you can use either for cash withdrawals from the bank, or to make payments without having to use cash. Life today would be impossible for many of us without the cheque facility. Just imagine carrying around £4,500 in £1 notes if you were going to buy a car, or always having to send cash through the post. Transmitting money by means of a piece of paper, which is protected by your signature and the details you must fill in on it, is obviously much safer than sending actual cash. Today, most banks give customers a cheque guarantee card, which covers cheques up to £50. The majority of customers now also get another card, which enables them to get cash from machines inside or outside the banks, which do away with queuing. The amounts customers can draw on these cards varies depending on how the bank rates the individual as a customer.

Another vital difference between current and other accounts is that you can have access to more money than you actually have – with your bank manager's permission. He may be prepared to allow you an overdraft, which will be fixed at a certain limit depending on your needs and circumstances.

Before agreeing to open an account for you, the bank will probably ask you for one or two references. Quite reasonably, the manager will want to know if you are who you claim to be, whether you can be relied upon to be honest and responsible, and whether your employers are prepared to recommend you.

There are several questions you should ask yourself before deciding whether the services of a bank would be useful to you and make the management of your money easier, or whether, when the glamour of having a cheque book wears off, you would really be throwing money away by having a current account.

1 Are you paid monthly or weekly, and does your money come in cash or by cheque or credit transfer? You can usually choose, but your employers may be reluctant to use one method for you and another for everyone else.
2 Do you have enough transactions to justify the use of a current account? This isn't just a matter of the cheque facility. Banks will deal with all sorts of payments for you: rent, mortgage, annual orders to clubs, electricity and gas bills and a host of others.
3 Is earning interest on your money less important to you than the very obvious advantages of having a cheque book? This makes it much easier for you to move money around, but at a cost.
4 If you need to borrow money, is the bank the best place? You can get money from building societies and finance houses. To borrow from a bank you will almost certainly have to have an account with a particular branch and a steady source of income coming in to pay off your debt eventually.

You may feel after answering these questions that a current account is not for you. You can take it that you do not need a current account if:

1 You are paid weekly in cash.
2 Your rent is collected from you at the door.
3 You always use cash when shopping.
4 You pay for your gas and electricity by putting coins in a meter.
5 You do not have a regular enough income to make an account worthwhile.

If you fit into this pattern, look at chapter 3 of this section on savings accounts.

Your bank manager

Remember that banks are more than a convenient place to put your salary and savings. They offer many services to their customers – travel facilities when you are going abroad, insurance, financial advice on investments, executor and trustee services, advice on setting up a company. I have dealt with these where they arise in other parts of the book, but mention them now to illustrate just how important a person your bank manager will be in your life.

So choose him with care. The best and most troublefree banking comes from a long-standing relationship with one bank. People who move about will be treated with caution. By all means, argue with your bank manager if you do not think you are getting the best possible service, but only change your bank as a last resort. It is better, too, if possible, to stay at the same branch. Over the years succeeding bank managers will get to know you well, and if you have conducted your affairs properly and within your means your bank manager will always be prepared to help you if you are in temporary difficulties, or, say, you want to expand your business.

Make sure your bank manager knows everything about you. Don't try to fool him; he is trained to notice subtle changes in your payment policy. So, if you get married or divorced, come into some money, start a new business, get a rise, make sure he is one of the first people to know about it. *Your bank manager is the best financial friend you can have.*

Bank charges

The basic difference between a deposit account and a current account is that your money will earn interest in the former whereas you will pay for having the facilities the latter offers.

If you manage your current account properly, however, you can reduce – and even eliminate – the charges you will have to pay. Every bank has its own rules, but there are some broad principles to follow if you want to keep your bank charges to a minimum. Remember, though, even if you pay no actual charges, you are in effect paying something because you could be earning interest somewhere else with the money you have in your current account.

This is why the banks are able to offer some of their customers charge-free accounts. They assume that the client's money carries a nominal rate of interest, so until that amount is used up in the carrying out of the services the account offers, account holders do not pay charges. Probably about half of the high street banks' customers do not pay charges today on their current accounts, because they meet the conditions laid down by the banks for charge-free banking. These vary from time to time and occasionally one bank will have the edge over the others. *It is not worthwhile changing your bank because of this: costs tend to even out over a period*. One rule which has irritated a great number of bank customers in the past was that they had to maintain a minimum of £100 in their current account each quarter, or pay charges for that quarter (some banks insisted on an average of £100 a quarter instead). The £100 minimum applied, even if the account dropped below that level for just one day. National Westminster, Barclays and Lloyds all had this minimum at the end of 1984, but the others – the Midland, Williams & Glyn's, the Co-op, National Giro, Clydesdale, the Royal Bank of Scotland, the Bank of Scotland and Yorkshire Bank – required only that the account was kept in credit – 1p would do.

Midland had always been in step with the other big three, but broke ranks in December 1984 by bringing in free banking to all current account customers who were in credit, heralding a new era in banking competition.

In December 1983, National Westminster had brought in a £3 quarterly standing charge as well as charges for each debit, but at the same time said that there would be no charges at all to current account holders who were in credit, as long as they kept a minimum of £500 on deposit with the bank. Barclays followed with a similar scheme a year later. It is wise to keep a watch on all developments in bank charges, because by moving a bit of your money around, you can often eliminate the charges.

If you find that you must pay charges, the rates for the cost of each direct debit or standing order vary between 12p and 20p, depending on the bank, and between 25p and 30p for cheques. These are quite high charges: it is obviously sensible to get charge-free banking, if you possibly can.

At the end of November 1984, the National Westminster Bank announced that in future it would send its private banking clients a breakdown of how the charges on their account arose. Other banks seem likely to follow suit and this should prove a valuable aid to customers, particularly if they think they are being over-charged.

Even if you fall below the qualifying level, however, you will not necessarily have to pay the full charges. As long as you are not actually overdrawn, the banks make some allowance for any money which you have in your account. This means that they credit interest to the account and deduct the total from the assessed charges. The interest allowed is usually two per cent below the particular bank's current seven-day interest rate.

Most banks offer charge-free banking to students, even if they do not have the required level of credit, and some now permit them to be overdrawn to £100 before making any charges. Such charge-free banking may continue for up to one year after graduation. Other banks make loans to graduates at special rates. The banks are relatively generous to students, because they see them as future profitable account holders. It is worthwhile looking around to check on the best offers to students before opening an account.

Clearing cheques

Clearing is simply the process used by all banks in cooperation with one another to get money from one place to another as fast as possible. That is what banking is all about – *the transmission of money*. In the past the system was a mechanical one, with cheques and money whizzing about the country. Today the computer has arrived and a company, Bankers' Automated Clearing Services, provides facilities for the transfer of magnetic tapes containing details of customer transactions from bank to bank. As well as this, of course, the banks themselves deal with transactions between their own branches. The system is fast and accurate, but mistakes can occur. So, if you decide to have a bank account, keep your own record of the payments you make and the money you pay in and check it against the statement of your account which the bank will send you from time to time.

This is how it works:

1 A cheque is a written instruction to your bank to pay a certain amount of money on your behalf, debiting your account.
2 When the payee received the cheque, either from you directly, or through the post, he deposits it in his own bank, or gets cash for it.
3 The cheque is then sent to London to be 'cleared'. To make the system fast and efficient cheques are not cleared individually, but centralized. All the cheques are added up and each bank gives just one payment to, or gets one from, its competitors. Putting the system on the computer has made this process even faster in the past decade.
4 The cleared cheque is then sent back to the branch on which it is drawn – that is, your bank. Your account is then adjusted for the amount of the cheque, assuming you have enough in the account to pay. If not, the bank may refuse to pay. This is known as 'bouncing' your cheque. So make sure you either stay in credit or have arranged an overdraft with your bank manager.

As you can see, this is quite a complicated procedure. Clearing usually takes only two days, as the banks are highly efficient.

Cheque guarantee cards

Being able to make payments by cheque is certainly the most important benefit offered by the bank to the account holder. But the system would not work if the people to whom cheques are made out are not virtually 100 per cent certain that they would be honoured by the bank. A shopkeeper must be sure that a cheque is as good as cash, and there are still a few – a very few – who refuse to take cheques at all.

In recent years the banks have taken steps to put the bank's backing behind the individual customer's cheque. They have introduced the cheque card, which guarantees that they will honour cheques up to a certain amount, regardless of the state of the customer's bank account. At present the level is £50. The customer produces his cheque card when paying or cashing a cheque at a bank branch other than his own, and if the number is noted on the back of the cheque by the *payee*, the bank guarantee payment. If the account becomes overdrawn the banks takes the matter up with the account holder. If the holder persistently runs into overdraft, or over his overdraft limit, the bank may take away the card. At the end of 1984, the limit for cash withdrawals was two cheques of £50 each per day. You could of course use other cheques on the same day for payments in stores, etc.

All the clearing banks now offer a cheque card. For customers of Barclays their Barclaycard counts as a cheque card as well as a credit card.

You should try to get a cheque card; the banks now automatically offer them to all their creditworthy customers. You may not get one if you are a student or have no regular income going into your account, but try to persuade your bank manager to give you one. Some parents are willing to guarantee their student children's cheque cards, and banks are usually happy to accept this guarantee. Remember, an honest face, or a driving licence, is no substitute for the guarantee of a cheque card.

There are some snags, however. A cheque drawn on a cheque card cannot be stopped in any circumstances, even if you instruct your bank before it arrives. So if you are buying something you may wish to take back don't use your cheque card.

How to use your account

Paying in

Banks are not fussy about the form in which you pay money in to your account. They will accept cash, cheques, money orders, foreign currency and postal orders. Nor are they fussy about where you pay it in. You need not go to your own branch, or even your own bank. At your branch you simply fill in a credit form; anywhere else you use what is known as a 'bank giro form'. Fill it in and the money will be credited to your account in a few days. You can also pay money into anyone else's account as long as you know their branch and account number.

Payments through the bank giro used to be free, but in 1981 Barclays and Midland began to charge 50p on cheques from other banks cleared through their branches. The other banks retaliated by charging 50p to Barclay and Midland account holders, so it is better and cheaper to use a branch of your own bank to cash cheques. The charge at Barclays rises to £2 for people cashing cheques on other banks on Saturday morning.

Writing a cheque

It may never have occurred to you that there are right and wrong ways of writing a cheque, but they are in fact one of the easiest things to add to or forge. Here are some sensible rules for cheque writing:

- *Never* give a signed blank cheque to anyone you cannot trust completely. I would even say never sign one at all, because it can be lost and then it's as good as cash.
- *Never* change your signature after you have given the bank a specimen signature for their records.
- *Never* leave any space either at the beginning or the end when you are writing in the amount, or putting in the figure. The pound figures should be as close to the sign as possible with a dash which does not allow a number to be slipped in and which finishes right up against the amount of pence.
- *Never* use Mr, Miss, Mrs or Ms, and, if you are a married woman, don't use your husband's name rather than your own Christian name (it can confuse the bank).
- *Never* write cash cheques for anyone you can't completely trust.
- *Never* lend anyone one of your cheques, or borrow from anyone else. Technically you can write a cheque on anything, but banks do not like this and will scrutinize very carefully any cheque which looks unusual.
- *Do* write in ink; pencil is legal but can easily be tampered with.
- *Do* date the cheque properly. Try not to date cheques ahead. This may worry the bank, or the payee, who may wonder whether you will have enough to pay when the time comes.
- *Do* write the name of the payee very clearly.
- *Do* write the figures in the box as well as writing out the amount fully. Since decimalization the banks have advised customers to use a hyphen and not a decimal point between the pounds and pence – £5-73, not £5.73. Always put two figures after the hyphen – £5-03 not £5-3. Write the figures carefully: a 3 can become an 8 or 9, a 1 a 4 or 7 written sloppily.
- *Do* cross a cheque which has to go through the post. Write 'A/C Payee' or 'not negotiable' on it. It is as well to cross *all* cheques; this means cash cannot be drawn on it, it has to go through the banking system.
- *Do,* if you have to endorse a cheque – sign it on the back – write in exactly the same way as you have written your name on the front. If that is not your usual signature, add it as well. Wait until you are depositing the cheque before you endorse it. If you lose an endorsed cheque, anyone can cash it.
- *Do* fill in the counterfoil. It's simple common sense and will help you to check statements, which are not as detailed today as they used to be. If you have no record yourself, it may be difficult for the bank to trace a lost cheque.

Protecting yourself against forged cheques

1 Follow the rules for writing cheques set out above.
2 Guard your cheque book as well as you guard your money. A cheque can be better than cash, because it can be written out for any amount.
3 Tell your bank immediately, by phone, if you lose even one cheque.
4 Check your bank statement for any discrepancies.
5 If you change your name, address or bank number, destroy all your old cheques.
6 Avoid a sloppy signature; it is much easier to forge.

If you are a shopkeeper accepting a lot of cheques, there are tell-tale signs to enable you to spot the possible cheque-bouncer. You should be suspicious of:

1 Anyone who does not have a cheque card.
2 Anyone who is impatient and tries to hurry you.
3 Anyone who makes a fuss about providing identification.
4 Anyone who tries to persuade you to take a cheque larger than the amount of the purchase and asks for change.
5 Anyone who drops names. It may be an attempt to make you believe he or she is well-connected.
6 Anyone who is a minor, that is, under eighteen years old. Minors are not responsible for their debts.

Stopping a cheque

When you sign a cheque you are in effect making a contract to pay the amount of money stipulated on the cheque to the person designated on it. It is therefore a serious matter to cancel a cheque before the payee has had a chance to pay it in. Such an action can lead to legal proceedings.

Nevertheless, sometimes in your banking life you may feel that you have to stop a cheque. You may feel that the payee has acted fraudulently towards you. Whatever the reason, think very carefully before taking this step.

For your action to be successful, you should get in touch with your bank as quickly as possible, and also the payee, unless you anticipate trouble. This means telephoning. Follow up the telephone call with a letter immediately. Give the cheque number, its date, the payee's name and the amount. If the bank has paid out before your instructions arrive, it's too late.

Cheques written under a guaranteed cheque card cannot be stopped. If you are in dispute with the payee, you will have to pursue your quarrel in some other way. Remember this when you are buying clothes, particularly shoes, if you are in doubt about the purchase.

Borrowing from your bank

Most of us at some time or another will need more money than we have in the bank. You may decide that none of the methods of hire purchase suit you, that you need a bridging loan between buying one house and selling the one you live in, that you want to renovate your house and do not have the ready cash, that you need some money to expand your business, or that you are temporarily short of cash. In circumstances like these the bank will consider your request for money, and if it feels you will be able to pay it back from your regular income will grant you an overdraft or a personal loan. An overdraft simply means that your current account is allowed to go from being in credit into debit without the bank bouncing your cheques. The bank will usually set a limit on the amount you can go into the 'red' and it is usually only prepared to lend money in this way for a short period. If it grants you a personal loan instead, this means you are getting money rather than goods on hire purchase. You get a lump sum and pay it off in fixed instalments. You will have to pay interest on both kinds of facility.

Overdrafts

An overdraft is now the unique feature of current accounts at the clearing banks. Today other accounts offer cheque books and loan facilities, but none of them allow customers to use more money in their account than they actually have. This is known as going 'into the red', as opposed to being in credit, which is 'in the black'.

There is no doubt that an overdraft is the cheapest way to borrow because you pay interest on a daily basis. It is usually charged at a few per cent above the bank's minimum base rate, depending on your credit rating by the bank. It means that the amounts you are charged fluctuates from time to time. It will go down as your wages or salary go in and then rise as the payments go out. *You are only charged on the amount you owe each day.*

The rate of interest you pay on your overdraft will depend on two things: the current base rate which the bank has set, and how your bank manager assesses you as a borrower. The rate can vary from as little as 1 or 1½ per cent above base rate to as high as 5 per cent. If your general financial position is not sound you are likely to have to pay at the higher end. It is generally the big industrial corporations which manage to borrow at the lower rates.

Banks are tough when it comes to overdrafts. Private customers provide most of the deposits which come into the banks, but get only one sixth of the loans, so getting an overdraft is not always easy. But money is always available to the right customers, even when getting any credit at all is difficult.

Remember, however, that no bank will let you treat an overdraft as a long-term loan. You cannot, for instance, buy a house on an overdraft, though today the banks are competing with building societies on mortgages (see chapter 8). You will probably be able to 'bridge' your mortgage by an overdraft, if you need to. Bridging is the time between your buying your new house and getting the money for the sale of your old one and banks do not like the period to be more than six months. If your roof falls in, the bank will very likely lend you the money for repairs while you negotiate with the insurance company. It may finance a short-term car purchase, or allow you to overdraw if you suddenly have a number of once-and-for-all bills to pay.

If you have difficulties in paying off the overdraft you may find you are an unpopular customer for life. The bank will want a good reason about every six months if you wish your overdraft limit to continue, for overdrafts are not designed to let you live permanently beyond your means.

Never go in to your bank manager with a request he can easily turn down. It is highly unlikely he will finance your holiday, or the purchase of a fur coat or a hang-glider. If that is your secret intention, be careful.

It will help if you have someone or something which will guarantee your overdraft. The bank manager may look more favourably on rather a frivolous request if you are prepared to lodge share certificates, or house deeds, with him, in case you can't or don't pay up. He will also accept another person as guarantor, if they can prove that they have assets to cover your overdraft. But remember that if you do not pay, your guarantor will have to. It is a lot to ask of someone.

Personal loans

These are an alternative to overdrafts, but they cost more because the interest is generally fixed for the term of the loan. The bank manager may prefer to lend in this way, not because the bank will make more profit – though it will – but because he may feel you should have the discipline of paying back a fixed amount each month. If you have a persistent overdraft, he may ask you to turn it into a personal loan and run your account in credit. Try to persuade him not to do this. A personal loan has some advantages, however.

First, you may have to pay regularly, but you can spread the payment over several years. Second, you can do what you like with the money unless you are borrowing under the bank's home purchase schemes. If your bank manager lets you have a loan, it is because he thinks you can pay it back, as with any hire purchase contract – though he will probably, but not invariably, ask you what the money is for.

Lloyds Bank have some tips for customers when they go to their bank manager for a loan or overdraft. First of all, they say, you must have the answers to these questions:

1 How much do you want?
2 What do you want it for?
3 When will it be repaid?
4 Where will the repayment money come from?

They also suggest:

- Be honest about your commitments.
- If you run into trouble, don't be afraid to shout early.
- Don't ask for too little, as it is as bad as asking for too much.
- Don't anticipate future income which may not mature, or legacies from relatives.

Tax relief on bank interest
There is a widespread – but inaccurate – belief that you can no longer get any tax relief on interest you pay to the bank. It is true that over the years tax relief has been reduced, but it still remains for certain items:

1 *Home loans.* More and more people are buying their houses on mortgages through the banks (see chapter 8).If you do this, you get full marginal tax relief on the interest on the loan just as you do with any mortgage. As with any mortgage, you are allowed a limit of £30,000 advanced and can only have relief on a loan on your principal residence.
   You can also get tax relief on any loan which is for improving your home, as long as you keep inside the £30,000 limit. This does not mean you can get tax relief on your current maintenance and repair bills; it must be a real improvement, like a second bathroom or central heating.
2 *Bridging loans.* It frequently happens when you are buying one house and selling another that the two deals don't coincide. When this happens you can get a bridging loan to tide you over, and can get tax relief on the interest on such a loan as long as you are not over the £30,000 limit. Without this tax relief many people would not go through with the deal, but usually the relief only lasts for twelve months, by which time you are expected to have your deal settled.
3 *Personal loans.* Applicable only if you are borrowing for strictly business purposes. It doesn't matter whether you are employed by someone else or self-employed: if you can prove that the purchase is strictly for business – say a typewriter, car or van – you will get tax relief.
4 *Overdraft.* Once again only if the loan is strictly for business purposes.

Other services offered on a current account

Standing orders and direct debits
Cheques are not the only means of using your bank account for making payments without using cash. There are two other ways: standing orders and direct debits. Standing orders have been in operation longer and cost more, and direct debiting is now taking over a great deal of this business.

If you have regular bills of a fixed amount – say, annual subscriptions, rent, or insurance policy premiums – you can pay them by means of standing orders. These can be very useful, because the bank takes over the 'remembering' for you and transfers the money on the particular date stated by you each year, month or even week. You will, of course, have to remember it yourself when checking your account. To arrange a standing order, simply fill in a form. It can be cancelled at any time.

Direct debiting is particularly useful when payments are likely to vary. The person or company to whom the payments are due is given the right to approach your bank directly and ask it to debit the appropriate amount from your account whenever a payment falls due, and credit its own account. This is cheaper than payment by standing order because the banks deal directly with one another. The customer is always asked for his permission before any new regular payment is debited.

But be careful: if you already have a standing order, it may be transformed into a direct debit without your being told. Some customers do not like this, and if you are one of them get the company and the bank to return to the standing order procedure.

Cash facilities

One of the problems for working people with bank accounts is getting to them. As I write, banks are open only between 9.30 a.m. and 3.30 p.m. from Monday to Friday, apart from Barclays, which opens some branches on Saturday mornings. Other banks will follow during 1985. The banks have also expanded their cash dispensing services to tide their customers over the times when they are closed, or when they cannot get to their own branches. As usual, each bank has its own system, but the services they offer amount to broadly the same thing.

1 *The cheque card.* This can be used at any branch of any clearing bank to obtain up to £50 cash twice in one day, just as it can be used for purchases. Some shops, too, will cash cheques outside banking hours for people they know.

2 *The cash card.* This is usually a small plastic card which can be inserted into a cash dispenser at some branches. You tap out on a keyboard your own personal code, and a fixed sum of money is delivered to you. The card is then returned for future use. Your account is then debited. Some cards deal in fixed amounts, others allow certain amounts to be drawn as arranged between the bank and the customer. Some bank branches provide this service outside the bank twenty-four hours a day, but others only inside the bank. All the latter does is help you avoid queueing; it does not effectively extend your banking hours. These new dispensers can sometimes do other things, apart from giving you the cash you need – provide you, during the week, with a written record of the balance in your current account; take an order for a statement of your current account; take an order for a new cheque book.

The snag about all these services is that they are not yet available at all bank branches. The machines are costly to install and it will be many years before there are almost as many machines as bank branches. Make sure, if you have a cash card, that you always carry a list of where the machines are.

Deposit boxes

These are used by people who wish to keep valuable jewellery, important papers, etc. outside their homes. There is no doubt that they are far more secure from burglary in the bank than in the average home. The bank takes as much care of its customers' personal items as it does of their money and charges a fee for so doing. Deposit boxes are in short supply and it is difficult to get one. Most people lodge what are called 'secure envelopes' at the bank instead. These may cost as little as £2 an item. Companies specializing in deposit boxes have grown up during the 1980s: they are usually situated in the major towns, particularly London.

Many people put things in security boxes because they wish to keep them secret. Banks don't ask what is in the box or envelope and they don't want to know. It is not unknown for people to store items illegally, and the banks don't want to be involved.

But banks do get robbed. They make it quite clear that they do not accept responsibility for loss or damage caused by criminals. To protect yourself you must take out insurance. Shop around. As with all insurance, the rates vary enormously. Any company which does household contents insurance will probably quote a special 'all risks' premium for the contents of your box.

Joint accounts

A current account need not be for one individual only. Many married couples have a joint account, and some banks require parents to hold one jointly with their child until the child reaches eighteen. You can, if you persist, make sure that only the child has drawing facilities and – though even more persuasion is needed – that only he gets the bank statement. In this case, the parent is acting as guarantor, and the bank will not be slow to inform him or her if the child gets into overdraft.

Joint accounts can be convenient for married couples, but they have serious drawbacks, which married couples should consider before pooling all their money:

1 Some banks regard the wife as only the agent and not the principal in a joint account. This means that they will send the statement to the husband only and in the event of his death will not allow the widow access to any money until probate is proved. Make sure that joint really means joint when you open the account.
2 Husband or wife may not always know what the other has drawn out. Unexpected moves into the red can cause family rows.

One possibility is to have a joint account to which you both contribute, if you are working, which is designed to pay household bills and nothing else, and separate personal accounts. An account just for bills is in any case useful, even if you are single, but it also means that married couples can keep their private spending quite separate – no one can complain if you are treating yourself on your own money, after making your contribution to the joint fund.

Bank budget accounts

If you are new to banking, uncertain about your money management, or have to make fixed regular payments every week or month, you may find that a budget account in addition to your ordinary current account will make your financial life easier. The banks have brought in this kind of account to help people who find that their bills come in batches, whereas their credits tend to be spread evenly throughout the year.

What you do is add up all the bills you expect to have to pay during the year, excluding those like rent or mortgages which you pay every month anyway:

rates	£600 (payable twice a year)
gas	£400 (payable quarterly)
electricity	£500 (payable quarterly)
life insurance	£90 (payable annually)
house insurance	£20 (payable annually)
car insurance	£120 (payable annually)
TV licence	£58 (payable annually)
season ticket	£500 (payable annually)

This sample gives a total expenditure of £2,288. Now divide this sum by twelve (or thirteen if you prefer) and transfer the money (£190.67 or £175.84) from your ordinary current account each month by means of a standing order or direct debit. If you can, add a margin to allow for increases in your bills. The bank will then supply you with a special cheque book to pay the specified bills. It does not matter if you run into an overdraft in one particular month. This will almost certainly happen, but you will end the year in balance.

A budget account is not free, but it can save you money because:

1 Annual season tickets are much cheaper – and save you still more money when fares rise – than weekly, monthly or quarterly seasons.
2 Car tax is cheaper if you pay by the year, rather than every four months.
3 Overdraft charges are higher than budget account charges.

The banks calculate the cost of budget accounts in different ways. Some charge a high basic fee based on the total amount passing through the account during the year, with no charge when you are overdrawn. Others charge a rather low fee, but there is an overdraft charge when the account goes into the red. Work out which one suits you best. If you pay out heavily at the beginning of the year, the first kind will probably pay off for you. If, on the other hand, you can build up a credit in the earlier part of the year, the second method will be best.

Before choosing your bank, consider all these aspects of the bank's services before you make your final decision.

The National Giro

The National Giro was set up by the government to provide some of the services provided by current accounts for people with no bank account. To begin with it offered just a simple and cheap money transmission service, but since it was set up in 1968 it has developed into something much wider.

When it started, a Giro account was much cheaper to run than a current account at a bank. Since then the clearing banks have reduced their charges a great deal, so that the difference is small. Nevertheless, there are some advantages in having a Giro account:

1 Deposits can be made at any one of the 20,000 post offices that do bank business. As with clearing banks, you can have your salary paid directly into your Giro account.
2 Most post offices are open for six days a week, including Saturday mornings, and as you can withdraw up to £50 in cash every other business day, you have access to your account more days of the week and for a longer business day. There is also a Giro cheque guarantee card, like the banks', for up to £50.
3 You can transfer your money by means of a Giro cheque free to other Giro account holders in the UK. All envelopes for postal transactions are postage paid and supplied by the post office.
4 Standing orders are free.
5 Statements are free.

You get all these services because you do not earn any interest on the money in your account.

Unlike current account holders, holders of Giro accounts cannot get an overdraft. A personal loan scheme for account holders has been introduced, however. You must be over eighteen and not live in the Isle of Man to qualify. Details are available at any branch of Mercantile Credit, and preferential interest rates are available to Giro account holders who have their pay credited directly to their accounts.

Trustee Savings Banks

The Trustee Savings Banks are gradually becoming more and more like the clearing banks and by 1986 at the latest the transformation will be complete. They offer cheque accounts as well as deposit accounts, and using one tends to be rather cheaper than using a clearing bank current account. Cheques and standing orders are free as long as you keep in credit. Otherwise, charges are 35p for cheques, standing orders and direct debits and for each use of the automated teller machines. The TSB also provides a cheque guarantee card for amounts up to £50, overdrafts and other loans.

TSB cheque accounts are very useful for those who wish to keep their bank charges down. TSB cheques, if backed by a cheque card, should be just as acceptable as any other cheques.

The TSBs also offer many other services. They sell certain government stocks at a low rate of commission, provide travellers' cheques, and have their own unit trust.

The Co-op Bank

Alongside the other banks is the Co-op Bank, which is linked to the familiar Co-operative Wholesale Society. For many years it paid interest – and still does – on its accounts and for that reason was very popular with people who felt they could not afford the luxury of a current account which paid no interest. As with the TSBs, there are no charges, if the account is kept in credit. The Co-op Bank is small, with seventy branches, less than one million customers, but it does have 1,000 'Handybanks' in the big Co-op stores. These are open six days a week and can offer most of the services of a full bank branch. There are also 3,500 'cash a cheque' points in other Co-op stores, where anyone with an account can get cash during normal shopping opening hours. The Co-op Bank has also launched its own in-store credit card, the Handycard, which anyone, not only account holders, can have. For these reasons, an account at the Co-op Bank is worth considering, as it provides a source for cash outside banking hours.

7 Getting a roof over your head

Deciding to buy a home

There are few of us who do not think about buying a house or flat some time in our lives. Normally it is a sensible thing to do. It gives you and your family a guaranteed roof over your heads, and eventually it can yield a substantial profit, which can either go to your heirs or, if your family has grown up and left home and you decide to move to a smaller house, provide a boost to pensions in retirement.

Since the end of the last war, house prices have risen just about twice as fast as the cost of living. This means that house buyers have beaten inflation handsomely. Of course the rise in house prices has not been uniform over the years. There have been 'bubbles' in the upward trend when prices have barely moved, and sometimes, allowing for inflation, they have fallen. So it is not enough to say that buying a house is a sound investment. You need to think about buying at the right time. If prices were at their highest ever, and all the signs in the economy indicated a general slump, you would be wise to defer your purchase in case you have a chance to buy at a lower price later. Of course most of us cannot choose the time we buy. You may marry, change jobs, see the house of your dreams, at a time which is economically inconvenient. Then you will have to make the best of the opportunities which come along.

During the 1950s house prices were fairly stable: the price of new houses rose by 1½ per cent a year, that of old houses by about 2½ per cent. During the 1960s house prices increased by around 7 per cent a year. Then in the early 1970s the house market went quite mad; between 1970 and 1973 the average price almost doubled.

A shake-out from these high levels was inevitable, and there were some very sharp falls in prices – though in some areas they remained fairly stable. In the past two years prices have risen by only seven and three per cent respectively. The very sharp increases of the early 1970s seem unlikely to recur, at any rate for some time.

This was what has happened to average house prices since 1973 according to the Nationwide Building Society:

1973	£9,760	
1974	£10,200	+ 4.5 per cent
1975	£11,280	+10.6 per cent
1976	£12,200	+ 8.2 per cent
1977	£13,140	+ 7.7 per cent
1978	£16,810	+27.9 per cent
1979	£21,950	+30.6 per cent
1980	£23,480	+ 7.0 per cent
1981	£24,170	+ 2.9 per cent
1982	£25,530	− 5.6 per cent
1983	£28,720	+12.5 per cent
1984*	£31,460	+ 9.5 per cent

*third quarter

You can see from this table that, if nothing else, your investment will be safe, though there are enormous variations from year to year. It was not surprising that after enormous increases in 1978 and 1979, the rise slackened off considerably.

Figures like these will seem enormous in relation to your wages and the various other demands on your financial resources. For most of us, buying a house is the single most important financial transaction of our lives. We should therefore go about it with care; mistakes are expensive. First, let's look in a bit more detail at the advantages of house buying.

Unless you are fortunate enough to have been left a property, you will have to pay money wherever you live – whether you buy a house or rent one.

A *cash payment* means that you will own your house outright. This may give you peace of mind, but it is not always the best way to buy a house. You pay what the pound is worth at the time you buy, whereas if you stagger your payments over a number of years, you will in effect be paying less because the value of the pound will decline.

Most of us buy a house on a *mortgage* (see next chapter); few people have the money available for an immediate outright purchase. If you have a mortgage you can take advantage of inflation, and – at the moment – get tax relief on any interest you pay. This means that the cost of a mortgage is relatively low no matter what the interest rate.

Rent is money down the drain. You can easily pay as much in rent as you do with a mortgage, and rents are more affected by inflation. So you lose in three ways: you have no asset at the end of the day; your payments may not go down, relatively speaking, over the years; you get no tax relief.

After weighing up all these factors most of us would decide to buy a house if possible. There are other plus factors in owning a property:

1 You can resell it at a profit.
2 You eventually stop paying for your house at all when you finish paying off your mortgage. Until then a mortgage is like a subsidized rent.
3 You can sometimes let off part of your house, either as a flat, or as rooms, and so provide yourself with an income. Be careful though: if you are still paying a mortgage the building society will want to know and you will need its permission. Some ban sub-letting outright.

Choosing a home

Once you have found a house or flat you like you should ask:

● Is the price right?
● Is the size right?
● Is it a good long-term investment?
● Is it in the right area?

Let's look at these aspects in turn.

The right price
This depends not only on the value of the house compared with others similar to it, but also on your ability to pay the deposit and to cope with the mortgage repayments and the running and maintenance costs. Here the building society manager may give advice. Remember the legal and survey fees involved in the purchase. You must also make some estimate for initial repairs or redecoration. You must decide what new household equipment you will need. Your old curtains may well not fit your new house; your old cooker and fridge may be too small, or too big. You must decide if you need central heating, if your proposed purchase does not already have it. Finally estimate your travelling costs to work, and you will have some idea – though only an idea – of the minimum cost of your proposed purchase.

The right size
Again this depends on what you can afford and what you want. A seven-bedroomed flat is no use to a couple whose children have left home, while a four-bedroomed house is sensible for the couple with a number of children who will be around for some time. Some families can manage with very little private space; others find a small place claustrophobic and unsatisfactory. Work out your family needs in a realistic way with regard to money. Try if possible to anticipate your future needs. Buy a larger house than you need at present if you intend to have more children – if you can afford it. The costs of buying and selling to meet the needs of a growing family can be prohibitive.

A good long-term investment?
You can *never* be certain, but you should try to assess whether your house will be a good long-term investment. First, go carefully over the points mentioned earlier and check the house itself fully before buying. It is a good idea to have the house surveyed for yourself instead of just relying on the survey done on behalf of the building society. Always try to have two houses in view in case one turned out to be full of dry rot or damp, for example. This way you can avoid being too disappointed.

Second, you need to know whether the value of the house you choose is likely to move up more than the general average for the country, or – much less likely – whether you could possibly lose money. Ask yourself some questions:

1 *Is the area in which you propose to buy changing in character?* It could become more or less fashionable. Islington in the London area, for example, from being an area where living standards – and therefore house prices – were low, has partly changed into a middle-class area. This district shows the possible pitfalls clearly. Some streets have not changed at all; others are unrecognizable compared with twenty years

ago. There have been vast profits in the latter sections, but only small ones elsewhere. Hastings, on the other hand, has declined as a resort in recent years and the rate of increase in house prices has been less there than in many other areas. This is typical of many seaside resorts.

2 *Is your proposed house near a projected motorway?* This can have marked positive effect on house prices in an area, if commuting to work then becomes a practical proposition. The same applies where the property is close to a good rail service. The closure of railway lines has had a dampening effect on areas which were previously well served by them. But new developments are not always an advantage. You can be too close to a motorway, or, usually worse, an airport.

Do not underestimate the importance of these points. They can make all the difference to whether or not your house is a good long-term investment – and a pleasant place to live in at the moment.

The right area?
There are a few more questions you should ask yourself about the area in which you propose to buy:

1 Are other municipal costs likely to mean that you are stretched financially? In London, for example, it costs ratepayers far more to live in the Camden area than in Wandsworth. If you are a house owner, you must pay rates, though there are rebates for those on low incomes.
2 Is the house so far from your work that commuting costs are likely to more than outweigh any benefit you get from a lower purchase price and lower mortgage repayments?
3 Are there suitable schools for your children? Will they have a long way to travel to school?
4 Is the area so remote that you will have to have a car to live comfortably?

Regional variations in price
House prices are not uniform throughout the country, and there is some variation between flats and houses, and between different types and ages of house. There are always individual variations within an area, but on the whole prices are higher the closer you are to the centre of a city, and highest of all in London and the south-east. Here are the third quarter of 1984 valuations put out by the Nationwide Building Society:

	New	Existing Modern	Older
All house prices	£36,070	£33,120	£28,840
Greater London	£43,160	£42,530	£41,510
Outer Metropolitan area	£49,290	£45,700	£44,380
Northern Ireland	£27,800	£29,290	£18,270
Scotland	£32,770	£32,080	£29,190
Outer South East	£43,740	£37,810	£33,150
West Midlands	£32,700	£27,690	£23,920
Northern	£31,350	£27,240	£20,360
East Anglia	£34,950	£31,710	£28,500
South Western	£36,400	£33,900	£30,150
Wales	£31,670	£29,440	£21,990
Yorks & Humberside	£31,750	£27,200	£19,060
East Midlands	£31,070	£26,750	£20,610
North West	£33,080	£28,850	£21,220

You can see that houses in London and the south-east tend to be more than 50 per cent dearer than houses in north-eastern England, and even within the London area it costs more to buy in Chelsea or Hampstead than in Willesden or Whitechapel. In some areas new houses are dearer than existing ones, whereas in others the reverse is true. New town houses will probably cost more than existing ones, because they tend to be in very modern developments in already expensive areas. But existing houses can cost more than new ones, especially if they are detached or semi-detached.

These figures are only averages, but they may give you some indication of whether your house is correctly priced for your area.

Freehold or leasehold?

When you are buying you must enquire whether the property is freehold or leasehold. The former means that the owner has sole and permanent control over his house and the land on which it stands. This is the way most of us buy today. But, particularly with a flat, you may find that you are only buying a lease and that somebody else owns the freehold. This means that someone else has the permanent right to the house and land, and that you have it only until the lease ends. Many years ago leaseholds were considered a bad thing, but successive government action has protected many leaseholders. When a lease runs out many holders now have the right to take on a new lease or buy the freehold – at a negotiated price – if they wish.

Some leases are so long – ninety-nine years is quite common for a lease on a newly-built house – that having a lease is virtually the same as owning the freehold. In such cases the annual payment for the lease – the ground rent – will usually be quite small, just a few pounds, and the freeholder's rights are merely technical.

If you live in Scotland or Northern Ireland, remember that customs and laws are rather different than in England and Wales. There it is the rule rather than the exception to live in leasehold rather than freehold property.

The buying process

You will probably buy your house through an estate agent, though people do sometimes advertise their houses privately. In any case it costs the buyer nothing to use an estate agent: it is the seller who pays his fee, which is based on the size of the house. Estate agents also advertise. They keep details of some of the houses on their books in their windows, and some of the bigger ones also send out lists of houses and flats. A new Estate Agents Act does not allow bankrupts to become agents and sets controls over deposits left with them, but does not protect the public against incompetent agents. No qualifications are required and anyone can become an agent. They do not always know what they are selling.

The first thing to remember is that the price asked is what the seller hopes to get for his house. It is by no means fixed, and you can always make an offer for a house you like, but do not think is worth the asking price. Some sellers state straight away if the price is not open to negotiation, but even then it may be worth a try, especially if the house is in need of expensive repairs. Many owners, however, deliberately fix on a higher price than they expect to get, so that the prospective buyer is more likely to think he is getting a bargain if he offers less than the asking price. But, even if you do have an offer accepted, things can go wrong and you may find yourself gazumped.

Gazumping
A gazumper is someone whose word in house-selling cannot be taken at face value, someone who will accept an offer for his house but still leave it on the market in case a better offer comes along. There is not much you can do if this happens to you, as unfortunately there is nothing in the law in England and Wales to prevent it. Deals are 'subject to contract' and either side can cancel it until contracts are exchanged, a process which usually takes at least one month. Gazumping is not possible in Scotland, where 'subject to contract' does not apply. A bargain is struck when the offer is accepted. Gazumping is a thoroughly reprehensible practice, and most unfair on the *bone fide* buyer. It usually only happens when house prices are rising sharply.

Selling and buying

Very few of us spend our lives in the first house or flat we buy. We marry, our families grow bigger, then smaller again as children grow up and leave home. As a result, our housing needs vary all the time. Nevertheless, it is important to think carefully before moving, because it is expensive. If you are selling, there will probably be estate agent's fees, which can be between one and three per cent of the sale price, depending on the area and price level; legal fees for the solicitor representing you in the sale, which vary a great deal and, as a guide, vary between one and three per cent; and moving costs to your new home. If you then go on to buy, there is another lot of solicitors' fees to put the deal through. This is called 'conveyancing' and you can do it yourself, but it is difficult for anyone without expert knowledge. At present, apart from the do-it-themselves conveyancers, the business is restricted by law to solicitors. The law will change shortly, however, to allow in licenced conveyancers, who may be cheaper. You will have to pay for a building society survey (incidentally ask to see a copy of it, or you will have to have another one done for your own peace of mind). There is no fixed fee for surveys and the cost can vary. It increases with the value of the property. You may also have to pay stamp duty, which is levied on all houses and flats costing over £30,000. It is at the rate of one per cent on the total purchase price. Some sellers are willing to put the price a little below the various levels and charge the rest as furnishings and fittings and this can save you money.

Here are a couple of examples of what can happen:

Selling a £15,000 flat and buying a £20,000 house

Estate agents (1%)	£150
Solicitor's selling fee	£100
Solicitor's buying fee	£150
Survey (say)	£75
Moving (say)	£200
VAT (15%)	£101.25
Total costs	£776.25

There is VAT to pay at the current rate on the estate agent's fee, the solicitor's bill and the survey, and the moving bill. You may feel that an additional £675 on to the purchase price of your new home plus VAT £101.25 is acceptable, but the picture is less good the higher up the range.

You are forced to move because you change your job and you exchange your £35,000 house for another one at the same price in the area into which you are moving:

Estate agent's fees (1%)	£350
Solicitors	£600
Survey (say)	£125
Stamp duty (1%)	£350
Moving (say)	£200
VAT (at 15%)	£191.25
Total	£1,816.25

Clearly, if you can persuade your existing or new employer to pay your moving expenses, it is a good idea to do so. If you are simply moving from one house to another in the same area, you should think very carefully before doing so.

Buying your council home

Under the Housing Act 1980 some council tenants have the right to buy their homes, if they want to do so. If you have been what is called a 'secure tenant' for three years (see Section five, chapter 7) of a local council, a New Town, or some housing associations, you have the following rights:

- To buy your home.
- To buy jointly with those members of your family who live with you.
- To a discount price of between 33 and 50 per cent of the market price.
- To a mortgage from your local or New Town authority, or the Housing Corporation. This does not stop you from getting a building society mortgage, if you prefer.
- The option to buy within two years, if you do not qualify for a mortgage big enough for you to buy immediately.

Applications should be made to the Department of the Environment, or the Welsh Office, if you live in Wales, or the relevant New Town authority, or the Housing Corporation. Your property will be valued and the discount worked out. This depends on how long you have been a tenant. The minimum discount is 33 per cent, if you have been a tenant for three years, going up by one per cent to a maximum of 50 per cent after twenty years as a tenant. If you do not think the valuation is fair, you can discuss the matter with the authority. Tenants have a legal right to a valuation by the district valuer, who is independent: his decision on the valuation is binding.

Housing associations

In the past twenty years a number of housing associations have been established. They work in a variety of ways, but basically a group of people get together to develop new or existing properties. Everyone pays rent and tenants who leave after a certain time, which is decided by the association, get some capital payment. In this way, people have been able to build up some capital, even though they do not have an individual mortgage. Under the Housing Act 1980 tenants in some associations have the legal right to buy their homes. The association must be registered with the Housing Corporation and must *not* be registered as a charity, have received public funds, be a 'co-ownership' or 'fully mutual' cooperative.

The buying procedure is exactly the same as that for a council house or flat.

8 Financing your house purchase

The advantages of a mortgage

Few of us today have suffecent cash to pay for the entire purchase of a house in one go, so what we do is buy on long-term hire purchase. This is known as a mortgage. Even if you do have the money, it is not always a sound idea for several reasons:

1 You are entitled to tax relief on any interest you pay on money borrowed for a single house or flat purchase, or home improvement up to a limit of £30,000. A married couple count as one person.
2 You can borrow in an insurance-linked way, so that if you die the insurance company pays up the full value of any remaining borrowing.
3 In a period of inflation the value of money is falling, so that over the years you gradually pay less and less in real terms, even if your repayments rise now and again because of rises in interest rates. Anyway, as the interest rises, so does the tax relief.
4 If you have ample cash available, it would probably be better invested in some other way, for the reasons given above. You can then build up your capital from two or more directions at the same time.

Basically, a mortgage is just like any other hire purchase contract. You put down the deposit and pay off the remainder of the purchase price in several different ways. The organization granting the mortgage keeps the house 'deeds' (the word for the papers defining the property and indicating the ownership) until the debt is paid off. Mortgages differ from most HP in that the contract almost always runs for a much longer time and borrowers are entitled to tax relief up to a maximum of £30,000 on the interest paid. The interest rate, too, normally varies over the period of the loan, though a few people still have fixed interest mortgages. These are excellent when interest rates are *low*, but it would be foolish to take one out when they are *high*, as there would be no benefit from a later fall in rates. Building societies anyway today do not grant such mortgages.

A mortgage is a cheap way of buying a house, not only because of the tax relief. Over the years, even if repayments increase with interest rates, the effective payment normally falls, because of inflation. As salaries and wages also tend to increase over the years as well, it usually becomes easier to make the payments. In building societies depositors provide the money for mortgages, but building societies sometimes do not have enough money to meet the demand, so you may have to shop around before getting a loan. The flow of money coming into building societies can change quite suddenly, however, so check before despairing of getting a loan.

Most of us still borrow from a building society and until the 1980s well over 90 per cent of mortgages were granted by building societies. But recent years have seen something approaching a revolution in mortgage lending, as the banks have increasingly come into the business. Mortgages are also available, though the total amount of money involved is small, from local authorities. Insurance companies, too, offer mortgage schemes, though these have become much less attractive since the ending of tax relief on (new) life assurance policies in the 1984 Budget. Endowment-linked mortgages always carry a slightly higher rate of interest, usually 0.5 per cent more than the current rate on repayment loans. Bank mortgages are often preferred by those who borrow large amounts of money, because many building societies charge those who borrow more than £15,000 an extra ¼–½ per cent interest. Competition from the banks has had an effect on building society practice, however, and some societies, particularly the bigger ones, now have a single rate.

Tax relief on mortgage interest

Tax relief is available on all principal residence mortgages up to £30,000 and, because of a new way of giving the relief, even those who are not tax payers actually pay less on their mortgages than the simple interest rate would demand. The new system is known as MIRAS (mortgage interest relief at source). Previously the borrower used to make full interest and capital repayments and the amount of interest eligible for relief was then included on his or her tax coding. This meant that take-home pay was higher than it would have been without the relief.

All this changed from April 1983, when it became the responsibility of the building society to allow for the tax relief at the standard rate in repayments. The society then informed the government of the amount of relief allowed. This immediately meant that most monthly repayments dropped by about one third, but that take-home pay also dropped by a similar amount. Not quite the same amount for most people, because of the way the building societies decided to run the new system. They worked on the basis of the average interest which would be paid for the full period of the loan, so that many people found themselves paying effectively more in the early years of their loan and often effectively for the whole of the period, as the average mortgage runs for about seven years and not the 15, 20 or 25 years for which it is taken out.

Under the old system, tax relief was at its highest when the loan was at its highest and fell as the level of the outstanding loan fell. For anyone who has a loan for the full period the net effect of tax relief is the same. But it is important for new borrowers to recognize that the way MIRAS is run – not the new system itself – can add to their repayments burden in the first half of their mortgage.

Tax relief is, however, available at whatever level of tax we pay, although the MIRAS system allows only for the standard rate of tax. Anyone paying the higher rates will still have those allowed for on his tax coding and the adjustment will be made at the end of the tax year. The standard rate allowance for higher tax payers comes with the monthly payments. Further, anyone with a loan above the tax relief limit of £30,000 does not come into the new system. The old method of the interest payments incorporated in the individual's tax coding still applies.

The non-tax payer also benefits, because he, too, is allowed the standard rate of tax on his payments, so is effectively paying less interest. Prior to MIRAS, such people could have option mortgages, which carried a lower rate of interest, but did not qualify for tax relief. These have now lapsed and been included in the new system. On balance, the position of the non-tax payer has not changed with MIRAS.

Relief on mortgage interest is one of the most generous forms of tax relief. As well as the £30,000 limit, each person is allowed relief on only one mortgage, what is called the 'principal residence'. This means, for instance, that you cannot get relief on two mortgages of £10,000 each, even though the total is less than £30,000. The government introduced this limitation because it was felt that too many people were getting tax relief on houses they never lived in and were perhaps making an income from.

Married people living together count as only one person (the normal rule in most tax affairs, unless special dispensation is applied for, and it is never allowed in the matter of mortgage relief), so husband and wife cannot each have a mortgage and tax relief. The average mortgage today is still well below the ceiling at a little under £21,500, so the limit affects only the relatively well off. Again, few people buy more than one house at any time, so that limit is rather academic as well.

The tax rules allow relief on two mortgages for a short 'bridging' period between selling one house and buying another, or on any money borrowed while you are waiting for your new mortgage to come through, but again the total limit for all these loans must not go over £30,000. People who marry and who each have a mortgage when they do are given some time to sell one house before losing the tax relief, or they must decide which house is to be the principal residence and they get tax relief only on that one. In cases like this, it is better to have as a principal residence the house which is likely to yield the most profit on sale, because principal residences are not liable for any tax on the profit made on them, though the 1982 Budget has taken a lot of the sting out of capital gains tax. Since then, only *real* and not *inflationary* profits are taxed. (See Section four, chapter 1.) Men who are divorced can get tax relief if they are paying two mortgages, one for themselves and one for their former wife, but the £30,000 total limit still applies.

How much can you borrow?

The amount of money you can borrow depends, generally, on three things:

1 The type of house or flat for which the loan is asked and the value that the lender sets on it.
2 The status, age and salary of the borrower.
3 Who you borrow from.

The type of house or flat

Lenders have all sorts of preferences. Some may not lend on flats at all; others do not like leasehold property, unless the lease is so long that it is equivalent to a freehold; some do not like older houses; others may not lend on properties in the centre of a city. If one source fails, shop around until you find someone who will at least lend you some money in principle.

Anyone lending money is bound to be cautious. Having accepted the house or flat as suitable for a mortgage, they will then have it valued independently before deciding the amount of the loan. They will want to be sure that the sale value of the property is enough to cover the amount of the loan they give you. This is why they are unlikely to offer you 100 per cent of the price – though this can occasionally happen with new property developments where the developer building the estate negotiates an overall deal in principle. The valuer will come up with a price. It may be the same as you are paying, or it may even be more, but usually it is less – if only a little less.

If the value of the house is set at less than you are paying for it, you will have to pay the difference. The mortgager (the person giving you the mortgage) will only lend up to the limits of his own valuation, and will set particular limits depending on the age of the house – and, of course, on the borrower's ability to pay, which we will come to later.

Say you are buying a house for £30,000 and the mortgager values it at £28,000, you will have to put down at least that £2,000 difference, and to be on the safe side the lender will probably not give you 100 per cent of his own valuation. If it is an old house you may only get a maximum mortgage of two thirds of the valuation, and almost certainly not more than 80 per cent. On new houses the percentage may be 90 or 95 per cent, or, occasionally, 100 per cent. Let's take the above example for an older house. Here the borrower will have to find a total of £11,160.

	£
purchase price	30,000
valuation	28,000
66 per cent of valuation	18,840
balance of valuation	9,160
difference between valuation and purchase price	2,000
total balance	11,160

But the picture is different with a brand new house at the same price. To begin with, the gap between the purchase price and valuation will probably be narrower.

	£
purchase price	30,000
valuation	29,500
90 per cent of valuation	26,550
balance of valuation	2,450
difference between valuation and purchase price	500
total balance	2,950

In this case the borrower will have only to find a total of £2,950.

So when the lender says he will offer you a 66 per cent or a 90 per cent mortgage, he does not usually mean 66 or 90 per cent of the purchase price. In the first example he is actually offering 63 per cent of the purchase price and in the second 88½ per cent. The difference between what you would regard as a certain percentage mortgage and what the lender does can be quite wide.

With the entry of the banks into the mortgage market (they claim to be getting thirty per cent of all new business), the old rules are changing. Some societies are offering 95 per cent of valuation and banks up to 100 per cent.

The status of the borrower

To get a mortgage you must basically be in work; if you are self-employed you must be able to produce figures to show you are capable of paying off the loan. It no longer matters whether you are a man or woman: under the Sex Discrimination Act, women in the same financial position as men must be offered a loan on the same terms. What matters is your earning level and the reliability of your earnings.

It is extremely difficult to set down fixed rules. What one lender finds acceptable another may refuse outright. Some lenders, for example, would not consider actors or writers – both notoriously erratic professions – but others accept them if their average earnings figure over a number of years is adequate. On the whole, however, to borrow easily you must have steady and regular earnings and your requirements must relate to your ability to pay. If you are self-employed, you may be required to produce several years' profit and earnings records.

As a general rule you will find that you cannot get a loan:

1 more than two and a half or at the most three times your current yearly wage or salary, or
2 which would involve you in repayments of more than one quarter of your monthly earnings. The average borrower spends 18 per cent of his or her gross pay on a mortgage.

These limits are set so that the lenders can be as certain as possible that borrowers will be able to repay the loan.

But salary levels on their own are not enough. The lender will want to know a great deal about you: your age, which may limit the length of time for which you can get a mortgage; your health, which may affect your ability to pay; your work record, which may suggest that you are an erratic employee; sometimes even details of your family and nationality.

A good mortgage prospect is a family man (or couple) in a good steady job with a record of past saving, preferably in the building society which will be lending the money. The worst mortgage prospects are those who work for themselves, on commission or in uncertain professions, who at the same time have a history of bad debts. So if your earnings pattern is at all uneven, do at least avoid bad debts.

Although today women are entitled to be treated in the same way as men if their incomes justify it it is still possible for a lender to refuse to take into account the whole of a working wife's income in deciding how much to lend a couple, particularly if she is young and likely to stop working to have children. Single women should find no more difficulty than men in getting a mortgage. If you think you have been unfairly treated, contact the Equal Opportunities Commission in Manchester for advice. Its address is Overseas House, Quay Street, Manchester M3 3HN.

The *ideal* borrower, then, is a happily married man with a steady job, earning about £12,000 a year. That is ample to support the current average mortgage of £21,500, or even a little more.

If you don't meet these conditions, don't give up your search for a mortgage. Few of us are ideal, and even if we are, we do not always choose an ideal house.

Who you borrow from

You may get better or worse treatment depending on whom you approach for a mortgage. Local councils usually limit their loans to people who already live and work in their area, or who are planning to move into it. Occasionally, too, they may give priority to a particular class of borrower. They may, for example, be trying to help the lower income groups, or to help people to buy the houses and flats they live in as council tenants. Councils tend to be rather more generous with loans than building societies; insurance companies tend to lend more on higher priced houses than either councils or building societies, and are often more flexible about the state the house is in. Building societies, particularly the smaller ones, may limit their loans to people who have been saving with them for some time. Banks are the most flexible.

You can often increase the amount of the loan you are offered by providing additional security in the form of savings or an insurance policy, and sometimes you can borrow more money from an employer or even your bank. But take care not to overstretch yourself financially by borrowing more than you can comfortably repay.

You may also be a borrower who is treated as a special case. This happens sometimes to tenants on a lease who have the opportunity to buy the freehold because the owner wishes to release some capital on his property. Certain leaseholders have the right under the Leasehold Reform Act to buy the freehold at a price which is generally well below the market price for the property. In such cases the lender may be persuaded to give a bigger mortgage than usual because the real value of the house or flat is way above the current asking price.

Where to get a mortgage

Mortgages, as we have seen, come from four main sources: local councils; building societies; insurance companies; and banks.

You can also borrow in a variety of other ways – all of which are eligible for tax relief if the loan is to help you buy a house. Friends and relatives may lend you money. Some employers have mortgage schemes for employees, which depend on length of service, status, etc. You may have a family trust fund which can help. Finance companies will sometimes 'top up' your mortgage with what is called a second mortgage, if you do not have quite enough to meet the purchase price. Occasionally

– though this is rare – the person selling the house may be prepared to let you pay him off gradually in the form of a mortgage rather than demanding the purchase price outright, at the time of sale. On the whole, however, except in exceptional circumstances, it is best to raise your mortgage through the usual channels.

Councils

If you can get a council mortgage, you may be going to the best possible source. Councils cover only 5 per cent of the total mortgage market, but they operate on rather different principles from building societies and insurance companies. They lend through a sense of social duty. They are trying to ensure that the people who live in their borough are decently housed, whether in council houses and flats or in owner-occupied homes. Many consider that it is cheaper in the long run to help you buy your home than to build new council-owned property. Not all councils operate mortgage schemes, however. Check to see if yours does. Because they view loans as part of social policy, councils tend to see their priority as helping the borrower, rather than balancing the value of the house with the ability of the borrower to pay. It is therefore sometimes easier to get a big – even a 100 per cent – mortgage from a council than from the other sources available, who are basically in the mortgage business either to balance their ingoings and outgoings (building societies) or to make a profit (insurance companies and banks). A disadvantage is that interest rates may often be higher than those in building societies and cuts in interest rates are infrequent. And in times of financial stringency they may suspend their schemes altogether.

Building societies

If you have read the chapter on savings (chapter 3 of this section) you will know that the building societies were set up solely to finance house purchase, though a new Building Societies Act greatly expanding the areas in which they can operate and the financial services they can provide will be passed in this Parliamentary session. Nevertheless, the bulk of building society business is still likely to be in the provision of loans for private home purchase and they provide more loans than all the other organizations that lend for house purchase put together. They use the money they get in deposits (paying interest at one rate) to lend to suitable borrowers (who pay interest at a higher rate). They do not make a profit, but the difference in rates covers the day-to-day running costs and provides a reserve in case of a sudden withdrawal of savings, or an unusually large failure rate in mortgage payments. Whatever changes we see in building societies in coming years, it is unlikely that any other financial institutions will edge them out of their predominant place in the home loans market.

Building societies tend to have stricter requirements for their loans than local councils or banks, but there is no doubt that the building society still provides the best opportunity for the average borrower to get a mortgage.

Building society rates of interest change relatively slowly, but they do follow the general pattern of interest rates. If they rise, mortgage interest rates will rise, and it is wise to remember this when taking out a mortgage. Try not to borrow so much that even a small increase in monthly payments will overstrain the family budget.

The amount available for lending by building societies varies from time to time, depending on how much money is going into them. This varies because building society rates of interest to depositors change slowly in comparison with interest rates in some other areas, so the societies are not always the most attractive way of saving in a period when interest rates are rising. When this happens depositors shift their money to areas offering higher rates of interest, and, correspondingly, there is less money available to borrowers. If mortgage money is tight, it is a good idea to save up in a building society if you are thinking of applying for a mortgage at a later date. It is no guarantee of a mortgage, but it does mean that your application will be looked at more favourably in a difficult period.

What else can you do to ensure you get a building society mortgage? First, choose the sort of house which building societies regard as a good risk. This means a house built after 1921, though older houses are not barred. They like the sort of houses that 'normal' families live in – not too close to the centre of a city, but not too far away to make commuting difficult. The semi-detached post-war house is typical of what they favour. They often do not like flats, unless they are purpose-built with a ground landlord who is responsible for certain services, which will maintain standards.

If after a few years you decide that you wish to extend your present house rather than buy another one, building societies will usually listen sympathetically to any request for a topping-up mortgage, as they see this as increasing the value of the house eventually.

Banks v. building societies

The commercial banks are becoming the biggest competitors to the building societies in the home loans field. Building societies still have the bulk of the business and will continue to so do for the foreseeable future, but the banks are likely to gradually take up more and more of the demand. The banks (including the TSBs) generally like larger mortgages. National Westminster lend a minimum of £12,500 to a maximum of £150,000 (late 1984), for instance, though of course the £30,000 limit for tax relief still applies.

We have seen in chapter 4 how the same interest rate can mean different things, depending on how interest is calculated. In the building societies, for instance, borrowers pay for a whole year on the balance outstanding at the beginning of the year, so that rate-for-rate borrowers are paying more if they borrow from building societies rather than banks. When interest rates are low, the switch is not worthwhile.

Getting a mortgage with a bank or a building society with which you do not already have a connection can be difficult. Building societies do not insist that you have saved with them before granting you a mortgage, but they do give preferential treatment to their depositors. Having said that, a savings account with a building society does not actually guarantee a mortgage, unless you fulfil the other criteria required of borrowers. It would, for example, be extremely difficult to get a mortgage, however long you had had an account, if you were unemployed. Building societies always insist that their loan is the first charge on the property. Banks and other lenders do not always do this.

The banks, too, have rules about the conditions under which they are prepared to grant mortgages.When they first offered mortgages these conditions were quite stiff. As the banks got more and more experience, they gradually relaxed the rules. At the end of 1984, for example, some banks did not even require borrowers to be customers of the bank. In tighter credit conditions than those prevailing at the end of 1984, of course, the rules might well be re-imposed. Previously, they have involved participation for a period in one of the bank's saving schemes, or a qualifying period as a bank customer, etc.

Insurance companies

Some insurance companies will finance the whole purchase of your house through a special insurance policy, but most link themselves with a building society, so that the borrower pays not only normal repayments on the outstanding loan but also a (sometimes hefty) insurance premium to cover the purchase in the event of death. This provides protection for the building society, which is then guaranteed to get its money back, and also gives security to the borrower's dependents in the event of his or her death.

It is useful to get the extra cover that an insurance policy gives to a mortgage, because building societies can then be persuaded to make bigger loans. The new borrower gets no tax relief on the insurance payments and this has made endowment-linked mortgages less attractive. The tax relief of 15 per cent on life assurance premiums remains on those policies taken out on or before 13 March 1984. There is no need to cash in an assurance policy when repaying a mortgage on a house sale: you can always transfer a current policy to a new mortgage and thus keep the tax relief until the policy matures.

In general most people will go first to a building society, but people who are seeking a higher than usual loan, or who are buying a house which may need a lot of money spent on it for it to become habitable, may find an insurance company or a bank more willing to listen to their request than a building society or a local authority.

Finance houses
These are not a major source of mortgages, but they will often lend on second mortgages (which are eligible for tax relief if they don't break the £30,000 barrier). They are useful if you are a little short of what you need, but they usually carry a higher interest rate than normal loans, and you must make sure that the loan is not so loaded with awkward condi tions as to be barely worth having. They are also useful for those who want to raise more money when they have been living in their house for some years, and can be used for home improvements. They are a useful standby, but no more than that, in the total mortgage business.

The rest
There are all kinds of other sources for mortgages, but remember, if you go in for any kind of private borrowing you will have to meet any terms the lender sets. So take great care and only borrow when the terms are fair and reasonable.

What kind of mortgage?

There are five basic kinds of mortgage:

1 Repayment mortgages: gradual repayment over the whole loan period.
2 Standing mortgages.
3 Endowment mortgages: repaid totally at the end of the loan, or on the death of the mortgagee if that is earlier.
4 A combination of 1 and 2.
5 Index-linked mortgages.

There are also other, less common kinds, including:

1 Joint-income mortgages.
2 Low start mortgages.
3 Escalator mortgages.

Repayment mortgages
These are the most common. They are repaid in monthly instalments, which represent the repayment of a combination of capital and income. They are eligible for tax relief. It is normal for lenders to suggest, or even insist, that these mortgages are a guarantee policy to protect the lender in

the event of the death of the borrower. Repayment mortgages were the first to be granted on a wide scale, but became less popular as more and more borrowers chose a life assurance link for their loan. With the ending of tax relief on life assurance premiums, however, simple repayment mortgages seem likely to return to popularity.

Interest-only mortgages (standing mortgages)
The borrower pays interest charges only. The interest is calculated at a maximum rate fixed over the whole period of the loan. The capital borrowed remains outstanding until redeemed. Payments are therefore fairly low and are wholly eligible for tax relief. When property prices are rising, repayment of capital normally presents no problems when the house or flat is sold. This is a relatively expensive way to borrow, but to those paying a lot of tax the high tax relief can be attractive.

Endowment mortgages
Standing mortgages can be linked to life assurance through endowment mortgages. The borrower takes out an insurance policy for the same amount as he wished to borrow. Its timing is the same as the loan period for the mortgage and it provides extra security. These mortgages are rather costly, particularly in comparison with an ordinary repayment mortgage, because not only must continuing high interest be paid on the loan, but there are insurance premiums as well. What the policy does is insure the mortgage for the full loan period and then redeem the loan at the end. Such mortgages taken out before the 1984 Budget carry tax relief at 15 per cent. Later ones do not, but like ordinary life insurance such policies can have a tax-free 'with profits' element (see under Endowment in chapter 13 of this section). They cost more but can provide a healthy extra profit at the end of the mortgage period. Like insurance policies, too, endowment mortgages carry a surrender value after a period.

Combined mortgages
A mortgage which combined repayments and endowment life assurance became increasingly popular in recent years and for many people provided the best of all worlds. The life assurance cover is cheaper than in a full endowment mortgage and borrowers, especially if they took out a with-profits policy, had a handy lump sum at the end of the mortgage period. The 1984 Budget, of course, also dealt a blow to these mortgages and the use of them seems likely to decline in coming years.

Index-linked mortgages
Index-linking has become increasingly popular in many financial fields in recent years and mortgages are no exception. The idea behind them is to

enable people to borrow rather more than their income would justify without taking on an impossible financial burden. Such loans are very useful for people starting off in their careers, when they may have excellent long-term prospects but low income when they are trying to buy their first home.

Index-linking means that monthly payments can be reduced in the early years of the loan and rise gradually over the life of the mortgage. Because payments are lower than they otherwise would be, the borrower can afford to take out a bigger loan, or consider home purchase from what in normal circumstances would be an inadequate salary. Loans may be fully index-linked, or – more usually – partly. What happens is that the repayments and balance on the loan, or that part which is index linked, are adjusted each year to allow for inflation. Inflation is measured in the same way as for the revaluation of index-linked national certificates, that is, by changes in the Retail Prices Index (RPI), which is published every month. As a rule, the year-end index is used in the revaluation. Another difference between a conventional mortgage and an index-linked one is that the interest rate on the index-linked part is fixed – and very low – for the full period of the loan, so that the borrower knows precisely what interest he will pay allowing for the upward revaluation each year. If there were no inflation at all, or – even more unlikely – prices fell during the year, the loan would either remain the same or be reduced by the amount of the fall.

In a conventional mortgage, the borrower would be unlikely to get little more than 2½ times his income; with an index-linked loan it could go to 3½ times.

To show how a loan might work, here is the plan offered by Nationwide Building Society. This is a loan, half of which is repaid in the normal way and half of which is index-linked. There are other points to note:

1 The interest rate on the conventional part is the normal published rate at any time and may fluctuate. That on the index-linked part is much lower and fixed for the full term.
2 The amount owed on the conventional part is a simple repayment mortgage and should fall as the loan repayment period proceeds.
3 The index-linked element is adjusted every 31 December, after allowing for any capital repaid at the end of each year in line with RPI.

Take a loan of £20,000 over a 25-year period. Say then that the interest on the conventional part – £10,000 – is currently 13 per cent and on the index-linked part 4 per cent, fixed for the term. Now supposing that interest rates do not change over a two-year period and that prices rise by 5 per cent. This is what happens to the monthly repayments:

Year 1 =	on the conventional part	£85.60
	on the index-linked part	£46.80
	Total monthly payment	£132.40
Year 2 =	on the conventional part	£85.60
	on the index-linked part	£49.14*
		£134.74

*£46.80 increased by five per cent to allow for the increase in the Retail Price Index.

Anyone borrowing in a conventional way totally would pay £171.20 in both years. But of course, we also have to look at what is owed at the end of the first year. The sum looks like this:

Year 1 =	on the conventional part	£9,882.80
	on the index-linked part	£10,204.40
		£20,087.20

You can see that the amount borrowed index-linked has increased beyond the initial £10,000. This is because £281.52 capital has been repaid during the year, as well as the 4 per cent interest, giving a closing balance of £9,718.48. This is then increased by 5 per cent, that is, the rate of inflation, giving an outstanding balance of £10,204.40.

It is clear that the amount borrowed on an index-linked basis will fall much more slowly than that borrowed in the conventional way – and in a period of high inflation it may go on rising throughout the period of the mortgage. If past experience is anything to go by, the rise in home prices will take care of that. It should not of course be assumed that prices will go on rising, regardless of economic conditions.

I have dealt with these mortgages in some detail because they are new and most people are unfamiliar with them. They are likely, however, to become an increasingly important part of the total mortgage picture, helping people on low incomes to buy homes and increase their payments as their incomes rise.

Joint-income mortgages
These are simply a variation of the ordinary repayment mortgage. The incomes of both husband and wife are taken into account in deciding the amount of the loan, and the repayments are phased in such a way that they are larger while both are earning and then tail off. This is usually done on a fixed formula, with the first, say, three years' payments at the rate of a fifteen-year mortgage and the rest on a twenty-five-year basis. You may find that you have to pay a slightly higher rate of interest on this type of mortgage, but it is very useful for a young couple who want to pay off as much of their mortgage as possible before starting a family.

Escalator mortgages

In these, payments start off low and increase steadily. They are useful if you know your income will rise, but the lender may well want proof that this is likely to happen. Mortgages are paid off faster and interest charges are lower, but they can be dangerous if your expected rise fails to materialize. Such mortgages are very rare now and will disappear altogether as index-linked becomes more popular.

Low-start mortgages

The borrower pays a reduced rate of interest for the first five years and then increases the payments. Once again these are attractive for people who know that their income will increase and so can take on rather larger commitments than their present income would justify. Mortgages like these are generally limited to professional employees or civil servants. There is a government low-start scheme, but as I write it is barely worth considering. It is strictly for low earners buying relatively cheap property. But keep an eye out for changes which may improve the scheme.

When interest rates change

As I have already said, mortgage interest rates change slowly, but they do eventually change if interest rates generally move up or down. Building societies tend to raise their rates after other financial institutions have done so, but they also lag behind when it comes to lowering them. When there is a change the amount of your monthly payments will change – though if you have a straight repayment mortgage you can extend or reduce the period of your mortgage rather than changing your monthly payment. The following table shows the monthly payment to building societies on every £1,000 borrowed over twenty-five years at different rates of interest. These payments do not allow for tax relief, which will usually effectively cut the payment by almost a third.

mortgage rate	monthly repayment
8½%	£8.25
10½%	£9.54
12%	£10.63
14%	£12.13
15%	£12.90

Remember, it is not possible on all mortgages to keep your payments steady, and even where you can there may come a point when you are in effect extending the repayment period for ever. The societies recommend, however, that you do not let your payments go beyond thirty years in a repayment mortgage. But extension is not possible with endowment and interest-only mortgages. Your monthly payment must increase or decrease in accordance with the revised amount that will be sent to you by the society.

Mortgage rates change rather more slowly than other interest rates, but even so, three or four changes in one year is no longer unusual. They have varied enormously over the past forty years and appear today to be much higher than, say, at the end of the Second World War. From 1945–52, for example, they stayed at 4 per cent. But inflation comes in here, too. Allowing for that, what appears to be a high interest rate may be very low indeed; in fact, it has on occasion been a negative rate. This means that, allowing for inflation, borrowers are paying nothing for their money. Having said that, however, at the end of 1984 true rates were higher than for some time.

This is how the Building Societies Association's recommended rates have moved in the past five years:

1979	22 November	11.75%
1980	12 December	14.00%
1981	13 March	13.00%
	9 October	15.00%
1982	12 March	13.50%
	5 August	12.00%
	12 November	10.00%
1983	22 June	11.25%
1984	16 March	10.25%
	13 July	12.50%
	9 November	11.50%

Since late 1983, the rates have been only 'advised' rates and not compulsory for members. This happened because some of the larger societies stated that they did not want to have to give 28 days' notice to the Association of a change in rates and also that they did not want to be confined to the recommendation. Since then, some of the bigger societies have charged rather more than the recommended rate.

When you cannot keep up repayments

If for any reason you cannot keep up your mortgage repayments, tell the lender immediately. Whether an institution or a private person, the lender has the right to foreclose on the loan and sell the house to pay the debt, but few will take such action immediately if you explain the circumstances to them. Building societies, for instance, may permit you to make interest-only payments for a time until your circumstances improve, and your local social security office may help towards these. If the situation persists, however, and the lender does foreclose, you are entitled to have any capital returned to you which you have paid off, less any expenses the lender may have incurred in the sale. If the situation does arise that your house has to be sold because you cannot pay the mortgage, it is best to try to do this yourself and then pay off the outstanding loan.

Mortgage protection

Your can buy mortgage protection or guarantees for your house to protect your heirs in the event of your death, even if you do not have an endowment-linked mortgage.

The guarantee is secured through a special insurance policy and should only cost a few pounds. It ensures that the mortgage will be fully paid off if you die. The payments can be added to your mortgage loan if you wish.

Protection costs more, but is useful not only if you die but also if you are unable to keep up your payments because of ill-health or unemployment. Premiums vary, but are rarely very high.

When you may not get a mortgage

Some properties are extremely difficult, if not impossible to mortgage. They include buildings which are not normally used as homes, like windmills, oast houses, old barns and the like. You may get a small loan on such a building, but nothing like the loan you can get on an ordinary house or flat. Many building societies are also reluctant to lend on thatched or timber houses. They require massive insurance (against fire risk), which again is more expensive than on an ordinary house or flat, before considering giving a loan.

First-time buyers

The government has introduced a scheme to help first-time property buyers. It was first announced in December 1978 and offers a tax-free cash bonus up to £110 and an interest-free loan of £600 for five years, provided the applicant has saved for at least two years in either a bank or a building society which is participating in the scheme. It is necessary to inform the institution right at the beginning that it is the intention of the saver to apply for the bonus and the loan after the period is up. There is a special form for this, HPA 1. Then, twelve months before the application is made, at least £300 must have been saved and a minimum of £300 must always be kept in the account. The larger the amount in the account, the bigger the bonus, as the table shows:

Minimum savings held during the 12 months before applying for benefits £	cash bonus £
300–399	40
400–499	50
500–599	60
600–699	70
700–799	80
800–899	90
900–999	110
over 1,000	110

The rules to get the interest-free loan are similar, but there is one difference. When the application is made, there must be at least £600 in the account. The £600 loan is added to the normal amount borrowed on the mortgage, but no interest is paid on it for a period of five years. Then it carries interest in the usual way. There is another proviso – the government has set maximum prices upon which it will offer the scheme. These differ from area to area and change from time to time, so check the levels if you are considering participation. The amounts of money involved may seem small, but don't look a gift horse in the mouth. The early years of paying off a mortgage are always the worst and the money could be very useful. If the bank or building society does not mention the scheme to you, remind them of it, if you want to participate.

Home improvement grants

Borrowing money for home improvements is rather cheap, as the interest you pay is eligible for tax relief, as long as you do not go over the £30,000 limit. But there is something much better, particularly if you are restoring a very dilapidated house or flat which is not up to modern standards. Or you may wish to divide a house into flats, if it is too large for your needs.

In certain cases, you will be able to get a home improvement grant. This is not a loan: it is a sum of money contributed by your local authority to the cost of renovations or alterations. *You do not have to pay the money back*. Grants go towards many different kinds of work – putting in a bathroom or lavatory where there is not one inside, for instance, or installing a modern kitchen, a hot-water system, or a new roof.

This is how you go about getting a grant:

1 Decide exactly what you want to do.
2 Get it properly costed.
3 Call at your local council offices and put your plans to the home improvement officer, who will tell you whether you are eligible for a grant, what sort of grant to apply for and how much money you may get.

There are four types of grants:

1 *Improvement grants* for major jobs or conversions. These grants are discretionary, which means that the local authority does not *have* to give you one. They can choose whether or not to approve your application. You cannot get one if your rateable value is more than £400 in Greater London, or £225 elsewhere. The maximum grant you can get for anything apart from a conversion is £13,800 in Greater London and £10,200 elsewhere. These are the limits for 'priority' cases. Non-priority limits are £9,000 and £6,600 respectively. Conversions are subject to the same limits, but more is available for houses of more than three storeys.

There are of course conditions attached to all grants. Broadly, they are that when the work is finished:

1 The home will have a useful life of at least thirty years.
2 It will be in reasonable repair.
3 It will have all the standard amenities (a fixed bath or shower, wash-hand basin, sink, hot and cold water supply and inside lavatory).
4 Meet a list of ten requirements which include adequate lighting, freedom from damp, proper drainage, good structure, proper cooking facilities, heating and thermal insulation in the roof.

The maximum grant for priority cases is 75 per cent, for houses in general improvement areas 65 per cent, and for all other cases 50 per cent.

2 *Intermediate grants*. These are assistance for the installation of standard amenities (see (3) above) and the maximum grants at the end of 1984 were as follows:

	Greater London £	elsewhere £
fixed bath or shower	450	340
wash-hand basin	175	130
sink	450	340
hot and cold water supply at a		
fixed bath or shower	570	430
wash-hand basin	300	230
sink	380	290
water closet	680	515
total	3,005	2,275

These grants are mandatory if you meet the conditions. There is a further £4,200 available in London and £3,000 elsewhere for repairs.

3 *Repairs grants*. These are grants for houses built before 1919 and to qualify the repairs must be substantial. The grants are discretionary and the limits are £4,800 for London and £6,600 elsewhere.

4 *Special grants*. These are discretionary and available to owner-occupiers to put in standard amenities, fire escapes in houses with multiple occupation and repairs and replacements associated with them. The limits for the standard amenities are the same as for intermediate grants, but there is a limit of £10,800 for fire escapes in Greater London and £8,100 elsewhere.

It is clear that these grants can be a great help in improving your home and, depending on the particular case, you may be eligible whether you are an owner-occupier, landlord or tenant. There are several booklets about home improvement grants, which are available from Citizens Advice Bureaux, Housing Aid Centres, Rent Officers and council offices.

A word of warning is necessary here, however. As I write, the Government is looking at the whole home improvements grants system. At present, it is the state of the particular dwelling which determines whether the grant will be made. It is quite likely that in the not-too-distant future, the income of the applicant will be taken into account and the more wealthy may well be refused grants.

A final point: there is special provision for the adaptation of homes for people who are disabled and there are no rateable value limits for such people.

9 Keeping down the running costs of your home

Wherever you live, certain costs are unavoidable: mortgage or rent, rates, water rates, and compulsory service charges if you live in a block of flats or an estate.

After that it is up to you to make the best or worst of the running costs of your home – though you may not always have a choice about every item of your spending. Your business may be such that you have no option but to have a telephone. Your home may already have electric central heating or storage heaters when you buy it, and you may not be able to afford to change them, or the area may not be served with gas, which might be more economical. Think about these things before you actually buy your home. Later on may be too late.

Remember that government policy may change. Some years ago many people bought electric storage heaters because of the favourable tariff available if they were used at night. That tariff has now been scrapped and owners are left with an expensive, and not always efficient, form of heating.

Remember, too, that the price of any service is likely to increase steadily. There was a rush to gas central heating when natural gas was discovered in the North Sea. It was thought it would make gas cheaper, but government policy has decreed that gas prices must come into line with the prices of other fuels and prices have risen steadily as more and more gas has been piped ashore.

The rule when you are setting up home and estimating running costs is *always assume the worst.*

If you are actually buying an appliance, buy soon rather than later – the price is sure to increase. When estimating your gas and electricity costs, assume a minimum rise in prices of 10 per cent a year to give yourself some leeway and ask yourself whether your funds are likely to increase enough to cover the higher costs. It is no use installing central heating if you are going to find it too expensive to use properly: far better to heat individual rooms separately, so that you have more control over the cost.

Your fuel bills

Electricity. Study the amounts of electricity you could use in any one week (of course, some of the items have a seasonal bias). The following are the average number of units of electricity the average family uses in a week, as estimated by the Electrical Association for Women. One unit is equal to 1,000 watts, or one kilowatt.

Approximate amount of electricity used by domestic appliances

appliance	units per week
refrigerator	5–10
freezer (12 cu. ft.)	12–18
cooker (family of four)	20–30
lighting (3-bedroomed house)	7
TV – black and white (9 hours' viewing for 1 unit)	3½
colour (6 hours' viewing for 1 unit)	5
dishwasher (1 unit per washload)	7
electric blanket – under	1
over – on all night	2
portable room heater (2 units per hour)	112 (8 hours'

appliance	units per week
	daily use)
washing machine – automatic cold fill (2 units per washload)	10–20
twin-tub (3 units per washload if water used once only)	12–24
tumble dryer (2 units per hour)	6
toaster (70 slices per unit)	1
shaver (1,800 shaves per unit)	–
clock	12 units *per year*
hair dryer (3 hours per unit)	1
immersion heater (only form of water heating in winter)	75

You will probably not have all these appliances, but it is easy to work out the weekly cost of any of them at the early 1984 national average rate of 5.59p per unit of electricity, and from that your total bill. This has two elements, a standing charge, which is always payable, and the cost of the units used. The Electrical Association for Women produces a very handy booklet, *Electricity for Everyday Living*, at £1.75 from 25 Foubert's Place, London W1V 2AL. It will tell you all you need to know about using domestic electricity.

Gas. There are, of course, fewer gas appliances, but those where a comparison can be made cost slightly less to run.

You will notice that I am looking at the running costs of domestic appliances before going on to the purchasing of them. This may seem like putting the cart before the horse, but it is the right way to go about it. Estimate what the costs will be *before buying*, even if you have the cash to buy or will have no problem getting a hire purchase agreement. No appliance is any use if you find it too expensive to run.

Let's assume that you are moving into a new house, or renovating a very old one, and have complete freedom of choice about what kind of appliances you install. Here are just a few examples of the differences in running costs. You can easily work out any others by consulting your local gas and electricity boards.

Heating
In winter, and perhaps during part of the spring and autumn, heating is likely to be one of the biggest items in your bills. As I write, these are some of the points you must consider when deciding how to heat your house:

- All central heating is expensive. You can ignore what advertisements say about 'cheap' and 'efficient'. It may be efficient, but it is never cheap.
- Oil is the most expensive form of heating, closely followed by electricity.

- Electricity has some advantages over the rest. It is very clean and easy to use. Gas requires rather more servicing, while solid fuel needs more work by the householder, but less professional servicing than either oil or gas. Electricity, too, is the only type of heating which does not need a flue or chimney. If by any chance you do not or cannot have one installed, you will have to have electricity, despite its cost disadvantages.
- Electricity is available everywhere. Gas is not, and if you choose oil or solid fuel you will have to be sure that you can arrange for regular delivery. Just as important, you should have enough storage space to allow you a reserve should your delivery be late.

Think about all these points and then ask yourself whether:

1 Your family is out all day (though you can get a time clock which automatically switches off your heating while you are out or sleeping).
2 You generally use only a few rooms and the others just occasionally.
3 You would find your total budget under pressure while you are paying for the installation and running costs at the same time. (This, of course, will not apply if you buy a house which already has central heating.)

If you decide against central heating, you will have to think about some kind of individual room heater for each room, or a heater which you can carry around from room to room. Among these, the dearest to run is the portable electric heater which blows out hot air. The cheapest are gas convector fires, though these must be linked in some way to outside air, and solid fuel closed stoves.

Paraffin heaters and gas radiant/convector heaters, for some considerable time after purchase at least, are, taking into account purchase price and running costs, the most economical.

Here are the end-1981 comparative running costs for centrally heating a three-bedroomed semi-detached house to 70 degrees for one week, in order of expense:

System	with insulation	without insulation
oil	£354	£444
LPG-propane	£463	£572
solid fuel	£327	£390
mains gas	£238–£278*	£295–£275*
electricity	£421–£448*	£326–£333*

*Including standing charges in the higher figure.

Until the sharp rise in oil prices, electricity was by far the most expensive form of central heating. This is no longer so and oil costs have overtaken electricity, a trend which seems likely to continue.

How to keep your heating costs down
First, insulate your house as much as possible. You can insulate the loft with the thick wadding which is available cheaply; you can have (more expensive, but only a once-and-for-all payment) cavity wall insulation; and you can install double glazing on the windows (the price varies according to whether you do it yourself or have it done professionally). *Efficient insulation can save you up to 50 per cent of your fuel bills, and up to 75 per cent of your heat loss.*

This is how the Government Energy Efficiency Office estimated the cost and the savings on insulation in 1984 for a semi-detached three-bedroom house:

| | Cost | gas | *Annual savings* | | | |
| | | | cheap rate electricity | full rate electricity | solid fuel | oil |
	£	£	£	£	£	£
Loft						
100mm loft insulation DIY	100	35	65	100	40	60
150mm loose fill	250	37	70	105	45	65
Tank						
Hot water cylinder jacket	6	15	18	40	15	23
Draughts						
Draught proofing	30	15	25	40	15	25
Cavity walls						
Cavity wall insulation UF foam	250	50	80	125	55	80
Cavity wall insulation mineral wool	400	50	80	125	55	80
Polystyrene beads	325	50	80	125	55	80
Double glazing						
DIY double glazing, secondary panes	300	25	45	70	25	40
Contractor-installed double glazing, secondary panes	1,500	25	45	70	25	40

Second, if you have central heating, find out the minimum temperature in which you feel comfortable. For every degree celsius lower that you fix your thermostat you can save up to 7½ per cent a year on your bills. Put individual thermostats in each room. A thermostat radiator valve in each room is the most economical. Use a time-switch if you are out a good part of the day. There is no point in heating when no one is at home. Check your radiators regularly to make sure they are all working properly.

Heating your water
If you have central heating, the price of heating your water will be included in the central heating costs. To make sure you are using it as economically as possible:

1 Make sure the tank is lagged. This can save you up to £50 a year.
2 Do not put the thermostat too high. This costs more, and is of no benefit if you always have to add cold water when you run any hot.
3 Use your hot water economically. Don't heat up a whole thirty-gallon tank when you only need a little. Use a pan or kettle instead for small amounts. Have showers rather than baths; they use far less water.

If you use a round 250 gallons per week – again the average consumption of hot water by the average family of two adults and two (not quite two) children in a three-bedroomed semi – this is how your costs work out. You may not believe that you use that much, but the average bath alone takes 10 gallons. If your family are all daily bathers, you are likely to be well over the average.

The following table shows the number of gallons of hot water you can expect per pence from the different forms of heating. They will probably rise by at least 5 per cent a year.

Electricity:	instant heater	1.2 gallons
	immersion heater	1.0 gallon
Gas:	instant sink heater	10.0 gallons
	instant bath heater	6.9 gallons
	boiler	4.0 gallons
Oil:	central heating boiler	3.0 gallons
Solid fuel:	central heating boiler – coke	3.0 gallons
Solid fuel:	central heating boiler – coal	4.0 gallons

These amounts are only approximations. They will simply give you an idea of the different costs of the various types of water heaters.

Lighting
Lighting uses very little power in comparison with heating. In a three-bedroomed house, you will be unlucky if you use on average much more than seven units, so the cost should not be more than 50p a week.

The dearest light bulb you can buy, combining initial and running costs, for a given amount of light is the longlife single coil, which has an estimated life of 2,000 hours. The cheapest is the pearl coiled coil. Pearl bulbs give more light than opal ones, and clear give the most light of all. But you may not like the glare which comes from a clear bulb.

As well as the three different finishes, there are also three different internal structures. These are the single coil, the coiled coil and longlife. The coiled coil gives out more light for the same amount of electricity than the others, but the longlife (which gives out less light for the same electricity and wattage) lasts twice as long as the other two.

Here is how you can save:

1 Hundred watt bulbs work out cheaper combining purchase price and running costs, so use them if your lighting design permits it, rather than the lower wattages. This applies whether you are considering levels of light or the cost of electricity.
2 Longlife bulbs are dearer to buy and give out less light, but if you do not mind this they work out cheaper to run if you are using a lot of light.
3 Fluorescent tubes can be cheaper than bulbs in the long run. You will need to buy special fittings and the tube itself is expensive, but they last up to seven times longer than an ordinary bulb and give out far more light for the amount of electricity used. Thirty watts from a tube will give as much light as a 100 watt bulb. But don't keep switching the light on and off. It will blow far more quickly if you do. You also have to ask yourself whether you can actually stand living in a room lit by flourescent lighting.
4 A light dimmer can reduce the amount of electricity you use, but it is only worthwhile if you use it often. If you use one three hours a night on average (and this is a lot if you take the summer months into account) the dimmer, if you buy one of the cheaper ones, might pay for itself in about a year. A dearer one would take four or five years to pay for itself. It is best, therefore, only to buy and use a dimmer if you like it for decorative purposes in your lighting.

Cooking
The cost of your cooker

There are three basic kinds of cooker. The two most popular are gas and electricity. The third is the solid fuel, sometimes called the Aga-type, which can also be run off gas or electricity and can be used to heat water. It is by far the most expensive to run, takes up more space, and costs more to buy. Gas and electric cookers both cost around £300 for a standard model, though you can pay up to £800 for a model with extras, and even more if you buy a split-level continental or American model. The Aga-type costs around £1,500, plus VAT plus fitting.

Gas is the cheapest to use, electricity will probably cost at least twice as much, and an Aga anything from nine times more if run on gas, to fifteen times more if run on oil. Solid fuel Agas will cost over £200 a year. Agas clearly are only for devotees of that kind of cooking, of whom there are many, particularly those living in the country.

How to cut the costs of cooking

No matter what you do, you will only save a few pounds a year, but with prices at their present levels and with further rises in the offing, we should consider all possibilities. Here are some suggestions:

1 Buy gadgets like pressure cookers, toasters, slow roasters, electric kettles and the like for use when appropriate. They are generally cheaper than using a cooker.
2 With an electric cooker, make the pans fit the ring as exactly as possible. On gas, do not use pans so small that the flames go up the side of the pan and waste heat.
3 Use very little water when cooking vegetables. This is not only economical; it is better cooking too.
4 Keep the lids on saucepans, unless you are cooking something which requires them to be off. You will cook more cheaply and quickly this way.
5 Use matches rather than a gas pilot light. It's surprising what a pilot light can add to your bill – it can be more than £5 a year.
6 Don't over-cook food. It tastes better, is more nutritious and costs less when lightly cooked.

I haven't mentioned microwave ovens yet. These are expensive – £200 to £300 – and have limited uses. You cannot, for example, cook beef which is crispy on the outside and rare inside, as the microwave oven cooks evenly throughout, but it will reheat frozen food very quickly and cook a joint in less than half an hour. It has its uses for those who are at work all day, or who use a freezer a lot. Microwave ovens are very cheap to run, but they are an extra rather than a first choice for the average family, because of the cost and their limited uses. In the last few years, however, the price has fallen, the machines themselves have become more sophisticated, and their use can be expected to increase.

Gas and electricity bills

If you do not pay your bills, the supply will be disconnected and will not be restored until you pay up. If you are elderly, or on social security, you are likely to receive help with paying your bills, and in many areas of the country, especially if you are elderly, the supply is no longer disconnected simply because in the winter months, when your bill is heavier, you are unable to pay.

For the vast majority of us, however, fuel bills have to be paid, however difficult we may find it. They come in four times a year and consist of a standing charge (for the use of the service) and a charge for the amount of fuel used.

How to pay

1 You can simply pay your gas or electricity bill as it comes in by cash or cheque.
2 You can open a budget account at your bank, so that it does not matter whether you have the actual cash when the bill comes in (see chapter 6 in this section).
3 You can make regular monthly payments which are one twelfth of your *estimated* bills for the year. If you do it this way, an adjustment is made either way at the end of the year. You can pay these either through a standing order at your bank or through a National Giro account or by vouchers issued by the electricity or gas boards.
4 You can buy special savings stamps issued by the gas and electricity boards whenever you have some spare cash and these can then be used towards paying your bills. If you bought one £2-worth of stamps each week, for example, you would have £26 towards the bill at the end of the quarter but you might as well put the money in the Post Office and get some interest on it over the period.
5 You may be able to get a slot meter, but this is costly and the boards are not keen to install them.

If you have a problem in paying, *tell the local gas or electricity office immediately*. If your difficulties are going to be only temporary, they may arrange a special easy method of paying off your debt over a period. If you are getting any of the allowances for poorer families set out in Section three, chapter 4, get in touch with your local DHSS office and tell the board you are doing so. Then the supply will not be turned off for at least fourteen days while your case is studied.

Your washing
This is the last really major item for most families. Prices of washing machines vary enormously, depending on what you want your machine to do. Automatic machines which do the whole process in one go, including spin drying, are usually the most expensive to buy; twin tubs are cheaper. There is quite a substantial difference in price between different makes. You can also wash by hand or use the launderette, or simply buy a spin or tumble drier after doing the washing by hand.

Taking our average family again, they are likely to be washing about a ton of clothes a year, so it is very important to work out the costs of washing correctly. The price of detergents must not be ignored, nor the cost of the electricity involved in an average wash.

The amount of electricity used in a washing machine will vary depending on the type of wash you are doing. The most expensive is the hot white wash; the cheapest, the cool wash with no spin drying. It is obviously cheapest to dry your clothes outside on a line, but this is not always convenient if you live, say, in a flat.

Let's assume you are washing clothes which need hot water, that the main drying is done in a machine, and that you are buying your washing machine on hire purchase.

Here, then, is the approximate cost of your weekly wash:

hand washing – dried on line	50p
dried in a spin drier	05p
dried in a tumble drier	£2.14
twin tub – dried on line	£3.10
dried in a spin drier	£4.08
dried in a tumble drier	£4.72
automatic machine – dried on line	£2.00
dried in a tumble drier	£2.50
launderette – two loads a week tumble dried	£5

There seems little advantage in using the launderette when you consider the inconvenience of having to go to it. If you have a service wash – that is, you leave your washing there for one of the attendants to do – you will have to pay extra. This may be well worthwhile if you have no space for a washing machine, or if you are out at work all day, and have little time to spare.

Twin tubs will, unless you are unlucky, cost less in repair bills than automatics. They also spin dry better and are quicker than automatics, but automatics are less bother to use, they rinse better, and usually have a bigger capacity than twin tubs.

Dishwashers
So far the dishwasher has not caught on very well in Britain. It is expensive – usually between £250 and £600 – and is obviously well down on any priority purchase list. It costs about 6p *every* time you use it, as against about 50p a week for washing-up by hand. It may also not be very good at washing very dirty pans, and you may find that you have to do these yourself. To be run economically, it should always be fully loaded, and this means you will need a reserve of plates and cutlery, etc., unless you have a large family always sitting down at one go. A dishwasher is very hygienic, but whether it saves time or not is a moot point. It takes time to load, sometimes as long as to wash by hand, and if you leave washing-up on the sink to dry and drain there is little to commend a dishwasher in its drying properties.

Freezers

In normal times it is unlikely that a freezer will save you a lot of money. What you save in bulk buying may be swallowed up by running costs. Freezers are basically for making your life easier, not cheaper. In times of inflation, however, when food prices are rising almost weekly, useful savings can be made. To save money on perishable foods, you will definitely need a freezer. Savings accrue in three basic ways:

1 You can buy food in bulk and pay less per pound.
2 You can save as prices rise by having bought earlier.
3 You can store your own produce, or buy when prices are seasonally low.

Against these advantages you must set the running costs:

1 Electricity. The cost of running a freezer is relatively low, but it will certainly rise as time goes on. The actual amount will depend on the size and type you choose; the length of time you leave the lid open and the number of times a day you open it; the average temperature of the room around the freezer and the temperature of the food you put in it.
2 Depreciation. Your freezer will usually last about fifteen years. Work out an average cost each year for depreciation, including in this any interest charges if you have bought on HP.
3 Insuring yourself against breakdown and food loss.

When you have worked out these costs, you will probably find that even with bulk buying you will not save a great deal by using a freezer, unless you have plenty of your own home produce.

You should also consider what using a freezer costs in non-monetary terms. You must plan your menus more carefully. You must find space for the freezer in your home. You must remember that it takes time to unfreeze food. Such irritations may outweighs any advantages of a freezer for some people.

However, despite the drawbacks, more and more people are deciding that the advantages of having a freezer far outweigh the disadvantages.

Choosing your freezer

Before you start looking at particular models, decide whether you want an upright or chest freezer, or a combined freezer/fridge.

Chest freezers take up more space than the other two types, and loading and unloading is more difficult. Make sure that you can reach the bottom when you bend over. On the other hand, chest freezers accumulate far less frost, use less electricity, and maintain a more even temperature than upright ones. They also offer a good extra working space in your kitchen.

Upright freezers are becoming increasingly popular because they generally take up no more space than a fridge. They are easier to defrost than chest freezers, but cost no more to run.

Only consider a combined *fridge/freezer* if you have no room for both separately. Usually the freezer space is relatively small, and there is almost always more room in the fridge than in the freezer section. Many people might consider this the wrong way round.

When you have decided which type you want:

- Buy as big a freezer as your space and income will permit. Reckon anyway on about four cubic feet for each member of the family and you will not go wrong. If you have a lot of your own produce you will need more space than this.
- Extras cost money. Decide whether you really need them. You can get automatic defrosting, interior lights, extra-fast freezing compartments, door locks, warning lights when temperatures change and special racks or baskets for storage.
- Shop around. Fix yourself a price and stick to it. Wait for special offers. Freezer prices can vary enormously on the same model.
- Always buy from a good dealer. Freezers are reliable and tend not to cost much in repairs, but things can go wrong and you will then need faults put right within twenty-four hours if you are not to lose all your food.
- Even if the guarantees all appear sound, insure the contents of your freezer against spoilage (see below).

If you follow these tips you are unlikely to go wrong, but before buying insist on:

1 A test run before delivery.
2 Proper installation. Do not let the delivery man leave the house until the freezer is in place – *and running*.
3 A lesson from the delivery man on the best use of your freezer.

Two final tips: have a special electric point which you use for your freezer and nothing else. Cover the on/off switch with sellotape, so that you cannot switch it off accidentally. I once lost a lot of food by accidentally switching off the freezer switch, which happened to be one on a panel of four. And remember, a full freezer is heavy. A big one can weigh as much as half a ton. Can your floors stand such a weight?

You've bought your freezer, had it installed, it runs properly – then *use it*. To get the maximum savings, fill it up as much as you can afford. Keep it full. Rotate its contents. Never switch it off, except for an annual clean-out.

Freezer insurance
I have already mentioned getting insurance to cover lost food. You should also remember that – though it is unlikely – your freezer can break down, and once it is out of guarantee repair bills can be high.

There are many freezer and breakdown policies available which automatically cover you for food loss and freezer breakdowns.

A typical policy should, if your freezer is less than ten years old, cost a maximum about £10 a year. This will cover food loss of up to about £100, labour and parts to about £150. As few freezers for the average family cost much above this, the cover is good enough.

Small appliances

Small appliances cost relatively little to run. Whether you buy them or not depends upon your priorities. Probably only a vacuum cleaner is a must. Using, say, a mixer or a liquidizer is always more expensive than doing the job by hand. Whether these sorts of appliances save time is also doubtful. What they save in preparation they very often lose in the more complicated cleaning and washing after use.

Buying your appliances

There are certain rules to be observed when buying your domestic appliances:

1 First and foremost, *buy the appliance which best suits your needs*. It is no use buying an enormous freezer if a small one would suit you better, or a small cooker if you have to supplement it by a number of gadgets.

2 *Look at* Which? *magazine*, the journal of the Consumers' Association. It comes out monthly and is extremely useful if you want to be certain you are getting the 'best buy' out of a range of models. One that costs more to purchase may be safer and more economical to run. Take time before making your final choice. Even after consulting *Which?*, insist that you are shown how an appliance works in the showroom. You might find, for instance, that *Which?*'s 'best buy' is at the wrong height for you to use.

3 *Shop around.* This is all important. Prices vary enormously. You may have to pay far more in a store which will deliver the goods than in one of the discount stores which encourage you to take whatever you buy away with you – and even if you don't they have relatively low delivery charges.

Discount warehouses are cheapest of all. They do an enormous amount of advertising in the national press, setting out their prices against what they describe as 'normal prices'. Sometimes the difference seems very large, but it is generally possible to buy below the higher prices stated in other stores. Nevertheless, savings can easily be of the order of 20 per cent. Specialist electrical and domestic appliance shops come next cheapest, with general department stores dearer, except at sale time. Some highly specialized shops may carry only the expensive ranges, and they usually charge top prices when they do so, particularly among radios, television and stereo equipment, which is very much a matter of individual taste and which I will look at in chapter 11 of this section. But the same considerations about shopping around still apply.

4 *Use the sales.* There is absolutely nothing wrong with sale goods so far as domestic appliances are concerned. They are just as safe and efficient as any bought at full price. Shops and stores, and electricity and gas showrooms, are simply clearing their stocks for new designs to come in. You can get real bargains.

Telephones and postage

Making a telephone call is becoming increasingly expensive, but so is postage and most of us have to keep in touch with some people at least in one way or another. As far as postage is concerned:

1 Always use second-class postage for non-urgent mail.
2 Pay your bills if possible through the Post Office Giro, or a bank. You can do this whether you have a bank account or not. The bank will always accept cash in payment for a bill. The bill you receive will tell you at which bank the organization you owe money to has an account. Try to pay in at one of its branches if possible, or you may find you have to pay a fee. Alternatively, if the gas or electricity office is close by, you can always call in there. Telephone bills can be paid directly at any post office, rather than by post. These may sound like small insignificant savings, but they do add up for those of us paying for gas, electricity, phone, rates, water rates, mortgage or rent, and credit payments.
3 It almost always pays to write rather than phone long distance.

The telephone, to many of us, is a vital necessity in our lives. It is a great temptation to use it, however, at times when it is unnecessary, when a cheaper letter or postcard would do just as well. Installation charges, quarterly rentals and the price of calls rise all the time, as does the reconnection charge should you not pay your bill and the phone be cut off. It makes sense, without being too parsimonious, to keep the cost down as much as possible and still get as much use from your telephone as you need. Here are a few tips:

1 Make your calls during the cheap period if you can. There are three different charge bands: the peak from 9.00 a.m. until 1.00 p.m., the standard from 8.00 a.m. till 9.00 a.m. and 1.00 p.m. to 6.00 p.m., and the cheap from 6.00 p.m. until 8 a.m. Using the cheap period can make a lot of difference to your bills – a ten-minute local call in the cheap period costs less than one third of one made in peak time. For long-distance calls, the difference is even more striking. Standard time costs come in between. For international calls, there is a cheap and a

standard time, cheap running from 8.00 p.m. until 8.00 a.m. British time. Clearly it is possible to make a large number of personal calls in the cheaper times rather than at peak.

2 Do not hang on, if you cannot be put through to the person you wish to talk to straight away. Call again, or ask them to call you.

3 If you need information, say what it is and call back for it, don't hang on while someone looks.

4 If you are travelling and want to keep in touch while you are away, arrange for your home to telephone you, rather than calling from a hotel. The prices can be very high and you have no control over them.

5 Limit the time of your calls. You can do this easily without looking mean.

6 Give your children, especially teenagers, strict time limits for their calls. If all else fails, put a lock on the dial so that they cannot make calls unless you are there.

7 Have an 'honesty box' by the phone. You never know, it might make phone-hogs think about your money they are spending.

8 If you think your bill is too high, ask the post office to check it.

You can buy telephone stamps (£1 to £5) from the post office to help you pay towards your quarterly bills, if you think that will make it easier to pay. You can also pay for your TV licence that way, or your vehicle excise licence (you can also give these stamps as presents, of course), but remember if you do that you are making a present to the government. There is no interest allowed on the stamps you build up, so perhaps it would be better to put the money into a post office savings account and earn a little, though it won't be much, interest.

Cutting your rates bill

The costs involved in home ownership – or indeed renting – do not end with mortgage repayments. All property is liable to a local tax: these are the rates. If you feel that you are paying too much in rates, you are in good company; it is estimated that several hundred thousand household-ers pay more each year than they need.

There are two ways of reducing your rates bill. The first is to check whether you are paying the same rates as people in similar accomodation in your area. If you find you are paying more, you can apply to the Valuation Officer, who fixes the rates, for a reduction. The second way is to persuade him that you are being overcharged, because the environ-ment in which you live has deteriorated. Such a claim could be made where a new motorway or airport is built too near your home, or a new factory pollutes the air. The closing of your local railway station, which makes your travelling to work more difficult, or a new or increased risk of flooding might make the Valuation Officer look with sympathy on your claim. If you think that your environment has been damaged in any way at all, it is worthwhile apply for a reduction. A useful little leaflet, 'Rating Appeals to Local Valuation Courts', available from town halls, tells you how to go about an application.

An easier way for most people to see if they can cut their rates bill, even if the valuation is not changed, is to see if they qualify for a rates rebate. Don't dismiss this out of hand: the qualifying level is surprisingly high, depending on the size of your family and the rates bill itself. Once you get a rebate, you have to re-apply every six months, in case your circumstances have changed. (See Section three, chapter 4.)

Marginal savings in rates are possible, too, in the way that you pay. They become payable on 1 April each year, but most demands come in twice a year. Some councils give a small discount if you pay the lot immediately, but it is better to leave the money in the bank until the final date they are payable and earn interest meantime. Most councils allow payments in ten equal instalments and that, too, is better than handing over the whole lot at the beginning of the period.

A warning: remember that if you improve your home, your rateable value will go up. This means that your rates will also increase. It may seem unfair to penalize you for improving your property, but the Valuation Officer calculates the gross rateable value on what a tenant would have to pay for the property. The better condition the house is in and the more facilities it has, the higher the rent would be. You are, however, under no obligation to tell the officer about the improvement, though he will find out eventually when all rateable values are reassessed. And, if you do anything which requires planning permission, the local authority will tell him anyway and he may increase the rateable value of your property without even seeing it. For these reasons, it is best to come clean at the start, or you may be in trouble. Improvements which change rateable values include a new garage, central heating, or a second bathroom.

10 Buying food

If you have read chapter 1 of this section, you will know that, after the rent or mortgage, food is easily the biggest item in the average budget. The days of cheap food which the British enjoyed for so long are gone, and the increases in prices are by no means over. Food is going to loom even larger in our total budgets, until finally we approach the European pattern, where in some countries it takes more than half of a family's available money.

It makes sense, then, to look carefully at the way we spend money on food and, if necessary, to change old habits for new and more economical ones.

Your basic groceries

The Grocer magazine has worked out a basic shopping basket. You probably do not buy exactly these items, but something very similar.

As you can see, the list consists of branded goods. If you use super-markets regularly, you will know that very often a particular store will offer what are called 'own brands' which can bring down the price of your 'basket' considerably. The prices you pay depend to some extent on the shop you use and to some extent on exactly where you live. You cannot do much about that, of course. It would be crazy to move house simply to get cheaper groceries. But it is quite useful to know where you stand nationally as far as expense goes.

Basic shopping basket

food	
Anchor butter	8 oz
Birds Eye fish fingers	10
Birds Eye frozen peas	1 lb
Cheddar cheese (UK)	1 lb
Cookeen fat	8 oz
Del Monte tinned peaches	15½ oz
Eggs (standard white)	6
Golden Delicious apples	1 lb
Heinz baked beans	15¾ oz
Heinz tomato soup	15¼ oz
John West sardines	4¼ oz
Kelloggs' corn flakes	500 g
McDougall's self-raising flour	3 lb
McVitie's chocolate home wheat biscuits	200 g
Mothers Pride sliced white bread	large
Nescafé instant coffee	4 oz
PG Tips tea	4 oz
Robertson's strawberry jam	1 lb
Stork SB margarine	1 lb
Tate & Lyle granulated sugar	1 lb
Wall's pork sausages	1lb

non-food	
Ajax scouring powder	1 lb 2 oz
Daz washing powder	E3 size
Fairy Liquid washing-up liquid	19 fl oz

Fresh fruit and vegetable basket	
apples	1 lb
carrots	1 lb
new potatoes	1 lb
tomatoes	1 lb

The Grocer has estimated that the savings in own brands could be as high as follows:

washing-up liquid	at least 30 per cent	tea	at least 10 per cent
scouring powder	at least 20 per cent	tomato soup	at least 10 per cent
self-raising flour	at least 15 per cent	washing powder	at least 10 per cent
sardines	at least 15 per cent	butter	at least 5 per cent
baked beans	at least 10 per cent	strawberry jam	at least 5 per cent
chocolate biscuits	at least 10 per cent	soft margarine	at least 5 per cent
coffee	at least 10 per cent	tinned peaches	at least 5 per cent
corn flakes	at least 10 per cent	frozen peas	at least 5 per cent
cooking fat	at least 10 per cent	pork sausages	at least 5 per cent
fish fingers	at least 10 per cent		

In 1977, when this book was first published, the average weekly shopping basket cost less than £5 each week. By the end of 1984, it was around £12.50, depending on which supermarket one visited. If you are spending more than the average on food each week, look at what you are buying and try to buy more sensibly, particularly if your overall budget is tight. You should also consider whether you are getting the best value for your money. Frozen foods and other convenience foods may be easy to prepare, but they are expensive relative to the nourishment they provide, and their taste is often very bland. It is far better to make a large casserole when you are cooking and freeze some of it for two or three other meals than to buy branded frozen stews.

The same goes for other products. Make jam when fruit is cheap and plentiful, rather than buying branded jam. It will keep for months. Freeze the bits you cut off the meat when you are making a casserole; they will mount up and provide you with a good stock, far better than a (relatively expensive) stock cube. Make your own bread; it tastes better than a sliced loaf. There are many means of economizing on food if you really want to and they need not involve you in a great deal of time.

You will find that wherever you live you can make a considerable saving by buying a grocery chain's own brands. Do not think you are buying an inferior product when you buy an own brand. It has probably been manufactured in the same place as the branded goods and the composition of the product is likely to be the same. Often only the packing is different – generally less elaborate in the own brand range. But why pay for packaging?

The saving in buying own brands applies wherever you live and is quite consistent throughout. You can save 10 per cent outlay, sometimes more, by careful selection of own brands.

The Grocer has estimated where the best bargains are available and how considerably overall prices differ from one grocery chain to another. Wherever you live, Key Markets are the cheapest for the full basket and VG the dearest. Asda and Tesco are a little dearer, followed by Fine Fare and the Co-op. Sainsbury's, Safeway and Waitrose are a little more expensive. Next comes International Stores. Dearest of all are the independent grocers and in particular the (usually London-based) chains which offer late-night shopping every night – at a price. The differences are small, however. It would hardly be worth making a long journey by car or bus to save the few pence involved.

The Grocer also does regular assessments of the cheapest places to shop in the various regions it studies. Consider changing from one chain to another, if one is cheaper and equally convenient to shop in. Here are its conclusions:

The Midlands. Asda was cheapest for brands and as cheap as any chain for own brands. Key Markets and Mac Markets came next, with Mac being a little cheaper in own brands. Key was cheapest for fruit and vegetables.

North. Asda and William Jackson came out best, with Asda being a little cheaper except for fruit and vegetables. Mac was about the same for own brands, but dearer for branded goods. Liptons was about the same as Mac, as were Safeway, Woolworths and Tesco.

Scotland. The Co-op was the best bargain here, if you collect stamps. Otherwise Safeway and Woolworths were cheapest for brands and own brands.

Greater London. Key Markets was cheapest for brands, and only Mac Markets was cheaper for own brands. Next best came Sainsbury's, Safeway, Woolworths and Tesco and if you collect stamps the Co-op. There was little to choose here. Tesco was marginally cheaper than the others for fruit and vegetables.

South-east. Here again Key Markets and Mac Markets came out on top, with Key slightly cheaper for brands and Mac for own brands. Next came Tesco, and the Co-op for the stamp collectors. Liptons and Woolworths were cheap for brands and Sainsbury's as cheap for own brands.

South Wales and the South-west. Key Markets came out best, followed by Tesco and the Co-op (with stamps), with the Co-op a bit cheaper for brands and Tesco for fruit and vegetables. Liptons, Woolworths, Gateway and International Stores were as cheap as any others for brands but not own brands. Liptons was cheapest of all for fruit and vegetables and Sainsbury's as good as the Co-op and Tesco for own brands.

You can see from this that, by picking and choosing between brands and own brands, and between supermarkets, you can make quite considerable savings – though interestingly *The Grocer* found that very often people preferred the atmosphere of the dearer shops.

Rules for supermarket shopping
You can follow all the rules for sensible shopping, go to the cheapest stores, choose own brands, and still waste money. To avoid this:

1 Make a list of what you need and stick to it.
2 Don't be tempted by anything new or exotic. The chances are that it is overpriced.
3 Take advantage of special offers when they occur, like so much off toothpaste or detergent, rather than waiting until you actually need the item, when the offer may be over.
4 Don't buy too much or too little. If you live alone, or have a small family, it is a waste of money to buy a bumper size and then have to throw some of it away.
5 Know exactly the price of what you are buying. This means working out the unit cost of every item you buy. This is most important.

Meat

When you are buying meat, remember that the cuts which you can grill or roast quickly will cost the most. This does not necessarily mean they are the most nutritious or even that they taste the best.

Even if you are out at work all day, try to organize your cooking routine so that you can take advantage of the cheaper cuts. If you have a freezer, this is easy. You can cook several meals at the weekend and use them during the week. Look out for seasonal bargains. Pork, for instance, is often cheaper after Christmas.

Here are how prices break down among the different meats:

Beef
Fillet steak is by far the most expensive, followed by sirloin and the best topside roast. Rib roast is rather cheaper. Chuck steaks and flank steaks can be grilled if the quality is good and they come cheaper than the prime grills.

Cheaper still are braising and stewing cuts, which will take a long time to cook. These are beef shank, brisket and shin beef. Lastly there is minced beef, which can be cooked slowly or quickly as hamburgers, meat balls and meat sauces.

Lamb

The most expensive cuts are the chops cut from the rib or loin and leg of lamb for roasting. Shoulder is far cheaper. It roasts well, and although more fatty it is often more succulent than leg.

Chump chops and best end of neck are cheaper, and cheapest of all are neck chops. These are not popular in Britain, but they do not need such long cooking as the cheaper cuts of beef and are excellent in casseroles.

Pork

Loin and leg for roasting are the dearer cuts. Shoulder is cheaper and also roasts well, but it is difficult to cut unless the butcher bones and rolls it for you. Chops, too, are expensive, as is pork fillet.

Only belly is cheap. This can generally be cooked quite quickly and makes a good roast if stuffed, boned and rolled – though it may be too fatty for some tastes. It also makes a beautiful hotpot-style dish, with potatoes and onions, which is cheap, tasty and filling.

Offal

This is often the poor relation in cooking in Britain – though in many countries it is regarded as a great delicacy. Except for calves' liver and, a little less dear, lambs' kidneys, it tends to be cheap.

Veal kidneys, hard to get but worth searching for, are remarkable value, and a little patience can make a good meal out of almost any kind of liver, kidney, tongue, heart, brains, sweetbreads or tripe. This last, much misunderstood food can be make into delicious casseroles for a fraction of the price of a beef or lamb stew. It is also very nutritious.

Veal

Veal is young beef and what goes for beef also goes for veal, though on the whole the stewing cuts of veal are leaner than beef, and more tender, so take less time to cook. Though the expensive cuts of veal are as dear as any meat, stewing veal is often a great bargain and can be used in as many dishes as stewing lamb or beef. It is a sadly neglected meat in Britain, so look out for it.

Poultry

Most poultry in this country is sold as a total bird. It is worth experimenting with larger ones and roasting, say, only a part and using the rest for stews and finally as stock for soups.

This applies particularly to turkey. When you buy a turkey, however, do not buy one so large that you have to go on eating it indefinitely. Probably more turkey is thrown away uneaten because a family becomes bored with it, than any other meat. It is no wonder turkey is generally only popular at Christmas; we spoil our appetite for it for the rest of the year. Try buying it in pieces and making escalopes of the breast, or roasting only one leg of an enormous bird.

How many portions per pound?
As a rough guide here is the number of portions you can get from one pound. Ham goes a little further than pork, because eating the fat is more acceptable to most people:

beef	
fillet steak	3
sirloin steak	3
other steaks	3
top rump roast	3
rib roast (with bone)	2
casserole beef	3
lamb	
leg	4
shoulder	4
lamb chops	4
stewing lamb	3
pork	
leg	4
shoulder	4
loin chops	2–3
loin roast	3
poultry	
chicken	2–3
turkey	2–3

Weight loss in cooking
When you buy meat you must also consider how much it will shrink when you cook it. This is why you do not get the same servings pound for pound from every kind of meat. Some lose more when cooking than others, and the more slowly you cook the less the loss will be. Frozen meat loses rather more than fresh meat.

The amount of meat loss is a measure of how much extra you are paying for one pound of meat. Chicken is generally the cheapest meat to buy, but it does not always work out cheapest when you consider the net weight after cooking. On the whole, New Zealand lamb shoulder, which originally costs nearly 50 per cent more than chicken, works out the cheapest meat of all, taking into account both price and weight loss in cooking. Here are some examples:

joint	weight loss
beef topside	37%
pork neck end roast	38%
sirloin steak	38%
pork loin	43%
English leg of lamb	47%
NZ leg of lamb	48%
English shoulder of lamb	48%
NZ shoulder of lamb	48%
pork leg	51%
beef rib roast	54%
frozen chicken	69%

When you are buying, you must allow for this loss of weight when calculating the real price of the meat. If you are making a casserole, the weight loss will go into the gravy, so do not use more water than you need if you want your casserole to have a rich taste.

Fish

Though we live on islands surrounded by waters rich in fish, the British have never been really big fish eaters. This is a pity, because ounce for ounce, fish is as rich in protein as meat and it is not nearly as fattening.

You can often eat almost twice the amount of fish as meat for the same number of calories. This does not apply to all fish. The more expensive sorts, like salmon and lobster, are heavy in calories. It is with the white fish like cod, haddock, hake, halibut, sole, plaice and turbot that the gains really come.

There used to be an enormous price advantage in buying fish rather than meat, but this has largely disappeared, except with fish like mackerel, herrings, sprats and coley. All these are rich in nutrition, but some people find them fiddly to eat. The small effort of filleting these fish can be well worthwhile.

The main thing when buying fish is to buy it fresh, preferably from a fishmonger. There will be nothing wrong with the frozen fish you buy in a supermarket, but its texture will have changed, and there is no doubt that fresh fish tastes nicer.

Prices vary enormously every day, so you should buy the bargain of the day. And try the cheaper fish, like coley and rock fish, which are excellent when cooked and have not climbed in price to the same extent as cod and other popular fish.

If you are thinking of freezing fish yourself, buy it as fresh as possible and get it home and into the freezer as quickly as you can. Never freeze shellfish yourself. You can buy it frozen and put it into your freezer, but there is a real danger of shellfish going bad if you buy it fresh and freeze, however quickly you freeze it. Never exceed the recommended maximum freezer periods, as given later on in this chapter.

Some fish, like lobster, salmon, prawns, turbot and halibut, are now definitely in the luxury class. They will be at least as expensive as the most expensive cuts of meat.

The only consolation is that there is very little waste at all, and far less is lost in cooking fish than meat.

Vegetables and fruit

Unless you have a freezer, or grow your own vegetables and fruit, you will be at the mercy of seasonal prices, for most fruit and vegetables last only a few days, and not only do they go mouldy, but with each day left uneaten they lose some of their nutritional content.

So buy only as much as you need at any one time, or as much as you can accommodate in your freezer. Always beware of out-of-season items. They may be tempting, but the prices are almost certain to be ludicrously high. If you have a freezer, soft fruits are generally a good buy in season and freeze very well.

The store cupboard

It makes good sense in these days of inflation to buy food now instead of later if it can be stored for a time, to keep ahead of price rises. The obvious way to do this is to buy tins, jars, bottles and packets. Food will go off, eventually, however. The length of time it lasts depends on the product itself and the way it is preserved. In the end seals will break and even tins deteriorate, letting in air and bacteria.

Rotate your purchases. Don't use the tins you have just bought. Bring older ones forward and you should have no problems. Do not keep food until it has lost its colour and flavour, even if it will do you no harm.

Running your freezer

Nor does food last forever in a freezer. Even if it has not actually gone 'off', some food changes texture, colour and even taste if left too long. To avoid disappointment in these ways, make sure you rotate the food in your freezer. It takes time, but you must move the food round, so that you do not take out first the things which you have only just put in. Here are a few fresh meat maximum storage times:

beef	12 months
lamb	10 months
veal	10 months
pork	9 months
mince	2–3 months
offal (liver, kidney, etc.)	2–3 months
sausages	6–8 weeks

Cured meat lasts less well than fresh meat in terms of taste. It also needs wrapping well, so that it doesn't dry out and to prevent all the contents of the freezer tasting smoked. Smoked bacon will usually last for four to ten weeks and unsmoked for three to six weeks.

If you are freezing composite dishes like stews and casseroles, or soups, try not to leave them in the freezer for more than three or four months.

Remember that if you go beyond the recommended storage times, the food may not necessarily be bad – though you are taking a chance on it – but it will probably not be worth eating.

chicken	12 months
turkey and ducks	9 months
game birds	6–8 months
white fish	12 months
salmon, trout and herring	9 months
shellfish	1 month
vegetables	6–12 months (depending on variety)
fruit	12 months
cream	3–6 months
butter, unsalted	4–6 months
butter, salted	2–4 months
margarine	12 months
cheese	4–9 months (depending on variety)
beaten whole eggs or yolks	6 months
egg whites	12 months
milk	3–6 months
bread	6–12 months
cakes	4–6 months

Not everything will freeze. Most salad vegetables go limp and watery. Frozen tomatoes can only be used for cooking. Bananas turn black. Mayonnaise curdles and single cream separates. Hard-boiled eggs get leathery yolks. So don't waste money freezing anything which is not suitable.

Don't freeze things, either, which can be stored better in another way. Pasta will freeze, but it keeps just as well and cooks as quickly if you start straight from the packet. Its texture is better, too.

These are just some of the traps to avoid. Buy a good book on freezing – there is a large choice. They go into enormous detail and can help you use the freezer in the most economical way.

Bulk buying for your freezer

If you shop haphazardly or just buy normally at, say, your local butcher, you will certainly not save any money by having a freezer. It is essential to plan your spending. Many butchers will give you a discount for bulk sales, but there are also companies who do nothing but sell in bulk. Be careful, though. If it is beef you want, make sure you are not being sold poor quality.

If your family will not look at liver and kidneys, or can't stand stews, it's no use buying big packs which include these. And, again, watch the quality before you buy. Is the meat properly trimmed? Is there too much fat? Would you be better off as far as your family's tastes are concerned if you bulk bought half a dozen legs or shoulders of lamb rather than half a sheep? These are all important considerations. Before you start buying, consult your family and try to tailor your purchases to their requirements.

Look carefully at any freezer food purchase plans. These can appear very tempting. You may get a rent-free freezer and a certain amount of food free to start you off. But there will be snags. You may have to sign up for a long-term contract, which you may not be able to afford. You may have to contract to buy a certain amount of food every month. The minimum purchase may be too much for your needs. Again, the packs may not suit your family needs, so they turn out more expensive than they look at first sight.

In all these schemes, use extreme caution before committing yourself.

Food coops

A new way of saving on food bills has been growing in popularity recently – the food cooperative. When a number of people get together to buy in bulk they can save 15 to 20 per cent. To start a cooperative you need at least a dozen people and not more than about fifty, otherwise the coop gets unmanageable. Around twenty-five is a good number.

Get together with your friends or even advertise for coop members. Make sure you run your coop in an orderly way. Have meetings about once a month, and keep proper books of your incomings and outgoings. Work out a cycle of ordering, buying and distribution. Charge a small membership fee to cover your distribution costs. Decide whether you will distribute from one point, or whether you can manage door-to-door deliveries.

Work out your expenses properly and be very careful that you do not underestimate them. These are the kind of savings you can expect:

1 Meat: between 15 and 20 per cent. But be careful: coop members will need freezers to take real advantage of bulk buying.
2 Fruit and vegetables: about 30 per cent. Once-weekly buying is all you can manage here. Don't buy highly perishable vegetables, or fruit that is too ripe.
3 Cereals, pulses: about 50 per cent.
4 Eggs and dairy produce: about 15 per cent. You will need refrigeration for this.

You will not save much on frozen foods and groceries – particularly frozen food – after you allow for running costs.

Some rules to follow:

- Search around for the best discount stores. Try buying from farmers directly. Local butchers will give you a discount, but not as much as meat wholesalers.
- Find out the smallest bulk order you can get.
- Find out if you can get delivery; this is important if no member of the coop has a large car.
- Find out if you must pay in advance.
- Find out if substandard orders can be returned.

Friends of the Earth, 377 City Road, London EC1 (telephone 01-837 0731), have produced a useful little booklet on food coops. It tells you the best buys, what to look for, and how to run your coop.

Tips for saving when buying food

1 Plan well head. Work out your menus. Do not buy more than you need of perishables.
2 Avoid buying ready-made meals if possible. These can be very useful if you have to leave a hungry family to take care of itself now and again, but for ordinary family catering they are total disaster pricewise.
3 Do not be taken in by fancy packaging, or, even more so, by fancy descriptions of food. It will rarely come up to the promise on the package.
4 If you know you will have leftovers, buy things you can easily use up.
5 Do not send anyone to do your shopping for you. Do it yourself, or you will end up spending more than you have to.
6 Avoid health foods unless you are buying them for the taste. They are expensive and there is no evidence – yet – that they are better for you than ordinary food.
7 Be flexible. If beef costs too much, rework your menu, so that you can take advantage of what is cheaper. This applies to vegetables, too. It is best to buy what is in season. All of us should be able to buy a

few strawberries or even asparagus when they are in season. Out-of-season prices may be three or four times higher, or even more. Try to avoid the beginning of the season, when prices may be at the absolute top, because the produce is so tempting.

8 Use your freezer sensibly and shop when items are in season for use later on.
9 Always check the unit cost of what you are buying, however rough your calculation is.
10 Try to work out the cost of every portion when you buy meat, fish or vegetables. If the cost per portion is too high, choose something else.
11 Try to make quality and quantity go together.
12 If you can buy by the ounce, gram or pound, you may well be able to save money. Unfortunately, because of pre-packaging, this is getting more difficult.
13 Do not buy in such quantity that your stocks will have finished their reasonable shelf life before you get round to using them. This applies particularly to dried goods like peas, beans, lentils and barley. The fact that they do not actually go off does not mean that the flavour is not impaired by keeping them too long.
14 Buy the size which is most useful to you. Do not be too mean or too generous. One way you will be forced to open another (relatively expensive) small package, the other you will be throwing things away.
15 Look at what you are buying and compare the price with other forms of the same food. Do fresh, frozen, tinned or freeze-dried peas work out cheapest for you? As a rule, frozen food is a bargain only when used in small quantities.

Know the cost of what you are buying
Packaging can be deceptive: elaborate labels, boxes, shapes and coverings can mask the real size of what you are buying – and so hide its true worth. Make sure that you are not one of the ones who are deceived in this way.

Very few people check the *unit* cost of what they are buying – this is the cost per ounce or pound, gram or kilo. By buying in quantity you can usually lower the unit cost, but not always. Rarely – but it does happen – the price per ounce or gram is higher for larger amounts, so it is wise to check before buying. This may reflect increased packaging costs.

It is a bore always having to make calculations as you go round a store, so try to memorize a few prices per pound and per kilo, so that you can do a quick check between brands and get the best bargains. You must always look for the *net* weight – the gross weight includes the packaging.

Learn to recognize the unit cost automatically. Carry a copy of the list below around with you for a time until you get used to it, or even take a small calculator with you to calculate unusual amounts. Many people – including me – do this today. Then you will know exactly what you are getting for your money.

Try at least to remember a few key amounts:

1 kilo is just over 2 lb.	¼ kilo (250 grams) is just under 9 oz.
½ kilo (500 grams) is just under 18 oz.	100 grams is rather less than ¼ lb.

11 Personal and family purchases

Clothes

The customer may always be right in theory, but certainly not in practice. More money is probably wasted on clothes than any other area of personal spending. That dress or suit which looked so good in the shop may be all wrong when it gets home. Nothing is lost – take it back immediately, unworn. You should get your money back and you don't have to settle for a credit note.

More often, clothes, and particularly shoes, develop faults after very little wear. If this happens, take them back. More and more shops automatically take things back today, but some still try to refer the buyer back to the manufacturer. Do not accept this. Demand your money back; it's the shop's job, not the customer's, to deal with the manufacturer who supplied the faulty item.

When you've decided what you want to buy, don't hand over your money until you have done your own quality check. Make sure, as far as you can, that you are getting value for money. Generally, the more you pay the better the quality, but beware of fancy trade names, where prices may be higher than the quality of tailoring justifies. Quality is in any case not always what people are looking for. Fashion garments, in particular, may be best bought cheaply and thrown away after a season. Examine shoes very carefully: there are more after-sales complaints about them than anything else.

The good clothes buying guide

Decide why you want to buy. Don't pay a fortune for something you intend to keep only for a season, or, conversely, pay too little for something you will want to wear for a few years.

Make sure you buy the right size. This isn't so daft as it sounds. Even the same size can vary; one size 10 may not be the same as another. Try on whenever you can. British, Continental and American sizes are all different. How they vary is shown opposite and overleaf.

Examine every garment for possible faults. Does the hem droop? Will it fall down? This is evidence of bad cutting and hasty sewing.

Are the seams skimpy? Is the sewing even? Will they split on wearing? Is there enough margin to allow alterations?

Will the buttonholes fray, the buttons fall off, or the zip break? Zips which are too light for the weight of the material, for example, will not last long.

Will the lining split because it has been too skimpily cut? This is a common fault in cheap clothes.

Will any decorations fall off in wearing, washing or dry cleaning?

Check whether a garment will wash. Dry cleaning is expensive. Many garments carry a dry cleaning label when it is perfectly possible to wash them. The manufacturer is protecting himself against deterioration in washing. If you take a chance and wash when the instructions say dry clean, you won't get anywhere if you complain.

These are commonsense rules, but it's amazing how many people try something on, like it, and buy it without any check. It's a very English habit. On the Continent, people care almost as much about the inside and basic quality of the garment as about the style.

Women's clothing

Dresses, knitwear, blouses and lingerie

British	American	Continental (bust/hip)
32 ins (10)	8	81/86
34 ins (12)	10	86/91
36 ins (14)	12	91/96
38 ins (16)	14	96/102
40 ins (18)	16	102/107
42 ins (20)	18	107/112

Skirts

British (waist/hip in ins)	American	Continental
24/36	10	42
26/38	12	44
28/40	14	46
30/42	16	48

Stockings

British	American	Continental
8	8	0
8½	8½	1
9	9	2
9½	9½	3
10	10	4
10½	10½	5
11	11	6

Men's clothing

Socks

British and American	Continental
9½	39
10	40
10½	41
11	42
11½	43
12	44
12½	45

Shirts

British	American	Continental
14½	2	37
15	3	38
15½	4	39
16	5	41
16½	6	42

Suits and overcoats

British and American	Continental
36	46
38	48
40	50
42	52
44	54
46	56

Shoes (men and women)

British	American	Continental
3½	5	36
4	5½	37
4½	6	37/38
5	6½	38
5½	7	39
6	7½	39/40
6½	8	40
7	8½	40/41
7½	9	41
8	9½	42
8½	10	42/43
9	10½	43
9½	11	44
10	11½	44/45
10½	12	45
11	12½	46
11½	13	46/47
12	13½	47
12½	14	47/48
13	14½	48

Avoiding the pitfalls in shoes

As I have already said, shops get more complaints from buyers about shoes than any other article of clothing. Most shoe shops now obey the law and give you back your money, but some still try to persuade you to take a credit note instead. Do not accept this, unless there really is another pair of shoes in the shop that you like. Complaints mostly arise from 'fashion shoes', which may look substantial but quickly fall apart.

Whatever the price of shoes, you can help avoid problems if you bear in mind a few things when you are buying:

1 Make sure they fit. This is not as obvious as it sounds. Your feet change size during the day. They are smallest in the morning and largest at night. So buy about midday.
   Don't just sit down when you are trying them on. Walk about. The height of the heel or the shape of the toe can reduce comfort as you walk. Don't cram your feet into a particular size because you think it is your usual one. The same size does vary with make and style. Don't try on just one shoe. Your feet are likely to be marginally different in size.
2 Spend most money on your work or walking shoes. Save on sandals, or shoes which only match a particular outfit.
3 Choose a style that will last. This probably means not buying the height of fashion, but then your feet will still look good after the fashion has faded.
4 Remember, children's feet grow quickly. Buying at sales is a false economy if the child will then not get enough wear out of them. Up to the age of fifteen, a new size is needed every few months, and even after that, many people's feet are still growing. It is best and most economical to limit the number of shoes a child has. Otherwise he or she may end up wearing shoes that are too small because they are not worn out.
5 Only wear shoes for the purpose for which they were intended. Fashion shoes will deteriorate very quickly if worn too often in the rain. If your shoes do get wet, bring them back into shape by stuffing them with paper and letting them dry slowly away from heat.
6 Try to change your shoes once a day. Shoes get tired too and will keep their shape better if you don't keep them on too long at any one time.
7 Remember, you get what you pay for. Leather is dearer than synthetic materials and it wears in a different way. Don't economize on uppers, but there is no harm in paying less because a shoe has some sort of synthetic sole and heel. Examine the shoe properly before you buy. Is it stuck or stitched together? What is the lining like?
8 Look at the name of the manufacturer and its source. If something goes wrong you are unlikely to be able to get an exact replacement for a foreign-made shoe, so you may be better off buying from a reputable British manufacturer.
9 *Always keep your receipt.*

Choosing your sewing machine

You can save an enormous amount of money by making your own clothes, and the key to success is your sewing machine. Choose the right one for your needs. There is no point in buying a complicated machine with every possible gadget that can do all sorts of embroidery if you are just going to make simple clothes. The basic choice is between hand-operated and electric machines. Most people today choose the latter because they are less tiring to use, quicker, and easier in that you have both hands free to work the material. But if you are a beginner, hand machines run more slowly and are easier to control, and some people choose them because they don't want to be tied to an electric power point. The chances are that you will choose electric.

If you are going to do anything more than simply sew seams, it is worth paying for a few extras. If you buy a machine which only does *straight stitching* you will find it difficult to sew stretchy or knitted fabrics. A buttonholing attachment is particularly useful; a *zigzag* machine often incorporates a number of different attachments; a special presser foot means you can sew on buttons, or hem. All these are well worth buying, because the additional cost is small and an enormous amount of time can be saved. Unless you think you will do quilting, smocking, cording, gathering, etc. – and not many people do – don't buy those attachments.

All machines on the market will sew competently for you, but designs vary a lot. Look for the following:

- The light: it is better to have one above the needleplate.
- The case: some are easier to carry than others.
- The weight: if you want to carry your machine around, don't buy one which is too heavy. Heavier is not necessarily better.
- Be sure you have extra bobbins, spare needles and any other bits and pieces.
- Check the guarantee. You should get five years on the machine and two on the motor and foot control.

Finally, make sure you have a demonstration before you buy. The specialist sewing machine shops may be most helpful, but you may find that you can get a discount in an ordinary shop or department store.

Having bought your machine, have it serviced now and again. Sewing machines are tough, but they run more easily for a little oiling and care.

Furniture

The kind of furniture you buy for your home is largely a matter of personal taste. No one can decide for anyone else what is or is not a good buy. There are, however, a few guidelines you should take into account, whatever style you choose.

Make a proper buying plan. Few people can afford to buy a whole house full of furniture in one go. Work out how much you can afford on hire purchase and do not go over your limit. Decide what is essential and buy that first. With some items it is best to pay for as good a quality as you can possibly afford. This applies in particular to beds. You will spend a third of your life in bed, so you might as well do it in as much comfort as possible.

You will be surprised how few things you need to get your house looking like a home. A bed, chest of drawers, settee, table and chairs and you are off. Put everything in the same room if necessary at the beginning to make it look lived in. Make it look individually yours with a few lamps, cushions, pictures and mirrors. Above all, do not be tricked into over-extending yourself to impress your family or neighbours.

If you really do not have much money to spend, buy as cheaply as possible and rely entirely on these accessories to give the rooms their own, and your, character.

And if you have very small children, do not buy expensive furniture anyway, unless you have a special room for the children to do their destruction in, or actually do not mind your furniture being ruined. You cannot expect a small child to appreciate the value of your treasured object.

Do not buy anything until you have inspected it thoroughly. Bounce on the bed, lean back hard in the chairs, wooden or soft, to see if they can take it, make sure a table you may have to work at is a comfortable height. Do not buy an 'easy' chair that is not easy and comfortable to sit in just because it looks attractive.

Be especially careful when buying carpets. These are often offered as 'bargains', which they may well not be. Cheap carpets are often not hard-wearing. Check the fibre content before you buy. Wool is the most expensive and hard-wearing but it must be mothproofed. Nylon and acrylic are less resilient and easy to clean.

Try to imagine everything in its setting in your home. What looks nice in a showroom may be totally unsuitable for your room. Think about the size. Is it too small for your rooms, too big, or the wrong shape?

If you will be moving soon, buy as cheaply as possible, in case some things do not fit into your new home.

Re-upholstery. Before you consider getting your furniture re-upholstered, find out what you will really save. If it is not much and the actual structure of your settee is showing signs of wear and tear, you might be better off in the long run buying a new one.

If you are going to re-upholster, get several estimates; they can vary tremendously. If you have a lot to do, consider doing it yourself. You can enquire with your local authority about classes, or, if you are naturally handy, there are many easy-to-follow books.

Delivery. Use your connections to get discounts. But if you use a discount store, check that its prices item for item are genuinely cheaper, because you may find you have to pay for delivery.

Delivery can be a problem, but do not let the store bully you. Ask when delivery is and make sure that they stick to the date. If there is any sign of doubt about delivery, shop around a little. Most items of furniture are similarly priced wherever you shop. Go to the firm which offers the best delivery terms.

Mail order

Buying on mail order may save you money (see chapter 4 of this section). Branded goods bought this way may be cheaper, quality for quality, than those bought in shops, though non-branded goods are usually dearer. The customer can also save on expensive shopping trips, particularly if he or she lives out of town. But there are snags:

- The customer cannot examine the product until he takes delivery, when it may well not come up to expectations.
- There is nothing to be gained from paying cash, as the quoted prices are always credit prices and there is no discount for cash.
- Delivery can take a long time, sometimes too long, and the product may no use when it finally arrives.

Taking the following precautions will save you both disappointment and money.

1 Make sure you fill in the form correctly – a lot of people don't. Have you ordered the right size, quantity, colour, etc.?
2 Order well in advance and allow at least a month for delivery – more at Christmas, especially if you are buying gifts.
3 Look at the conditions attached to the sale. Is there a guarantee? What are the money-back terms?
4 Don't rely on any illustration in an advertisement or a brochure. Read the description – its weight, colour, size, contents. If anything is missing, don't buy.
5 Don't pay cash if you can avoid it. A cheque can always be stopped. But you cannot get a refund (unless the mail order firm is prepared to give you one) if you use a credit card when you are buying.
6 Examine the product as soon as it arrives to make sure the contents are as stated.
7 If you want to send the product back, do so immediately. Give your reasons in a letter attached to the parcel. Keep a copy of your letter.
8 Use only reliable mail order companies. If you buy through a national

newspaper you have some protection at least on delivery. The papers have a fund which reimburses people who do not receive the goods they ordered or get their money back.

You must claim within three months of making your order, and the fund covers only undelivered goods. If you have a quarrel with the company over quality, you must take it up direct with them.

Remember, you have the same protection and rights in law if you shop by mail order as you do with personal shopping.

Seasonal buys

If you do not have to buy at any particular time, you can often save a lot by buying at certain times of the year.

You may not wish to buy your clothes in the sales if you are very fashion-conscious, but in this 'anything goes' era for clothing, being up-to-the-minute is less important than it was previously. In any case, you can buy underwear, tights, socks and children's clothing in the sales.

Sometimes buying in bulk – three pairs of socks in one pack, for instance – will save money. If this is not possible, wait for the cheap 'season' to buy whatever you want. Shops and stores like to keep trade moving in months when people would not normally buy, and they also need to clear their stocks to make way for new designs.

Garden furniture comes cheaper at the *end* of the summer, not the beginning. Fridges may be cheaper in the winter. Central heating can often be installed at bargain prices in the summer. When you are buying, think whether you could buy more cheaply if you waited a few months. I cannot give a totally exhaustive list, but here are a few items and the cheapest months to buy them:

product	time to buy
bedding	winter and summer sales
bikinis	summer sales from July onwards
blankets	late winter
camping equipment	late summer
clothing	
spring	summer sales
summer	summer sales
autumn	winter sales
winter	winter sales
crockery	winter and summer sales
seconds	any time
Christmas presents	any month except December
domestic appliances	
fridges	winter sales
cookers	winter and summer sales

product	time to buy
washing machines	winter and summer sales
dishwashers	winter and summer sales
furniture	winter sales particularly
furs	June to September
gardening equipment	August and September
home furnishing	winter and summer sales
ski wear and equipment	March
toys	January and February

This short list shows that the best time to buy is generally the time when most people are not buying. It makes sense to think about whether what you are buying has a 'low' season and take advantage of it.

Cutting the cost of your entertainment

Entertainment at home

We all need some relaxation in our lives and most of us have it, even if it is only the *television*. One thing to be said for television is that it is cheap to run. If you watch it for four hours a night, that will take up most of your leisure time and will cost just 3p an hour for colour or 1p for black-and-white – excluding the cost of buying or renting. Spread that among a family and it is highly unlikely that you will find any form of relaxation cheaper, apart from walking, and even that uses shoe leather.

When you include the cost of buying, say, a 22-inch colour television set, which lasts you for five years and costs little in repair, the cost of an hour's viewing will rise to between 11p and 13p an hour, depending on where you buy your set. If you get it at a discount warehouse or store, the price is likely to be more than 25 per cent less than in an ordinary store.

Or you may rent your set. If this is a black-and-white one, you may well pay less than 50p a week, particularly if you have had a long contract. This way you have no repair bills to think about, and if the set breaks down totally it will be replaced by the rental company.

But renting has been less attractive since the advent of colour television. Rentals are much higher and if you are going to keep your set for more than two years, which is likely, you will be better off in the long run buying.

If *music* is your hobby, you will need rather more expert advice on record and cassette equipment than I am able to give. Try to get this for nothing. Go round several stores, describe your needs and accommodation, and decide what equipment you would like. Then buy at a discount.

A good stereo system costs about 1p an hour to run, without taking into account your buying costs, or the cost of records or cassettes, whichever you are using. Listening to music is therefore a much more expensive hobby than watching television. Anyone who buys a dozen records a year and listen for about ten hours a week, will find that the overall cost comes to 35p an hour. The more you use it, the lower the average cost per hour.

There is a very wide price range for hi-fi units and this is an area where the quality of the reception you get can vary enormously. Remember that you only get what you pay for. Take advice, and listen to several machines before buying.

Entertainment outside the home

If you think the figures above are high, think what entertainment outside the home might cost an average family in a week. A family doing all this is likely to be paying out up to £50 a week on family entertainment. Not many of us can afford that much:

parents:	
one night a week at the cinema	£5
or the theatre	£15
one meal out each week	£20
mother:	
two nights' bingo (say £3 a night)	£6
father:	
one night at the pub	£3
children:	
dancing lessons	£1 (each)
piano lessons	£2 (each)
going to football match	£2 (each)

Drinking at home

If you confine your drinking to your home you will certainly save money. Pub and bar prices have a service element built into them. If the brand you buy does not particularly bother you, shop around various wine merchants. You may find the following discounts:

liqueurs and sherry	up to 40%
port and wine	up to 30%
beer	up to 25%
vermouth, vodka and rum	up to 15%
gin and whisky	up to 10%

It is also worth looking in your supermarket: the brands they have on offer are more limited, but often cheaper. They occasionally have own brands, too, which are sometimes, though not always, cheaper. Do not buy these bulk, however, until you have tried one bottle to see if you like the taste.

This is particularly important with wine. Today anything only a little over £2.00 a bottle is usually rubbish. It is impossible to sell a decent bottle of wine at such a price and make a profit. This is how the price of a 70cc bottle of wine builds up:

transport, distribution and marketing	61p
duty	84p
VAT	27p
bottling and labels	20p
producer's profit	14p
total	£2.06

You can see from this that, even if you pay only 4p for the wine and the grower's profit, you will have to pay £2.10 a bottle and that allows nothing for the distributor's profit. If you pay £3 a bottle you are obviously getting much better wine, as the overheads will be the same. The quality of wine rises quite sharply after the basic costs are covered.

Costing your sporting activities

This book is not the place to go through every sport, working out the possible costs you may face if you are to take it seriously. But before you embark on what could be an expensive pastime, here are some questions you should ask yourself:

1 Have you got the time to take it seriously, or would it interfere with your other activities?
2 Just what, if anything, will it cost each time you play?
3 What are the transport costs involved in getting to and from the venue? Are they prohibitive?
4 What will equipment cost?
5 Will it involve you in a lot of expensive socializing after the match or game is over?
6 Is it dangerous? If so, have you got yourself properly insured?
7 Is it so expensive that it would virtually prevent any other member of your family taking up any sport or activity they would like?

These questions may seem trivial at first glance, but any hobby, once taken up seriously, can be difficult to give up. When times are hard, resentment can build up in a family which sees money going in one direction when other members feel it could be better used elsewhere. Always discuss your hobby and what it will mean in time and money with your family.

12 Insuring your home and your possessions

Insuring your home

Once you have bought your home, you should insure it even before you set foot inside the door. In fact, you should do it as soon as contracts are exchanged. If you are buying on a mortgage, the insurance company or building society will insist that you insure the building for at least as much as the original mortgage they allow you.

At one time, you had no choice over the insurance company you used; the building society would simply include the annual premium in your mortgage repayments, so that there would be no question of the policy lapsing. Now you have some choice, but there is so little to choose between the bigger insurance companies that it is not worth making a fuss about it.

The lender may wish you to insure your home for rather more than the amount of your mortgage, or indeed for more than you have paid for the house. This is because he is basically insuring himself against the total destruction of the building. He will want to be sure that if this happens there is enough insurance money to replace the building. He may reckon that this will cost far more than the amount of the mortgage and set the insured value accordingly. This will be the value of the house, not the land on which it stands.

You need not insure your house for its market price; that includes the site. But take care, because the market value is often *less* than the cost of rebuilding.

If you are buying your house for cash, you should make the same calculations. If you own the freehold, you will have the land no matter what happens, but the cost of rebuilding your house will rise steadily with inflation. For this reason, you should steadily adjust the amount for which the house is insured as time goes on.

Even if you have some insurance via your mortgage, it is worth considering taking out additional cover yourself on the building. If you are renting property, check to see if the landlord has arranged the house insurance. If not, do it yourself to safeguard your position.

How to go about it

1 Sit down with a reliable local insurance agent and talk the matter through. He will have a good idea of basic values in the area and will be able to advise you. He will take into account the exact location and condition of your house. A swimming pool or garage would obviously add to the cost of insurance, for instance. If you do not know an

insurance agent, ask your bank or solicitor to help you. Or try the local Citizens Advice Bureau.

2 If the house is new, get the builders to give you some sort of estimate of its replacement cost. It may well be more than their costs, even if the house has only just been completed.

3 If you have bought from someone else, try to find out if you can what they had the house insured for. If they had lived in the house for some time, however, it is highly likely that they were under-insured – most people are – so use their estimate of value only as a starting point.

4 If all else fails, call in a surveyor and ask for his estimate of the value. While you are doing this, you can also have the contents of your house professionally valued, which will be a help when it comes to insuring them.

Once you have decided on the value, you are ready to go ahead with the insurance. Your policy will be basically a replacement policy for the whole house, but it will also cover you for damage from burst pipes, leaking roofs, etc. For small jobs, however, the lessor or owner of a property may be required to pay the first £15 or even sometimes £50 of damage himself.

Check with your building society to see that the value for insurance purposes is adequate, then keep the insured value of your house up to date all the time. If the insurance company feel you have under-insured they may scale down any claims you make, even for minor damage. Some policies today are index-linked. Get one if you can afford it, then you are safe.

Do not make trivial claims. If the insurer gets several from you every year – particularly if, say, your roof always seems to be leaking, or your pipes bursting – he may well put up your premium.

What your policy can cover
Although most policies give the same kind of cover, there is actually no standard house insurance policy. Though they may make certain exceptions, or load the premiums in certain locations – if you live in an area known to be subject to flooding, for example, you will probably have to pay more than normal for that risk – most insurers will cover the following:

1 Fire, lightning, explosions or earthquakes. These can all happen in Britain. In 1976, for instance, there were many claims for earth tremors, if not for quakes.

2 The escape of water or oil from a water or heating installation. This includes such things as burst pipes.

3 Aircraft or car damage. This is becoming increasingly important, and many people, since the advent of supersonic aircraft, are trying to cover themselves against any damage sonic booms could do to their houses. This is particularly important if you are on a known flight

path, though there have been some difficulties so far in proving that broken windows or cracks in the wall were caused by sonic booms.

4 Riots or malicious damage. Obviously this is more important in some areas of the country than in others. The centres of big towns are the most prone to this kind of damage, as we saw in 1981.

5 Storms or flood. We know all about these in Britain, but is this cover enough? Check your drought cover. The summers of 1975, 1976 and 1984 have shown that we can have droughts, and these can lead to serious damage. Drought can cause subsidence, leading to cracking walls. In the autumn and winter of 1976–7, many insurance companies had more claims for leaking roofs, because of the cracking and shifting of tiles due to the long drought, than ever before. Frost damage is often excluded, as I have found to my cost! If you live in an area liable to flood, tell the company when you take out your insurance; otherwise, your claim may not be met.

6 Theft. Burglars rarely steal a house (it has been known) but it is remotely possible that you may have an integral part of your house stolen.

Remember, policies do not cover normal wear and tear. You can see from what I have said that your house insurance policy can cover most contingencies. As far as burst pipes, floods, riots or malicious damage are concerned, the householder will usually be required to pay the first £15 of damage. If you want to avoid even this payment, your policy will probably cost you an extra £4 a year. You can also increase your cover to allow for further items – say, damage from falling trees. If you decide you want to be covered for 'all risks', most insurers will give you this for a slightly higher premium.

Normal house insurance is not dear. It varies from between £1.50 and £1.90 for every £1,000 worth of building, usually with a lower limit of £10,000 and an upper one of £250,000 for a normal family house..

Subsidence cover

Most risks are well known, but from time to time new ones arise and the householder may then discover that he is not covered for them. One such instance is subsidence, which can cause minor or quite severe damage to a house. Areas of subsidence are well charted and include not only natural geological areas of subsidence, but also those created by old mine workings or other man-made underground activity.

In normal weather circumstances it has always been thought that at most one per cent of British homes would be liable to subsidence. The percentage was so small that it was not until 1970 that insurers provided cover for subsidence at all, and then it was included in the general policy. This meant that many householders were insured against a risk they did not face.

The dry summers of 1975 and 1976 changed all that. Many thousands of claims for damages have come into the insurance companies, from minor cracking and leaks to the severe sinking of a whole house. To cut down the costs to themselves of such claims insurers have been writing what are called 'excess clauses' into their policies to cover subsidence. Insurers may require householders to pay the first £500 of any subsidence claim, or 3 per cent (sometimes as much as 5 per cent) of the sum insured, whichever is greater. This means that, if your house is insured for £10,000, you may have to pay the first £500, even though 3 per cent is only £300, and £600 at £20,000.

This presents a dilemma for many householders: if they increase the value of their overall insurance to keep pace with inflation and make sure that their cover for, say, fire damage is adequate, they are at the same time putting themselves at risk of having to contribute far more than they can afford if they are forced to put in a subsidence claim.

So far the insurance companies have not yet come up with a solution to this problem. All the householder can do is raise his insurance to keep up with inflation if he is fairly certain he is in an area which is not subject to subsidence. However, if he lives in one that is, he must balance the chances of finding himself inadequately insured should there be a fire against the more likely eventuality of having a smaller bill for subsidence damage. Not a pleasant choice to have to make.

Problems like this come up all the time in insurance, so you should pay constant attention to your house insurance. Not only do replacement costs rise, but the actual incidence of various forms of damage changes. Do not be caught out with a totally inadequate policy.

A warning
Read your policy carefully to make sure that it covers all the risks you may face. If it does not, find out what it will cost for extra cover and take it out. There is a further risk which not everyone is aware of. Some building societies today have one massive policy to cover all their mortgages. This has the advantage of being cheap to everyone because the individual risk is small. But it may not cover a particular risk in some properties. Make sure you see a copy of the policy to check that you are properly covered. If not, you are free to take out your own insurance policy: the society might not like it, but it cannot stop you from withdrawing from the bulk policy.

Insuring your possessions

Once you have got your home adequately insured, you must look to its contents. Remember that insuring your possessions is entirely your responsibility. They will not be covered by your house insurance. If, for example, you have a burst pipe which damages your carpets, your house insurance policy will cover you for the damage to the fabric of the building and the repair itself, but any replacement for the carpet or the cost of any cleaning will have to come from the policy on your possessions.

If you are arranging all the insurance yourself, however, contents can sometimes be included in an extras section. The rates of the two types of insurance are different, but there is the advantage of having only one premium to pay if you can have everything dealt with in the same policy.

The first steps

First of all, make an inventory of all your possessions. This means furniture, domestic appliances, pots and pans, curtains, carpets – everything. Work out what they all cost and what you would have to pay to replace them. Break down the list into several sections:

1 Normal household furniture and equipment.
2 Pictures, antiques and anything else with no simple replacement value. If necessary, take photographs of these. They may be useful to show to the police or your insurers in the case of burglary or fire damage. Get a professional valuation on anything particularly valuable.
3 Any very valuable items, like paintings, furs, jewellery or watches. These should be insured separately. It is highly unlikely that you would be able to persuade your insurer to give you the full value of a £1,000 diamond ring, if it was lost or stolen, unless it was separately insured in a list vetted by the insurer, and the premium for that part of the policy calculated accordingly.

When you have have added up the value of everything you have, you will probably be surprised at what it amounts to. It has been reckoned that it costs £2,000 to replace the average living room, £1,500 for a bedroom or kitchen and £1,200 for a dining room. This puts the average contents of a three-bedroomed house at a value of close on £10,000.

When your list is complete, put one copy away safely, then take another to the insurance agent or broker, or the insurance company if you are dealing with them direct.

The cover provided by different companies can vary considerably. It might be sensible, therefore, to use an insurance broker, who would be able to look at all the possibilities available and find the one that suits you best.

Remember, your insurance needs may change. As you add to your possessions, whether they are personal belongings or part of your family home, include them on your insurance.

How much cover do you need?

You may be able to get a single 'all risks' policy for everything you have, but this is likely to be extremely expensive. It is generally more economical to split your belongings into sections.

1 *Your normal belongings*. There can be insured at various standard rates, depending on the area in which you live. Central London is the most expensive – more than twice as much as in the depths of the country – followed by the other major cities. You can put quite expensive items on your normal policy, but mention them specifically when you take out your insurance, or you may find that you get only a proportion of the value when you make a claim.

The standard form of insurance policy will probably have certain restrictions on it, regardless of the total value. It may only cover the loss of money up to a certain amount, say £50, or 5 per cent of the total sum which you have insured. All your jewellery and other personal effects, like furs, may be regarded as not worth more than one-third of the total sum insured. 'Wear and tear' will be taken off before you get the amount of a claim. If you have been using an armchair for fifteen years and it gets burned beyond repair, it is highly unlikely that you will receive the full replacement cost, unless you take out a 'new for old' policy which costs about 5p more for every £100 insured.

If you want to cover yourself for full replacement costs, regardless of the age and condition of your effects, you may be able to take out a policy which allows this. If you do, you will have to insure for the full cost of replacing everything in the house. Consider very carefully whether this would be worthwhile: in not too many years the total of the premium may well add up to more than any expected benefit from the replacement of one particular item.

2 *Belongings which have a particular value*. Could be a piece of furniture, or a picture, but more often single items of jewellery or watches, cameras and other equipment which you might carry around with you, including some items of clothing. These are commonly insured at a higher rate under 'all risks'. You may be able to get a worldwide 'all risks' policy, which means that wherever you go you can take these items with you, secure in the knowledge that if they get damaged or stolen they will be replaced.

Try to get an 'agreed value' for all these items, because once something is lost it may be difficult to reach any agreement. You may need a receipt. If you have not got one, say, when you have been given a present of jewellery, get a jeweller to give you a professional valuation. When you have arrived at a total value for everything you want to insure, add on a little more to cover anything you may have forgotten, and anything else you may buy during the coming year.

You may be able to cover damage or loss of clothes under your 'all risks' policy, but you will generally have to pay the first £10 or more of any such loss on the wear and tear principle. It is, of course, always possible to get these insured separately. If you are a professional entertainer, for example, you will probably have to pay a fairly high premium, not only because your clothes are worth a lot, but also because you travel around a great deal and therefore expose them to greater risk of damage or theft.

What your policy will not cover
Now you may think you are completely protected, but even 'all risks' does not cover everything. Certain mishaps are excluded:

1 The breakage of anything brittle, unless it is done by thieves, or fire. If you are dusting your Ming vase and drop it, the insurers will not pay a replacement value for it. On the other hand, if you drop your non-waterproof watch in the bath and it stops, you could then argue that the damage was caused by 'external means'. Whether your claim was met would depend upon the particular insurance company.
2 Damage caused by moths or vermin. Try to mothproof anything which may need it, and make sure that your possessions are as safe as it is possible to be from rats or mice.
3 Breakdown, gradual deterioration, or wear and tear. An insurance policy does not mean that you will never have to replace things; you will when they break down or wear out. The idea is to replace anything lost by accident, whether through theft, fire or sudden damage caused in any other way.

What it will cost
Normal cover for your household belongings is not very expensive, it costs about twice as much as cover for the building. You may be able to get most things covered for 30p for each £100-worth. This means that if you have £2,000-worth of furniture and equipment, you can insure them for £5 a year. £20,000-worth would cost £60.

This rate covers most of the country, but if you live in the centre of a big town, and particularly the centre of London, you are likely to find yourself paying more. This is because insurers believe – and the crime statistics confirm this belief – that theft is more common in city centres. Theft is the biggest area for claims, yet another reason why it is a good idea to have photographs of as many of your valuable items as possible.

You may also find yourself paying a slightly higher premium if you live in one of those fashionable and expensive areas outside towns which are such a natural magnet for thieves – for example, the so-called 'stockbroker belts'. If you live in such an area, your insurance company may want to inspect your house to satisfy itself that it is adequately burglar-proofed. In these areas, normal 'indemnity' policies cost at least 75p per £100-worth and 'new for old' 80p.

Always shop around for your contents insurance; you may be able to save money. Premiums vary considerably from company to company, as do the areas which different companies regard as high risk. You may be able to save between 15 and 20 per cent on your premium for the same cover, wherever you live. Rates in inner city areas, particularly London, Glasgow, Manchester and Liverpool, are set to rise sharply as I write. In November 1984, the Prudential – by far the biggest insurance company in Britain – doubled its rate in those regions from 75p to £1.50 per £100-worth 'new for old'. At the same time, the company also announced that those customers would have to pay the first £200 loss themselves on any claim for theft in those areas. The move, which was designed to cut the losses the company had been making on that business in recent years, may also have aimed to discourage people in inner cities from insuring their contents, at least with the 'Pru'. Other companies did not immediately follow suit, but they have been making losses, too, and may follow before long.

At the same time, the 'Pru' lowered its rates in some country areas. Changes like this occur frequently in the insurance industry, so it obviously pays to look around. There are no 'no claim' bonuses either, so there is no benefit in sticking with a company just because you have had a policy for some years. Each time renewal comes round, check that you are getting the best and cheapest cover to suit you.

If you keep making claims for thefts, the company may well refuse to continue to insure you unless you change to better locks, put gates across your windows, or install a burglar alarm. If you go to another company, they may well ask you how many times you have been robbed and stipulate the same conditions before they agree to insure you. If you have a great deal of jewellery, you may be asked to keep a safe in the house, or, if it is extremely valuable, to leave it in the bank for safe keeping.

It is impossible to set out any rate, or even an average rate, for the cost of an 'all risks' policy. It will depend on who you are, where you live, the sort of life you lead, your job, the particular type of item you are insuring and the total value of everything you have on 'all risks'. It is likely to be most expensive (yet again) if you live in London or any large city, or if the total insured is extremely large.

Making your claim

You are entitled to claim when anything is lost or destroyed, damaged, or stolen.

Inform your insurers right away. In the case of anything lost or stolen, inform the police immediately too, particularly if you discover the loss at night or in the evening when it is not possible to contact the insurers for some hours.

Do not touch anything until the extent of the damage has been seen by the insurers. You can only do essential repairs before informing the insurance company if by so doing you can prevent the damage from getting worse. For example, you could repair a burst pipe to prevent it from damaging your carpets still further.

If you have any doubts about getting an agreed value, you should employ an assessor. He will be able to haggle with the insurance company on your behalf. But you will have to pay his fee out of your own pocket.

You will have to fill in a claim form. Then the insurer may pay up, or he may wish to inspect the damage for himself before deciding what, or whether, to pay out on your claim. They do not always come themselves and may send an 'independent adjuster' to negotiate the claim with you.

Do not be surprised if, when the adjuster arrives, he tells you that you are under-insured. As I have said elsewhere, this is almost inevitable if you have kept your insurance at the same level for a number of years. Making a claim from your insurance company is one way – the hard way – of finding out you really are under-insured.

The insurance Ombudsman

In 1981, the insurance industry set up an Ombudsman organization to deal with complaints. It is designed to deal with grievances from the public about the way in which their policies are interpreted, or their claims met, by the companies. Most of the major companies belong to the bureau, which is financed by the companies themselves.

In cases where the Ombudsman finds the complaint justified, he can make an award of up to £100,000, which is binding on the company involved. Before considering a complaint, the Ombudsman must be satisfied that the complainant has taken reasonable steps to reach agreement with the company, nor must any proceeding have been started in a Court of Law. Complaints must be made within six months of the company making its decision about the claim known to the complainant.

The Ombudsman covers all insurance cases from life assurance to motor, household and legal expenses. He does not accept that the complaint is justified in all cases. In 1982, for instance, only 141 complaints were confirmed and a further 38 revised out of a total number of complaints of 2,504. Very often, complaints arise because the policyholder has not read the documents carefully. Make sure that you do this before taking out a policy: you may well not be covered for what you need to be.

13 Assurance at all times

Most people's mistake when they come to insure themselves is that they do it too late. When they are sick, they suddenly discover that they could have covered themselves for periods away from work. When they get round to thinking about life insurance, they all too often find that they have missed the best terms.

So sit down early – in your twenties – particularly if you are a man and married, and consider whether you have insured yourself properly against accident or sickness and whether you have adequately catered for your dependents in the unfortunate event of your unexpected death.

If nothing happens, and you have insured yourself properly, you will have acquired a relatively pain-free way of saving over the long term.

There is a difference between *assurance*, which covers something that will definitely happen some time, and *insurance*, protection against something which may or may not happen. This chapter deals mainly with assurance.

Different kinds of life policy

A straight life policy is called a *whole of life policy*. You pay premiums every week, month or year for the rest of your life and the insurance company pays your heirs the sum assured after your death. The sum assured is agreed between the insurance company and the customer at the time the contract is taken out. There are two other kinds of policy which are now far more popular with the public than whole life.

1 *Term assurance*. You pay premiums for a fixed number of years – this is unlikely to be less than ten years, but may be twice that. If you die during this period your heirs will be paid the sum assured. If you survive until after the term has ended, the company pays nothing.

2 *Endowment policies*. These give the best of both worlds. You pay premiums for a fixed number of years. If you live until the end of the period, you receive the sum assured. If you die while you are still making payments, the money will go to your heirs.

All life assurance policies can be purchased either 'with profits' or without. With-profits policies cost more, but if you can afford the premiums you will get far more out than you put in if you survive the term, or your heirs will get the amount of profits credited until the point at which you die. 'With profits' simply means that each year the insurance company gives you some of the profit it makes from investing your premiums.

Most people do not think of *annuities* as insurance, but they are the same as whole life insurance policies in reverse. Instead of paying premiums until you die, you pay a cash sum to begin with and then you are paid a certain agreed sum of money at fixed intervals until you die. Then the annuity usually dies with you.

So that you understand what you are getting when you insure, let's look at some of the possible benefits:

1 First and foremost, you can protect your family from financial hardship in the event of your death. You can do this by providing for some form of regular income, or a lump sum payment. If you are buying your house

on a mortgage you probably already have an insurance policy which will repay your mortgage if you die when it is still outstanding.

2 You can save regularly for a nest-egg which matures when you retire, or provides a lump sum if you die first.

3 If your policy has been running some time, you can use it as security for a loan from your bank.

4 You can gear your endowment policies to mature at certain points in your life – when your children go to secondary school, when they leave school at sixteen, to pay for their further education, or even, if you want to splash out in a big way, for their wedding.

5 The maturing of an endowment policy can be an excellent tax-free wedding gift to your child.

Whether you go for whole life, term or endowment policies, there are some differences within each type.

● If the policy cover remains unchanged throughout its life, it is known as *level term*.

● If the policy includes an option to change it later into a more valuable policy of the same kind, or even a different one, it is called *convertible*.

● If the sum assured declines steadily to vanish at the end, it is known as *decreasing*.

● If the sum assured is to be paid out in regular instalments in the event of the policyholder's death, rather than in a lump sum, it is called *family income*.

What life assurance costs

The amount of premium which is paid on a policy is based on risk. Just as we saw in the previous chapter that people living in areas where burglary is common have to pay more to insure their possessions than people in safer areas, so the higher the risk of early death, the higher the life assurance premium.

On the whole, this means that the younger one is when taking out life assurance, the cheaper the premiums. Secondly, the greater the promised benefits, the higher the premium. Thirdly, sex come into it. Women on average live seven years longer than men. Insurance companies do not give them the full benefit for that, but age-for-age treat a woman as if she is four years younger than a man, so she pays less for her life assurance.

For most routine life assurance policies, the life companies set out in tabular form the level of premiums which must be paid, depending on the age at which the policy is taken out. *This does not mean that premiums rise with age once the policy has been taken out.* It is the starting age which determines the level of premium for the whole of the life of the policy, so that the earlier one takes it out, the less the monthly or annual cost and the greater the benefits.

Generally, simple term assurance is the cheapest. A premium of £1 a month over twenty years should cover a man of 20 for £10,000. A man of 40 taking out a similar policy would pay £4.10 a month. Next comes whole life without profits and here a man of 20 would pay around £5 for £10,000 cover, compared with around £12 for a man of 40.

Endowment is far more expensive than the other two, but premiums do not rise so much with age until the mid-50s. A with-profits £10,000 basic sum assured for a man fo 20 would cost about £27; for a man of 40, it would be about £30 for a policy over 25 years.

These are normal premiums for people in good health and in relatively safe jobs and there is some variation, though not a lot, between companies. Anyone with a serious medical condition or in a risky job may well have to pay more. This is called 'loading'.

In fact, very few people are loaded and insurance companies have been getting more generous about whom they accept at normal rates. And there has been one recent development in the opposite direction. In the past, there have not been discounts for those in exceptionally good health, or at exceptionally low risk. Today, however, many companies are offering discounts of up to one-third of the total premium. This is a tremendous saving, which you should take advantage of, if possible.

What kind of assurance do you need?

Whole life
Whole life insurance is suitable for anyone who wishes to leave his family or heirs with a lump sum when he dies. This will usually be a married man with children.

One problem is that the premiums usually must be paid until death, and after retirement it may become difficult to keep them up. You can get round this by taking out a *limited payment policy*, under which you pay full premiums until retirement, after which they stop.

With-profit policies are dearer than straight policies, but you can take out something called a *decreasing whole life with-profits policy*. The premiums are calculated as if the sum assured actually decreased over the years. This does not happen, because the with-profits bonus payments more than make up the gap. Eventually the sum assured reaches rock bottom and the decreasing period ends. You then stop paying premiums and the policy begins to appreciate in value rapidly.

The snag about whole life is that you can never touch the money yourself. If you have a policy for, say, fifty years, you may begin to think that you could have saved or invested the money more profitably somewhere else, particularly if inflation has eaten away at the true value of the sum assured. It is, however, not a particularly expensive form of assurance.

Term

This is the way of getting the biggest cover for the least outlay. You do not get any money if you survive the term. People who do dangerous jobs or engage in dangerous sports often use term insurance as a means of getting high cover at comparatively low cost.

It is also popular with many people who have mortgages, especially the *decreasing term* type, more commonly known as a mortgage protection policy, when a decreasing sum is assured as you pay off your mortgage. A building society may even insist that you take out this kind of policy for the period of your mortgage. It is an additional security for them. There are varieties on the basic term policy: sometimes you may even get a paid-up whole life policy at the end of the term, or a cash payment.

Obviously this sort of insurance is suitable in some cases and some situations, but it's not in the end much use to anyone unless the policyholder dies before the term ends.

Endowment

Quite rightly, endowment with-profits policies are the most popular in the United Kingdom today. They are quite expensive, but they provide the policyholder with a means of protecting his dependents in the event of his death and also with the prospect of being able to enjoy the money should he survive the full term.

The with-profits elements can be most attractive, and may even mean that the policyholder gets well over double the sum assured. If you have read the chapter on mortgages, you will know that this kind of policy is most popular with building societies when they are arranging a mortgage. The policy is used as additional security for the loan.

Endowment with-profits policies are also the basis of most equity and any other linked contract investment schemes (see Section five, chapter 5). What happens is that part of the money paid each month by the investor goes into an insurance policy which protects the saver.

Endowment policies come in all sorts of forms and for all sorts of purposes. Education policies have been growing in popularity in recent years. The parent pays premiums, usually but not always and not necessarily linked to the father's life, which guarantee that an agreed sum for a child's education will be paid for in the event of the parent's death, or that an agreed sum will be provided for an agreed number of years, when it is needed. As the policy is activated, the premiums rise. These policies vary enormously in what they offer. If you are thinking of taking one out, there are two rules you should always follow:

1 Take out the policy as soon after the child is born as possible.
2 Gear your premiums to much higher school fees than at the time you take out the policy. Fees have risen enormously in recent years, and

what looks adequate today may be a mere flea-bite in a few years time (see Section three, chapter 2).

Grandparents can also take out endowment policies to benefit their grandchildren. They insure themselves against dying before the child, and the policy ends when the child comes of age with either a cash payment or a fully paid-up life policy.

Endowments are very attractive to many people, but they can seem relatively expensive in the initial stages. If you are forced to surrender your policy before it matures (see later in this chapter), the cost can be high, so be sure that, unless something totally unforeseen happens, you can meet your commitments.

Annuities

When you buy an annuity you are taking a gamble on how long you will live. It is the reverse of the gamble you take when you take out a life assurance policy. You pay a capital sum to give you a regular income until you die: the older you are when you buy the annuity the shorter that time will be, so the higher the income in return for your capital payment the insurance company will be prepared to pay you. It goes almost without saying that you will never be asked about your state of health when you buy an annuity. The sooner you die, the more profit to the company.

As men have a shorter life expectancy than women, they usually get a slightly higher income at the same age than women. The longer you survive, the greater your chance of making a profit, though it always takes some years at least before you recover the capital sum that you have paid out. How long this takes will depend on your age when you take the annuity out.

There are various types of annuities:

- Guaranteed annuties, which give some form of capital repayment on death as well as lifetime income.
- Immediate annuities, where you pay a lump sum and start receiving the income six months later, and afterwards in half-yearly instalments.
- Deferred annuities, which you buy before you wish the payments to begin. These are bought on an instalment basis, and may include a cash option as well as income.
- Joint survivorship annuities, which are for husband and wife together. When one partner dies, the amount of the annual annuity usually falls by about a third.
- Minimum annuities, which guarantee a fixed income for a certain number of years, usually five. At the end of that period the person who holds the annuity has the option of a cash payment instead of continuing with the annual income. This is useful if you suspect that you may be able to get a better deal five years later, when the cost of buying annuities has fallen.
- Reversionary annuities are another form of joint annuity. They can be

taken out by someone who wishes to assure an income for a companion if he or she dies. If the purchaser dies first, the companion get the annuity, but if the companion dies first, the annuity dies.

Annuities are useful because they provide attractive tax concessions which vary and would not be available if you simply invested your capital sum and lived on the income from it. With annuities you can usually get double the income you might get from investing in the stock market.

How much assurance do you need?

There is no fixed amount for you to aim at in the matter of assurance. If you are a young man or woman with no ties and responsibilities, you may well feel that the business of assuring your life can wait. And you may well be right. But once you are married with responsibilities you will need some kind of assurance to protect your dependents.

Many women feel that they need not concern themselves with assurance, but their death can bring considerable financial hardship to a family, particularly today when many wives work and the overall standard of living of many families is dependent to some extent on the wife's income. For this reason a married couple should plan their assurance together.

If you still need convincing, one of the major assurance companies has produced the following facts: 7,000 married women under the age of forty-five die each year in Britain. This means they are still likely to have children living at home. Housewives, too, are said to have a replacement value of well over £200 a week. Though we should not take these figures too seriously, they do show that life assurance can be just as important for women as men. Yet only one in four wives is assured in any way at all. You could try, for example, to get joint life assurance on your mortgage. Discuss all these aspects with your broker when deciding what level of joint cover you need.

First of all, decide what income the surviving partner will need if the other dies. If it is the woman who is left, she is unlikely to be earning as much as her husband, or may not be earning at all, and will need to replace her husband's income as nearly as possible. A surviving man may not need so much, but it is wise to remember that if life is to be at all manageable some extra help in the home will probably be necessary – and it generally costs more than a wife.

Second, calculate your outstanding commitments should you die and try to make sure that any money coming from the insurance company will cover them. Additionally, you may want to insure your children's education and a variety of other projects.

All the time, take care not to commit too high a proportion of your total income to assurance. We are nearly all worth more dead, but it is foolish to make life miserable just to ensure that this is the case.

Below is the sort of life assurance programme that the Life Offices' Association and the Scottish Life Offices suggest that a man should follow through various stages of his life, from marriage to retirement.

First step: age 25 (newly married: intending to start a family)

Newly married, starting to buy their first home on mortgage, intending to start a family shortly, husband in company's pension scheme

Take out	Monthly premium	Cover initially provided
(a) **Mortgage protection policy** to cover £15,000 building society loan repayable over 25 years	£2.00	£15,000 initially
(b) **Family income benefit policy** on husband's life for £3,000 a year for remainder of 25 years	£3.00	£75,000 initially (£3,000 a year for 25 years)
(c) **Family income benefit policy** on wife's life for £3,000 a year for remainder of 25 years	£2.80	£75,000 initially (£3,000 a year for 25 years)
(d) **Whole life policy,** with profits or unit-linked policy. Premiums to cease at age 65	£6.00	£3,000
(e) **Permanent health insurance policy** to provide £120 a week if husband is unable to work through illness for 26 weeks or more	£7.00	—
Total monthly premium	**£20.80**	**Providing initial cover of £168,000**

Second step: age 35 (budget allows more saving)

Budget allows more savings

Take out	Monthly premium	Cover provided at age 35
Endowment policy with profits or unit-linked policy payable when husband retires at 65	£14.00	£4,000
Previous policies		
Mortgage protection	£2.00	£13,575
Family income (husband)	£3.00	£45,000
Family income (wife)	£2.80	£45,000
Whole life	£6.00	£4,770
Permanent Health Insurance (PHI)	£7.00	—
Total monthly premiums:	**£34.80**	**Providing cover of £112,345**

Third step: age 43 (eldest son leaves school)

Eldest son leaves school

Take out	Monthly premium	Cover provided at age 43
Further endowment policies with profits or unit-linked policy payable when husband retires at 65	£17.00	£3,500
Previous policies		
Mortgage protection	£2.00	£9,660
Family income (husband)	£3.00	£21,000
Family income (wife)	£2.80	£21,000
Whole life	£6.00	£6,915
With profits endowment	£13.80	£5,800
Permanent Health Insurance (PHI)	£7.00	—
Total monthly premiums:	**£51.60**	**Providing cover of £67,875**

Retirement

Husband aged 65

Mortgage protection policy had stopped when the mortgage was fully repaid.

Family income policies had both stopped after the 25 year period.

Now, the endowment or unit-linked policies mature providing a lump sum to supplement the pension:

First policy matures with benefits of:	£19,900
Second policy matures with benefits of:	£11,580

The **whole life policy** still goes on providing cover of £18,330 including bonuses and can go on increasing the total sum although no more premiums are to be paid

Copies of a booklet explaining this plan are available from LOA/ASLO Information Centre, 60 Cheapside, London EC2V 6AX.

Surrendering a policy

I cannot repeat too often that you must take care not to overload yourself with assurance. If you have to give up a policy before it has run its course you will find that the penalties are severe, especially with a savings-linked or life endowment policy. Many people make the mistake of over-committing themselves, only to find that they cannot keep the payments up. *Nearly half the life assurance policies taken out are given up within ten years of starting*, long before the policies have matured.

When a policy actually acquires a surrender value varies from company to company, and you should check this before taking your policy out. Some policies acquire a surrender value after the very first payment, but most companies insist that you pay for a minimum of two or three years before the policy gets a surrender value, and some companies may make the policyholder wait as long as five years.

Let's consider a man of thirty taking out a with-profits endowment policy for £10,000, maturing after fifteen years. A typical annual premium could be £698.

Surrender after two years and a payment of £1,396 in premiums will bring him a repayment of only £912; after five years the figures are £3,490 and £2,280. It is only after about seven years that the repayment will equal the premiums paid. After that there is a profit, and when the policy matures after fifteen years and a payment of premiums totalling £10,470, he can expect a minimum payment of £18,905 – a very nice profit.

This final payment is likely to be more than you would have got from regular saving in the bank or a building society, but they would have been earning interest right from the start.

Why are assurance policies so different? When you surrender a policy you are paying a *penalty* for not giving the assurance company enough time to cover its costs in issuing the policy. It costs money to assure you, and expenses and commission have to be paid to whoever sold you the policy.

To avoid losing your money:

1 Stop and think before you commit part of your salary on a regular and long-term basis.
2 Don't just listen to the assurance salesman. He makes his living out of selling policies. Make sure he describes the contract and explains the surrender terms. Get independent advice. You will have no comeback once you have signed the contract.
3 Do your own check on anything long-term. Set the spending against your other commitments. Make sure the policy is what you want.

Tax and life assurance

Until the 1984 Budget, life assurance premiums carried tax relief at the rate of 15 per cent or up to one-sixth of total income. On 13 March, the Chancellor of the Exchequer abolished all that. It would not be true to say that the change was a bolt from the blue: the industry had long been expecting relief to go or be reduced, but it had expected consultations first. As it was, anyone taking out a new policy found himself paying 15 per cent more for the same cover than would have been the case the previous day.

The Chancellor did not, however, remove the relief from existing policies, which continue to benefit from the 15 per cent relief and will do so until the policy matures. This means that anyone thinking of surrendering a policy should think even more carefully than before, because not only would any new policy cost more, as the policyholder would be starting it at a later age, but there would be no tax relief, either.

Tax relief remains on self-employed deferred annuities. (See Section five, chapter 9.)

How to buy life assurance

You can get your life assurance through:

The insurance company directly. This can be a good idea if you know that the particular company offers good rates and returns, or has a deal which will suit you particularly well. But if you are buying through one company, you do not have the benefit of being able to shop around, so it may not be the best you can do.

Remember the different kinds of companies. They are:

- Proprietary companies. They are ordinary incorporated companies. Some of them may be very old and have been formed under Acts of Parliament or under Royal Charter. This makes no practical difference to the way they operate.
- Mutual companies. These have no shareholders; anyone who has a policy with them is a 'member' of the company, sharing in its profits and, of course, when they occur, its losses. Losses are extremely rare, because some mutuals are limited by guarantee, and have not happened at all for many years.
- Mutual indemnity associations. You are unlikely to come in contact with these; they sell to the professions rather than the public in general.

An insurance agent. These include people like solicitors, accountants and bank managers, who deal with money every day and are often asked for advice by their clients. Car dealers are often insurance agents as well, though they, of course, limit their activities to car insurance. As a rule, they work only for one company, so dealing with them has the same kind of disadvantages as dealing with the company direct. They make their money by commission on sales, so they won't charge you anything.

An insurance broker. All in all he may be your best bet when searching for life assurance, especially if your needs are a little complicated. He sells any sort of insurance, and although he, too, will tend to do regular business with certain companies, he should know where the best bargains are to suit your particular case. An insurance broker will:

- Look at your particular circumstances.
- Design total cover in all areas in the most efficient and economical way.
- Look for unusual cover for you.
- Review your policies from time to time to see that they still fit your needs.

- Deal with your claims for you promptly.

Insurance brokers must now by law be members of either the Federation of Insurance Brokers, the Association of Insurance Brokers, or the Corporation of Insurance Brokers before they can describe themselves as brokers. Prior to this law, which introduced other rules for practising this business, these were 9,000 'brokers'. Immediately afterwards the number almost halved, so a great number of unprofessional operators were weeded out, though it has to be said that this number included many who chose to become agents rather than call themselves brokers and who had high skills.

If you have any doubts about the status of anyone who says he is an insurance broker, check with the Insurance Brokers Registration Council. The people who operated before without fulfilling the rules can still carry out insurance business: they simply cannot use the word 'broker'.

Friendly societies

New-style friendly societies were becoming an increasingly popular vehicle for small with-profit assurance policies during the early 1980s because of the unique tax benefits they offered. Since the 1984 Budget such societies have been able to offer only very small – but profitable – business. Friendly societies were originally set up in the nineteenth century to help poor families in times of sickness or death. Because its objectives were charitable, all the profits of any society were completely free of tax. This benefit has continued and is now being applied over a wider area – but the sum assured is now limited in law for many societies to £750. The policies, which are often called bonds, are generally with-profits and, although it is not yet possible to see how they will turn out after, say, ten years, because no policy has yet been in operation that long, investment experience in the past suggests that the final payout could be up to three times the original sum assured.

Like all life assurance policies, the proceeds at maturity are of course tax free. But friendly societies have one big advantage over life assurance companies. The latter must pay tax on their investment profits before paying the proceeds to policyholders. Friendly society profits are tax free, so they start off with a built-in 37½ per cent profits advantage to distribute to their policyholders.

Those who have the policies taken out when the limit was £2,000 should do very well from them and should not surrender them. The surrender terms on such policies are fixed at a maximum of the gross premiums already paid, so the profits come only at the end. All these policies still have the benefit of life assurance premium tax relief, because they were taken out before the 1984 Budget.

Fringe insurances

Today it is possible to insure yourself against an enormous variety of things, for either long or short periods. It is impossible for me to list here all the possibilities, but here are just a few you might consider worthwhile:

1 You could cause accidental injury to someone. We can all do this, but if you drive a car a great deal in your job it might be worth covering yourself against this eventuality.
2 You can insure yourself against having twins, a good idea if twins run in the family. If they do arrive, the extra money always comes in useful. You take out the policy as soon as you are pregnant. This costs about £5 for every £100 insured in each pregnancy, but will vary depending on how strong the family record on twins is.
3 In addition to your own life and that of members of your family you could also insure the life of a favourite pedigree pet, or a horse. You can also cover yourself for veterinary fees.
4 You can insure bits of yourself: your voice if you are a singer, your hands if a pianist, your legs if a dancer or footballer.
5 You can also insure yourself when you go on holiday, or against being unable to go as planned (more details in chapter 18 of this section on holidays).

14 Covering yourself against sickness

If you are ill, you will have enough to think about without worrying about money. On the other hand, employers may well ask themselves why they should pay you when you are not at work. You can help solve this problem in many ways.

State sickness benefit

First of all, there is the state sickness benefit. We pay for this each week or month when we are working, through our National Insurance contributions. Like most benefits, this has risen over the years, and is likely to continue to do so. Rates change each November and from November 1984 were:

men, single women, widows and married women paying full contribution	£27.25	additional payment for: wife, or other adult dependant	£16.80

This means that a married man with two children will get £44.05 to support his family with while he is away from work sick. Additionally, a wife will get £13.70 total child benefit each week, bringing the family income up to £57.75. It is not a great deal, particularly for a family buying a house and trying to run a car. This is generally partly overcome by the additional payment of an earnings-related supplement for twenty-six weeks. The rates and earnings levels change each year, like most social security benefits. The employer has now become responsible for paying the first 28 weeks of benefit: previously they paid for eight weeks and then the Department of Health and Social Security took over.

No payment is made if you are away from work three days or less, and nowadays it is almost unheard-of for an employer to make deductions for the first three days. It is just not worth anyone's time and money to go through the necessary administration. Of course, anyone who does piecework or happens to be employed by the day will not get any money, but this is rare. The earnings-related supplement is not paid for the first twelve days.

These benefits apply whether you are employed or self-employed, but if you are unemployed you will continue to receive the usual unemployment benefit. The self-employed do not get the earnings-related portion.

To get the benefit at all you must have a medical certificate, which now goes under the title of MED. This is a statement by your doctor that you are unfit for work. When you are ready to return, he will produce a further certificate stating this and your benefit will cease from that date.

Since 1982 people have been allowed to fill in their own sickness certificates for the first week off.

Most people assume that the state benefits will be enough to see them through. They do not expect to be ill very often and feel that it will be enough to tide them over difficult periods. Their medical treatment itself will, of course, cost them nothing if they use the National Health Service, apart from prescription charges.

Company sickness funds

In addition your company may have what is called a sickness fund. When you are sick you get a payment from the fund to help you out. There are almost as many varieties of these funds as there are firms. The fund may be provided entirely free by the company itself; more likely, employees will pay in a small contribution each week, and membership of the fund will be optional.

If it is a company scheme, your employer will very likely have taken out a permanent health policy to cover all his workers similar to that available to the individual (see later in this chapter). The insurance company will generally insist on its own doctor examining the person for whom the claim is made, to make sure that there is no malingering. The payment is usually made to the employer rather than directly to the employee. That way it is regarded as earned income and treated better from the point of view of tax. Were it paid to the employee direct it would be regarded as investment income, which often bears a higher rate of tax.

Where the sickness fund is contributory, the rate of benefit will depend to some extent on how much is in the fund and will be adjusted from time to time.

Private insurance

You may feel, nevertheless, that your benefits are not enough, and wish to take out extra insurance for periods when you are ill. There are various forms of private insurance.

Hospital cash insurance
You can cover yourself for any period that you are in hospital. This is not the same as having *private* medical treatment in hospital, and the money can be used for any purpose you want: your family may have a long and expensive way to come and visit you; maybe you would like a private room, or a semi-private one. A premium of between £60 and £120 a year will give you cover of £20–£30 a day while you are in hospital. This is a rather high premium if you are not going to be ill very often, but only you can calculate that risk. It covers you only while you are in hospital (the average stay is ten days, and one in ten of the population spends some time in hospital every year), and not while you are at home convalescing. The insurance company will not normally pay out to patients in mental or geriatric hospitals. On the whole this insurance is not enough, and the premiums may rise if you make several claims. You would be wiser to look around for something more substantial to cover you for the total period that you are ill.

Permanent health insurance
It is far better to take out permanent health insurance. Once you have this the insurance company cannot cancel it, no matter what happens to your health, or how many claims you make.

If you want this kind of insurance, it is a good idea to take it out as young as possible. Premiums may rise sharply with age, as you become more likely to be taken ill. You may find, if you are a woman, that illness or absence from work through pregnancy and childbirth are excluded from all these policies.

What you get is a weekly payment if you cannot work because of sickness or accident, and the payments will go on as long as you are not working, or until you reach a particular age, which is set beforehand. As a rule, the payments do not start as soon as you are ill; they usually begin after thirteen weeks.

A policy for a 29-year-old married man with two children, providing £5,000 a year, with payments starting after six months away from work, would cost about £5 a month. As in any insurance, premiums in PHI are based on how likely you are to be ill for a long period. The lower the risk of your becoming ill, the less you will have to pay. so premiums rise with age. They are also usually higher for women. PHI policies are still relatively new and most of the policies have been taken out by men. Insurance companies claim that women are a greater risk and that they tend to be ill longer and more often than men, even after excluding pregnancy and any effects from it.

As a result, fewer women take out policies, because they find that they may have to pay premiums which are anything between 20 and 80 per cent higher than men for the same cover. How true the insurance companies claims are is difficult to say. Women have challenged the companies and, as I write, one case is before the European Court. Many people believe, and I am one of them, that the level of business from women in Britain so far is not enough to assess whether they are in fact a bigger risk than men. The companies may be relying on figures from America, where PHI is more popular, but American patterns need not necessarily be repeated here. A few companies charge men and women the same rates, but these tend to be companies with higher-than-average rates anyway, so that is little help to women. If women win the case, their premiums will have to come into line, though it may mean that companies will be more reluctant to offer PHI policies at all. Non-working wives anyway already find it difficult to get this cover: only a small number of companies offer it, those who do not say that problems of assessing inability to do housework make it an unacceptable risk for them to take.

After six months your state sickness benefit stops and is replaced by an invalidity benefit, which is much less, so your income drops still further in comparison with what it was when you were working. This makes permanent health insurance particularly useful.

If you take out permanent health insurance, the insurer will generally let you insure yourself for up to three-quarters of your earnings, less any state benefits you are allowed. You can choose when the payments will start – either one, three or six months after you become ill. The longer you defer payments, the cheaper the insurance is. If you are prepared to wait six months, you will probably find that your annual premium will be half as much as if payments were to start after one month. A man just under forty with a hitherto good health record will pay about £10 a month for a benefit of £5,000 a year paid after three months sickness. Premiums vary a little, however, from company to company.

Permanent health insurance may not be suitable for all of us, but it can be a great help to the self-employed and to those who have high incomes, whose standard of living would be most affected by long-term inability to work. Talk to your employer first and find out how long he will be willing to go on paying your salary in the event of your being ill, and fix your insurance policy accordingly.

Accident insurance

You can also insurance yourself against accidents at work. This is fairly cheap and may be advisable if you are in the kind of job where accidents do occur. You will naturally have to pay more if you are, say, a manual worker on a building site than an office worker.

Policies against accidents are often sold in 'units'. One unit may offer, say, £2,500 on death within twelve months of an accident, £5,000 for permanent disablement or loss of limbs, temporary weekly benefits to replace income for a particular length of time. For this kind of cover, annual premiums would be £6–£7 for dangerous jobs down to around £4 for the safest.

Private medical treatment

In addition to securing a reasonable income for yourself while you are ill, you can also insure yourself for private medical treatment, either in hospital or out of it.

It has to be said straight away that you will not get better treatment because you pay for it privately. What you will get is a private room or a bed in a small ward, and you will be able to have the treatment immediately, or when you want it, even though your case may not be urgent. You can also choose your own consultant.

If you use the National Health, you may find that for a hernia, tonsils or varicose veins you have to wait up to three years for treatment, and that you then have to go for treatment whenever you are sent for, even if it is inconvenient, otherwise you may lose your place in the queue.

Many people, however, cannot afford the very high fees which must now be paid for private treatment, and to cover themselves they take out insurance to pay for it should the need arise. About three million people are covered by medical treatment insurance in the UK. They either take out this cover themselves or belong to the group schemes which are run by many companies.

Full cover, if you take out an individual policy, can cost a 30–40-year-old married man with two children between £300 and almost £600 a year, depending on the company chosen and the area in which he lives. Cover will provide for the surgeon's fees and accommodation in hospital. Group schemes are about a third cheaper. Sometimes the employer will make a contribution, sometimes not. Occasionally he may offer it free to some or all of his employees as a fringe benefit, though the employee has to pay tax on the benefit. As medical costs have risen, so has the cost of policies, and some companies are now devising new schemes where the cost of the insurance is much lower but the patient agrees to pay the first £1,000 or so of treatment.

If you are attracted by the idea of private medical treatment, make enquiries with your employer first. If he has nothing to offer you, write to one of the non-profit, making organizations that specialize in this type of work. The three biggest are:

British United Provident Association, Provident House, Essex Street,
    London WC2R 3AX.
Private Patients Plan, Eynsham House, Tunbridge Wells,
    Kent TN1 2PL.
Western Provident Association, Culverhouse, Culver Street,
    Bristol BS1 5JE.

All these companies offer basically the same sorts of schemes, but the specific benefits vary, as do premiums, from one company to another. Write to find out what they offer. All exclude some things, which may or may not be important to you. Treatment during pregnancy and child-birth is always excluded, although sometimes you may be covered if a caesarian section is necessary.

You will always have to pay for your own gold fillings, or trips to health farms, osteopaths or acupuncturists, and for a variety of other treatments. You will also have to declare any existing illnesses or medical condition and, unless you come to a special arrangement with the company, you will not be covered for treatment for these. There may also be a limit on the contribution which the insurer is prepared to make.

Do remember, if you want private treatment and have to pay for it yourself, accommodation and nursing can cost you up to £140 a day for a private room in a London teaching hospital and £100 in the provinces. Scotland and Northern Ireland are cheaper than in England and Wales. You can get cover for up to a year in hospital through private medical schemes. Nevertheless, think carefully before you take out this form of insurance. If you do not mind being in a ward or waiting for a minor condition to be treated, do not take it out. If you are suddenly struck down and need an operation immediately, there is no more delay with the National Health Service than with private medicine.

15 Buying and running your car

The cost of motoring

We take motoring so much for granted these days that it is sometimes difficult to appreciate that it is entirely a twentieth-century development. Indeed, it is only in the last twenty-five to thirty years that car ownership has become widespread.

To begin with it was the preserve of the wealthy; its growth has been linked with the growth in disposable income. It was still a status symbol in the 1950s and 1960s, but has now become an indispensable part of the way of life of millions.

Yet its cost is still formidable. This cost is not always realized at the time a car is purchased, and is all too often later ignored. As a result, a family may have to sacrifice many other things in life simply to keep their car, which may or may not be providing a service which justifies the expense.

Today there are 56 million people in Britain and over 16 million cars. The figure is not staggeringly large, but it has quadrupled in the last twenty years and doubled in the last ten. But most cars today have more than one driver – half the adult population possesses a driving licence.

Motoring has always been expensive, and never more so than now. Have no illusions about it. All calculations comparing the costs with the costs of public transport show that it is an expensive way to travel.

Just because you can get four people from Manchester to Sheffield in a car ostensibly more cheaply than by train, or fill your car up once a year with your family for a holiday, does not mean that it is cheaper overall to have a car than to use public transport. Your car, as we will see later, costs you money even when it is standing in your garage.

For a few brief years at the beginning of the 1970s, it looked as though the cost in real terms of buying and running a car would fall. Then in 1973 the oil war came and these hopes were dispelled. The following year motoring costs rose faster than in any other year since motoring began, and more and more motorists found their car was costing them as much as – and sometimes more than – their mortgage.

We are still feeling the effects of the events of 1973, directly and indirectly. The price of petrol (early 1985) is over £2 a gallon, while servicing, repairs and insurance have all gone up by half as much again. All this means that the motorist's out-of-pocket expenses have risen sharply. Worst of all, the cost price of a new or second-hand car has more than doubled. If you already have a car, trading it in for another one may not present such problems as a first purchase, though the upsurge in prices upset many drivers who had felt that once they were over the hurdle of the first car, all problems were over.

If you had bought a brand new Mini in the summer of 1973, you would have had some change out of £700. If you had sold it a year later, you would probably have been pleasantly surprised at how little it had depreciated in price. But a year later you would have had to pay £80 more than the original showroom price to buy it back, and in the meantime a *new* Mini had more than doubled its price tag. By the beginning of 1985, the price of the Mini Mayfair, the most popular Mini, had risen to £5,000.

In spite of this, you may feel that the car is still a source of pleasure for you and your family and still a comparatively inexpensive way of enjoying leisure activities.

More important, the reduction in public transport and the resulting relative isolation of many parts of the country mean that a car – no matter how expensive – is sometimes essential if you are to get around at all.

Buying your car

Before you buy

First, ask yourself whether you really need to own a car. If you live in a city and need your car only for occasional outings and summer holidays, hiring one whenever you feel you need it may make more economic sense than buying one. Using a taxi every day for your needs can be cheaper than running a car, and you then have no worries about parking. Even with the charges hidden away in most car hire company's contracts, a fortnight's hiring fees represents only one third of what a year's garaging could cost in a major city.

Second, if you have decided that you really do need a car, spend some time deciding what kind you want. It is useless to choose a two-seater sports car with a jump seat if you have a family who will expect to be taken out in it. An estate car is a good buy for a growing family, or for anyone who uses a car for holidays and touring. If you are a young and inexperienced driver, do not choose a sports car because you think it suits your personality. Insurance companies are aware of the temptations of such a car to the young, and the cost of insurance is correspondingly heavy. Do not buy an enormous car, which is costly to run, if you will generally be driving alone, or if you live in a city where parking can be difficult.

Third, make sure you can pay for the car – both for the actual purchase and for the running of it. Make sure you have enough cash or can get a loan, whether from your bank or from a finance house, or possibly through the car dealer. The cost of borrowing varies enormously, so look around rather than immediately accepting the first deal you are offered.

Fourth, if you are using a dealer:

1 Make sure he is reliable. Make enquiries with the professional dealers' organization before you start the process of buying.
2 Compare the different guarantees that dealers offer. What do they cover? How much are they for?
3 Do not automatically take the dealer's word that you are getting a bargain. It's highly unlikely that you are. Have the car checked independently. The AA and RAC do this.

You may find that you get the best service from a local dealer, rather than one of the big, more anonymous ones. He will depend for the successful continuation of his business on local recommendation.

Second-hand cars
It is likely, if you are buying your first car, that you will buy second-hand – unless you are a woman; women apparently prefer new cars. As many as two-thirds of all Britain's motorists drive cars they bought second-hand, and many who could afford a new car prefer one about a year old, which has been run-in properly and had all the snags ironed out.

As the price of new cars increases, so demand for one- or two-year-old cars also increases; this applies even to company cars, which will generally have done around 17,000 miles in the first year, compared with the private motorist's average 9,000. At least these cars have been regularly serviced and maintained, while the private owners may well have neglected their cars because of soaring garage costs.

One great attraction of buying second-hand is that you will not have to face such heavy depreciation as on a new car.

One snag, if the car you buy is three years old or more, is that it will need an MoT (Ministry of Transport) test every year. The test is now tougher than ever, and will cost you £10 (1984) whether the car passes the test or not. Reasons for failure can range from such vital matters as steering and inadequate brakes and seat belts to minor faults like a defunct horn, worn windscreen wiper blades and blocked screen washers, or even a dud bulb in the stop lights.

Try to get a second-hand car which carries a guarantee from a reputable dealer. If it does not, have it checked by the AA or the RAC, the independent motoring organizations. They will charge an inspection fee – an amount well worth paying to know that the car is in good order. Some dealers offer cars complete with an independent AA report.

How much can you afford to pay?
Set yourself a maximum price that you are prepared to pay before you start – and stick to it.

New cars. With a new car the price is usually known beforehand, but there are still several ways of saving money. Extras can put the price up a good deal. Some of these are more or less compulsory, but others are genuine extras. Some manufacturers include delivery, and the price of number plates and seat belts (which are now compulsory), in their prices, others do not. Most family cars are made with two kinds of interior, standard and 'de luxe'. If you are set on one particular model, you may find that you have no option but to take the de luxe model, and the expensive trim can add between £150 and £300 to the basic cost of the car. This is not all bad, however, because the car will keep some of its de luxe aspects when traded in, so you may be able to recoup some of your money.

Second-hand cars. When you are buying a second-hand car, remember that you will never get a bargain unless you buy privately. All dealers, and many private sellers too, know exactly what the car or cars they are selling are worth. If you get a few pounds knocked off the price, that will most likely be because the dealer had intended all the time to knock them off.

If the car you are buying genuinely costs less than most other similar models, take great care and have it thoroughly checked to see why it is being offered so cheaply. There is likely to be something wrong with it. Do not always believe the mileage reading. Milometers can easily be tampered with. Learn the tell-tale signs which will give you an idea what mileage a car has really done:

- One that has driven 15,000 miles will still have a good deal of tread on the tyres.
- One that has driven 25,000 miles will have a worn tread on the tyres and the battery may have been replaced.
- One that has driven 30,000 miles may have a brake pedal which is wearing out.

Test drives
It does not matter whether you are buying new or second-hand, always ask for a test drive. Surprisingly, less than half the buyers of new cars ask for a test drive. The fact that a car is new does not necessarily mean there is nothing wrong with it.

If you don't think you will spot any faults yourself, get someone with more experience and some technical knowledge to drive it for you. Do not simply drive along the road and back. Test the car for hill starts, try it on a poor road surface if possible, and in congested traffic conditions. Alternatively, do not test-drive the car at all: this may strengthen your position if you discover a fault later (see Section six, chapter 2).

Check the car carefully for scratches and dents before you drive it away. If you do not do this immediately, it may be difficult later to have things put right for nothing by the dealer.

Having test-driven it, check the boot to see that the spare tyre and any tools are all there. Do not leave the dealer until you are sure you have the logbook, warranty and handbook and, very important, the MoT road-worthiness certificate, if the car is more than three years old. Do not forget your insurance cover (see next chapter).

Negotiating the price
Once you have chosen your car, you should start negotiating on the price. Even when you buy a new car, you need not always accept the listed price, particularly if you are paying cash.

A main dealer gets a discount of about 18 per cent on a new car. Try to persuade him to give some of it to you. If you are lucky, you may get between 5 and 12 per cent off the list price. If the first dealer you try will not do it, try another.

Drive a hard bargain when you are trading in your car for another one. Take it to the dealer in tip-top condition, cleaned up and polished and with minor faults put right. The dealer will usually offer you between 20 and 25 per cent less than he expects to sell it for later on. You may find that it is better to sell your car privately first. That way you may get a higher price – but do not underestimate the problems of selling privately. Advertising can be expensive, and anyone buying from you will probably also try to drive a hard bargain. Remember that a dealer's second-hand price should include VAT (see Section four, chapter 3).

Time your trade-in properly. Your repair bills may begin to get out of hand after you have driven 60,000 to 70,000 miles. Every car will vary, but do not trade in before you have had your car three years; and after six years, you might as well drive it into the ground and then sell it for scrap.

Running costs

Once you drive your car away from the showroom, you begin to spend money. It disappears in several ways, apart from petrol costs.

Depreciation. A 1,000–1,500cc driven on petrol, depreciates in value by almost £600 in the first year. That's nearly £12 a week, more than £1.70 a day. Allow around £200 a year for every 500cc increase in engine size. If you buy a new car, it will probably lose more than a third of its value in two years and half in three years.

Standing charges. Then there are the costs you incur without going anywhere. These are reckoned to amount to £885 a year if the car in your garage is between 1,000 and 1,500cc – the most popular range owned by nearly half of Britain's motorists. As well as depreciation, you must allow some interest for the amount your money would have earned if it had not been invested in your car. Garaging costs money, either in rent or extra rates. Other expenses are road tax, your driving licence, insurance and the MoT certificates, where applicable.

If you are wise, you will also join one of the motoring organizations. They are always useful, and not just when something goes wrong.

Repairs and servicing. Repairs can be a major item, even on the most carefully driven car. When you buy, look at the recommended servicing intervals – some models go 3,000 miles in between servicings, others as much as 6,000. Clutches on some cars take two and a half hours to replace, on others up to eleven hours. Now that labour charges have reached over £16.10 an hour on average, the time a job takes can make a considerable difference to your final bill.

Do not run your car without proper servicing. It will only cost you more in the long run. If you wait until something goes wrong, your repair bills will be much higher. Regular servicing should bring to light any problems which might be developing before they become too serious, and replacement parts may not be necessary if a fault is found early on. Try to do some of your servicing yourself. It is not too difficult. Already over four million motorists have taught themselves how to do some, if not all, of the basic work. To help yourself in this, try to buy a car where all the areas that need servicing are easily accessible.

Beware when you buy an imported car – spares may be 20 per cent or more dearer than those for British-made cars, and their servicing garages may be few and far between, with the result that servicing and repair jobs are not only costly but also take longer. You may have your car off the road – costing money – for some time.

Petrol. This is the main cost involved in taking your car out on the road. As a rough guide, the AA says that small cars do 35–40 miles to the gallon, medium cars 30–35 and larger ones 20–30. If you have a GT version of your car, you will find you get five miles less to the gallon. Some very large cars manage only a few miles to the gallon, and if you drive mostly in town you will use up petrol more quickly than outside it. There is no point in choosing, buying, and maintaining your car sensibly and then throwing all these savings away by paying too much for your petrol. Here are some ways of making sure you get value for money at the petrol pump:

- Do not buy high octane fuel if your car does not need it. Over half the cars in Britain do not.
- Get out of your car when you are buying petrol, so that you can keep an eye on where the petrol is going.
- Make sure that the pump reading is at zero before the attendant starts to fill up your tank, or before you do if it is a self-service station.
- Watch carefully to see that your bill matches the amount you receive.
- If the garage is making any kind of special offer, be sure you get it, because you will be paying for it in one way or another in the petrol price.

Other running costs include replacement tyres, oil and batteries. And car parking fees, parking meters and (inadvertent) fines can add more than £100 a year to your motoring bills.

Total running costs for a small petrol-driven car, according to the AA, now add up to almost 10p per mile, which together with the fixed costs means that if you drive 10,000 miles a year it will cost you altogether 22.6p per mile, including depreciation, or £43.50 per week, a formidable sum of money for many average wage earners. A 1,000–1,500cc car costed in the same way works out at 26.4p a mile and the very biggest cars, between 3,000 and 4,000cc, at 63p. Diesel-driven cars up to 2,000cc cost 27p a mile, those over that which cost less than £10,000 new come out at 33p a mile and the more expensive at 45p.

Good driving can cut your costs

If you want to cut your motoring expenses, good driving will help:

To save petrol. Accelerate smoothly and get into top gear as quickly as possible. Brake gently and take the correct line into a bend.

To reduce wear on your tyres. The tread wears almost as rapidly at 70 mph as at 45 mph, especially in hot weather or when driving on curved or rough roads. Avoid striking sharp objects such as kerbs, rocks or holes in the road, and maintain the manufacturer's recommended tyre pressure. Do not do wheel-spinning starts.

To avoid unnecessary repair bills. Do not over-rev your engine or slip your clutch unnecessarily. Above all, keep your car in peak condition by regular maintenance. Choose the service agent with care. Try to get to know the mechanics who do the job.

Motoring for most of us is still worth every penny it costs. But make sure you and your family get maximum pleasure for the minimum amount of money from your car.

16 Insuring your car

The best insurance for you

We generally have an option whether to take out insurance or not. There is one legal exception to this – car insurance. It is against the law in this country – and most others – to drive a car without insurance. However, you can choose what kind of insurance you have.

The minimum insurance required by law must cover your legal

liability should you injure someone else on the road, including your passengers. Very few people have this minimum insurance by choice. If you have a very bad record it may be all you are likely to be offered, but if you are *that* bad you will probably already have been banned from driving.

You must get your car insured before you drive it away from the showroom or dealer. If you have not yet fixed up your permanent insurance, a temporary cover note will do. This can only be for a limited period, and can be issued to you by an insurance broker. The proper insurance certificate can come only from the insurance company with which you are dealing. Remember, if you let the temporary note run out – or, indeed, your proper insurance – you are breaking the law if you drive.

In recent years, the cost of motor insurance has increased very sharply. Even so, as with home contents insurance, most companies show a loss on this business. Recent surveys have shown that today people tend to spend more insuring their cars than their lives – a natural development when there are so many demands on one's total budget.

We know that the price of most things has risen, but motor insurance seems to have outstripped many other items. The temptation, then, is to reduce the amount of cover to keep premiums within reason. Even so, the average driver of a small car spends £240 a year on insurance. There are three main types of car insurance:

1 *Act only (third party)*. This is the kind I have referred to above. It covers only your legal liability for the injury to others, whether you knock them down as you drive, or they are passengers injured in a crash in which you are involved. It applies only to people and does not cover damage to your own car or anyone else's.

   This does not mean you will not have to pay if you damage someone else's car and the accident is entirely your fault. It simply means you will have to find the money out of your own pocket, and this could spell financial ruin if the damage is extensive. Clearly you should if at all possible have more insurance than this.

2 *Third party, fire and theft*. Third party covers any damage to people and their property. Property here usually means someone's car, but it could extend to the windows of a house you have driven into, or a wall you have knocked down. Third party does not cover damage to yourself or your own car.

   If your car either catches fire or gets stolen, it will be a write-off as far as you are concerned, so it is only sensible to be covered for this. Most claims in this area are for theft. You will not get the money immediately, however. The insurance company has to be satisfied that the car has disappeared for good before handing the money over to you.

If you have an old car, which is not worth too much money, third party, fire and theft is generally the best sort of insurance for you.

3 *Comprehensive*. Basically this means you are covered for damage to your own car as well as others, and it is not relevant how this damage is incurred. You, however, get all kinds of extras to your basic comprehensive policy, including:

- Cover for any other person or persons when driving your car with your permission. Driving without your permission can also be covered.
- Cover for third party liability when you yourself are driving someone else's car, again with their permission.
- Extra cover for your heirs should you be killed driving the car. This is unlikely to be allowed at much more than £1,000.

Whatever you do, you will probably not have covered every eventuality. If your car is a write-off, for example, you will not get the price you paid for it, but the depreciated price allowing for the age of the car. Repairs due to ordinary wear and tear are not covered.

It makes sense to have the widest possible cover, if you can afford it. If you cannot, you should ask yourself whether you can actually afford to run a car at all.

Working out the premium

When you have decided which kind of policy you want, that is not the end of the matter. The insurer may want to know the purposes for which you intend to use the car, and he may raise or – more rarely – lower the premium accordingly. On an ordinary car the highest premiums are paid by commercial travellers. If you use your car for business as well as private purposes, you may pay rather more than if you use it simply for private motoring.

The most common type of policy, which carries the standard premium, covers a car for social, domestic and pleasure purposes. It also covers the policy owner and nobody else if it is for business or professional purposes.

There is not, alas, one premium for one type of policy and one kind of car. The insurer will want to know a great deal about you when you apply for insurance, and if you do not tell the truth you will invalidate the policy. You will be asked some, if not all, of the following questions:

1 How old are you, and what is the age of anyone else who will drive the car?
2 What sex are you? And, if you are a woman, will men be driving your car?
3 How long have you been driving and what is your record? Have you had any accidents? Have you ever been disqualified?

4 What is your profession? Is it likely to put your car at more than normal risk?

5 What make of car is it, and what model? Is it a sports car?

6 How much is the car worth?

7 Where is it when you are not driving – in a garage, or out in the open air?

8 Where do you live?

9 If you were not born and brought up in Britain, where do you come from?

Those questions all mean something to the insurer, and on the basis of past experience, called 'actuarial experience', he will assess your desirability as a policyholder. From the above questions you may have guessed that it is better not to be too young or too old; to be British; to have a clean record, a steady job and a not too speedy car.

The *worst risk* is a young man, under twenty-five, living in central London, with only a couple of years' driving experience, who has had a few major or minor accidents already. He will have been born in Latin America, and drives a sports car worth many thousands of pounds which he lets all his friends drive. He will be charged a very high premium, or the ordinary insurance company may refuse to insure him at all. He may have to go to the Lloyd's underwriters for a special policy. His premium will run into hundreds of pounds.

In contrast, actuarial experience shows that the *best risk* is the teetotal housewife in her thirties, who drives a solid family car, which she uses infrequently, perhaps to drive children to and from school and her husband to the station. She lives in the country, having been brought up there, and is the only driver of her car. Women, despite views to the contrary, have a better driving record than men. Her premium for exactly the same cover will be far less than the young man's. Some insurance companies are offering discounts to women drivers who are prepared to guarantee that men will not drive their cars. The discount can be as high as 15 per cent.

Age is an important factor. If you continue to drive blamelessly for fifty years, it is unlikely that your insurance company will put up the premium just because you have reached seventy. But should you try to change to a new insurer, you would probably find that the premium immediately shot up.

Apart from your own personal circumstances, two other considerations are all-important: where you normally garage the car, and what model it is.

Where you live. Insurers divide the country into various sections. Generally, if you live in town you will pay higher premiums. Greater London is the most expensive, then the other major conurbations. The countryside is cheaper, and Devon and Cornwall cheapest of all.

Sometimes the premiums in the lower-rated areas may be only half as much as those in the towns, but rates vary greatly from company to company. Some companies, for instance, charge almost as little for cities as other companies do for Devon or Cornwall. You may get the worst of all worlds if you live in the suburbs: premiums may be as high as in towns, even though you never actually drive to town.

What model car you have. The various makes of car (with the exception of some of the real sports cars, which are rated individually) are also divided into different categories. There will be many makes of car in a particular range in one category, so you can at least get a rough idea of the premiums before your own circumstances are taken into account.

Very few motorists pay the full premium, or a loaded one. That only happens when you first take out insurance cover for a car you have bought or where your circumstances are adverse from the insurer's point of view.

As a rule, the more powerful the engine of the car, the more you will pay for insurance. Companies divide cars into nine groups, with the models most of us drive coming into the first six. Sports cars, or the very expensive cars, are in the last three categories and foreign-made cars are often in a higher group than their power would suggest. Other factors, apart from engine size, determine the category into which a car is placed – the sort of driver to whom the car usually appeals, and previous claims experience overall for that particular make.

If you are young, you may find yourself paying a higher premium, and if you have a poor record and have not earned any no-claims bonus, you will be similarly penalized. It may happen that you will not be penalized in your premium for being young. Instead, the insurer might insist that you pay the first £50, or sometimes even £500, of any bill for damage.

How to earn a no-claims discount

Obviously we should all aim at getting a no-claims discount. If you can build this up over a number of years, you can reduce the cost of your car insurance considerably.

To begin with, you must have been driving your own car for some time. You do not normally get a no-claims bonus when you first take out insurance for your own car, even if you have had years of trouble-free driving, using other people's cars or hiring cars.

Some insurers may allow you a discount of about 20 per cent if you come into this category, but not all. Otherwise, the first cut in your premium comes after the first year of claim-free driving. The discount builds up over the years to a maximum of 60 or 65 per cent after about four or five years. You may not always lose your entire bonus if you have made only one claim during the year, but you will slip back a bit in the discount scale.

If you have a minor mishap, especially if you are near the maximum no-claims discount, it is often worth paying for the damage yourself rather than risking your bonus.

Insurers are now beginning to bring out policies which do not offer a no-claim bonus. The normal premium is, however, rather lower than the initial premium in a normal policy. Some people may find this attractive.

Other discounts
In addition to the no-claims bonus and the discount to women, other discounts are available which can bring down the cost of car insurance. One driver (plus spouse) costs less than a car which is insured for any driver. The discount may be as high as 10 per cent. Then, if you are prepared to pay the first part of any bills yourself, further discounts may be available. Paying the first £25 will get you a cut of 7½ per cent on your bill and the first £100 a 17½ per cent cut.

Discounts vary from company to company, so shop around, because careful selection can reduce your bill for car insurance substantially. Take the basic comprehensive premium quoted for a 1600cc car; a woman-only driver in her 30s or 40s with a full no-claim bonus, paying the first part of the bill herself, would be paying a mere 20 per cent of that.

If you have an accident

Knock-for-knock agreements
When you and another car bump into one another, both cars and persons may sustain damage. To deal with this, most insurers operate what they call knock-for-knock agreements, whereby each pays the damage to the car which it has insured. No regard is paid to which driver is responsible for the damage. A condition of knock-for-knock agreements is that the policy on the car must cover the damage risk in full.

This is all very well for the insurer, who is able to pay out any claim more quickly, thus saving on the administrative costs of dealing with another insurer and also avoiding litigation.

These agreements are not so good for the driver, however. He may find that he will not be paid for the amount of any excess damage under his policy, and he may lose his no-claims bonus when coming to renew his policy. It is up to the motorist himself to put a claim in for the excess, if he regards himself as in no way to blame for the accident. This can lead to litigation, though usually it does not. If the driver succeeds in his claim, it is evidence for his own insurers that he was not responsible for the accident and the no-claims bonus should remain intact. If you were sure that you were not responsible for an accident, persist in your claim – otherwise you will lose your bonus.

How to make a claim

Rule number one is to tell your insurance company as soon as possible. Delay on your part could result in some loss to you. Your insurers will then send you a claim form, which you should try to fill in and send back by return of post.

If your car is a write-off, either through fire or a crash, the insurance 'assessors' (the company's experts who specialize in working out the value) will decide the market value of your car immediately before the damage was done. Try to get an 'agreed' value at the beginning of each year of insurance. That way, you will have no problems if the car is a write-off. The same applies if your car is stolen, except that you will probably have to wait at least six weeks before the claim is settled.

You will be lucky to get the whole value of any necessary repairs paid out to you. Your policy may well limit this, but in any case the insurance company may argue that the car is in a better state than it was before the repair and that the motorist must pay for part of this 'betterment'.

Even if you do not make a claim, however, your insurers have a right to know every time your car is damaged. They should be informed in writing, and are on record as saying that this information will not affect your no-claims bonus.

If you read the small print in your policy, you will see that under its terms you are required to do this. This rule is really to safeguard the motorist. You can never know when claims may come from the driver of another car. If you have not told your insurance company, it will have some awkward questions for you.

If your insurance is not valid

If you are responsible for an accident, someone may claim against you. There should be no problems here, apart from the loss of your bonus, unless for some reason your policy is invalidated. This could happen if you had been driving your car in a totally unroadworthy condition – perhaps with faulty brakes – or if the person driving the car was under the permissible driving age of seventeen years (eighteen if they were driving abroad).

If this happens, you could find yourself saddled with a very large bill, particularly if in the most unfortunate chance someone is killed as a result of the accident. What happens then is that the injured party's damages are paid by his insurance company, or the Motor Insurers' Bureau. Then, however, either the insurers or the MIB can take steps to recover the money from you. As your own insurance was invalid at the time of the accident, you will find no one to help you.

When your insurance runs out

As the car owner, you are responsible for keeping your insurance up to date. As a general rule, your insurance company will warn you that it is running out and send you a temporary certificate with a reminder. But they are under no legal obligation to do so.

If you have genuinely forgotten to pay, and can prove it to your insurers, they will generally accept the premium as soon as you send it, dating the new policy from the date the old one expired.

In some cases, they may even be willing to handle a claim for you during a time when you have been legally uninsured. If you suddenly remember that you have not renewed your policy, get on to your insurers immediately by telephone. *Never forget that a delayed renewal payment can leave you in serious trouble*.

The renewal notice will give you fifteen days' extra cover from the date your policy expires. Do not be under any illusion that you are getting fifteen days free – the new policy will date from the expiry of the old one. The fifteen days' grace only gives you the minimum cover required by law, and it only applies, anyway, if you are intending to renew with the same insurers.

Some motorists run into trouble because when they see the renewal premium they decide to look for something cheaper and to take advantage of the fifteen-day temporary cover while they look. This can be a serious mistake. If he has an accident after he has sent a proposal form and cheque to another insurer but before it has been accepted, the driver will find that he is covered by no one. By sending off another proposal form and cheque, the motorist is clearly indicating that he has no intention of renewing his old policy, and any claim under that policy will be rejected if the accident occurs after the original expiry date.

Filling in the proposal form

Similar problems can also arise if you do not complete the proposal form properly. This may mean that you cannot claim, even if your insurance has not run out. It is dangerous simply to sign the form and then leave the rest to the salesman.

Supposing a proposal form did not indicate previous convictions for dangerous driving; the car owner might not have mentioned them to the salesman simply because he hadn't been asked. Should the car be a write-off later, the owner would have to reveal these convictions on his claim form. The chances of the claim being rejected out of hand are very high.

Where to go for your policy

There are many insurance companies which do motor insurance, and you will have seen a lot of them advertising in the national and local press. You can also go to the underwriters at Lloyd's. A few insurance companies do not handle motor insurance. There is nothing to stop you from walking into a local branch of an insurance company and doing your business directly with them, or you can fill up a form and do your deal by post. Otherwise you can use:

1 *An insurance broker*. He may filter through the various companies to find the one which suits you best, and therefore can save you time. If you want to deal with Lloyd's anyway, you cannot go there directly and you must use a broker. He will normally not make any charge to you for this service: the money he makes will come from the insurer.

It is worth finding out if the company you work for has a particular insurance broker through which it does its business. If this is the case, the broker will often make a special effort on behalf of employees, though the particular policy may not amount to much in terms of total business from the firm.

2 *An insurance agent*. Many of the larger insurance companies have full-time or, more often, part-time agents. They may use a firm of solicitors, for example, or a large garage or car dealer.

3 *The motoring organizations*. The Automobile Association or the Royal Automobile Club may make the arrangements for you.

4 *A bank*. Banks sometimes offer motor insurance, though it is not their usual work.

Give your instructions clearly and precisely to whoever you ask to act for you, or to the company, if you are dealing directly with it yourself.

Whoever is acting for you may come up with a number of quotations. and you should always insist on seeing at least two and preferably three. *Do not leap automatically for the lowest one you are offered. Make some enquiries first.* You will want to know the attitude of the insurer to claims, for the chances are that some time in your driving life you will make at least one claim. When you do you will want it settled quickly, without fuss, and in full. So choose the quote which best balances price and service.

If you have any problems later on, you are entitled to the benefits of the Policy Holders Protection Act. Details of what can be done to help are available from the Policy Holders Protection Board, Aldermary House, Queen Street, London EC4.

Extra insurances

Motor insurance need not necessarily end with a fully comprehensive policy. You can take out a variety of other insurances to give yourself even more protection:

1 If you travel a lot and leave your car out in the street for some considerable time, you might choose to take out an additional policy to

cover any personal belongings that you might leave in it. Approach your own insurance company for this. Your claims under such a policy should not affect the no-claims bonus on the motoring policy, and you can insure quite cheaply for losses of high value.

2 If you can never manage without a car, it is worth taking out extra insurance to cover the cost of hiring a car any time when you do not have access to your own, either because it is being repaired after an accident or because it has been stolen.

You can insure yourself against the cost of hiring even if an accident happens through your own fault, but if the accident is someone else's you may be able to claim from them in any case.

Occasionally this type of insurance may be included in your overall policy, but check to be sure.

3 You can take out extra insurance against your car being written off or stolen. This will mean that you will get a guaranteed sum of money and will not have to face the almost inevitable arguments under your basic policy about how much you are entitled to.

4 You can insure yourself against being disqualified from driving. This insurance allows you to hire a driver for up to a year, if you are disqualified under the drink and driving laws, or if you have three speeding offences.

It is not cheap, so do not take it out unnecessarily; it will cost between £30 and £175 a year. Far better to use one of your family to drive you about if the worst happens. You can get up-to-date details of these policies from St Christopher Motorists' Security Association, Cheltenham (telephone 0242 20471).

5 There are various policies to cover you if your vehicle breaks down and needs to be towed a long distance – the motoring organizations also provide a service for their members. Details from National Breakdown Recovery Club, 21a Claremont, Bradford, Yorkshire BD1 BB.

6 If you do not think that the warranty on your car is good enough, write to Autoplan (Insurance Services) Ltd, Mont Cantel House, 146 Wellington Road, Bilston, West Midlands WV14 6AZ.

7 If you are towing a caravan or a boat, you may need extra insurance. It is unlikely that your car policy will need to be amended, but check to be on the safe side. Then ask your insurers to give you extra cover for the caravan, if it is your own. For details of caravan rental and its implications, move on to chapter 18 of this section on holidays. You will also find information there about taking your car abroad.

17 Cutting the cost of your travel

Travelling within the UK

We have already looked at travel by car and seen that it is likely to cost you 22p a mile, just for petrol and servicing. It has always been more expensive than public transport and will remain so, even though increases in public transport fares sometimes narrow the gap for a time.

So far as public transport is concerned, buses are always the cheapest method of travelling – though not of course as cheap as actually walking, or, as is becoming increasingly popular again, cycling. Trains are dearer, but if you have to commute to work they are the only practical means of travelling in the time available.

1 *Walking.* If you do not have far to go, this is certainly the cheapest way to travel. Only your shoe leather gets worn and the exercise is good for you.
2 *Cycling.* A new bicycle today can easily cost you £150–£200, though you can still get second-hand ones cheaply. The new small-wheeled bikes are good for towns, but unsuitable if you are a serious cyclist and want to cover a fair distance.
3 *By bus.* Buses are useful for short journeys in towns and for longer ones outside. Prices vary enormously, depending where in the country you live.

   If you are a regular bus user, get a season ticket, if they are available in your area. Not only do they save money, but they save fiddling about for change every time you use a bus. If you are retired, see if you are entitled to concessionary fares. Your local authority may allow you to travel free all the time, or at least outside the rush hour. Or there may be a reduced fare for pensioners. Children are also entitled to reduced fares. Those under five years old travel free. Half-fares are available up to fourteen or sixteen, depending on where you live.
4 *By train.* Commuter trains are relatively expensive per mile and they certainly cost far more than buses, but they save time – and time means money to many people, particularly those going out to work. Cost per mile varies, depending on where you live. It is much more expensive, for example, to travel in Greater London than it is in Scotland. British Rail say that the average cost per passenger mile at the end of 1981 was 4.8p.

   In recent years British Rail has introduced a variety of cards which cut the cost of rail travel to selected groups of people. These are (late 1984):

- *The student railcard*, which has now been extended to all people under 24. It costs £12 a year and the holder can travel for half fare.
- *The senior citizen's railcard*. This comes in two varieties, the £12 one which offers half-price train travel at any time, and the £7 one, which is only for Awayday tickets.
- *The disabled person's railcard*. Again these offer half-price tickets for a £10 annual payment. This is available to registered blind or partially sighted people, and those who get mobility or attendance allowances, industrial disablements benefit, a war or service disablement pension, or a DHSS car or private car allowance.

On these three cards, the half-price concession applies to both first- and second-class tickets. There are some restrictions on the British Rail services which can be used, particularly on Sealink and Seaspeed and boat trains. There are minimum fare conditions for students on weekdays and some Friday restrictions for them.
British Rail's most recent card is:

- *The family railcard*. This also costs £10 and enables up to four adults to travel together for half price each and up to four children for just £1. There must always be one adult and one child in the family party and the group must stay together for the whole journey. The group does not, however, have to be related, so two women friends, say, with a child each could travel on one family ticket. The added restriction here, in addition to those on other railcards, is that it can only be used for second-class travel.

Remember: you must always have your railcard with you to take advantage of the concessions. British Rail also ask that anyone severely disabled lets them know in advance, so that they can make special arrangements to ensure that the journey is as comfortable as possible.
Wherever you live, *get a season ticket if you use the train regularly during the week*. It will almost always save you money, unless you are in a job which enables you to travel off-peak all the time. Let's take someone living in Brighton who travels to London and back every weekday, a total of 100 miles a day. There was a choice of a variety of fares at the beginning of 1985, as follows:

1st class ordinary return	£17.40	2nd class ordinary return	£11.60
1st class cheap day return	—	2nd class cheap day return	£6.50
1st class season ticket:		2nd class season ticket:	
weekly	£43.00	weekly	£28.70
monthly	£165.00	monthly	£110.00
quarterly	£474.00	quarterly	£324.00
annual	£1,707.00	annual	£1,147.00

Rail savings become available immediately if you are able to travel after the cheap-day concession comes in at 9.30 a.m. or if you buy a season ticket. For instance, five first-class returns would cost you £121.80 a week, whereas a seven-day costs only £43. The saving becomes greater the longer you buy the season for. An annual first-class season costs £1,707, as against £4,524 for separate first-class returns for 260 working days in a year.

Most people travel second-class, however, and the savings there are just as good. Your second-class ordinary return costs you £11.60 a day, or £67.28 a five-day week, and a weekly season £28.70. By the time you reach an annual ticket (and remember there may well be a fare increase meanwhile which you won't have to pay), the figure comes out at £3,016 for separate daily tickets and only £1,147 for an annual season. In fact, if you can pay a year at a time, you can travel first-class for more or less the same price as 260 daily second-class off-peak return fares.

Even if you allow for a month's holiday each year, there is still a vast gap between the two costs. Buying a season can make all the difference between being able to live out of town if you wish and being forced to move closer to your work.

All very well, you may say, but I cannot pay out £1,147 in one go, let alone £1,707. This is where your bank comes in. For this reason, if no other, it is worth considering opening a budget account (see chapter 6 in this section). If you do, you will be able to pay out these sort of sums before you actually put the money into your account each month. Ask your bank. Some companies, too, will advcance interest-free loans to employees, so that they can buy season tickets. Wherever you live, a season ticket will save money. Ask at your local railway station for details.

If you travel irregularly you should try to travel in the off-peak period; second-class cheap day returns can save you up to 40p in the pound. Ask at your railway station about any discount fares for two people travelling together, and any special excursions. British Rail also offer weekend returns for journeys over seventy miles one way. These run from Friday to Monday. There are also a variety of longer period mid-week returns worth considering.

5 *By car.* The Brighton–London–Brighton drive would cost you a minimum of £113 a week in the smallest car, allowing for running costs, fixed charges and depreciation, nearly twice as much as you would pay for a second-class weekly return on the train.

The petrol, of course, would be only a small part of this cost, so you might not be aware of the full cost as you drive. It would also take you longer than the train, be more tiring and is really not worth doing unless you have four people in your car who can contribute. Even then you should have special insurance cover, and your passengers are likely to want to contribute only towards the petrol used and not towards the other costs, which mean nothing to them.

It makes sense, as a rule, to leave your car at home.

6 *By air*. If you are travelling a fair distance between towns which are both served by airports, you can fly. The flight generally take a much shorter time than the train ride, but you must add on the drive to and from the airports, and the waiting time at each end. You can then find that from city centre to city centre there is not much to choose between train and plane as far as time goes. The plane costs more than the train and the train costs more than a coach. Let's look at the London–Manchester run (one way) at the end of 1984. You can go three ways:

air   £37–£46*
train: first class   £31.60, second class, £21.50
coach   ordinary, £10, express, £13.50

* Depending on type of fare.

The plane takes about 40 minutes, but you have to travel to and from the airports as well. The train takes between 2½ and three hours, the slower coach 4 hours 15 minutes and the express coach 3 hours 45 minutes. Clearly, if you have time to spare there is a lot to be said for the coach, particularly as return fares are very cheap indeed at £11.50 ordinary return and £15.50 express. Even the cheapest excursion return on the train was £17 at the end of 1984 and that was hedged around with restrictions.

Air travel outside the UK

The further you go, of course, the greater the advantage of air travel in terms of both cost and time. If you fly outside the UK, there are many ways of cutting the cost, not only because there are a variety of fares on any one route, but also because on some routes advance booking charters bring down the cost substantially.

Take the London to Paris return (end-1984):

type	return fare	conditions
Excursion	£64	Outbound and inbound must be booked at same time. Cancellation charge. Must stay one Saturday night. Restricted departures.
APEX	from £71	Must include a Saturday night.
Economy	£136	
Club	£168	
First	£256	

You can see that, by timing your journey properly, you can save a considerable amount of money, whatever the current level of air fares. Insist that the airline gives you details of all possible fares. And there is no point in flying first-class to Paris, except for the snob appeal. The flight only lasts forty minutes, hardly time to need the extra space for stretching out or the free champagne, which are what first-class air travel gives you.

But Paris is not too far away. You can get there in just over eight hours, even by coach. This is about the cheapest way to go. There are, however, various combinations of different modes of travel at varying prices which you might consider. Consult a travel agent, who will know about them all.

Now, what about longer distances? London New York–London is a good example, but beware, prices change all the time and do not necessarily go up.

London–New York return fares – late 1984	
Concorde	£2,516
First class	£2,095
Club	£1,248
Economy	£622
APEX	from £329

There is a discount of about 10 per cent for children between two and twelve. Infant fares are about 10 per cent of the full fare, though this is not always exact. Although these are the official published fares, you can pay less even for first-class travel, if you accept certain conditions and restrictions attached to your travel.

In addition, there are charter flights and other cut-price fares which can bring the cost of a return flight from London to New York down below £300. These may have restrictions and require that you book and pay in advance – though not always. You may find if you do not actually travel that you do not get your money back. As with most things, you can insure yourself against this eventuality. The cost will depend on the price of the ticket. But you must do this when you book, otherwise you will be refused cover.

British Airways and other carriers have now introduced APEX bookings to most parts of the world. This has had the effect of cutting economy return fares by almost half, and bringing foreign holidays that much more within the scope of the ordinary family holiday. You must book and pay in advance.

You can also book on other kinds of charters. They may be very cheap indeed, but not always reliable. Some travel agents sell flights on scheduled airlines at rock-bottom prices, but there are risks and if you lose your money you have no one to blame but yourself. If you think it is worth the chance, the fares are less than one half of the ordinary economy return.

One comfort: air fares are likely to come down in price in real terms over the years, one of the few things which will in this period of inflation. The ordinary first-class and economy fares will probably continue to rise for those who have no option but to book at the last minute where there are no stand-by tickets, but more and more 'deals' can be expected for those who have time to plan.

When you are travelling, try to make a total flight plan. If, for example, you are going to America, make all your reservations at one time, as this may save you money. There are all kinds of discounts – fares are anyway much cheaper in America than in Euorpe – covering wives and families.

Some European airlines offer these sorts of discounts too. Where this is the case, fly with that airline rather than any other. Planning takes time, but it can cut the cost of your travel by up to 50 per cent, or more if you are travelling in a group.

18 Getting the most out of your holiday

Just over half the population of Britain take a holiday each year away from their homes. As a general rule, this annual break is taken during the summer, and most people stay in another part of the UK, though a growing proportion go abroad each year. There are hiccups from time to time in the increase in foreign travel, but they are minor and the clear trend is upwards. Few people take a winter holiday as their main break, and those who do mainly go skiing. The travel business has developed enormously over the past twenty years, and a trend towards two holidays – a main one in the summer and another shorter break during the winter months – is beginning.

Holidays may be one of the first things to be abandoned when the family budget becomes too tight. Yet the travel industry has suffered very little from our economic crises, which shows how it has kept its prices within the pocket of the ordinary family. There are again signs, however, that many of the smaller travel companies are finding trading extremely difficult and the number of bankruptcies is increasing. Where such companies are members of the Association of British Travel Agents (ABTA), holidaymakers are protected by an insurance bond and get their money back if their holiday is cancelled. Choose an ABTA member, if possible.

In many cases, travel today is much cheaper than it has ever been. The development of the commercial airlines has brought foreign travel to many who previously could never have afforded it. Tour operators have been able to get extremely cheap flights because they have been able to guarantee a certain number of seats to the airlines. As a result, they have been able to offer all-in 'packages' of flights and accommodation at prices which are often only marginally higher than the price of buying the airline ticket on its own.

Just as important as the growth in air travel has been the increase in car ownership. This has enabled families to travel together in a reasonably economical way.

Depending on the amount of money you have available, there are enormous holiday opportunities to suit every pocket, from camping and caravanning to staying at boarding houses, private hotels or the large licensed hotels.

Let's see first how the travel market breaks down. As I said, most people still take their holidays in the UK, but in recent years an increasing number have gone abroad. If present trends continue, it will not be long before foreign holidays are more popular than those at home. In 1980, 48,500,000 holidays of more than four nights were taken by the British in the UK. This was a fall on the previous year, whereas foreign holidays taken rose to 36,500,000.

This table shows where people stay both in Britain and abroad:

	Britain %	abroad %
licensed hotel	15	60
unlicensed hotel or guest house	8	6
holiday camp	3	1
camping	5	5
towed caravan	5	1
fixed caravan	8	2
rented flat	2	4
other rented	3	4
paying guest in private house	3	2
with friend or relative	50	19
second home	1	1
others, or in transit	3	11

Note. These columns need not necessarily add up to 100 per cent, because many people use several kinds of accommodation in one trip. Figures are from the British Travel Authority.

One-week holidays taken in Britain cost on average around £67 a head for accommodation. This figure allows for people taking holidays with friends or relatives. Taking a holiday in a hotel, holiday camp or boarding house would cost much more.

If you go abroad, the average cost immediately rises to £287 per head. Many package holidays come within this price range, and, of course, include flights or other transport and sometimes full board.

It would seem from these figures that most of us could afford at least one short break a year, even if there is no convenient friend or relative to stay with.

Of course, accommodation is not all. You will certainly spend more on food, unless you are staying with friends, camping or caravanning, or staying in rented accommodation which enables you to do your own catering. You will probably drink more and spend more on general entertainment than you do in an average week at home. And you will almost certainly have invested in special holiday clothes (if you are sensible you will have bought these at sales).

All in all, a holiday may become a very substantial item in an overall budget. Plan your holiday spending just as carefully as any other spending.

Where to spend your holiday

There are two main factors you must consider:

- The money you can spend.
- Your interests.

Money is, of course, all important, but it would be foolish to have a very cheap holiday skiing if you hate skiing, or a week lying in the sun doing nothing when what you like is plenty of activity. To make sure you have enough money to do what you want, try to make holiday saving a normal part of your monthly budget.

When you have got your money together you must then decide whether you will take your holiday at home, elsewhere in the UK, or abroad.

At home, or elsewhere in the UK?
The only thing to be said for staying at home is that it's cheap. The chances are that you will not have a holiday at all, but will simply be at home instead of at work. If you really do not mind this, fine. But if you really want to benefit from your holiday, you need a change of scene.

Do not assume that by staying in the UK you will necessarily spend less than going abroad. The only advantage may be that you can actually work out your costs fairly accurately before you go away.

Abroad

When you go abroad there may be all sorts of expenses you have not thought about. You should never assume that prices abroad are the same as, or lower than, in Britain. Before you go, try to find out the general level of prices from your travel agent. If he is a good agent, he should know this sort of thing.

You can take it now, for example, that London is one of the dearer capital cities in the world. Almost everywhere in Western Europe and North America is now expensive. The low level of the pound sterling when related to many other currencies in recent years, has meant that places like, say, New York have become comparatively even more expensive for the British. By the end of 1984, the pound was worth little more than half in dollar terms what it was two years before. What goes for capital cities tends to go for the rest of the country. Do not think either that journeying to some little, rather undeveloped spot will automatically be cheaper. The amenities which are available may be costly.

Read as much as you can about the place you choose, and write for any information you need to the travel office of the country concerned. These offices exist to help you; you are going to spend money in their countries, and in return they should provide all the relevant information you need.

Here are just a few of the things you need to know:

1 The price of food or restaurant meals compared with Britain.
2 The price of drinks.
3 Any extras, like transport to beaches, towns, etc.; any special taxes.
4 Whether you are covered by reciprocal health arrangements.
5 The kind of clothes you will need.
6 What facilities are available for children.

You will have your own individual preferences, so ask if what you want is available. For example, it is no use going to a 'dry' country if you like drinking.

Most people want value for money when they go abroad. This used to be quite possible. The pound was worth great deal in many foreign countries, so prices were at bargain levels. Sadly, this is no longer true: the value of the pound has slumped, and today you will find most places relatively expensive compared with Britain.

The cheapest place to go is probably Gibraltar, which has the added advantage of using sterling, so there is no currency problem. The next cheapest holiday places are Spain, Italy, Turkey, Greece and Yugoslavia, and these are countries in which the value of the pound in relation to the local currency has not declined and may even have risen.

Just because the cost of living may be higher in a country, say West Germany, this does not mean that holidays there will automatically be dearer. The travel industry cuts its costs to the bone, particularly for package tours, and you may be able to find real bargains. Naturally, the further afield you go, the more you will have to pay. Even allowing for the cheap fares made available to package travellers, the fares to places like Australia, New Zealand and the Far East still run into hundreds of pounds. Spain is by far the most popular choice for the British, followed by France, then Italy and Greece. The Greek island of Corfu is actually the single most popular foreign resort for British visitors.

You may be tempted by the newer holidays offered by tour operators in faraway places. The basic packages are relatively cheap, but when you get there you will find that anything you have to buy is extremely expensive. Even in countries where living costs are relatively low, prices to tourists for drinks, food and souvenirs may be very high indeed. If you are going to the Caribbean, for instance, you should allow a minimum of £2.50 for every drink, soft or alcoholic (1984).

Making sure that you are acquainted with the level of prices in the area you are going to can do much to make your holiday budgeting satisfactory and therefore your holiday more enjoyable.

Where to stay

It is likely that the cheapest holiday you can take at home or abroad will be with a friend or relative. Here, in ascending order of expensiveness, are the other sorts of holiday you could consider:

1 *Camping.* This is cheap, but is really only suitable for families with children, or the unusually active.

   If you take your own equipment – which can cost as much or as little as you please – you can either use the general facilities of a camping ground, which will cost only a few pounds a week, or you can camp for nothing, if you can find a convenient field.

   There are also camping sites with fixed tents, where everything is provided. These are dearer, but still not expensive. Site prices vary between £1.50 and £4 a night, depending on facilities. The actual cost depends on the facilities available. Some camps are quite luxurious (especially in France), particularly as you get nearer to the Mediterranean. Take great care that you know where you are going and exactly what facilities are available before you set out.

2 *Caravanning.* Basically the choice is the same as in camping. Later in this chapter I will go into the costs and insurance aspects of towing a caravan.

3 *Staying in a holiday camp.* These are particularly popular in Britain, though there are some (including a few British-owned ones) abroad.

   They provide a means for a family to go away together, but then to get away from one another once they have arrived. They probably provide the easiest and cheapest babysitting facilities for those with small children, for instance.

4   *Staying in a hotel*. This ranges from bed and breakfast in a private house
to full board in a de luxe hotel. You must decide what you can afford. This
of course also applies to renting a house or flat. And, having made a price,
stick to it. If you allow yourself to go over your budget early in your
holiday, you can end up ruining the rest of it.

Once you have booked into a hotel you have entered into a contract with
the proprietor. This has certain implications.

If you do not turn up, you will be liable to pay for the room, less a
suitable amounty for electricity, laundry, cleaning and food. All a hotel has
to do to claim money from you is to show that it has done all it could to let
the room. If you do have to cancel a booking, give the hotel as much notice
as you possibly can. However, if the hotel has a lot of rooms empty you
may still have to pay, regardless of how long before you cancelled your
booking.

On the other hand, if the room is not ready when you arrive, or the hotel
fails to provide you with it, you can claim damages for general
inconvenience. This would include any amount it costs you to find and go
to another hotel, and the difference between the prices of the two rooms, if
the substitute hotel is more expensive.

The hotel can keep your luggage (though not your car), if you cannot
pay the bill. But the proprietor or manager cannot hold you in the hotel,
unless he has reason to believe that you are guilty of fraud and calls the
police. After six weeks, if the bill has still not been paid, he can auction
your luggage to offset the cost.

In law, hotels are bound to provide travellers with food and drinks at any
time of the night, but you may find that you have to be satisfied with a few
sandwiches. If you think a hotel has been unreasonable in refusing to
provide you with food, you can take action and they may be liable for a
fine.

Nor can a hotel refuse to give you a room, if it has any vacant, unless you
are clearly undesirable. Court cases are rare, but it might be worth
insisting on your legal rights in an emergency. This ruling does not apply
to boarding houses or pubs.

What you get for your money in 1985

Seven nights' holiday for two adults and two children

Under £100	Camping in the United Kingdom
	Caravans in the UK
	Some self-catering in UK holiday camps
	Some simple camping and caravan sites, Europe
	Cottages, bungalows, self-catering, UK
Under £150	Cottages, self catering, Europe, excluding fares
	Coaching/camping holidays, Europe
	Caravans, Europe
	Camping/drive, Europe

Under £250	Holland, self-catering in holiday homes
	Boating, UK
	Minorca bungalows, self-catering, flight included
	Camping, Israel
	Austria, ½ board, transport included
	France, apartments, self-catering, flight included
Under £450	Tunisia, full board, flight included
	Greece, self-catering, flight included
	Teneriffe, ½ board, flight included
	Sweden, car for camping and camping sites
	Majorca, half-board, flight included
	Costa Brava, full board, flight included
Under £500	Rimini, Italy, full board, flight included
	Valencia, full board, flight included
Under £600	Portugal, B&B hotel, flight included
	Ibiza, full board, flight included
	Yugoslavia, half-board, flight included
	Bulgaria, full board, flight included
	Spain, full board, flight included
	Britanny, self-catering, transport included
Under £1,000	Madeira, half-board, flight included
	Mainland Greece, half-board, flight included
	French Riviera, bed and breakfast, flight included
	Sardinia, half-board, flight included
	Malta, half-board, flight included
Over £1,000	Almost anywhere, but certainly all holidays in America, Africa and Asia. It now costs over £1,600 a head for a two-week trip to China, not allowing for spending, for example.

If you travel in a 'package', however, you are likely to get better accommodation cheaper than if you travel independently. The table above shows how costs can vary, depending on location and what is provided. It shows a selection from 1985 brochures. Prices have risen rather sharply in recent years.

Package holidays

When you book a package holiday, look carefully at the small print, because if you are forced to cancel it for any reason you may find that it costs you almost as much as going. The simplest way to safeguard yourself against this is to insure yourself in the event of cancellation. Normally, however, you will not have to pay the full cost; most booking forms lay down a sliding scale of charges which must be paid on cancellation. The nearer you are to the departure date, the more you will have to pay. If you find you do have to cancel, do so without delay. The more reliable firm you choose, the more likely they are to refund your money.

In 1974, several package tour companies went bust and many holidaymakers found that through no fault of their own they had lost not only their holiday but also their money. Following these failures, steps were taken to see that this situation did not recur; now, if a firm which belongs to the Association of British Travel Agents fails, those who have booked with it get their money back. As a safeguard for travellers, ABTA makes a tour operator lodge up to 10 per cent of the value of its total bookings with ABTA.

This protects the holidaymaker. To protect the tour operator, ABTA have also tightened up the final dates by which the full money for a tour must be paid. You will now be expected to pay up at least six weeks before departure and cancel after that for only the most extreme reasons – say, that war breaks out. If you book less than six weeks before you are due to go, you will have to pay in full immediately.

Remember that packages can be taken anywhere. They are available in Britain as well as abroad. Remember, too, that not all packages mean that you travel in an enormous group. Package tours can be quite individual, and you may well not be aware that you are on one. Admittedly this applies mostly to the dearer packages, but not always. No matter how well off you are, it is worth considering a package; you will certainly be travelling at a very heavy discount compared with the independent traveller.

Some rules for package holidays

1 Shop around. Otherwise you may spend more than you need. Tour operators, using exactly the same flights and the same hotels, rarely charge exactly the same price.

Each operator will have done its own special deal with the hotel and, depending on the numbers he can guarantee, the operator will be set an individual price for each room used. Some tour operators have 'loss leaders', and for a period will offer very favourable terms in an area they are trying to build up.

2 When you have chosen, check that the package is exactly what it says it is. If it claims the hotel is near the sea, make sure it is. A sea view should be a real view, not a distant glimpse. Go over the package detail again and again before paying your deposit.

3 Check what you will get in the basic price. Is it bed and breakfast, breakfast and one meal (half-pension) or full board? This can make a lot of difference to the final overall cost of your holiday. Does the basic price include excursions?

4 Does the package give a guarantee that the price you pay will not change, no matter what happens to the value of the pound? More and more tour operators now guarantee that there will be no surcharges to pay, whatever happens to sterling. You will be wise to stick to one that does.

5 Make sure that the insurance cover that the package offers you is enough. If not, get the travel agent to top up the insurance for you, or make your own arrangements. It is also a good idea to insure yourself against the possibility that you are unable to go on holiday, so that you are covered for the cost. You will have to do this as you make the booking. If you try to do it later on, the insurance company is likely to refuse to cover you – they will think that you have already decided not to go.

Getting your money back

If something goes wrong on your holiday and you are dissastisfied, you may be entitled to your money back. Remember, though, that if your package deal turns out to be disappointing, it may be simply because you did not read the brochure properly and expected something that you were not in fact offered.

The contract you sign sets out the conditions under which you travel. Tour operators may say that they do not accept that the holidaymaker has any right to compensation if anything goes wrong, but in law it is not possible for an operator to protect himself against any misleading statements in the event the holiday turns out not to be what is set out in the brochure.

If you feel you have a case, you can take it to the county court under the Misrepresentation Act 1967, or complain to the trading standards officer under the Trade Descriptions Act 1968 (see Section six, chapter 2). If you win your case, the court can order the operator to pay you compensation.

It is better, however, to see if you can get your money back without resorting to legal action. You should write, setting out your complaints, and make a request for compensation. Give the firm time to reply. If the company is at all reliable, they will investigate your complaint and write back to you. If you have heard nothing after ten days, write again, saying you intend to take action, preferably under the Trade Descriptions Act. Once the trading standards officer is informed, he will investigate your complaint.

You may also get help from the Citizens Advice Bureau and, if the operator is a member of ABTA, their free conciliation service may be able to help. Write to them at 55-57 Newman Street, London W1, giving all the details and sending copies of any correspondence.

Always write, never telephone. Preferably send your letters by recorded delivery. Then you have proof that they arrived.

You have a year in which to bring your complaint if you have dealt with the firm in writing, but if you *have* complained over the telephone you must take legal action within six months. Obviously the quicker you write on your return – or even while still on holiday – the more chance you are likely to have of settling the matter without going to court. If you decide to take legal action, be sure of your case; it is often very difficult to prove. Consult a solicitor.

Taking your car abroad

As your car costs you such a lot of money just standing in your garage, it is a good idea to make the most of it by using it as your main form of transport on holiday. This is one time when the car is likely to be full and therefore used as economically as possible. This is particularly true if you are going abroad.

Before you take it, however, there are some things that you must bear in mind.

Car insurance

Will your normal insurance cover your car when you are abroad? If your insurance does not cover foreign trips, ask for a 'topping up' insurance for the period, or go to one of the companies which specializes in this form of insurance.

You will almost certainly need more cover than your insurance policy automatically gives you, and it is highly unlikely that your Continental cover will be as full as the cover for the car when it is in the UK. The best plan is to arrange with your insurers to have full cover extended for the time that the car will be on the continent. You will have to pay an extra premium for this. There is no standard charge for the extension of your insurance. The cost will depend on where you are going, how long for, and sometimes the model of your car.

Your insurers may give you a European Accident Statement, which they advise you to sign if you are involved in an accident. *Signing it is not a confession of guilt (which you should never make).* Completing the form is not compulsory, but is encouraged; the form should then be sent to the insurers with any completed claim form or accident report form. Whoever you bump into should also have a form in his or her own language.

As a rule, when the cover for your car is extended, it will also cover any journey you have to make by sea which takes up to sixty-five hours by a recognized route. This includes hovercraft ferries, as well as boats.

If you are travelling by sea for more than sixty-five hours – which is unlikely – you will have to pay an additional premium. This ferry cover does not extend to taking your car by air, but the carrier normally makes himself responsible for any damage which might occur while the car is in the air. To be on the safe side, check before you go.

Green cards

The 'green card' is the most convenient way of proving that you are adequately insured to travel abroad. You no longer need one when you are driving on many parts of the Continent – EEC member states, Austria, Czechoslovakia, Finland, the GDR, Hungary, Norway, Sweden and Switzerland – but it is still a very good idea to have one, as it is the quickest and best way of proving, if you are involved in an accident, that you are adequately covered by insurance. It is still essential in those countries where a British insurance policy does not automatically give the minimum cover required by law in whatever country you are driving in. Anyone in the group who is planning to drive should sign the green card.

If you decide that you do want a green card, apply for it at least three weeks before you leave. Tell your insurers the date of your trip, the countries that you are visiting, and any others that you may have to cross in an emergency. Some countries do not accept green cards, so check before leaving. When this is the case your insurance company may not be prepared to extend your insurance and you may have to go to an insurance broker to get the sort of cover you need.

Spain

There are special rules for motoring in Spain. If you are driving there, you will need a bail bond as well as your green card, and this will cost extra. The reason for this is that, under Spanish law, a car and its driver may be detained by the authorities following an accident, no matter how trivial.

If you want to get the car and yourself released, you must insure yourself against the possibility of any civil or criminal action against you from which damages may arise. You will also have to guarantee your presence or legal representation at any proceedings which may follow.

This costs money – far more money than you will probably be able to afford to take with you. So you buy a bail bond, which is acceptable to the Spanish authorities. It will cost you about £2.50 for £1,500-worth of damage (280,000 pesetas). Your company may offer you only a £500 limit. This is most certainly not enough. Get at least £1,500.

Caravans

You may also want to take a caravan abroad. If you buy one and use it for all your holidays, it is certainly a good investment and will pay for itself eventually. Indeed, caravan prices have been rising so sharply that if you keep your caravan in good order you may be able to sell it at a profit later.

It is impossible to give an average figure for the cost of a caravanning holiday. It all depends on where you go and when you go and the size of the caravan, if you are hiring. All one can say is that, whatever way one looks at it, a caravan holiday is one of the least expensive ways to get a break. Prices at caravan sites vary. A 'certified location' – that might simply be a farmer's field – could cost as little as £1.50 a night for four. One with plenty of facilities, such as showers, possibilities for being plugged into main drains, electrical points, etc., or club houses, could be £3.15 or more in peak season. The size of the caravan and the number of people using a single site also affect the price.

Travelling with one's own caravan is of course cheapest and rental for a four-berth caravan can cost between £30 and £90 a week, depending on its size and whether it is motorised or for towing. If you want to take the caravan you rent abroad, that will be much more expensive and the hirer will want a £15 or £20 hire insurance deposit to cover himself in the event of damage to the caravan. This will be returned in full if the caravan is returned undamaged.

Insurance for your caravan

You should tell your car insurers that you propose to pull a caravan. Your policy may cover this, but check to be on the safe side. If it does not, there will be a small extra premium to pay. Then, if you own the caravan or it is not fully insured by its owners, ask for extra cover on your car policy to cover that, too.

If you have a green card, make sure it shows you are towing a caravan. If you borrow a caravan from a friend or relative, it is even more important to see that you are fully covered by insurance. The same applies if you are towing a boat.

It will cost you at least £100 to get a fourteen-foot car plus a caravan plus a family of four across the Channel and back. But prices vary enormously with routes and season, and when you book, so check this.

Your foreign currency

When you go outside the UK, you cannot spend sterling. Every country has its own currency and you will have to take foreign bank notes or traveller's cheques. You will have to take enough foreign currency with you to cover all your spending once you get abroad, if you are travelling privately, and anything over and above the accommodation and food you get if you are on a 'package'. You can also use your cheque book to cash two cheques a day up to £100 each, but you will need a special Euro-cheque card for his. Your normal cheque guarantee card which you use in Britain will not do. Unlike the British card, the Eurocheque card is not issued automatically to you; you must apply for a new one each year. The banks believe that this special Eurocheque card is one way of keeping down fraud.

The first rule is to be realistic about what you need. There is no point in ruining your holiday by worrying about money all the time. Work out what you will need in the currency of the country you are visiting and then work back to the equivalent amount in sterling.

Your first question will naturally be, what happens if the value of the pound falls while you are away, so that your money does not go as far as you estimated. To avoid this, you can exchange your money before you go. Of course the pound could rise in value, so that you would lose out by getting your currency before leaving Britain. You can't have it both ways; it is up to you to decide which risk you want to take.

There are no limits today on the amount of money you can take out of Britain. You can remove everything you have if you wish. You can open a bank account abroad and send money to it. This is useful if you tend to spend your holidays in one place, because the money can go by bank transfer and you need not carry any money or traveller's cheques with you.

You get foreign currency through a bank, even if you are not a customer of that particular bank, or do not have an account at all. Give the bank a few days' notice, especially if the currency you want is rather unusual.

There are various ways of taking money abroad:

1 *Cash.* You can decide to get all your foreign currency in cash before you leave, providing the bank has enough to cover your needs. This is another reason for giving the bank some notice. You may also find that the country you are going to puts a limit on what you can take in, so you may not be able to take all your currency in cash. The regulations change all the time, so check with your bank, which will know the current position. You must take some of your funds in cash to cope with your arrival. Cash has the *advantage* of making sure you don't lose by a fall in sterling, but the *disadvantage* that if it is stolen you have no means of recouping the money, and that you won't profit by any increase in the value of sterling.

2 *Sterling traveller's cheques.* These can be purchased from any bank. You can cash them for local currency when you arrive at your destination. The rate of exchange you get depends on the level fixed in the local area that day. Sterling traveller's cheques have the *advantage* that you are protected from loss. The bank keeps a note of the numbers of the cheques. You sign the cheques when you receive them and countersign when you cash them, which makes fraud difficult. But there is the *disadvantage* that if the pound falls between the time you buy the cheques and the time you cash them, you will get less for your money than you expected. You will find, too, that you get less for them in shops and hotels than you do if you cash them in a bank.

3 *Foreign currency traveller's cheques.* These are probably the best means of carrying foreign currency. They are protected in the same way as sterling cheques, but have the added *advantage* of fixing the amount of foreign currency you will have available at the time you buy them. Their only *disadvantage* compared with cash is that you are dependent on banks being open to cash them, and in some countries they can only

be cashed at a branch of the bank which issued them. Foreign currency traveller's cheques are also not available in all currencies.

4 *Currency transfer*. You can buy currency at home and have it lodged in a bank abroad in your name and draw it when you arrive. This is an excellent way to transfer your money. It has the *advantage* of being safe and easy to withdraw as long as you can prove your identity satisfactorily, but the *disadvantage* that it is really only appropriate if you are staying in one place. It takes time to transfer money, so if you are doing it this way, give the bank plenty of notice.

5 *Credit cards*. These cannot be used to get cash, but they can be used to pay many of your bills in shops, restaurants and hotels. They have the *advantage* of being just as – sometimes even more – acceptable as cash or traveller's cheques, but the *disadvantage* that they are not universally accepted Also, the card company will charge you in sterling at the rate of exchange prevailing when they pay out the bill, not when you used the card, so you never know exactly what rate you are paying. If you use American Express or Diners Club you will pay two lots of currency exchange, first into dollars and then out of them into sterling. If you have an American Express card, they will issue you with new traveller's cheques from their offices – if you are near one.

If all these means fail and you still run out of money on holiday, your bank will usually send you more money if you cable them and give them the name and address of the bank where you want to collect the money.

All in all, it's difficult to find yourself completely stranded abroad without money today. If it does happen, contact the nearest British consulate or embassy. They will provide you with enough money to get home. You will have to repay it later.

Traveller's cheques

All the banks advise their customers on how to protect their traveller's cheques. National Westminster, for example, suggest that you:

- Carry your passport and traveller's cheques in a safe place – not just flung in a beach bag.
- Fill in the detachable slip you will find in your traveller's cheque book, and keep this record of your cheque numbers in a safe and separate place from the cheques themselves.
- *Don't* countersign unless in the presence of the person who is cashing the cheque.

They also advise:

- *Do* check rates of exchange when you cash your cheques.
- *Don't* ever get into the awful position of finding yourself abroad and flat broke. Do use traveller's cheques.

- *Don't* exchange traveller's cheques or cash with street traders. There is always the chance that you will get forged notes in exchange, and in some countries you will be committing a criminal offence.

Remember, it is common practice abroad for the encashing agent to call for some proof of identity when accepting traveller's cheques. Take your passport with you when you want to cash money.

Returning from abroad
1 Pay attention to the foreign currency regulations in the countries you visit. Many countries restrict the amount of actual cash you can take out.
2 Bring back as few coins as possible, as you will probably not be able to change them at the bank when you get back. If you can, the rate will be very poor.

Duty-free allowances

We are all tempted by the words 'duty-free', particularly when applied to alcohol or cigarettes, living as we do in a country which taxes both very heavily. And it is true that *sometimes* up to 50 per cent of the price can be saved by purchasing 'duty-frees'. But there are snags.

First of all, you are severely limited in the amounts you are allowed to bring back. The allowances change from time to time, and should eventually disappear altogether for countries in the Common Market, as EEC duties and taxes become more uniform. The table shows how they stood in late 1984.

Many people go into a duty-free shop and expect massive bargains. The things are indeed duty-free but they are not profit-free, and sometimes the mark-up is enormously high. You may well be better off shopping outside, where the choice will be wider and prices lower because of the greater competition.

Remember, if you go over your duty-free allowance *you must declare the goods to the customs*. You will have to pay duty on them – and sometimes this is heavy. The penalties for not declaring are severe. It is simply not worth trying to slip something through undeclared.

	goods bought in ordinary (not duty-free) shops in EEC countries	goods bought outside the EEC, or in a duty-free shop inside it, or on the plane
Tobacco		
cigarettes	300	200
cigarillos	150	100
cigars	75	50
tobacco	400 g	250 g
Alcohol		
over 36.8% proof (22.2% alcohol) (generally spirits)	1½ litres	1 litre
not over 36.8% proof, or fortified or sparkling wine plus	3 litres	2 litres
still table wine	4 litres	2 litres
Perfume	3 fluid oz (75 g)	2 fluid oz (50 g)
Toilet water	13 fluid oz (375 cc)	9 fluid oz (250 cc)
Other goods	£163-worth	£28-worth

Holiday insurance

Things can go wrong on holiday, wherever you go. Most things do not matter very much, but sometimes they can cost money – money which you can ill afford. It is only sensible to take out some kind of insurance against the most likely mishaps, particularly if you are going abroad.

This should include:

Medical insurance. It does not matter where you are taken ill in the British Isles, medical treatment is available, and available free. This is not the case in most countries, though members of the EEC have some reciprocal agreements with one another for emergency medical treatment.

Such agreements, however, do not apply to the self-employed, and you may find anyway that you have to pay and then reclaim the money later on form E 111, which you must make sure you have before you go. Getting this money can be a long and laborious process. You may feel it is not worth it and that you would be better off taking out insurance.

If so, then you must:

- Make sure it is enough. You will need a great deal of cover if you are going to the USA or Canada. It does not take long to run up a bill of £1,000. Certainly any less than £500 cover will be totally inadequate. Ask your insurer how much you will need where you are going. Skiing accidents which result in a broken leg, for example, are always costly.

- Tell the insurer about any medical condition you suffer from, which may recur at any time. Otherwise you will not be covered for it while you are away.
- If you are sent to hospital, give them details of your cover. The officials will check directly with your company.
- Keep all bills and receipts, even for prescriptions at the chemist.

Car insurance. Apart from extending your ordinary inusrance cover, if you take your car abroad you should consider getting cover for the following extras:

- Hiring a car if your own breaks down, is irreparably damaged, or is stolen.
- Transport costs for all your party, if you are unable to drive home.
- The cost of bringing the car back to Britain, if it proves impossible to repair abroad.
- The freight costs of flying out spare parts for your car, if that is necessary.
- Customs charges which you may incur if your car is either stolen or completely destroyed by fire or accident while you are abroad. The AA S–Star and RAC Cordon Bleu policies cover these items.

Cover for yourself and your belongings. This is important. You may be involved in an accident. You may lose your luggage or have it stolen. You may lose your money, your traveller's cheques, or your tickets.

If any of these things happen, report it immediately – at the airport, hotel or wherever you are. Do not forget also to inform the local police and make them confirm in writing that you have reported the loss to them. Make sure you have a copy of their confirmation. It will probably be a condition of your policy that you report any loss within twenty-four hours. *It is not always possible to report back to Britain in that time, so make sure you lose no time locally.*

You can also insure for rather more unusual things. For instance, people used to insure themselves against the possibility of rain spoiling their holiday. This is less fashionable now, following a few good summers, but you can still do it. You can also insure yourself against being hijacked: this gives cover for injury to yourself, loss of your belongings and accommodation and repatriation expenses.

Holiday insurance is not expensive, and a few pounds spent can make all the difference to your enjoyment,but check the policy carefully to see that it fully provides the cover you need. Many do not. The British Insurance Association suggests the following cover:

- Luggage and belongings, between £500 and £1,000.
- Holiday cancellation or curtailment, £750 to £1,000.

- Delay, usually £50 a person.
- Personal accident, up to £15,000.
- Medical expenses, mainly up to £100,000.

A policy including all this should not cost much more than £10 for an adult for 14 days in Europe, though premiums will be quite a lot higher for Canada or the United States. Worldwide cover, excluding the USA and Canada, is about 2½ times the level for Europe.

What you must remember
Before you go
1 When you take out the policy, be sure it covers the full period you are away and a little extra in case of delay. Make sure it covers all the countries you may visit.
2 Be realistic about how much cover you need.
3 Check that the age limits cover your whole party.
4 Make a list of the contents of your suitcase.

On holiday
1 Do not forget to take the policy with you.
2 Keep receipts of all medical bills.
3 Report any losses immediately.
4 Tell the police, as well as airport/railway/hotel officials, wherever you are, of any loss.
5 Ask for confirmation in writing that you have reported the loss.

On your return
1 Fill in your claim form and produce all receipts and written reports.
2 Give a list of contents of your suitcase, or of the numbers of your traveller's cheques if they are lost or stolen.

If you are travelling on a package tour, you may not have to do any of this. Some carriers take out insurance for the whole party and charge an extra fee for it. But check: not all operators do this.

Section two
Your money and your job

1 Choosing your career

The career you choose will have an impact not only on your own standard of living, but on that of your family as well. So choose your career carefully.

Average salary per annum (£)	
medical practitioners	19,832
personnel or industrial relations officers	14,872
marketing and sales executives	14,664
office managers	13,577
journalists	13,468
mechanical engineers	13,312
ships' officers	13,291
general managers	13,083
electrical and electronic engineers	12,755
scientists and mathematicians	12,324
architects/town planners	12,298
civil engineers	12,152
accountants	12,126
public health inspectors	11,351
metallurgists	10,982
senior sales representatives	10,384
welfare workers	9,329
costing and accounting clerks	6,978

Source: *New Earnings Survey*

These are only average salaries. People just coming into the various professions will earn much less and the very experienced can earn a great deal more, though this does not always follow. Nevertheless, it is clear that salaries vary enormously from profession to profession and the qualification or amount of training required is not always an indicator of what salary can be expected.

If you are a parent, make sure your child is properly advised. If the school does not do this well, use all the official resources which are available through your local Department of Employment. Try to guide your children into careers with a future. Steer them away from declining industries. Persuade them to avoid the low-paid professions if possible. (Note that this is a book about money, not careers. There are many excellent books available to help you choose a career which will satisfy you both in terms of personal enjoyment and in terms of financial security.)

If you are in your thirties, the sorts of salaries you could expect to get in managerial jobs in mid-1984 are shown in the previous table. From this you can measure just how well or badly you are doing if you are in one of these jobs. Whatever your job, check on average salary levels and make sure you are being paid what you are worth.

In recent years the position of professional managers has got worse in comparison with those who have gone into the civil service and local authorities. Salaries there are sometimes higher than they are in comparable jobs in private industry. There, too, jobs are more secure and pensions higher, usually geared to the rate of inflation. The civil service, however, is difficult to get into today: numbers are being cut rather than increased.

As I write, there are well over 3,000,000 unemployed people in Britain and all sectors have been affected. It is difficult to find a job today which will guarantee security for the whole of your working life. Even teaching, once regarded as a very secure job, has become just like the rest, as more and more teachers have been qualifying to teach fewer and fewer children. We must all hope that real economic recovery will come. When it does, the job opportunities will open up again.

Think very carefully before you decide on your career. High salaries at the beginning do not automatically mean you will not fall back later in your career. Try to make sure that your earnings are on par with others. As I write, the average per week is £178.80 for a man and £117.20 for a woman. You should aim to beat that average, not fall below it.

Jobs to avoid are those which come below the average. Some are well below, including hairdressers, catering staff (though both of these get tips), shop staff, laundry workers, clothing industry workers, toy makers and agricultural workers. You will see from this that, apart from catering and agricultural workers, most of the low-paid jobs are those in which women predominate. Turn to chapter 9 of this section, where you will see that there is no need to settle for a low wage just because you are a woman.

Even in the better paid manual jobs, there are quite large variations in wages. Print compositors in London were way ahead of the rest in 1984, earning close on £300 a week. Coalface mine workers are usually up there with them, but there were no comparative figures for 1984, because of industrial action. At the bottom of the list were hotel and catering workers, averaging only £109.10 a week (but before tips), then agricultural workers, on £115 a week (plus, probably, accommodation). Here are the rankings:

print compositors (London)	£298.40	food industry workers	£160.40
police below superintendent	£244.20	shipbuilders	£158.60
banking	£226.40	postmen	£155.20
steel workers	£196.60	engineering workers	£153.70
school teachers	£195.90	ambulancemen	£150.40
print compositors (provinces)	£191.50	water workers	£149.30
coalface workers (1983 levels)	£188.60	nurses	£136.60
gas fitters	£177.10	garbage disposal workers	£135.20
civil engineers	£175.70	textile workers	£133.10
chemical workers	£174.00	food retailing	£127.70
car workers	£168.40	agricultural workers	£115.00
railway workers	£163.50	hotel and catering staff	£109.10

As well as variations between different jobs, there are also different averate rates, depending on where you live. Among the manual trades, workers in the south-east get paid the most, an average of £160.50 a week, and Greater London has the highest rates of all, £169.80 a week. This compares with the south-west where manual rates are only £142.90 a week on average. In the non-manual area, the south-east again leads with £228.20 a week (£224 for Greater London) and the East Midlands have the lowest rate at £191.20. In that area, workers in the Tyne and Wear district get the lowest pay of all, an average of £189.20 a week.

What your contract of employment should tell you
By the time you have been working full-time for thirteen weeks, most of you (there are some exceptions) should have received a written notice from your employer setting out the terms of your employment. This should tell you:

1 The date you began working.
2 How you will be paid – weekly or monthly.
3 The starting level of your wages or salary.
4 Terms and conditions of hours of work.
5 Holiday entitlement.
6 Terms upon which sick pay is paid.
7 Pension.
8 The length of notice required on either side.

9 Any job title.
10 Any previous employment which counts as part of continuous employment.
11 Disciplinary rules, and grievance procedure, if one exists.
12 The date of expiry of the contract, if the term of employment is fixed.

You may not receive this notice if you work for sixteen hours a week or less, or if you already have a written contract of employment which includes all these details.

2 If you are unemployed

What you are entitled to

Most people today are eligible for benefit if they become unemployed. To make a successful claim you must:

• Have no work.
• Be able and willing to take up another job.
• Have paid a minimum of twenty-six Class 1 national insurance contributions.

To get the standard rate of benefit you must have been paid or credited with, in the relevant tax year, Class 1 contributions of at least fifty times the lower earnings limit (£35.50 from 6 April 1985) for that year. If you do not meet this requirement, your benefit will be less.

Leaflet NI.12, issued by the Department of Health and Social Security, sets out all the rules in great detail and in simple language which is easy to follow.

At present there are two rates of benefit, one for men, single women and widows, and one for those married women still eligible to pay the lower rate. From November 1984 the single person's allowance is £28.45 a week. A married woman can also get benefit at this level if her husband is getting an invalidity pension, retirement pension or any unemployment allowance.

Further claims can be made for dependants. As a general rule, these will be for a wife and children. The married man's weekly rate is £46, £17.55 a week more than single person's benefit.

There are further allowances for adult dependants. These could include male relatives who live with you and are incapable of supporting themselves, if you pay for at least half their keep, and female relatives in the same circumstances, but who are also earning no more than the standard amount of an increase for an adult dependant which is shown in the DHSS leaflet NI.196. In certain circumstances, too, there is an allowance for women with child dependants.

The current figures mean that the 'average' family, consisting of husband, wife and two children, will get a basic total unemployment benefit, on the husband's qualifications, of £46, plus, of course, child benefits, which (usually) go to the mother. At current prices this is often clearly not enough to support a family. If you do become unemployed you should visit your local DHSS office to find out what other benefits you may be entitled to. I have spelled these out in some detail in Section three, chapter 4.

Your benefit may be affected if:

- You get any lump sum from a former employer.
- You still work part-time.
- You have an award from an industrial tribunal under the Employment Protection Act 1975.

And you may lose your benefit altogether if:

1 You put restrictions on the kind of work you are prepared to do to such an extent that you make it virtually impossible for the Employment Service Agency to find you another post. This means that you will have to be flexible in your demands, and sometimes be prepared to take work which is unfamiliar to you.
2 You leave your previous employment voluntarily without just cause. It is up to you to show 'just cause' for leaving.
3 You have been forced to leave your job because of misconduct. In this case, however, it is up to your former employer to prove 'misconduct', which can range from failure to carry out instructions to dishonesty.

If you repeatedly turn down or fail to apply for jobs which are offered, you may be disqualified from receiving benefit for up to six weeks. This will most often occur when you are offered 'suitable employment', which generally means your usual occupation – though if you are unskilled it would cover a wider range of jobs.

How to claim
You must go to your local unemployment office on the first day that you are unemployed. At the same time you should register that you are available for new employment at the local office of the Employment Service Agency (the old Labour Exchange). When you go, remember to take your P.45 (which your employer will give you when you leave) or a note of your national insurance number with you.

If you do not claim on the first day you are unemployed you may lose some of your benefit, so this is very important.

Payment of benefit
You will usually get your unemployment benefit sent to you as a Giro cheque through the post. Benefit, which includes earnings-related supplement if applicable, will be paid to you for up to 312 days of unemployment (not counting Sundays) in any one period of uninterrupted unemployment.

Once you have had the 312 days' benefit (equal to one year, excluding Sundays) you cannot qualify again for unemployment benefit until you have been back to work for at least thirteen weeks and have worked a minimum of twenty-one hours for each of those weeks.

If you are still unemployed after 312 days you will have to apply for the kind of benefits which I have set out in Section three, chapter 4.

Remember, benefit levels change each November, so check the position if you are making a claim.

3 Redundancy and dismissal

Redundancy
Industries flourish, then falter, new technology may require less labour, economies boom and slump. These are just some of the reasons why you could find yourself made redundant. Redundancy comes as a shock to many people and can change their lives radically.

Periods of notice
Over the years, government-sponsored protection for employees has increased and, although no one can be completely cushioned against redundancy, dismissal which is not through one's own fault, there are now strict rules which employers must follow when dismissing employees. Employers, too, have corresponding rights; they are entitled, for example, to have proper notice given to them when an employee wants to leave.

Employer and employee can come to an agreement themselves over periods of notice, but the periods set must be as long as or longer than the legal minima. When there is no such agreement the minimum periods of notice are:

length of employment	period of notice
4 weeks to 2 years	1 week
2 years to 12 years	1 week for each year
over 12 years	not less than 12 weeks

In all cases the employee must give at least one week's notice.

This law only applies if the employment has been continuous. You are allowed to be ill for periods of up to twenty-six weeks without affecting your entitlement, and those weeks are included as if you had been working.

Periods when you have been on strike do not break the continuity of your employment, but they are taken off when the full period is calculated. If you happen to have been with the same firm before and after a period in the armed forces, your continuity is not broken, but the time served does not count as part of the full period of employment. If you are offered other suitable work instead of dismissal, you may lose your right to redundancy pay if you refuse it.

Redundancy payments
When dismissed as 'redundant', an employee has the right to go to an industrial tribunal for compensation, as long as he has been employed with the firm for a minimum of two years, if he thinks that the redundancy is not genuine and is just an excuse to get rid of him.

Many companies today have special redundancy agreements of their own, particularly if the industry is running down or the technology is changing, in an attempt to persuade people to leave the industry voluntarily. These voluntary agreements usually give better financial terms than the legal minima, which are:

for each year of employment between the ages of	employees' minimum payments
18 and 21	half a week's pay
21 and 40	1 week's pay
40 and 65 (men)	1½ weeks' pay
40 to 60 (women)	1½ weeks' pay

The maximum number of years counted is twenty and the maximum pay is £145 a week. This means that, if you are earning, say, £200 a week and are made redundant, there is no redundancy payment for £55 of that (£200–£145).

These terms recognize that the older you get the less likely you are to be able to transfer to a new job which pays as well as the old one. If you are offered redundancy, you should consider the matter carefully before accepting or rejecting it.

If there is no special redundancy scheme in your company, the maximum payment you can get is £20 (for twenty years)×£217.50 (1½ weeks' pay), or £4,350. Such a sum might be quite useful to someone of forty who was fairly certain of getting another job; redundancy might then seem rather attractive. But to a man of sixty, with five years to go to retirement, it is not such an attractive proposition. Redundancy payments are tax-free, so the maximum of £4,350 is equal to £5,655 before tax at the current standard rate of 30 per cent.

Privately-arranged redundancy schemes often set no limits either on the time worked or on the amount earned. In a scheme which gives, say, one week's pay for every year worked, a man who is made redundant after forty years' service when earning £10,000 a year, or about £200 a week, could end up with £8,000.

Redundancy is clearly something you must think about carefully if you are offered voluntary redundancy, as is often the case in private schemes.

Defining redundancy
Employers only have to make compensatory payments when employees are dismissed for redundancy. It is therefore vital to the employee that he should be able to prove that he has been made redundant.

You will get redundancy pay:

1 If your employer declares you redundant.
2 If your employer's conduct justifies you in leaving, for example if you are demoted for no reason and – very rarely – if your wages are not paid.
3 If there is a lay-off or a period of short-time working of four consecutive weeks, or of any six weeks out of thirteen, you can claim redundancy pay. It will only be disallowed if your employer can prove that full-time working will recommence within four weeks.
4 If an employer refuses to renew a fixed-term contract when it expires.

You will not be able to prove redundancy, however, if your employer has made a written offer of suitable alternative employment and you have rejected it unreasonably. But no tribunal will regard your decision to reject as unreasonable if you are offered a much lower position, or a job which is quite outside your capabilities. Conflict is inevitable in some cases, however.

If you find that you cannot reach an agreement with your employer, you may have to go to a tribunal. You may well prove your point if your employer is known to be running down or closing his business, or if a particular part of it is being run down or closed.

When a firm is moving headquarters, so that continued employment with that firm requires an employee to move house, it is normal for companies to work out special 'one-off' redundancy agreements. There are many reasons why employees may not wish or be able to move, and their employment cannot simply be terminated without compensation simply because of this.

The same thing often happens where companies have been the subject of a successful takeover bid. You may feel that it will be difficult for you to claim redundancy if your employer resists, but remember that the onus is always on the employer, not the employee, to prove his case at the tribunal hearing. (When employees go to the new area, they are usually helped with removal costs.)

Claiming redundancy pay

You must follow special rules when making your claim, otherwise it may not be allowed by the tribunal.

The most important requirement is that within six months you must either have agreed and received your redundancy money (after that, except in very special circumstances, it is too late to put in a claim), or have made a claim to your employer in writing, or have already referred the claim to an industrial tribunal.

Some exceptions may be made to these rules in certain cases. If you have left your claim too long it may still be considered by the tribunal.

In some cases, an employee may find new work before the period of notice runs out. This does not necessarily mean he or she will not be entitled to redundancy money.

Golden handshakes

When you are made redundant, your employer may offer you more money than he has to in law, or even in a particular house agreement. These are called 'golden handshakes', because the first £25,000, which covers most of us, is completely tax free. After that, special rates apply (see Section four, chapter 5).

Unfair and wrongful dismissal

Occasionally employers sack workers and staff for no good reason. When this happens, as long as the person involved has been employed for more than two years, he can take action against the employer and claim compensation. At the outset it is important to distinguish between *unfair dismissal,* where there is a statutory right under the Industrial Relations Act 1971 for every employee who feels that he has been unfairly dismissed to go to an industrial tribunal for compensation, and *wrongful dismissal* when an employee feels that there has been a breach of contract, which can lead to a common law action in the civil courts.

Unfair dismissal

If you feel you have been unfairly dismissed, or are not getting redundancy money to which you are legally entitled, you should make your claim on a form which is available from the offices of the Department of Employment.

Once the claim has been made, it is up to the employer to prove that the dismissal was fair and justified. If he makes no such claim the tribunal will award compensation to the employee.

Find out what the employer is required to prove; then you can work out how good a chance you have of succeeding in your claim. He must show one of the following:

1 The qualifications and capability of the employee were inadequate for his job.
2 The conduct of the employee was such that the dismissal was justified.
3 The employee was redundant (in which case he is entitled to redundancy pay.)
4 The employee could not carry on working where he was, without either the employee or the employer contravening some statutory restriction or duty.

If the employer proves his case and is held to have 'reasonable' grounds for dismissing the employee, the claim will fail. What is held to be 'reasonable' is a matter for each industrial tribunal to decide. If the case goes against the employee, there is a right of appeal. If he wins, the tribunal will ask the employer to take the employee back. If the employer refuses, he will be given compensation.

This will consist of a 'basic award', calculated in almost the same way as a redundancy payment, and an additional 'compensatory award' decided by the tribunal. This latter will take into account such things as:

● The extent to which the conduct of the claimant led to the dismissal.
● The loss of earnings which resulted and the prospects for new employment.
● And, recently, some award for 'hurt feelings'.

There is no minimum award for unfair dismissal. The maximum is £11,850, plus a further £3,370 if reinstatement is refused (end 1984). Even though in theory there is a lot to be said for going to a tribunal, in fact it is rarely in anyone's interest to go to the tribunal if it can be avoided. If you feel that you have been unfairly dismissed, either talk to your employer yourself to see what he is prepared to pay you to leave without taking further legal action, or, if you cannot do this yourself, get a solicitor to act for you.

If you get a good solicitor, he may be able to get you a payment which you think is fair, with the former employer paying all the costs. If you can get the equivalent, say, of two years' salary, you should be content: you are unlikely to get more from a tribunal.

Whatever the offer, you must then think very carefully. Just how strong is your case? Is the compensation you may get at the tribunal likely to be more or less than the offer you already have? Remember, a large company will often have better legal advice than an employee. And though you will not have to pay anything for your application to be heard by the tribunal, you will of course have to pay a solicitor if you want legal advice.

If you find yourself in this situation, do not turn down a reasonable offer simply through greed, or because you wish at all costs to meet your employers publicly at the tribunal (you can conduct your case yourself if you wish). You must be very sure of your case and the evidence you can produce, or you may find that you get nothing at all in the end.

Remember, too, that you cannot be dismissed on grounds of sex, race or marital status. For example, you can no longer be sacked automatically because you marry, as often used to happen to women. There are few occupations today which can legally be limited to one sex. If you think you have been acted against illegally on these grounds, get in touch with the Commission for Racial Equality, which enforces the Race Relations Act, or the Equal Opportunities Commission, which deals with the Sex Discrimination Act.

Wrongful dismissal

This applies when an employee feels that the conditions of his contract of employment have not been observed in the manner of any dismissal – though the dismissal itself may have been 'fair'. You might claim that you have not had proper notice as set out in law, or, if you have a fixed contract, that you were dismissed before the end of the term.

If the case is proved, compensation will be given only to the level of the lost earnings which have resulted. In some cases damages may be awarded for any potential earnings lost. These damages look only to the future and not at the existing situation. You cannot, for instance, get damages because you feel that your reputation has been damaged by the dismissal. In these cases, the employer can cite the behaviour of the employee as a contributing factor to the dismissal. If he proves this, the employee may lose the case, even though this is a wrongful, not an unfair, dismissal case.

Legitimate dismissal

Not all dismissals are unfair or wrongful. There are quite legitimate reasons for even summary dismissal. These include theft, gross incompetence, negligence and insubordination. Of course, it is possible to argue about some of these. Though it would be difficult to disprove dishonesty if you were caught in the act, cases of alleged insubordination or negligence have been taken up.

If you find, for instance, that you were sacked for one isolated act of mild 'insubordination', you would probably have a good case for wrongful dismissal. If you were persistently rude or persistently disobeyed instructions from your superiors, you would find your case much more difficult to uphold.

Help for removal

In times of severe unemployment, the government does all it can to persuade people to move to areas where jobs are easiest to get.

A system of grants and allowances has been instituted to help people with removal and travelling costs associated with moving to a new job in another area in certain cases. The rules about who qualifies are very strict. However, if you do manage to persuade the authorities that you are a deserving case, the 'approved contractors' estimate of removal is met in full.

4 If you are self-employed

As you read through this book, you will see that the self-employed are disadvantaged in many ways, particularly when it comes to the social services and pensions. For example, they are not eligible for the new 'earnings-related' part of the Castle pension scheme which started in April 1978 (see Section five, chapter 9). They pay a flat rate of £3.50 a week then a further £3.40 if they wish to qualify for the basic pension and a limited range of other benefits. Some also have to pay a 'Class 4' contribution of 6 per cent on profits they make between £5,000 and £14,000, but 50 per cent of that has been allowable for tax since April, 1985.

The self-employed should take care of their retirement adequately themselves and to supplement the flat-rate pension (see Section five, chapter 9). They are also disadvantaged over unemployment pay and sickness benefit (see chapter 1 of this section, and Section one, chapter 14).

Before you decide to be self-employed, you should consult your bank manager, an accountant and a solicitor. There are many practical difficulties and pitfalls which may beset you. The National Federation of Self-Employed Limited may be useful to you: their address is 32 St Annes Road West, Lytham St Annes, Lancashire FY8 1NY (telephone 0253 727075). It operates a service for the self-employed, which includes the issuing of a number of booklets discussing the practical problems of being self-employed and listing sources of funds for small businesses. You may also find your local chamber of commerce very helpful. They will be able to put you in touch with one of the many organizations which help small businesses.

Despite the possible problems, being self-employed can be very rewarding personally. You will have to remember, however, that you will need capital not only to develop and expand your business but also to provide for your family in case you hit a sticky patch (for sickness insurance see Section one, chapter 14) or have a long period of illness. Remember, too, that you will need a dedication and purposefulness which you do not always need if you are employed by someone else. There is no one for you to fall back on, if you are trying to develop your business alone.

5 Setting up a partnership

You may decide to set up a partnership. Be very clear in your mind what the differences are between operating alone, in partnership or through a company.

If you operate alone you carry all the responsibility for the business – its successes, failures, profits and losses.

In a company the liability of the owners is limited to the stake they have in the company.

In a partnership you have the advantage of the use of the various skills of the partners. All the profits can be shared out among members of the partnership, but at the same time the partners are totally liable for losses. This means that if a partnership fails with heavy debts, each partner is liable up to the limit of all his or her personal assets and possessions.

There may also be 'sleeping partners', who put up money for the business and get a share of the profit, but take no part in the running of the business. They are liable only for the amount of money they have put into the partnership. This kind of limited partnership must be registered at the Companies Registry, at the addresses given in the next chapter.

Most self-employed people choose to operate alone. Few form companies. Some choose the partnership way. This is particularly popular in professions like stockbroking or jobbing, law and accountancy, where a number of individuals get together to run a business. In fact, partnerships are rather more popular than they used to be. Until 1967 private companies were allowed to keep their accounts private. Now they cannot. Limited partnerships are the only option open to anyone who wants to keep his financial affairs secret at the same time as limiting his liability. The most famous example of a limited partnership is C & A, the well-known clothing retailers. It was a private limited company until the Companies Act 1967 was passed, and then became a limited partnership. This means that even today no one has any idea of the profit levels of this group.

In theory, every partner can be limited, but the business would then have to be run by paid managers.

How partnerships work

When a partnership is set up, it is covered by the Partnership Act 1890, unless a specifically different separate agreement is made. It is a contractual arrangement which runs for a certain length of time.

Ending a partnership. You can choose to set a date on when the partnership will end. If you do this you can always set up again, if you wish. But most partnerships are what is known as 'at will', and continue until a partner either gives notice that he is leaving or dies.

This notice must be given in writing, and if it is not so given the other partners are entitled to assume that the person is still a partner with the same rights and responsibilities as everyone else in the partnership. If a partner acts in a way which damages the partnership's business, the other partners are not protected against his actions and must take responsibility for them.

The rights of partners. Unless there is a special agreement to the contrary, they must all have:

- Access to the partnership books.
- A share in the profits or losses, either on an equal basis with all the other partners or in a way specified in the partnership agreement.
- Voting rights. Again these may be equal or in proportions laid down in the partnership agreement. Senior partners sometimes have veto rights.

Partners cannot be dismissed because the partnership contract is for a fixed period, unless there are special powers written into the agreement. Similarly, a new partner may not be taken on unless all the existing partners agree.

Partnership agreements. These cover points such as whether partners may have other business interests outside the partnership and how directly they can go into competition with their previous partners if they decide to leave.

These rules must not be too strict, otherwise they would be difficult to enforce. It would be difficult, if not impossible, for example, to enforce an agreement which said that former partners could not operate in their particular line of business for a considerable number of years. However, it might be easier to enforce one which limits partners' future activities to outside the area – which must be clearly defined – where the partnership does most of its business. Even this might be regarded as too strict in, say, the broking business in London, where most partnerships do their business in the City.

As you can see, there are complications in forming a partnership. You must be very aware of the risks and responsibilities you carry as a partner. Seek legal and financial advice before you make a decision to go ahead.

Never draw up the partnership agreement yourself without the help of a solicitor and an accountant. If you do so, you could be storing up a great deal of trouble for yourself.

6 Forming a company

If you are self-employed, the chances are that at some time you will consider setting up a company. The stage at which this becomes desirable will vary, depending on the nature of your business, but once it becomes at all complicated it is well worth taking some advice on forming a company.

The overriding advantage of having a company is that you can limit your liability for business debts. If you are in business alone – what is known as a 'sole trader' – or with a business partner, you are responsible for any debts you may incur. In contrast, a company has a legal identity of its own, quite separate from that of its owners, and their personal liability is limited to the value of the shares they have in it.

Since the war there have been three main Companies Acts, in 1947, 1967 and 1980, and these apply to all companies registered in Scotland, England and Wales (a separate law applies in Northern Ireland). These Acts distinguish between two forms of companies, public and private, but all limited companies have to file what is called an annual return at the Companies Registry. A new Companies Act came into force in 1982, bringing British company law practice into line with EEC directives. This actually cut back on the information small companies (with turnover less than £1.4 million, balance sheet total not more than £700,000 and less than fifty employees) have to file with the Registrar. They no longer have to put in a profit and loss account and need file only an abridged balance sheet. The Act also permitted companies to buy their own shares, a practice which was previously illegal. The other provisions in the Act do not affect small businesses to any great extent.

The private company

It is highly unlikely that your first step will be to form a public company. It is far more usual to begin as a private limited company. The basic difference between the two is that private companies are not allowed to offer their shares to the public; the Acts insist on strict control over the transfer of their shares. Also:

1 There must be at least two shareholders and not more than fifty, excluding any employees. There is of course nothing against employees being shareholders.
2 There must be at least one director and a company secretary.

It is clear that, if you are operating a business completely on your own, you will have to bring in at least one other person and give or sell them a share, however small, in the business before you can set up a company.

Having thought over the pros and cons, if you want to go ahead, go to a solicitor and ask him to help you prepare the company's memorandum of association and articles of association and some other statutory declarations and certificates. The memorandum of association is a kind of charter which sets out the activities of the company. The law states that it must include:

- The full name of the company, with 'Limited' as the last word.
- A description of the objects for which the company was formed.
- The address of the registered office of the company.
- Details of the capital structure of the company, including the category, number and denomination of the shares.
- A statement that the liabilities of the members are limited.

The articles of association set out the rules by which the company is managed. By law they must include:

- The rights of the shareholders.
- The rights and duties of the directors, including their borrowing powers.

A company can either draw up its own articles or adopt the ones laid down in

Schedule 1, Table A, of the Companies Act 1948. Before you can go ahead three more statements must be drawn up. They are:

- A declaration by the solicitor involved in forming the company, or the company secretary, or a director, stating that all the requirements of the two Companies Acts have been met.
- A notice of the location of the company's registered office which need not and often is not the same as the main place where the business is operated.
- A statement of the nominal capital of the company.

When you have all these documents you are ready to register your company. It costs £50 to register a new limited company and £40 to register a change of name. All individuals or companies trading under names which are not their own must register the name of the business at Companies House, 55–71 City Road, London EC1 1BB.

You will also have to pay a capital duty of £1 per £100 on the nominal capital. This means £1 for a company with £100 capital, £10 for £1,000, and so on.

The documents and the money should now be lodged with the Registrar of Companies at:

- For companies in England and Wales:
     The Registrar of Companies,
     Companies Registration Office,
     Crown Way, Maindy, Cardiff CF4 3UZ.
- For companies in Scotland:
     The Registrar of Companies,
     Exchequer Chambers,
     102 George Street. Edinburgh EH2 2DJ.
- For companies in Northern Ireland:
     The Registrar of Companies and Commerce,
     Law Courts Building,
     May Street, Belfast BT1 4XJ.

You can do all this yourself, but you will find the whole process much easier if you use a solicitor, or one of the businesses which specialise in setting up companies.

You can start trading as a private company as soon as the Registrar has studied all the documents and found them satisfactory. He will then issue a certificate of incorporation and you are in business.

The public limited company

The certificate of incorporation does not entitle you to trade as a public company. To do that, another document, a trading certificate, is also essential. As I have said, it is highly unlikely that from being a partnership or a sole trader you will become a public company. But this step may come in time, so it is worth considering a few of the differences between the private and the public company.

A private company may decide to go public for a number of reasons: to release the original capital invested in the business to the people who started the business; to pay for death duties; to finance expansion by selling shares to outsiders; to establish a public value for the shares of the company. To have securities and shares publicly quoted, it is necessary to 'go public'. These shares, whatever type they are (see Section five, chapter 1), are then 'traded' – that is, bought and sold on a recognized stock exchange.

The first visible step comes when a company offers its shares to the general public by issuing a prospectus; this is also run as an advertisement in a newspaper, with a coupon for anyone wishing to buy the shares. If more want to buy than there are shares available, the applications are all scaled down, and when a great number of people want a small number of shares there is in effect a raffle.

A lot of effort goes into preparing a prospectus, and there is no way of doing this without professional help. Anyway, Stock Exchange regulations require that a public issue of shares is made through a recognized issuing house. Most of the merchant banks have a subsidiary for this kind of business, and there are some independent specialist firms, too.

This is a very technical subject and requires expert advice. There are a few points to consider, however, before you spend money 'going public'. The Stock Exchange Council has very firm rules about what companies it will allow to have their shares quoted publicly:

1 The total market value of the securities quoted must be at least £500,000, and if more than one kind of share is issued any one kind must have a market value of £200,000. So a company must be of some size before going public.
2 Though you do not have to sell off all your shares – you can keep some, even the majority, for yourself and your family – you will be expected to issue at least 35 per cent to the public. There are some exceptions to this, but not many.
3 You will have to produce a balance sheet and a profits record for some years back – at least five is insisted upon at the moment. Companies with profits of less than £100,000 before tax are not especially liked.

As a rule, companies which come to the market have a market value of £2m–£3m and smaller companies pay very dearly for having a share quotation. In 1980, however, an unlisted securities market was opened (the USM) by the Stock Exchange and smaller companies can more cheaply be introduced there (see Section five, chapter one).

Once you have become a public company you are free to raise money in a variety of ways. But you will, of course, have to comply with all the stock exchange rules concerning disclosure of details of your business. These include half-yearly figures, total sales and profits figures, and a number of other business details which on balance you may prefer to keep secret. There are, of course, legal requirements which apply to *all* companies. If this is the case, you should not set up a company. There are other ways of raising money to finance expansion, as we will see in chapter 8 of this section.

7 Your company's annual accounts

If you set up a company, you will have to produce accounts once a year. You must draw up a balance sheet, showing what assets the company has and what liabilities, if any. You must also produce a profit and loss account, showing what income you have had during a particular period and what outgoings – the balance between the two indicating whether you have made a profit or a loss in your business.

Making up your own accounts is important, and vital to your business. But reading other companies' accounts is important to investors and businessmen. By a careful study of two years' figures, you can discover what has been happening in a company above and beyond the simple statement of profits.

The balance sheet

This tells you what your total assets and liabilities are at a particular moment in time. It should be worked out in what is called the 'double entry' system of book-keeping. This means that total assets will always equal total liabilities.

Let's take an example. Our company ABC Ltd is set up on 1 January. Its share capital is £10,000, which has been put up by its directors. As it begins to trade, its balance sheet will look very simple, with liabilities on the left and assets on the right:

Liabilities		*Assets*	
Ordinary shares	10,000	Cash	10,000

This, very simply, is the double entry system. The company has £10,000 in its bank account to finance its business – its sole asset; this money is owed to the shareholders who put the money up – its sole liability.

On its first day of trading, our company buys new machinery costing £2,000 and raw materials costing another £2,000. It pays cash for the raw materials, but buys the machinery on credit. If it were to draw up a balance sheet, then it would look like this:

Liabilities		Assets	
Long-term		*Fixed*	
Ordinary shares	£10,000	Machinery	£2,000
Current		*Current*	
Creditors	£2,000	Raw materials	£2,000
		Cash	£8,000
£12,000		**£12,000**	

Notice that the assets have become divided into *fixed* and *current*. Fixed assets are those which are unlikely to be changed except over a long period, like land, buildings and machinery. Current assets are either cash or assets which can be changed quickly into cash. Liabilities, in turn, are divided into *current* and *long-term*. Current will include anything owed to people outside the business – the bank, suppliers or the taxman. Long-term will include the money owed to the shareholders of the business and mortgages.

This picture of the business will change with every day that the company operates. To see what it will look like at the end of the first year's trading, let's suppose these transactions have taken place:

- You buy £20,000 worth of raw materials in the first year, but use only £15,000 for the goods you produce during the same period. The £5,000 left over will be shown as stock and work-in-progress in your balance sheet.
- You buy your factory premises, paying £3,000 cash and taking out a £7,000 mortgage.
- You rent a showroom after nine months and pay one year's rent of £1,600 in advance, so that you have nine months' rent in hand at the end of the year (£1,200).
- As you have not paid for all your raw materials, you still owe money to your creditors (£8,300) and to your bank (£1,300). These are shown under liabilities.
- Not everyone has paid you for the products you have sold to them, so a figure for your debtors (£12,000) will appear under assets in your balance sheet. You prudently assume that you may not always get

241

payment in full, so you allow something (£500) for bad debts, giving a net debtors' figure of £11,500.

- You have been using your £2,000 worth of machinery for a year, and you reckon that it will last for twenty years, so you make an allowance for depreciation (£100).
- You make a profit of £5,000 which is owned by your shareholders.

All these transactions must appear in one form or another *on both* sides of your balance sheet. This will probably be drawn up for you by an accountant, whose calculations will then be checked by an auditor, who is there to see that accounts are properly drawn up. Remember, every asset will be reflected in a liability. A balance sheet is not a profit and loss account; it simply shows the distribution of your assets and liabilities. Your balance sheet will look like the one shown below.

Liabilities		Assets	
Long-term		*Fixed*	
Ordinary shares	£10,000	Factory	£10,000
From profit and loss account	£5,000	Machinery (£2,000 at cost, less £100 depreciation)	£1,900
Mortgage loan	£7,000		
Current		*Current*	
Creditors	£8,300	Stock and work-in-progress	£5,000
Bank overdraft	£1,300	Debtors £12,000, less £500 provision for bad debts	£11,500
		Cash at bank	£2,000
		Advance payments	£1,200
Total	£31,600	Total	£31,600

This is of course a very simple balance sheet, nothing is allowed for wages, for example. The situation will become more complicated with each year. There are certain points you should bear in mind when looking at any balance sheet, however:

1 It only shows what is happening to a company at a *particular specified moment*. The situation can change rapidly, and it is not unknown for a company to manipulate its invoicing to show the company in the most favourable light. This is a bad thing to do and is difficult to keep repeating.

2 It shows only the financial situation. Only in the broadest way will it indicate how a business is doing – the state of the company's bank account, the stock situation, the level of debtors, and things like that.
3 It will not always set down assets at their current market value. Stocks may be valued at their original purchase price, so too may machines and factories. It doesn't really matter how you do your valuation, so long as you are consistent from year to year.

The profit and loss account

This is much simpler to prepare than your balance sheet. You simply tot up all your receipts and all your costs and the difference is your profit or loss.

Depending on the nature of your business and the size of it, the costs can be varied. You must include not only the costs of your raw materials and labour, but also any bank interest or promotion and distribution costs, for example.

8 Help with business expansion

If your business, partnership or company is doing well and you want to expand, it is possible that you will have to look outside for at least some of the money for that expansion.

First of all, work out exactly how much money you will need and how long you will want it for. Then draw up a plan to show the potential lenders. Be thoroughly familiar with this plan, so that you can answer any questions which may come up.

Lenders regard anything up to one year as short-term, between one and ten as medium-term and anything over that as long-term. If you make the wrong decision at the start about how long you want money for, you can get into a mess. If you get only short-term money, you may have to borrow later on penal terms to pay off your loan. On the other hand, you could tie up too many of your company's assets in long-term borrowing. *Take professional advice from your accountant right from the start.*

Getting a short-term loan

The bank
Your automatic first choice for short-term finance will be your bank. The

best and cheapest way of borrowing from a bank is to have an overdraft facility which you can use when and how you wish, as long as you keep within the limit you are given. It is usually relatively easy to renew the facility at the end of the agreed period, as long as your business prospects remain good. Remember, though, that if you borrow money at low rates of interest and you have to ask for an extension when they are high, this could damage your business.

The bank may also make you a 'term loan', at a fixed rate of interest for a fixed period of time, though generally they like these to be for more than a year.

Trade credit
It can be extremely helpful for the small businessman if his supplier will allow him to pay over a period. This kind of loan does not carry interest rates as such; in effect, the rate is the difference between what is paid over a period and the discount which will be offered to anyone who pays cash within, say, one month of delivery.

Discounts vary, but they are usually around 2½ per cent, which means that, in effect, you pay 30 per cent a year for the credit. This is far more than you would pay a bank, but it is nevertheless a popular means of getting credit and may suit a great number of businesses. Trade credits come in short, medium and long varieties.

Bills of exchange and acceptance credits
These are provided by the discount houses and the merchant banks, which you can read about briefly in Section one, chapter 2. They have been operating this type of credit for many years. A bill of exchange is a written promise to pay for goods received now at a later specified date. This date is normally three months in the future. The bills can, however, be bought and sold (i.e. are negotiable), so that the person who is owed the money need not wait the full three months for the payment; he can offer the bill to a bank or a discount house as security for a loan.

The bill can either be held by the purchaser until payment is due, in which case it is called a 'trade bill', or sold to the bank, in which case it is known as a 'bank bill'. Acceptance credits come in when a bank agrees to accept bills regularly from a particular company, for which the company pays the bank a commission charge. These are 'prime bank bills' and are bought – discounted – at the most favourable rates. Before an accepting house takes you on, it will investigate your credit-worthiness.

When bills are due for payment, whoever holds them gets the money in full and receives the amount of the discount as income. Discounts vary and are linked to interest rates, but they are a fairly cheap form of financing.

Factoring

A new service has grown up in recent years to help businesses over their short-term financial problems. It is called factoring, and it involves the allowing of credit against the invoices which a company sends to people who have bought its products. The factor gives money to the company in exchange for the invoices, usually about 80–90 per cent of their total value. This means that if the factor manages to collect all the debts, he will make a good profit, while the businessman will pay between ½ and 3½ per cent for the service. That may seem a lot, but the businessman is then rid of all the problems of chasing people for money, and the saving in administrative costs can often make up for the percentage lost.

Besides, the factor is taking all the risk. Some companies do not like their customers to know they use a factor, because before taking on an invoice the factor will want to investigate the credit-worthiness of the customer. Some customers may resent this. It also costs money, and the factor's client may find he is paying up to 25 per cent in the early stages of the service. This charge falls as the relationship is established.

You are likely to need an annual turnover of £100,000 and an average invoice value of £100 before a factor will take you on, so it is a limited but useful form of financial help. You can have confidential invoice factoring, whereby the customer does not know you use a factor, but to maintain confidentially a great deal of the administration will remain in your own hands and may be more costly in the end, even though the initial cost of the service may be lower.

Factoring companies offer a wide range of services; you will see advertisements in the paper. Write to them if you are interested.

Medium- and long-term finance

Though some sources of finance are limited to either medium- or long-term loans, it is well to put these together: the basis of the arrangement is similar whatever length of time you are seeking the loan for. The exception to this is the raising of equity capital, which means bringing outside partners into your business, which you do through the Stock Market, the Unlisted Securities Market, the over-the-counter markets, the business expansion scheme, or by private arrangement.

The bank

It is unlikely that you will be offered a long-term overdraft, but the clearing banks have been moving into medium- and longer-term loans in a big way in the past five years. Small businesses can now get loans specially tailored to meet their needs, and funds from £2,000 to £250,000 are available for suitable cases. Repayment can be anything up to a period of ten years.

Before you get any advance at all from any bank, you will be expected to show that lending money to you is a good business proposition. This does not simply mean showing your past record and reasonable estimates for future business, but also that you run your business in a proper manner, with proper financial control.

Even if all that is satisfactory, you may still not get a loan, because the banks prefer a few reasonably large borrowers to a greater number of small ones.

Hire purchase and leasing arrangements

If your company is very small, these may be your best bet. Hire purchase is offered in exactly the same way as to individuals, but tends to be for rather larger amounts. Certain companies specialize in this kind of business, including some of the factoring companies mentioned earlier. Finance companies also handle it.

You can also lease rather than buy equipment, though there can be tax disadvantages in doing this. If you buy on HP you will be treated by the taxman as if you were the owner of the equipment and will be entitled to any investment grants or allowances which may be available. If you lease, it is the person doing the leasing who gets any such allowances.

There may be problems, in any case, if you are very small. The lessor companies may be unwilling to do business with you, so you will have to be very persuasive. Make sure, too, that you know exactly what rates of interest you are being charged.

Mortgages

You can get these for any length of time, but they are most useful as a way of getting long-term finance. They work like any mortgage, with a repayment date and a rate of interest. You will be able to raise up to 70 or 75 per cent of the valuation put upon the fixed assets of the business, and as values rise you may be able to extend the loan.

Insurance companies and pension funds are the main lenders of mortgages to businesses. The building societies are severely restricted when it comes to lending to industry. Again, your whole operation will be looked at; it is not enough just to have sound premises. You may find it difficult to borrow less than £50,000.

Sale and lease-back

This is in some ways the same as getting a mortgage, except that you give up your right to the freehold of any premises which are covered by such an operation. You sell the freehold for a sum of money and then take out a lease – usually a long one – on the same premises, so that you can continue to run your business from them. After that, a rent is paid to the freeholder. The rent includes an interest charge, which fluctuates with interest rates.

Sale and lease-back arrangements may be available to anyone with premises worth more than £25,000, generally from insurance companies and property companies.

Government loan guarantees for small businesses

These schemes are operated by the banks, which scrutinise your proposal, decide whether or not it is sound, then, if it is, pass you application on to the Department of Industry. Your proposal would be one which the bank itself would normally *not* lend on.

There is an approved format and a considerable amount of detail is required about the directors, the amount of money required and why, the business, current profits performance and some forward projections. Loans are for up to £75,000, repayable over two to seven years. Monthly or quarterly payments of interest must begin immediately, but sometimes the repayment of the capital can be delayed for up to two years. These loans are relatively expensive.

Public sector funds

There are a great number of these, well over 100 and they include central and local government, some agencies and the European Economic Community. As a general rule, funds are mainly available for local and regional projects. To find out about them, read *Financial Incentives and Assistance for Industry – a Comprehensive Guide*. This is published free by Arthur Young, McClelland Moore & Co., Rolls House, 7 Rolls Buildings, Fetter Lane, London EC4A 1NL.

Industrial & Commercial Finance Corporation Ltd (ICFC)

This company was formed in 1945 and is now the major source of finance for small businesses, both new and existing. It is owned 15 per cent by the Bank of England and 85 per cent by the English and Scottish clearing banks. It concentrates on privately-owned businesses and will lend anything from £5,000 to £2 million. Most of its loans, however, are for around £100,000.

Do not be put off by the fact that ICFC on the whole makes rather large loans: it will consider all applications. If you want a loan, make sure that you present your case in a full and proper manner and take advice from an accountant as to the way to show your business in the best possible light. ICFC has a great deal of experience and can provide you with a full financial package to cover your particular needs.

This brief outline by no means includes all the available sources of finance. There are many excellent books which will give you a great deal of detail on the subject. There are also management courses you can attend which will help you understand how to run your business efficiently. The commercial banks, the merchant banks (accepting houses), discount houses and a variety of governmental and private organizations exist today to help the small businessman or woman. A practical starting point, however, is your bank manager.

Useful organizations

Here is a list of just a few of the organizations which may be able to help:

Accepting Houses Committee
Roman Wall House, 1–2 Crutched Friars, London EC3N 2NT (01-481 1896)

Banking Information Service
10 Lombard Street, London EC3V 9AR (01-626 8486)

British Bankers Association
10 Lombard Street, London EC3V 9AP (01-623 5511)

British Export Houses Association
69–75 Cannon Street, London EC4N 5AB (01-248 4444)

British Overseas and Commonwealth Banks Association
10 Clement Lane, London EC4N 7AB (01-623 7500)

British Overseas Trade Board
1 Victoria Street, London SW1H 0ET (01-222 7877)

Charterhouse Investment Trust Ltd
1 Paternoster Row, London EC4M 7DH (01-248 3999)

Department of Trade and Industry (Head Office)
Millbank Tower, Millbank, London SW1P 4QU (01-834 2255)

Equipment Leasing Association
18 Upper Grosvenor Street, London W1X 6PD (01-491 2783)

European Investment Bank
2 Place de Metz, Luxembourg (Luxembourg 435011)

Exports Credits Guarantee Department
Aldermanbury House, Aldermanbury,
London EC2P 2EL (01-606 6699)

Finance Houses Association
18 Upper Grosvenor Street, London W1X 6PD (01-491 2783)

Foreign Banks and Affiliates Association
16 St Helens Place, London EC3A 6BT (01-283 1080)

ICFC
91 Waterloo Road, London SE1 8XP (01-928 7822)
(There are also some local offices)

Issuing Houses Association
Roman Wall House, 1–2 Crutched Friars, London EC3N 2NT
(01-481 1896)

London Discount Houses Association
39 Cornhill, London EC3U 3NU (01-623 1020)

National Research Development Corporation
PO Box 236, Kingsgate House,
66–74 Victoria Street, London SW1E 6SL (01-828 3400)

Small Business Capital Fund
88 Baker Street, London W1M 1DC (01-486 5021)

Most major towns now have a Small Firms Centre and you can find its address in the telephone book. The Council for Small Industries in Rural Areas deals with places where the central population is under 10,000. Its services are available to businesses employing fewer than 20 people. The local offices are usually in the county towns. If you have any problems in locating an organization which might help you, go first to your local chamber of commerce.

9 Women at work

There is no reason today why a woman should expect to do less well in her career or accept less money for the same work than a man, just because she is a woman. The Sex Discrimination and Equal Pay Acts have seen to that.

Equal pay

The original Equal Pay Act laid down that women were entitled to equal pay with men if they were doing the same or broadly similar work, or if their job had been given the same value as a man's under a job evaluation scheme. It did not incorporate of the idea of equal pay for work of equal value. All this changed, however, after several women had taken their cases to the European Court using the equal value concept, which applies under Common Market regulations. As a result of their success, the British government changed the rules to include the work of equal value. It has to be admitted, however, that cases are not always easy to prove to the satisfaction of the industrial tribunal, however clearcut they may appear at first sight.

The rules apply to all work, manual and non-manual, full- and part-time, in factories, shops, offices and anywhere else. But as a rule you can only compare your work with a man working in the same establishment or for the same employer (though there are exceptions).

Taking action

If you think you have a case, the first step is to try to settle the matter with your employer, either personally, through your trade union if you are a member, or through the official arbitration body, ACAS (Advisory Conciliation and Arbitration Service).

If this fails, you can go to an industrial tribunal, which will settle the matter, and you can appeal if you think the tribunal has been unfair. Tribunals cost nothing. They are not frightening, and you can represent yourself or use a lawyer. *It is better to have a lawyer, but make sure the lawyer has experience of tribunals.*

You can also seek the advice of the Equal Opportunities Commission, Overseas House, Quay Street, Manchester M3 3HN, before taking action. They may decide to back you officially.

Job opportunities

The Sex Discrimination Act, which the Equal Opportunities Commission also monitors, deals with those cases where people feel they are losing out in their jobs, or have been refused jobs, just because of their sex. This Act applies *equally to both sexes,* though it is women who more often encounter discrimination.

Discrimination has been defined in five ways:

1 *Direct sex discrimination.* This means treating a man or woman less favourably at work just because of their sex. This includes passing someone over for promotion or refusing them a job, simply because of their sex.
2 *Indirect sex discrimination.* An example of this is demanding a qualification for a job which is not really relevant, but which only one sex is likely to have: for example, insisting that a hotel receptionist has an O-level in domestic science, a subject which girls rather than boys usually take, or that a trainee manager in a shop has an O-level in woodwork, a subject which mostly only boys study at the moment.
3 *Direct marriage discrimination.* This means treating a person less favourably because he or she is married. This includes sacking someone because they have got married.
4 *Indirect marriage discrimination.* This includes making conditions of employment which make it more difficult for married people to apply. This could arise, for example, if an employer refused to take on anyone with children.
5 *Victimization.* If an employee was treated less favourably than other employees because he or she had asserted rights under the Equal Pay Act, or the Sex Discrimination Act, this would be victimization.

It is obvious that this Act is particularly important for women. It

250

opened up the whole area of job opportunities for women. Better jobs means more money and an increase in the economic power of women.

Taking action
As in disputes over equal pay, you can take your complaint to an industrial tribunal, but common sense dictates that you try to settle the matter with your employer before taking this step. Again, it is worth getting in touch with the Equal Opportunities Commission before taking action.

Working women

If you are a woman, the chances are that there are different considerations for you in choosing a job than there are for a man.

If you are single or your children are grown up, your case probably does not differ much from a man's – though the chances are you will still have some extra domestic responsibilities. You should choose your job taking account of these.

Remember that going out to work will probably mean that your housekeeping will cost more. You will have less time for cooking and therefore be less able to take advantage of, say, cheaper cuts of meat, which need long cooking; you may need a cleaner; you may need someone to take care of the children after school before you get home, or even full-time if they are less than school age.

Your wages may push your family income into the higher tax brackets (read the section on tax and married people), and you may have to take a job which allows you to take time off in case of family illness, which may effectively rule out a lot of jobs.

These are just a few of the things most women have to think about when they take jobs. Unless you are very dedicated, the chances are you will not want a job which means that you actually lose money after you have paid out the extras. So sit down and work out just what financial benefit you and your family will get from your working and ask yourself whether it is worthwhile.

I'm not suggesting that women with domestic responsibilities shouldn't go out to work – I have always worked myself – but the hidden costs make the real contribution to improving the family's standard of living far less than it appears when you just consider the salary you are offered.

You should try to ensure that there is some 'tiredness money' left over from your wages for yourself – money for little extras which give you a lift and make you feel that your extra effort is worthwhile. This could be money for the hairdresser, a few extra clothes, or an extra treat or holiday for the family which you all enjoy and which saves you doing the chores. These are all important in keeping your family contented and keeping yourself happy at work.

Section three
Family finance

1 The wedding

Who pays for what at the wedding

Fashions in marriage change and today it is less common for a father to 'splash out' in a big way for his daughter's wedding. But some still do, and anyway most couples plan some kind of celebration to go with their marriage ceremony, whether it takes place in a church, chapel, synagogue, mosque or registry office.

One decision where money should not be a consideration is whether to have a religious ceremony or a registry office wedding. One expense which is quite unavoidable in either is the marriage licence. If you want to get married quickly – that is, within twenty-four hours – you will need a 'special licence', which costs £6.50 for the entry of notice, plus £33 for the licence; but if you are prepared to wait three weeks or more you will pay £6.50 (£13.00 if you do not both live in the same district) for a marriage certificate.

The registry office ceremony is usually cheaper than the religious ceremony, but that is obviously not the point. Those who are religious will automatically choose a wedding in church. A simple church ceremony is not expensive, but as you add an organist, a choir, extra flowers and church bells, the bill rises accordingly. In most churches, the officiating minister, vicar, priest or rabbi must be paid a fee, often according to what the couple feel they can afford. It may be waived if the couple has strong church connections. Apart from this fee, all costs are optional.

It will not come as a surprise to many people that the average wedding and reception usually end up costing far more than was budgeted. The problem is remembering everything, and very often a significant item is overlooked until the last minute.

It isn't very romantic, I know, but it is best to sit down and work out all the possible costs before you embark on an elaborate wedding. Tradition has it that the major expenses are borne by the bride's family, a remnant of the old dowry tradition. More and more today, however, the bride and bridegroom's family share them – a trend which is only common sense when women work and make a contribution to the family budget after the marriage.

The first decision to be made is how big the reception should be. If a big wedding reception is going to mean, say, not enough for a deposit on a house, sensible couples are going to think twice and ask for the money instead. However, weddings are very often not really for the benefit of the couple involved but for their families and friends. So rule number one is try to not to upset anyone, but don't give into pressure, particularly if you are going to be paying for it for years, when the memory of the day will have dimmed and other more mundane but essential items of living have had to be sacrificed.

If you decide to go ahead and have a reception:

- Just as in any other transaction, get several estimates for the reception.
- Check the cost carefully – are the charges for food, drinks and service all included. Is VAT included? Does the estimate leave you open to any extra unforeseen charges?
- Do not spend more than about a quarter of your total budget on the bride's, bridesmaids' and bride's mother's outfits.
- Make sure you know the cost of the invitations, any announcements, special transportation. Get several estimates for the cost of photographs.
- Remember, formal dress for everyone, including the bride, can be hired.
- Add about 25 per cent to your budget for the things you haven't thought about.

If the costs are being borne in the traditional way, by far the biggest bill goes to the bride's family. Here are the items the bride usually pays for:

The church fees (the officiating minister, organist, choir, bell-ringers, etc.).	Bridesmaids' clothes.
The flowers in the church.	Invitations.
The cost of the reception.	Announcements.
Presents for the bridesmaids.	Transport.
	Photographers.

The groom pays for:

The bride's engagement and wedding rings.
The marriage licence.
The stag night dinner.
The bride's flowers, any flowers for the mothers and buttonholes for the men.
Presents for the best man and the ushers.
The honeymoon.

Engagement and wedding rings

This is a tricky one. You can save money, but you must ask yourself whether an economy in this area will get you off to a bad start with a reputation for being stingy. A way out is to go window-shopping beforehand, deciding jointly on the price range, and sticking to it. Then:

1 Choose a reputable jeweller.
2 Tell him the sort of price you want to pay.
2 Try to pay cash.
4 Insure the ring.

Incidentally, having a wedding ring is only a custom, it is not essential, and today some people do without one altogether. In contrast, many men wear wedding rings today. The bride pays for it.

Saving on your wedding and honeymoon
1 Have the reception at home. Make it simple. Do the catering yourself. Without looking mean you can control how much drink you need buy.
2 Have a buffet, or even just cocktail snacks, rather than a meal. Many guests prefer the informality.
3 Buy a wedding dress you can wear again. The same goes for the bridesmaids' outfits.
4 Plan your honeymoon well ahead. This may well be the one time you don't want a package tour with other people, but individual packages can be arranged by reputable travel companies and by booking ahead you can save money on individual air tickets (see Section one, chapter 17).

Wedding presents

Wedding presents are often a headache – and not just for those buying them. Ending up with twenty-five toast racks or twelve pepper mills is no joke, and a quantity of household linen that does not match your colour scheme is disappointing. And it's just as disappointing for the giver if his gift is not appreciated.

The couple must make the first move and produce a wedding present list, which can be left with a department store or stores. This should be as detailed as possible, indicating preferred brands, designs, colours and quantity. It should also cover a wide price range to cater for all pockets. If no list is available then:

1 Decide how much you want to spend. Don't be competitive with other guests when you can't afford it. It doesn't impress anyone.
2 If you know the couple well, try to match their tastes, not your own.
3 Try to fit your gift to the way they will live. Sophisticated designs are wasted on those who live a rural life, or garden implements on flat dwellers.
4 Don't give money, unless you are a very close relative. It's in bad taste.
5 If you are really stuck, give a gift voucher from a reputable store with a

wide range of goods. These are always appreciated to fill in gaps among gifts.

A second wedding, incidentally, is usually much cheaper. It is quieter, clothes are less elaborate and receptions smaller. Very often the couple will say that they do not want presents.

2 Home and family

Setting up and running a home

The build-up to marriage, the ceremony itself and the honeymoon are often the most exciting period in our lives. But the setting-up of a home and the starting of a family soon brings realism, and many couples find that the early years of married life are financially the most difficult they ever face. The pooling of resources can bring a pleasant feeling of financial security, but it may not be long before the considerable expense involved in setting up and running a home begins to be felt, particularly if the couple is suddenly reduced to living on one wage with an (expensive) addition to the family. Let's look at some of the costs facing a young couple living in, say, the north-east of England.

The house. If you buy one at around the current average price for a new house of £31,460, you will probably have to find at least £3,146 deposit (10 per cent) before you can go ahead with the purchase. It is a good idea, if possible, to try to get this money together before marrying. If you can start off in your own home, the financial strains and stresses will be less than otherwise, and you will always have an asset which can be cashed in in case of emergencies. The building society will fix the maximum loan they are prepared to offer you, but it is only sensible to try to keep your repayments to no more than one quarter of your gross income before tax.

Rates, gas, electricity, telephone, water rates. It is impossible to set a figure for these, for they will vary with every house. But work them out properly for your own home and take care not to underestimate. You should be able to find out what the rates are from the estate agents who are selling you the house. Each house has a rateable value of £X; the rates due are expressed as Yp in the £1. The Y element may change annually. Your local authority will give you the rate.

Travelling costs to work. Is it cheaper by car? Can you both use it?

A house or flat is not a home without *furniture and essential fittings*, and you should set out to buy these carefully (see Section one, chapter 11). But it is very difficult today to find even the bare essentials for a house or flat for less than £2,000. Of course, you can always buy some things on hire purchase, but remember that you are probably already buying your house in this way, so take great care not to over-extend yourself. You can always save by buying second-hand.

You may decide you want to start a *family* straightaway, or this may happen without any planning. Even if you have decided to wait a year or two, try to work out your budget to allow for the arrival of a child.

To make sure that your marriage gets off to a good financial start, you should both be entirely honest with one another about your wages or salary. Those marriages where husband or wife refuses to tell their partner what they earn, cannot start off in an atmosphere of mutual trust. I do not suggest you pool all your resources (see Section one, chapter 6 on bank accounts), but that you pool a certain amount, keeping back agreed amounts for your own private spending. When you marry, you will have to follow the rules for personal budgeting far more closely than you did when you were single. If you begin sensibly, quarrels about money need never arise.

Wives and children are entitled to the maintained by a husband or father, but they have no entitlement in law to a specific amount from him. When working out the areas of responsibility as far as payments go, the husband ought to make sure his wife has enough to cover hers, and for him to adjust payments upwards as bills increase, or circumstances change. Wherever possible, some small personal allowance should be included; there is nothing worse for a wife who does not work than to have absolutely nothing for her personal spending. Wage and salary increases should be shared out properly as well. Too many wives face a 'wages freeze' long after the husband has received a rise.

Family planning

The possibility of planning the maximum size of our families lies within the reach of all of us today. Gone are the days when contraceptives were costly. Every kind of contraception is free under the National Health Service if your doctor supplies the service, apart from the condom, which varies in price.

If you join your local Family Planing Association office and pay your subscription, you will be able to get the condom free there as well.

If you have decided that you absolutely do not want any more children under *any* circumstances, you can consider the possibility of sterilization. There is usually a waiting list, which can be up to five years in some areas, for a vasectomy, as the male form of sterilization is called. You can also have the operation done privately, if you wish. The cost will vary to some extent, depending on how quickly you wish to have it done. At the end of 1984, the cost was around £65.

Female sterilization is also possible, but is much more complicated than vasectomy and not so often recommended. Again, where this is decided upon, it can be done free on the NHS. Otherwise, private charities, like the Well Woman Clinic, charge £125 where a local anaesthetic is use, or £140 for a general.

Abortion

Sometimes all the precautions fail and you find you are going to have a baby which you have not planned for and do not want. When this happens, most women, especially if they are married, decide to make the best of it and go ahead and have the baby. In some cases, however, for a variety of reasons, the woman involved, with the agreement of her husband if she is married, may feel that under no circumstances can she face the prospect of a child.

Today the law allows abortion in certain conditions on the National Health Service. In these cases it is free. But it is not enough in this country simply to want an abortion. We do not have abortion on demand. It is necessary for two doctors to agree that there are sound medical grounds for performing an abortion. These need not be strictly physical grounds, however, and include cases where the two doctors judge there are, or could be, serious emotional as well as physical risks to the mother and the baby, or to the family into which the baby would arrive.

Abortions on the NHS can sometimes be delayed, in certain parts of Britain, for so long that there would be a serious physical risk to the mother if one was performed. This can also happen if a woman does not discover she is pregnant for some months. In cases like these, where the grounds for an abortion can be proved, it is possible to get an abortion more quickly in the private sector of medicine. Charities like the Well Woman Clinic will perform abortions for £133, but the cost may be between £200 and £400 from a private clinic. Don't think that by paying for an abortion the operation is any safer than under the National Health. So, if you do want an abortion, try to get one on the NHS.

The cost of having a baby

Fortunately, the arrival of a baby is a joyous event for most people. The vast majority of babies, planned or unplanned, are welcomed into the family unit. Nevertheless, now that people do have a choice about how many children they want to have, they tend to have fewer than the average family of the past. Many parents today prefer to have fewer children and cater for them all adequately rather than have more and have to make serious sacrifices to maintain them properly.

The ideal family size is something we all have our own views on, and the best way to bring up children is the subject of as many divergent opinions as there are families. Some may feel that it is important for a family to be limited, so that the children can live in a house rather than a flat, be educated privately, go on annual holidays and have plenty of clothes. Others feel that material possessions are not so important and that the love of a large family more than makes up for a few sacrifices. Whatever your own view, it is a good idea to look at just what a child can cost in money terms from when it is born till it reaches the school-leaving age of sixteen.

Any child born in 1985 is likely to cost its parents around £10,000, allowing for inflation, from pregnancy to the age of sixteen, taking into account all the state benefits, like maternity grants and child benefits. This figure does not, of course, take into account any of the mother's lost earnings, if she gives up a job after having children. If all benefits were simply maintained at the 1984–5 level, which they will not be, the state would contribute over £6,000 to the upkeep of the child from birth to 16.

The average child – and remember no one is actually average – has a state education, first at a primary school and then at a comprehensive after the age of eleven. At the comprehensive, it generally requires three sets of school clothing or uniform and games kit.

Let's start first of all with the pregnancy. All treatment for pregnancy, including the confinement and after-care, is free on the NHS. Prescriptions for pregnant women are free, and this concession continues until the baby is one year old. Dental treatment for the mother is also free for the same length of time. Milk is also available free to pregnant women who already have two children under the age of five.

Think carefully before embarking on private treatment in pregnancy. All too often you will be paying out unnecessarily.

Private confinements
You can of course choose to have your baby outside the National Health Service and there will always be some people who prefer to do this, particularly as it is increasingly difficult today to persuade NHS doctors to let you have your baby in your own home, as some women prefer.

First of all, remember that pregnancy and childbirth are not illnesses, but perfectly natural conditions which are assisted as needs be by doctors and midwives. There is no need to pay for expensive medical services which will almost certainly not be needed. The only reasonable case for private treatment is for those mothers who want privacy desperately, and this can sometimes be secured even on the NHS. Amenity beds are available in some hospitals at a small cost of about £10 a day for a single room, or about £5 a day for a bed in a small ward with two or three others. Check with your local hospital before you consider private treatment.

If you do decide to go privately, the consultant's fees may cost as much as £300. This does not include blood tests, X-rays or anaesthetist's fees if you turn out to need a Caesarian delivery, or an epidural injection – a local anaesthetic designed to ease discomfort. It does include your postnatal examination.

If private beds are available in National Health hospitals, they can cost from £100 a day in an ordinary district hospital to £140 in a London teaching hospital, if you have your own consultant. A nursing home can cost anything up to £225 a day, but a fee between £75 and £150 is usual for a private room, or £35 upwards for a bed in a small ward. Some nursing homes operate a scheme whereby you pay for your bed and make an extra payment should you need a consultant at the birth. The length of time you will stay in hospital varies. Some hospitals and homes will let you go home in little more than twenty fours, if there are no complications, others insist you stay a week or ten days, so the cost could be anything between £500 and around £2,000. Your NHS family doctor can supervise the birth in a nursing home and is not permitted to charge a fee, but if he is unable to attend and you use the nursing home doctor, he will be acting on a private basis and you will have to pay.

Medical insurance policies do not normally cover childbirth, but some do include emergency treatment like Caesarians. Check this point if you have private medical insurance.

Pregnancy and birth

A great deal can be free if you so choose during pregnancy, but there are nevertheless some unavoidable costs, mainly for clothes. Taking some average prices from the Mothercare catalogue, the costs look like this:

2 support bras (£3.99 each)	£7.98
2 girdles (£4.50 each)	£9.00
2 nursing bras (£4.50 each)	£9.00
2 pair support tights (£1.99 each)	£3.98
1 pair corduroy trousers	£12.99
2 tops (£12.99 each)	£25.98
2 maternity dresses (average £50.00)	£100.00
2 maternity slips (£3.99 each)	£7.98

This would be a basic minimum for most women for a first baby and it totals £176.71. You could easily spend double that. A basic list for the baby is at the top of page 259.

This brings us to a grand total of £541.22 for mother's and baby's basic needs: second and subsequent babies come cheaper.

The government has recognized that having a baby can break the family budget, so it has devised several allowances to help parents out. First, there is the maternity grant. At the present time, this is a lump sum of £25 and goes to every mother who has been resident in Britain for more than twenty-six weeks in the year before the week of the birth.

basic layette (clothes, nappies, etc)	£53.80
extra clothing	£30.00 (minimum)
cot and mattress	£65.00
baby bath	£6.75
2 blankets, 4 sheets	£18.30
carry-cot and transporter (£50–£100)	£75.00 (average)
high chair	£34.99
playpen	£37.50
potty	£1.99
bottle pack	£6.99
bouncer cradle	£13.99
toys, rattles, etc.	£20.00

But this is only a small contribution to the total cost. There is a further allowance to women who have worked and paid fifty weeks' full stamps in the twelve months ending fourteen weeks before the baby is due. The formula is a complicated one and you should enquire at the DHSS to see if you are eligible. The allowance is paid for a maximum of eighteen weeks, starting eleven weeks before the expected date of birth. At present the rate is £25 a week, so if paid in full the allowance is worth a total of £450, but for every week that the prospective mother works after the tenth week before the birth she loses a week's allowance. If you wish to apply, you should get in touch with your local office of the Department of Health and Social Security or clinic. To collect either benefit, you will have to produce a certificate of expected confinement, which your doctor or hospital will provide.

Maternity leave

You may decide that you want to go on working after your baby is born. In recent years, women's rights at work have improved a great deal and it is now forbidden by law to dismiss a woman simply because she is pregnant, whether she is married or not.

It is also the law that women are entitled to return to their jobs any time within twenty-nine weeks of the date of confinement. And even this period may sometimes be extended by four weeks, if the mother or baby requires it.

If you are pregnant and you want your job back after having your baby, you must have had the job for two years and stay at work at least until the beginning of the eleventh week before you expect the baby. You must also tell your employer in writing that you wish to return at least three weeks before you leave. If you don't do this and then change your mind, it is too late; you have surrendered your rights. Women have not had these rights for very long and from time to time there is pressure on the government to reduce or abolish their protection. So do not assume that your rights will remain as set out here: check the position if you are pregnant and wish to return to work after the birth of your baby.

- *This means that a woman can quite legally take 39 weeks away from work to have a baby without risking getting the sack, or not getting back the same job she previously held.*

The cost of bringing up a child

From birth to five years

By now the baby has arrived, and if you have received the full maternity allowances from the government you will just about cover your costs. It is with the birth that the expenses really start, though many couples find that friends and relatives are generous in their presents, especially for first babies.

By the time your child is five, you can reckon on having spent something like the following, assuming that in all health matters you use the National Health Service.

food (£6 a week)	£1,560
clothing (£80 a year)	£400
nursery heating	£110
bed (after two years)	£80
holidays (£50 a year)	£250
toys, books, presents (£1 a week)	£260

Look at the individual items. You will see that they are not extravagant; indeed, you could very easily spend more, though the average cost per baby will come down with each new arrival, as clothes, prams, nappies, baby equipment and toys can be passed from one baby to another.

From five to eleven

The child is now ready for school. The food bill goes down slightly if the child is having school dinners, but the clothing bill goes up and items like pocket money begin to appear. I will discuss how to work out allowances for children later on. Here is what the bill may look like between the ages of five and eleven:

food (£6 a week)	£1,875
clothing (£135 a year)	£810
pocket money (average of £1 a week)	£312
school meals, holidays, other school expenses	£500
bicycle	£50
toys, presents, books, etc.	£250

This means that, by the time the child goes on to secondary school, he or she has cost the parents around £6,500, before allowing for child benefit.

From eleven to sixteen

During the years from eleven to sixteen the child gradually gets more expensive. All children differ in their interests, but a common pattern goes like this:

food (£7 a week)	£2,340
clothing (£3 a week)	£936
school uniform, games gear (three changes)	£500
fares (a year)	£240
pocket money (average £2 a week)	£624
holidays, school trips, projects	£480
bicycle	£80
books, presents, etc.	£450
musical instruments and tuition	£284

This is the kind of overall picture you will see at present prices, if you are educating your children through the state system and using the National Health Service. This situation is quite different – and much more expensive – if you decide to educate your children privately.

Child benefits

The sums above are a bit pessimistic, because they do not take into account the fact that mothers will have been getting child benefits from the moment the child is born. These benefits were introduced in April 1977, and the old tax allowances, which had generally gone to the father, were phased out, except for a few special cases. For the year November 1984–5 the rate is £6.85 for each child from birth until it reaches sixteen, or finishes schooling, if that is later. Single or divorced parents get an extra £4.25 a week for the first child.

I have worked out child benefits as if they will be unchanged from the time the baby is born until he or she is sixteen. Of course, this will not happen. All benefits increase with inflation, though not always by as much as it. These increases are likely to be balanced out, however, by increased costs.

The costs are typical for a first child. Later children come cheaper, as layettes and cots, etc. can be used by successive children.

Educating your child privately

Many parents set the private education of their children above very many other aims they have in life. It is a tremendous commitment, particularly if a couple has more than one child, and quite severe financial sacrifices may be called for. The private education of one child can add up to well over £20,000 more to the cost of bringing up a child. And that will only include straight fees to the end of compulsory education at the age of sixteen; it does not allow for school uniform, and travelling costs if your child is at boarding school.

Private schooling is still popular, despite rising school fees. At present (1984), parents of more than 300,000 children are choosing to send them to one of the 1,000-plus independent schools in the country. The fees may seem high, but they are not as high as they might be, because most of them are charitable trusts and so are eligible for tax relief. Should their status as trusts change, fees are likely to rise sharply.

The Independent Schools Information Service puts the average cost per term for boys who board at over £1,000, with £600 plus for day boys. Girls' schools are generally cheaper, but there are wide variations within the average. London day schools, for example, tend to charge way above the average. These are not often the sort of fees that even the relatively well-off can contemplate paying from taxed income, particularly where there is more than one child to be considered.

School fees generally rise by about 12½ per cent a year, though between 1975 and 1976 they increased by as much as a third in some cases, and there is no guarantee that rises like these will not recur. At the beginning of 1982, top boarding schools were charging an average of £3,500, but it was possible to board for a little under £2,000 in the minor schools. Day school fees averaged around £2,500 for leading schools, £1,500 to £2,000 for those lower down the scale and a few less than £1,000. London had the most expensive day schools and girls' schools tended to be marginally cheaper than boys'.

As with all things, you get what you pay for. The higher the fees the more the facilities and range of subjects. You may not always have to pay full fees. Quite apart from scholarships and bursaries awarded by some of the schools themselves, places at some public schools are paid for by central government and local authorities. There are some ways, however, of cutting the cost.

1 Take out a life assurance policy, designed to help with school fees. Such policies work quite simply, and the terms vary, depending on how much money you are trying to raise. What usually happens is that you pay a certain premium until the child reaches school age, or the age at which you wish to send him or her to an independent school. This entitles you to a sum of money for a set number of years which must be used for schooling. Once you start to draw the money, the premium goes up. The problem is to decide just how much help you will need. In any case, the chances are that, in addition to the money from the policy, you will have to dip into your own pocket as well before the child's school days are over.

When you take out the policy, make some enquiries about the current level of fees at two or three schools you would like your child to attend. Add 12½ per cent on the fees for each year before the child starts school to get more or less the starting fee for your child. Then work out the total cost over the years, adding a further 12½ per cent for each year, and try to get a policy which will give you an annual sum which is an average of that. You draw the amount you need each year. The premiums will be quite high, but a policy like this spreads the cost of schooling over, say, 20 years and the total proceeds from the policy will be far more than the premiums you pay. Take out the policy as soon as possible after the child is born. The later you leave it the more you will pay, and you may find that you are still paying the higher premiums long after your child has left school. You may be able to switch it from one child to another, and if you do not draw the money as school fees, it works like an ordinary endowment policy.

2 *A covenant.* You may have an elderly relative who wishes to help you with school fees. He or she can arrange for a payment to be made to you on behalf of the child. Covenants can be made for a variety of purposes and last for seven years (see later in this chapter). It is unlikely that a covenant will cover all your education costs, but it can be a considerable help and very tax-efficient.

3 Try to get a contribution to the fees from your company if your job is such that you have to have your children educated at boarding school. This applies to people who have to travel a lot, or get overseas postings to places which are unsuitable for children at school or where educational standards are very low.

School fees when you are educating privately are only the beginning. You can buy a £12 railcard, if your child has to travel a long way often, but even so, if your child is at boarding school, his travelling expenses and your own for visits to the school are becoming increasingly expensive. School uniforms are usually more extensive and expensive than for children in the state sector. All these items can add a further few hundred pounds to your total annual school bill. Do not forget them when making your calculations of the total cost.

Advice about schools, help with fees
If you are undecided about which school to send your child to, the Independent Schools Information Service, Albany Mansions, Victoria Street, London SW1 (telephone 01-222 7353), may be able to help you. *The Public and Preparatory Schools Year Book* and *The Girls Schools Year Book*, both published by A. & C. Black, may also be useful. These set out some details about the independent schools, but not their fees, which can change from term to term. You can usually find the books in the reference section of your local library.

Crises arise in all our lives, and school fees which have been managed on the family budget can suddenly become a great burden. This can happen in cases of redundancy, divorce or death. You need not despair, however, as some help is available through charitable trusts. The Educational Grant Advisory Service, founded in 1862, deals with about 3,000 applicants a year and grants some form of help to all but about 500 of them. It operates from The Family Welfare Association, 501 Kingsland Road, London E8 4AU (telephone 01-254 6251). This is probably the biggest, but there are other smaller foundations which may also be able to help you. Here are just a few, in alphabetical order:

Buttle Trust,
Alderley House, Vauxhall Bridge Road, London SW1

Gabbitas-Thring Educational Trust,
6 Sackville Street, London W1

Professional Classes Aid Council,
10 St Christopher's Place, London W1

School Fees Insurance Association Educational Trust,
10 Queen Street, Maidenhead, Berkshire

Thornton-Smith Young People's Trust,
4 St Mary's Road, Patrixbourne, near Canterbury, Kent.

Education after sixteen

If your children stay on at school after the age of sixteen, they may be eligible for a grant from the government, via your local authority, to help them financially during their extended schooling. The level of the grant depends on the amount of parental income and the system works broadly as follows.

In order to qualify for a grant, the person applying for the grant must have been resident in the United Kingdom for the three years preceding the proposed course of study. If the applicant has been living with parents who are working abroad or in the British Forces overseas, the right to a grant is not affected, but it might be if he had taken a year out of schooling to work abroad or even taken a long holiday.

Discretionary or mandatory grants

Grants are divided into two kinds, discretionary and mandatory. Local education authorities have considerable powers over the granting of discretionary awards.

Discretionary awards are usually given for courses lower than degree standard and go mainly to sixteen- to eighteen-year-olds and mature students. They cover a very wide range of courses, for example drama, music and chiropody, but they are also available for some professional examinations, like the Law Society and accountancy exams. As many of these courses are taken by women and only discretionary grants are available, women and girls often find it more difficult to get their qualifications than men, if they are not able to support themselves during their studies. If you fail to get a grant on your first application, it is well worth trying again.

Mandatory awards – that is those which are automatic – are given for designated courses which are degree or degree equivalent. Those who receive them normally have at least two 'A' levels or their equivalent, and the grant will be for at least three years. From September 1985–6, maximum mandatory grants will be:

undergraduates away from home in London	£2,165
undergraduates away from home outside London	£1,830
undergraduates at home	£1,480

Basically, these maximum grants go to anyone whose parental qualifying income is £7,600 or less. After that, the grant decreases gradually until, depending on family circumstances, the student gets only a basic £205 grant which goes to everyone. The assumption is that the rest of the money a student needs will be provided by his or her family. There is, however, no law which obliges parents to pay the money out and some of the 'poorest' students today come from families where the income may be relatively high, but very little of it is reaching the student. Any money earned during a vacation does not affect the amount of the grant, though earnings over £400 in term-time do.

There is no denying that students are now being treated far less favourably as far as grants are concerned compared with some years ago. Not only have the maximum grant was abruptly halved to £205 for the 1984–5 academic year. It was even more abruptly removed altogether for the 1985–6 year for students whose parents had a 'residual income' of £20,000 a year.

The basis for calculating the parental contribution has also changed. The government assessed the parental contribution depending on 'residual income' on the following basis:

Residual earnings	notional parental contribution
£9,000	£148
£12,000–£14,000	£674
£14,000–£16,000	£1,074
£16,000–£18,000	£1,524
£18,000–£20,000	£2,024
£20,000–£22,000	£2,405

Residual income is not the same as total income. It is income before tax, but less mortgage interest or rent, company and private pension contributions, plus some allowance for other dependent children or adults, apart from one's spouse. Where there is more than one student in the family at any one time, the maximum contribution parents will be expected to make is £4,000.

If you come from a family where the qualifying income is high, it is worth seeing whether you qualify for independent status. This means that your grant is not assessed on parental income and is always therefore the maximum.

To qualify, you must fulfil one of the following conditions:

1 You must have supported yourself out of earnings for at least three years before your course begins. You are allowed up to six months' unemployment in this period, and for married students time spent at home looking after children is counted. Or,
2 You must have reached the age of twenty-five.

If you are over twenty-six when you begin your course, you may be eligible for a further annual payment, which is related to your age.

There are other grants, including some for dependants, and it is worth enquiring about them. There are also additional allowances for divorced and separated students. For example, you may also be given something towards special equipment, if you are taking such courses as music, medicine, veterinary science, ophthalmic optics, architecture, landscape architecture, town and country planning, art and design, physical education or domestic sciences. Disabled students are eligible for a special grant.

Covenants

It is now possible for parents, as well as relatives or outsiders, to help their student children over the age of eighteen by making what is called a Deed of Covenant. This is particularly useful for those parents whose earnings put them above the level where their children do not qualify for any grant. What happens is that the parent agrees to make an annual payment to the child (paid annually, weekly or monthly). So what, you may ask, we all give our children money, why have a legal agreement about it? The answer, quite simply, is tax relief. Because as long as the annual payment is not more than the single person's tax allowance (at present £2,205) the parent pays the money to the child net of tax and he or she then claims the difference between the gross and net payments from the taxman.

Let's say you decide to covenant your child for £1,800 a year. With standard rate tax at 30 per cent, this would mean that you paid out only 70 per cent of that, or £1,260. The child would then be able to reclaim the remaining £540 from the Inland Revenue, making £1,800 in total, the amount set out in the covenant.

There are a few points to watch:

1 If the amount of the covenant is more than the single person's tax allowance, part or all of the relief is lost.
2 When you have decided the amount, you must stick to it. If you decide to give your child more, then the tax relief will not be available.
3 The taxman may have a few questions to ask to assure himself that you are not just trying to dodge tax.

4 Covenants must be witnessed or they are not valid and payments cannot start until after the deed is signed.
5 An Inland Revenue form R185(AP) should be filled in by the parent each year and the student should fill in form R40 when making a claim.

You can word a covenant yourself, but take care. The Inland Revenue has produced a special form IR47, 'Deed of Covenant by Parent to Adult Student', which can help you. If you get the wording wrong, you may find the Deed is not valid.

Children's allowances

Only foolish parents do not give their children an allowance each week. A child needs to learn to manage money and this cannot start too soon. The parent who indulges a child's every whim and supplies him with money on demand will eventually find himself with an adult who will never learn proper money management.

Family circumstances vary, but regardless of how much you can afford there are some general rules which will help both parents and children:

- Give a child an allowance as soon as he realizes that money can be used to buy the things he wants.
- Make it clear what the allowance covers. The older children get, the more responsibility they can have over their spending, until by the time they leave school they have experience of running a mini-budget.
- Take into account the allowances the child's friends get. There is nothing worse than being given less money than one's friends, but those who have far more than their friends may find things equally difficult.
- Give advice when asked for it about how an allowance should be spent, but *never* give instructions. Be flexible. There is no point in spoiling a child's enjoyment by refusing *ever* to make an advance on the following week's allowance.
- Review the level of the allowance from time to time, annually if possible. When deciding to increase an allowance, explain your decision and give the child a chance to put his own views forward.
- At the start, you may have to give a small child a little of the total weekly allowance every day. Later you can move to a week and then longer periods. If your child is likely to be a student getting a grant three times a year, try, if you can manage it, to do the same thing.
- Try not to make an allowance dependent on a child doing 'jobs', or at least give them a basic, plus extras for any tasks you agree.

As a guide, the *Sunday Times* reckoned, in August 1984, that pocket money, gifts and money for odd jobs totalled 84p for 5–7-year-olds, rising gradually to £3.79 for 14–16-year-olds.

Children and bank accounts

Most children enjoy having money in the post office or in a bank. The post office is more visible, easier to use, and more suitable for children who have little money. Some children are ready for this kind of account by the age of seven.

A current bank account is another matter. The teenager who can control his money properly is fairly rare. Only the parent can judge such cases as these, but if a child has shown consistent common sense by the time he is fifteen, I think it is worth a try. When children are under age, the bank will usually insist that an account is joint with one of its parents, so that the parent can see the statement and keep a tactful check on how the account is managed, retiring gracefully once the child becomes a wage earner.

Credit cards are a different matter and only in very exceptional cases would I advise a parent to underwrite them. Some parents, however, may trust their children enough to allow them to use their (the parents') own accounts.

3 When marriages go wrong

Divorce

Not all couples live happily ever after. As many as three out of ten of all marriages end in divorce and the younger you are when you marry the greater the chances are that your marriage will end not in death, but in divorce. In marriages where one or both partners are less than twenty, for example, there is a fifty-fifty chance that they will eventually divorce.

This book is only concerned with the financial aspects of the breakdown of a marriage, but money becomes interwoven with emotions when there is a separation or a divorce. The first consideration, then, is to think clearly and not allow feelings of anger, revenge or outright vindictiveness to influence you in coming to a proper financial arrangement.

To some extent these arrangements are covered by law. No court will order a man to pay so much in maintenance that he finds it difficult to survive financially himself. No court will turn a woman out of her home just because her marriage has broken up and her husband, or ex-husband, wishes to sell the house, except in very rare circumstances where there would be no hardship.

Let's look first at the current cost of a divorce:

1 The basic cost of filing a suit for divorce is £40.
2 Filing fees for any separate application for financial support are £12.

These are the legal charges, but the major cost you will probably face is that of a solicitor, and possibly a barrister. Solicitors' charges vary enormously. They are unlikely to charge you less than £40 an hour from the work they do for you and you may pay a great deal more, particularly in London. So clearly, the more a couple can reach agreement between themselves before going to solicitors, the more money they will save. It is no use being vindictive and letting the costs run away with themselves because you expect your husband or wife to be saddled with them. The more a divorce costs, the less money there is available in any settlement, and you cannot always be sure to get your costs paid by the other side, even if you are the 'innocent' party.

It is impossible to work out just what a barrister costs. He charges not just for the time he spends in court, putting your case, but also for any work and advice he offers before his appearance; £350–£500 would not be unusual for a good junior barrister in a simple case. But if you start to disagree on, say, custody of children or financial matters and he is asked to give an 'opinion', he will charge you much more. Try to find out before you embark on a divorce what the solicitors' fee will be and what he will be doing for that fee. Ask about possible extras. If the divorce goes through quickly and easily, you should know the extent of your bill roughly before you start, but a solicitor cannot estimate in advance for any unforeseen problems which may arise and which could put the bill up.

The Divorce Registry is very helpful in cases of divorce where the couple are agreed and there are no children and the divorce should cost no more than the basic £40. There is no need any longer for 'do-it-yourself' kits, or the like. If a couple can agree about this, a great deal of money can be saved. There are several excellent books which explain how you should go about it. If you have children under the age of eighteen, you will have to appear in court in any case, so that the court can be satisfied that their welfare is assured.

Order for costs

In most simple divorce cases the petitioner, particularly if it is the wife, will ask for an order for costs to be made against the respondent. This will usually be granted. There are cases, however, where no order for costs is made or where the petitioner and respondent are each ordered to pay their own costs. This would happen if the court felt that the petitioner had acted in such a way as to make the divorce far more expensive than it otherwise need have been. In divorces by post the cost works out at only around £20 each, a sum hardly worth bothering about. If you decide on legal separation instead of divorce, the financial rules are the same.

If you think your lawyer has charged you too much, you can ask for an itemized breakdown of the bill. If it still seems too high when you have looked at it, get your solicitor to obtain a certificate of reasonableness of his costs from The Law Society. If, when you see the certificate, you are still not satisfied, you should contact The Law Society, 113 Chancery Lane, London WC2A 1PL, or, if you live in Scotland, The Administrative Secretary, The Law Society of Scotland, 27 Drumsleigh Gardens, Edinburgh EH3 7YR. If you have a low income or are not working, you may qualify for legal aid (see Section six, chapter 1). You may get some reduction in your costs this way.

The 'best' way to divorce

Divorce is always a sad business, but it does happen and should be faced sensibly. The 'best' way to divorce is either to do it by post, if you have no children under eighteen, or, if not, by consent after two years' separation with all questions of maintenance and custody worked out with your solicitors before the divorce hearing. That way you may both save thousands – and I mean thousands – of pounds and your divorce should not cost more than a few hundred pounds at the most. If you are poor, you may be able to get legal aid in your divorce suit. Women qualify far more often than men. Nevertheless, there are pitfalls. Should the matrimonial home be sold at a later date, for instance, the person who has had legal aid is quite likely to have to pay it back from his or her share of the proceeds. So access to legal aid should not tempt anyone to drag out the proceedings and make them more expensive.

Maintenance

The rules about maintenance have changed over the years, reflecting changes in the attitude to divorce and the increasing financial independence of women. A new Matrimonial and Family Proceedings Act came into force late in 1984. It has not been in operation long enough, nor have there been many cases brought under the Act, to indicate what difference, if any, it will make to maintenance payments.

The Act produced for the first time ever in Britain the concept of the 'clean break'. Previously, the partner paying maintenance (usually the husband) was liable to maintain an ex-spouse for the whole of their joint lives. In theory, a wife may now be awarded only temporary maintenance, say for about five years, while she returns and re-establishes herself in her job, or the children go to school, or she undertakes training or re-training. However, 'first consideration' will be given to the welfare of the children of the marriage, who will continue to receive their maintenance from the paying parent until they leave school. Further, the conduct of the warring spouses will be taken into account in assessing maintenance levels.

Whatever the new law says, few courts are going to demand of a former wife that she returns to the work-place after being at home for a long period and if she is, perhaps, in her late forties or fifties. Such wives are most unlikely to find that their maintenance is curtailed after a few years. It is the younger wives, who could quite easily return to their careers, who will face the clean break. The major problem under the new law is conduct. On the whole, in the past few years, conduct had to be extraordinary before it had any effect on the level of maintenance awarded. A wife could leave her husband, move in with another man with her children and still find that courts were prepared to order her husband to go on supporting her. Courts seem likely to look at such cases more sternly in future, but if the concept of the 'first consideration' being the children is adhered to, some still might feel that maintenance to a wife or ex-wife, however bad her behaviour, must continue. One thing seems certain: there will be a temptation for couples to go back to the bad old days when they charged and counter-charged one another in the most lurid terms about their respective conduct.

Notwithstanding the new law, it is clearly a good idea if couples can work out their maintenance arrangements in as amicable a way a possible, whethere these are for the long- or the short-term. It is still the man who usually pays to support his former wife and children – though today a woman can, theoretically at least, be made to support a former husband.

It is advisable, too, to give this agreement legal standing as soon as possible, because there are financial advantages for both husband and wife. While a husband is paying maintenance voluntarily, he gets no tax relief apart from the normal allowances for a wife. As soon as the agreement becomes a legal one, i.e. accepted by the court, he is able to pay maintenance net of tax at the standard rate, while the wife and children (who will get the full single person's tax allowance) are usually able to reclaim part of the tax he has paid.

If a husband finds that a wife is unwilling to come to a legal agreement – and sometimes this happens even though the financial advantages are clear – it may be best for the husband to apply immediately to the court to sort the matter out, or force his wife to go to court herself by withholding maintenance. This may sound extreme, but the sooner these financial matters can be settled, the sooner any other problems will sort themselves out.

The sensible wife will apply to the court for maintenance, permanent or short-term, for herself and for the children of the marriage, which will last until the children either leave home or go out to work. She can go back to the court if her husband is paying either not enough, or not regularly enough. In the majority of cases, this matter is settled fairly amicably between the couple, and the court will merely be rubber-stamping their agreement when the divorce suit goes through.

Maintenance levels
The most important thing to remember when you are getting divorced is

that the overwhelming probability is that both husband and wife will have to accept a lower standard of living, at least temporarily. If you do not accept this, the chances are that you will go on squabbling about money at (sometimes) enormous cost to both.

If previously only the husband was working and supporting the family, his salary will now have to keep up two separate homes, until his wife either remarries or gets a job and eventually becomes fully self-supporting. The wife will be trying to live on a much smaller proportion of her ex-husband's income, unless she takes a job to supplement the amount she gets from him. If he remarries, she may find that getting any 'extras' over the basic maintenance for herself and the children becomes virtually impossible.

All rights to maintenance for the spouse cease as soon as an ex-wife (or ex-husband if the wife is maintaining him) remarries, but rights to maintenance for the children continue until the child or children have completed full-time education, or reached the age of seventeen. There are no absolute rules in deciding the level of maintenance, but as a general guide the court will start with of about one third of the husband's income before tax for the wife, plus something extra for each child. Obviously, the provision for children is only a guide: were it at a fixed rate, a man with three children, for example, might have nothing left from his salary to live on himself. Sometimes, where the husband gives up all rights to the matrimonial home, the court may order him to pay less maintenance to his former wife as a compensation for giving up his only capital asset.

If the wife was also working, the one-third rule applies not just to the husband's income, but to their total gross income added together. If a man has remarried and his current wife is earning, her income may be lumped together with his, either wholly or in part, in assessing a first wife's maintenance. Many second wives feel that this is unfair, as the court does not always make any reduction in maintenance when a man remarries a non-working woman. The court, however, is concerned only about the amount of money to which the husband has access and they assume that the second wife makes a financial contribution to family expenses, thus cutting his, if she works.

Here are a few examples to show you how it can work.

husband's income	£9,000	husband's income	£6,000
wife's income	nil	wife's income	£4,000
		total income	£10,000
total income	£9,000	one third	£3,333
one third to wife	£3,000	wife already has	£4,000
maintenance order	£3,000	maintenance order	nil

husband's income	£12,000
wife's income	£3,000
total income	£15,000
one third	£5,000
wife already has	£3,000
maintenance order	£2,000

Few cases are as simple as these. Where a wife gets the house, for example, the court will allow for that in assessing maintenance, because the husband is giving up his share of the asset. So her maintenance may be reduced below the one-third level. The court may also cut maintenance if they think a wife is able but refusing to work.

As you can see, the husband benefits from his estranged or ex-wife working. It may be a temptation for this reason for a wife not to work, even where she is able. This is a mistake, not only for financial but also for personal reasons. It is good idea to get out into the world to make new friends and achieve some financial independence after a marriage ends. Under the new law, of course, she may find that she has little option, because her maintenance will eventually cease if she is young and/or clearly able to work, or her children are off her hands.

Where a husband's income is very large or very small, the one-third rule may not be followed, and in marriages which have lasted only a very short time, particularly where there are no children, the court generally now awards a former wife no maintenance.

When you are trying to work out maintenance levels, remember that if you are unable to settle and have to go to court the two factors which will be taken into consideration are, first, the wife's standard of living before the break-up, which the court will seek to maintain as far as possible, and, second, the husband's income and ability to pay, which may be affected if he decides to remarry. Obviously, unless a man is very wealthy or very poor, these two aims may be incompatible. Settle for the best you can reasonably expect. The level of payments can of course be modified by the court if circumstances change. The husband may earn more, or lose his job; the wife may start or stop working.

Maintenance payments are usually paid at regular intervals, but occasionally a couple will agree that a once-and-for-all-lump sum should be paid to the wife. This can be paid in instalments, but once agreed it cannot be varied. Lump sums may become more attractive to ex-wives under the new law, if maintenance is to cease, anyway, after a time. The same applies if a lump sum is ordered for children. Clearly, if a woman is planning to remarry quickly, the payment of a lump sum is more attractive than periodic maintenance payments. Lump sums may also be more attractive to the working wife. If the couple did not own their own house, a lump sum can be the deposit for a new house and, therefore, a prospect of long-term financial security, or it can be used to start a business. Think carefully before you make your claim and discuss all the possibilities with your bank manager or solicitor. Check, too, on any pension rights you may have after a divorce: this is one area where former wives often lose out. Try to get some guaranteed provision, or at least an annuity from your former husband's estate should he die. Under the present rules, you will probably have some claim on his estate. It is worthwhile, however, considering insuring an ex-husband, or getting a life-assurance policy in an ex-wife's favour, written into a divorce settlement to provide a guarantee of some capital on the former husband's death.

Children
Maintenance for children is a very thorny area financially, and children are involved in 75 per cent of divorce cases. Maintenance payments for children usually end on the birthday following the age limit for compulsory schooling. At present that is sixteen, so payments will normally end on the seventeenth birthday. If the child continues in full-time schooling, or is unable to work for any physical or mental reason, the payments may continue. A couple should try to work out a sensible arrangement for the maintenance of children. It is no use taking so much money away from the man that he is unable to spend any money himself on his children, over and above the payments to his ex-wife. The man may have his children at least for some weekends and holidays and that will cost him money. The court will usually order a husband to pay at least £5 a week for a child, if his income justifies it. Non-working wives should prepare themselves for the day when maintenance to children stops – very often they are unable to make the same financial contribution to the home as the husband did. Courts today are unlikely simply to switch the total payments to the former wife.

Short marriages
For a woman, marriage used to be a passport to financial security for life. This is no longer so. Maintenance is now often more generous than in the past, but the court pays attention to the particular circumstances of each marriage. One which has only lasted a few years, where the couple are still young, and there are no children, is now often simply dissolved by the court with no order for maintenance to an able-bodied wife who is quite capable of getting a job.

The court may make a nominal order of '5p a year' in certain cases. This order is designed to cope with changed circumstances, for an order, once made, even for 5p, can be varied. At a later date, should an ex-wife become incapacitated or without an income for any reason, she can go back to the court and ask for the order to be varied. Sometimes a lump sum, though smaller than after a longer marriage, may be paid to the ex-wife.

In a marriage where a wife has always worked and there are no children and the marriage has lasted only a few years, there is no good reason why the husband should be bound in any way to maintain an ex-wife. A solicitor would advise potential ex-husbands to resist any maintenance claim, however small it may seem. You don't want to be remarried for twenty years with four children, only to find an ex-wife turning up with a new claim.

Getting your maintenance

One big worry after divorce can be actually getting the maintenance you have been awarded. To make this as sure as possible:

1 Keep proper records of all payments and when they arrive.
2 If you think your ex-husband or wife may not pay, you can ask the court to have the payments registered in the magistrates' court. When this happens, the payments go first to the court, which then passes them on to the recipient.
3 Try to make sure you know where your ex-spouse is living and working. If he or she has disappeared, there *may* be no official help forthcoming to locate him or her.
4 You can sometimes get an attachment of earnings. Under this section the employer withholds the amount of the order from (usually) the husband's salary and sends it to the wife.
5 If arrears have built up, you can go to the court, which will either issue an attachment of earnings or a committal order. The maximum for which the ex-spouse can be committed to prison for contempt of a court order is six weeks. The threat of committal is usually enough to make most people pay up. The procedure for getting arrears differs, depending on whether you go to the magistrates' court or the county court; your solicitor will advise you as to which court you should go.
6 Apply for social security. Then the local office *will* help you to trace a missing ex-spouse.
7 If you feel that your maintenance is insufficient and the salary of your ex-spouse has risen sharply, you can apply to the court for more money. If your husband's (wife's) salary has fallen, however, he can similarly apply to have the amount reduced.
8 If your ex-spouse has gone abroad and fails to continue payments, check to see whether Britain has a reciprocal arrangement with the country involved to collect maintenance payments.

Division of assets

The matrimonial home

When a marriage breaks up, there are assets which must be divided fairly between the couple. The most important of these is normally the matrimonial home. If the home is held in joint names, both are entitled to live in it until the matter is settled by the court, or the couple reach an agreement. Obviously, in most cases it will be the wife who stays, or at least the partner who is caring for the children, and this will usually be the woman. The house cannot be sold by either party without the agreement of the other.

If the house is in the name of only the husband, or the wife, the situation is more complicated. Many women fear that their husbands could force them out of the house, or sell it from beneath them. This is not the case, and under the Matrimonial Homes Act 1967 both husband and wife have the right not to be evicted, or excluded from any part of the matrimonial home, unless the court decrees it. Nor can the house be sold without a court order. A spouse with no proprietorial right to the house can register a claim to his or her occupation rights. This claim is filed at the Land Registry, so that any prospective buyer will know that a person other than the owner has the right to live in the house – a right which takes precedence over the rights of any other person who may buy the house. Do not forget to register this claim; without registering, you cannot claim your rights.

The law has changed considerably over the years to give women financial rights to their homes, even if they are not joint owners, or do not go out to work, so that the financial contribution they can have made to the home is minimal or non-existent. The Matrimonial Proceedings and Property Act 1970 set out for the first time that a wife does have some financial rights, and it recognized her contribution to the home as a home-maker caring for a family.

What happens varies in each case. The court may instruct a husband to turn the house, or his share of it, over to his wife or ex-wife. Alternatively, it may allow him to maintain an interest, but state that the home must remain intact while the children are being educated. It may then decide that, once the children are grown up, the house must be sold and the proceeds divided. Obviously, it is best for the wife if she can secure absolute ownership of the house; her maintenance should allow for the mortgage payments. In a case like this, if she remarries and decides to sell the house, she will be entitled to all the proceeds. A court does not normally consider the remarriage prospects, unless these are stated when maintenance is being decided. In law, the husband can make the same claims in similar circumstances.

The only problem, then, as far as occupation goes, is the building society or insurance company where there is a mortgage outstanding on the house. If the payments are not kept up, the building society will eventually simply repossess the house and the Land Registry filing then becomes irrelevant. This can be a problem for many wives, who will have to find some way of keeping up the payments if the husband fails to pay them, or their maintenance is insufficient. This is yet another reason for making a legal agreement as soon as possible. Building societies are not monsters, and if they are informed of the situation they will do all they can to help, even altering the terms of the mortgage in some cases, to bring down the monthly repayments, or suspending them for a time until a wife has been to court or got herself a job which enables her to meet payments. If all efforts fail and the house is sold, the wife (or, indeed, the husband) can claim a right to part of the proceeds. *It is advisable not to let things go this far.*

This is roughly the situation for owner-occupiers. A solicitor will describe the rules in more detail for you, and there are also several excellent books to help you which are on sale at most large bookshops.

The same sort of protection goes to husbands and wives who live in rented property and whose home is covered by the Rent Acts (see Section five, chapter 7). A court can order that the tenancy be transferred to the other spouse, whether it is privately rented property or council housing. This is very important for women, because, unlike in owner-occupied houses, where joint ownership is now the rule rather than the exception, tenancy agreements are usually between the owner and one spouse, that one generally being the husband. If a tenancy is transferred, all the rights and responsibilities go with it, the responsibility for paying the rent, the responsibility of maintaining the property (if the lease stipulates it) and the right to continue living in it.

Other assets

Most people today have assets other than their home. To begin with, there are the contents of the house. Normally these will go to the wife, or whoever is taking care of the children, with the exception of personal belongings, such as family paintings, antiques, or other things which one partner has brought into the marriage. These do not become joint property, so it is no use a wife hanging on to her husband's personal belongings, or a husband on to his wife's. He or she can sue for them under section 17 of the Matrimonial Property Act, and there is no way a wife or husband can claim something which does not belong to him or her. Wedding presents are held to be joint property, unless specifically given to one partner, a rather unusual occurrence. This is a very tricky area, and a couple should try to sort this out amicably – but be warned, it is often the sticking point in an otherwise fairly amicable agreement.

Living together

Although marriage has never been more popular, the moral attitude to it has changed and many couples live together at least for a period before marrying. Many other couples live together happily for many years, for one reason or another. Maybe one partner is already married and has not been prepared to push an unwilling spouse into a divorce, usually on religious grounds. Some of these relationships are successful and life-lasting; others, just like marriages, founder.

If you are living with someone, you should remember that it is not exactly like being married to them. There is no marriage contract and therefore none of the financial rights that go with marriage. Nevertheless, although the law does not recognize the so-called 'common-law wife', the courts today are taking a much more sympathetic attitude, particularly towards the woman, in cases like these. If there are any children, a woman will certainly be awarded maintenance for them on very much the same terms as for the children of a marriage and she is quite likely to be awarded something for herself. If a couple has lived in a house or run a business which the woman can prove she has contributed to, a court may award her a share in it. If you are living with someone, the best way to protect yourself is to have a legal share in everything. Then, if the relationship breaks up, you will at least be guaranteed your share in the home and its contents.

Single-parent families

In the vast majority of divorce cases, one partner ends up with the main responsibility for the day-to-day care of any children of the marriage. There are around 1,600,000 single-parent families in Britain, and in 90 per cent of them it is the mother who is caring for the children.

Most couples who divorce usually manage in the end to sort out their financial affairs, but there are always a few cases where the mother may find it exceedingly difficult to get any money out of her ex-husband, even where there has been a legal agreement. Endless forays into the court to collect arrears or secure an attachment of earnings to ensure payment can be a costly and wearing business. In some cases, it is not possible to find out where a former husband is.

When this happens, there is almost inevitably financial hardship for the family. Very often they are entitled to the sort of government benefits which go to all poor families and which I have outlined in the next chapter, and there is an extra £4.25 a week for the first child in a single-parent family, as well as the usual child benefit. But these are not enough to ensure a good standard of living, and in order to achieve this the mother often has to return to work. This step will be easier if she has a proper career to go to in which she already has experience or training. If you are a woman and marrying – although it sounds unromantic – try to make sure:

1 That you have some basic skills which you can always use if you are widowed or divorced, or your husband is unable to work for any reason.
2 That you have some experience in your career before giving it up. This will make it easier for you to return to it later.
3 If you have a sound and flourishing career, that you consider very carefully before giving it up when you have children. The legal maternity leave is now generous and you may find it worthwhile to continue working, even when your children are small.
4 That you try to stay in touch with developments in your particular field, so that you do not get rusty.

Bear these things in mind, then if you suddenly find you have to go out to work again, it will be far easier to restart than if you have been cocooned in your home for years.

There are some organizations which exist to help single-parent families, both emotionally and, where possible, financially.

Here are a few of them:

Families Need Fathers
23 Holmes Road, London NW5 (01-485 4226), open afternoons only, 2–6 p.m.
Formed to help men who feel they are not getting proper access to their children. Both men and women may join.

Gingerbread
9 Poland Street, London W1V 3DG
Membership is free and the organization is open to both sexes. It welcomes voluntary contributions.

The National Council for One-Parent Families
255 Kentish Town Road, London NW5 2LX
Gives advice either by post or in person.

The National Federation of Clubs for the Divorced and Separated
13 High Street, Little Shelford, Cambridge.
Represents clubs throughout Britain, and gives advice on housing, finance, problems with children, etc.

Single-Handed Limited
68 Lewes Road, Haywards Heath, Sussex.
This organization tries to find resident housekeeping jobs for single mothers in the homes of single fathers. It will also bring together two women, both with children, who would like to share responsibilities. There is a fee for these services.

4 Help for poorer families

Over the years, as the welfare state has developed, state benefits have been introduced to assist those whose income is temporarily or permanently below certain levels. The income levels at which these benefits are made available are revised upwards from time to time, as are the rates of benefit. Announcements can be made at any time, but as a rule the major changes are announced by the Chancellor of the Exchequer in his annual Budget in late March or April, with the new rates of payments starting in the following November.

As I write, the whole system of benefits is undergoing a thorough review. It may bring radical changes in the level of benefits and who gets them. With the present government aiming to cut expenditure in many areas, it is unlikely that benefits will be effectively increased in the next few years. Here the benefits set out are those which applied from November 1984 to November 1985.

It is important to recognize that social security benefits are a right, not a charity. Most of us at some stage in our lives pay through our taxes and national insurance contributions for benefits for others, but most of us at some time receive benefits, even if it is only the state pension, or free medical treatment on the NHS.

Not everyone appreciates this and some people do not like to ask for benefits. It has been estimated that the only state benefit fully taken up is the child benefit. As many as 35 per cent of pensioners who are entitled to supplementary benefit do not apply for it. Only 50 per cent take up their rent allowances or family income supplement. This means that many people are living unnecessarily at a lower standard than they need, or should.

Family income supplement

Family income supplement (FIS) is designed for people in full-time employment who have at least one dependent child and whose normal gross weekly income (that is, before tax and national insurance contributions) is below a certain level set by Parliament.

At the end of 1984, the qualifying level was an income of under £90 a week for a family with one child, rising by £10 a week for each additional child. Full-time work means that you must be working for more than thirty hours a week. Anyone can apply, but where a couple is involved it must be the man who is in full-time work and it does not matter whether you are employed by someone else or self-employed. All your children under sixteen are included and any over that age who are still at school, if they are living with you. The qualifying level of income is the same whether you are single or married. There are some things which are not taken into account when assessing your income, which will normally include both a husband's and his wife's earnings. They are:

- children's income or child benefit
- the first £4 of a war disablement pension
- the whole of any attendance or mobility allowance
- rent allowances
- payments for children boarded out with you

What you get
The amount you will be granted is half the difference between your family's total income and the level of income set by the government for your family size. The maximum payment is £23 for families with one child, rising by £1.50 for each additional child. Here is an example, using weekly payment figures:

income level below which you qualify	£90
total family income	60
difference	30
family income supplement payable (half of £30)	£15

This second example shows how the maximum can be less than half the difference. This usually happens with a single woman with dependent children:

income level below which you qualify	£90
total income	£35
difference	£55
family income supplement payable (maximum payment)	£23

If you get FIS, other benefits also go along with it when you are in need. These are:

- Free school meals for children at school.
- Legal aid, with certain limits.
- The refund of fares for members of your family attending hospital.
- Free prescriptions, dental treatment and glasses on the NHS.

Remember that the lower income level tends to move up each year, so check at any time to see if you are eligible.

Claiming
Get form FIS.1, which is available at all social security offices. Fill it in and send it to the Department of Health and Social Security, Family Income Supplements, Poulton-le-Fylde, Blackpool FY6 8NW. Post

offices and social security offices keep the forms and will also supply you with a stamped, addressed envelope. All applications are treated confidentially. You must send either five weekly pay slips or two monthly ones. If you are self-employed, you must send your last profit and loss account.

If your claim is allowed, you will be sent a book of orders which can be cashed each week at the post office of your choice. As a rule the book will cover fifty-two weeks and is not affected if your circumstances change during that time.

Child's special allowance

This allowance goes to those divorced women whose ex-husbands have died, or if they have any children and the husband was contributing, or had been ordered to contribute, towards the support of the children. The allowance, which is not paid if the woman remarries, is £7.65 for each child (1984–5). Single parents also get an additional £4.25 on top of the ordinary child benefit of £6.85 for each child.

Any claim must be made within three months of the former husband's death or some benefit may be lost, and it is based on his national insurance contribution record. Leaflet NI.93, available at post offices or social security offices, will tell you all about it.

Getting it free

Under the National Health Service, basic treatment is free, but there are charges for prescriptions, glasses and dental treatment. Certain people are exempt from these charges, mainly the young, the elderly and people who are receiving state benefits of some kind.

Prescriptions. The following are exempt:

1 Children under sixteen.
2 Men over sixty-five and women over sixty.

Also people who have exemption certificates:

1 Expectant and nursing mothers.
2 People who suffer from certain medical conditions.
3 War or service disablement pensioners.
4 People and their dependants who are receiving supplementary benefit or family income supplement.

Prescriptions can also be free on the grounds of low income. Leaflet PC.11, which is available at most post offices and local social security offices, explains the arrangements and also includes a claim form. Income is assessed in more or less the same way as in claims for supplementary benefits. You can also get leaflet FP.91/EC.91 at post offices. This describes the arrangements for exemption certificates.

Dental treatment. The following are exempt:

1 Children under sixteen.
2 Those over sixteen who are still at school full-time (there is no upper age limit). School here does not mean any college of further education.
3 Anyone between sixteen and twenty-one who has left school.
4 Expectant mothers.
5 Women who have had a child in the previous twelve months.
6 People and their dependants who are getting supplementary pension, benefits, family income supplement or any other state allowance.
7 Anyone, and their dependants, who is exempt on grounds of low income (leaflet PC.11 explains this).

The same applies for *glasses* with standard National Health frames and lenses, except that expectant and nursing mothers are excluded and so are young people over sixteen, unless they are still at school full-time.

Milk and vitamins. Seven pints of milk a week (or one 20 oz packet of National Dried milk) and vitamin A, D and C drops and tablets are available free to:

1 Expectant mothers and all their children under school age in families which are already receiving supplementary benefits or family income supplement, or have special needs because of low incomes.
2 Any expectant mother who already has two children under school age. Income is irrelevant here.
3 All but the first two children under school age in a family with three or more children under school age, again regardless of income.

Free milk also goes to handicapped children between the age of five and sixteen who are not registered pupils at an ordinary school or special school, and also to all children at an approved day nursery or playgroup.

Drugs and appliances supplied by hospitals. Drugs, elastic hosiery, wigs and fabric supports are usually charged for by hospitals. Drugs and elastic hosiery are exempt to the same people who qualify for free prescriptions. Wigs and fabric supports also go free to anyone over sixteen in full-time attendance at school.

Help for school children

Free school meals are available to children of poorer families, generally those who are already getting benefits of some kind. Qualifying incomes are worked out by taking gross income and subtracting expenses like rent, rates, mortgage repayments, income tax, national insurance contributions, trade union subscriptions, superannuation and fares to work.

The level of qualifying income changes all the time. There are also some education maintenance allowances for some families whose children are still at school after the age of sixteen, but not all authorities have these schemes. Again, some, but not all, authorities contribute to school fares for children attending state schools. These allowances do not usually go to children in private schools.

Some local authorities provide free school milk for children under seven, but this is not mandatory.

Those between seven and twelve may also get free milk, if it is recommended on health grounds by the school medical officer, and sometimes children at special schools get free milk. Where this is the case, each child generally gets one third of a pint a day.

Local authorities may also help with clothing and sports gear; the decision is at their discretion. Your local education office or education welfare officer will give you details.

Supplementary benefits

Supplementary benefits are rather different from most social security payments. They are designed to provide income on a non-contributory basis for people who are not working full-time. You will get a supplementary benefit if your income, whether it comes from part-time work or social security, is judged not enough to meet your requirements. 'Scale rates' are worked out by the Department of Health and Social Security and individuals' requirements are worked out according to these rates, with additional allowances for rent and any special items. Whatever you are earning is then deducted from this total. The difference is made up by the supplementary benefit. You may qualify for Family Income Supplements as well.

For the purposes of calculation, family income is lumped together and only the husband can claim. Couples who are living together, but not married, are usually treated as if they were married. This means that a woman who is living with a man as if they were married is likely to lose any benefits she would have got on her own account. If you are receiving supplementary benefits, you will also be entitled to free school meals, prescriptions, dental treatment, etc. These are the end-of-1984 levels of income below which people qualify:

weekly scales	under pension age	over pension age
married couple	£45.55	£57.10
single householder	£28.05	£35.70
any other person		
18 or over	£22.45	£28.55
dependant child		
under 11	£9.60	—
11 to 15	£14.35	—
16 to 17	£17.30	—
over 18	£22.45	—

There are also rate and rent allowances and, in certain cases, because of age or illness, heating, laundry and domestic help contributions to cost. Source: Department of Health and Social Security.

Rate and rent rebates

Rate and rent rebates and rent allowances are available to some owner-occupiers and tenants; you do not have to be getting supplementary benefits to claim. There are no income limits and, depending on the size of the family, quite high incomes still qualify for the rebates and allowances. Your local Citizens Advice Bureau, or DHSS office, should be able to help you. These benefits are well worth investigating, because they can contribute as much as 60 per cent towards your total housing costs.

Housewives' invalidity pension

There is a non-contributory invalidity pension available to married women. But it is very difficult to get. Women who have applied have alleged that one has to be almost completely immobile before one is allowed the pension.

Theoretically, all married women who have lived in Britain for twenty-eight weeks and have been continuously incapable of working in that time are eligible, if they are between the ages of sixteen and sixty. The benefit is, however, hedged around with so many qualifications that very few women actually get it. It is payable only when a housewife is unable to do her housewifely duties. Proving this is often difficult and the process involves a long questionnaire which many find impossible to answer correctly as it applies to their own case. If you are turned down, it is worthwhile appealing, because rather more attention is paid to appeal cases by the authorities. As I write, a number of women's organizations have complained to the government about the difficulties in getting this pension, so the situation may change.

A quite different rule, but with a similar discriminatory effect on women, is worth mentioning. A man can get a tax allowance towards help in looking after a disabled wife; a woman cannot get one if she is caring for a disabled husband. The reason given for this is that the Revenue is concerned only that there is a woman in the house to perform household tasks. As a result, families in this situation have to choose between living on social security, or the wife going out to work and paying someone to care for her husband during the day without the benefit of any tax relief.

Mobility allowance

Some disabled people, who meet certain conditions, are entitled to a mobility allowance. From November 1984 it was £20 and tax free. Applications should be made to the DHSS.

For details of other state benefits turn to the following chapters:

Unemployment pay	Section two, chapter 2
Child benefit scheme	Section three, chapter 2
Pensions	Section five, chapter 9
Supplementary benefits for the aged	Section five, chapter 9

5 Caring for your dependants

Making a will

If you make a will, when you die your assets will be transferred to your dependants in the way you choose; you must appoint an executor to see that your wishes are carried out.

Not everyone makes a will; many people are quite superstitious about it, taking the view that if they do they are in some way signing their death warrant. You should approach making your will in a positive way, however. It is likely that as your life develops your situation will change, and you will make not one will in the course of your life but several. Just one example: you will want to protect your children in totally different ways when they are small than when they are older with independent lives of their own.

The longer you delay in making your will, the more difficult it will become. Death is nearer the older we get, and thinking about a will can become very hard. Do it while you are relatively young and healthy. That way, it will be part of your financial thinking for many years.

Intestacy
If you die without making a will, you are said to have died intestate. This is an irresponsible thing to do, even if you do not have a great deal of money. For example, where a married couple have a joint bank account, the bank may not allow the wife to draw on the account in the event of her husband's death. Where there is no will, the process of releasing the money can take a very long time. (For a wife's rights, see chapter 7 in this section.).

But, and it is an important *but*, even if you make a will today it can be challenged by anyone who thinks they should have benefited and did not, if they have been dependent on you. This means that children can claim, or mistresses and (less often) lovers.

Six good reasons for making a will
1 Your money and other assets will usually go where you want them to when you die.
2 You can choose the people who will administer your estate. They are called your executors. Decide on them carefully and do not always pick a relative, as this can lead to quarrels. If your estate is at all complicated, have more than one executor.
3 You can give your executors wider powers of investment than they normally get under the law. This way you can help your family and other people or organizations to whom you leave legacies improve and secure their financial future.
4 You can arrange a particular financial plan to suit your family's special needs.
5 The business of looking after your estate is cheaper than if you leave no will.
6 You can save your beneficiaries money. With the help of professional advice, you can arrange your affairs so as to make provision for your dependants while you are still alive, and lessen capital transfer tax (see p.293) which will be due on your estate when you die. You can also adjust any other taxes for which you may be liable.

In contrast, there are *no* good reasons for not making a will.

Using a solicitor
There is no need to use a solicitor when you are making a will. As long as you state your wishes and find two witnesses to your signature at the end of it, it will be perfectly valid. But not using a solicitor may be a false economy. There are many legal rules and regulations, and what you write down does not always mean exactly what you intended, so the actual phrasing of the will is quite important.

A solicitor is useful because he will not only help you to draw up your will correctly, so that you are sure that your wishes will be carried out in the way you want, but – especially if he is a family solicitor who knows your circumstances well – he may be able to point out things which have escaped your notice. He will point out, for instance, that you cannot have as witnesses to your signature any person who will benefit under your will.

Doing it yourself

If you decide that you really do not wish to pay the rather modest fee a solicitor charges and you feel that your affairs are so simple that you do not need one, at least buy and read a book on will-making before you go ahead and make a will yourself. If you just fill in one of the will forms which are on sale in many stationers without guidance, you could make a mistake. Obviously, these forms have a particular set formula, and this could result in you not expressing your wishes as clearly as you want to. It is much better to follow the instructions in a book and, if you reach a point where you have any doubts at all about whether you are expressing your wishes properly, get in touch with a solicitor.

If there are no problems, draw up the final version of your will and get two witnesses to verify your signature. You need not show them the will; it is your signature they are witnessing, not the contents of your will.

After your death, details of your will are available to the public. If you do not wish anyone except the beneficaries to know what you have left, you can leave special instructions. But this really does need the help of a solicitor. The taxman will have to know the details, of course.

Choosing your executors

Your will must state who you have made your executor, or executors. You may think you are flattering someone by making them your executor, but it is not always an easy task. It may require a lot of work, as we will see later on, so the choice must be made with care. It is no use, for instance, making your husband or wife one of your executors, and then choosing another one with whom you know they will find it difficult to agree. As a courtesy, consult the person or people you have chosen. You need not do this, but unless prior consultation has taken place he or she need not take on the job. If a person you have chosen as executor dies, you will have to find a replacement immediately.

Five suggestions for choosing your executor
1 One of the tasks of an executor is to arrange the funeral. For this reason, even if you choose at least one professional executor, it is useful to have someone else as well who is close to your family and will find the personal dealings with them easier at this time.

2 One's husband or wife is a reasonable choice. They will normally be the chief beneficiary of the estate and will want – and should have – some say in how it is administered. But we all get older and some husbands and wives would welcome a co-executor. If your children have grown up they could make a good second choice, provided your will is fairly simple.

3 You may prefer, however, not to burden your spouse with the problems of sorting out your will. In that case, choose a family friend you can trust and who has some experience in legal or accounting fields. If you cannot think of anyone suitable, use a solicitor. Solicitors are quite used to dealing with this kind of work and will charge you an additional fee. As you will see later, when a will is proved it is usually necessary to use a solicitor; this 'charging fee', as it is called, is not often a particularly heavy extra burden on your estate.

4 If none of the above are suitable, you can go to people who specialize in this kind of work. Most of the big banks have executor and trustee departments. Most bank branches have booklets on display which set out the sort of services they can provide. This is a more expensive way of operating, however, because the bank will charge a fee in addition to the fee charged by the solicitor employed by the bank. But there is a lot to be said for banks. They do not die, so that you get continuing service from them at any time.

5 You can go or write to the Public Trustee, who operates from 24 Kingsway, London WC2. This office was set up by the government many years ago, and if you name him in your will he will act as executor, administrator or trustee of your estate. He is particularly useful for people with small estates, but the banks charge relatively less the bigger the estate.

The tasks of an executor

At some time in our lives, many of us will be asked by one or other of our friends or relatives to be their 'executor'. What this means is that on that person's death you become his or her legal representative, taking on all legal rights and responsibilities, and carrying out the wishes of the *testator* – the person who make the will. Before agreeing to become an executor, make sure you understand exactly what it means. Sometimes the task is an enormous one. You will have to collect together all the assets of the estate, pay all debts, which incidentally include tax, and then distribute what is left in accordance with the will.

First of all, before the work of settling the estate can begin, you must get probate. Probate is the process required by law before the court accepts the will as valid and empowers the executor to set about his work (see below).

The responsibility of an executor starts at the moment of death, and any delay in getting probate can cause problems for relatives. Insurance companies, for example, may not pay up immediately on policies, and banks sometimes limit access to a bank account, until probate is granted. It is not unusual for widows and dependants to find that they have no money for day-to-day expenses – a problem which is not automatically solved by couples having a joint bank account (see Section one, chapter 6).

How to get probate

1 *Prepare an Inland Revenue affidavit.* This is a statement of all assets and debts at the time of death. Changes afterwards do not usually count, though you can charge funeral expenses against the estate. If you think there will be capital transfer tax to pay (see later in this chapter), get a professional valuation done as soon as possible. The Inland Revenue officer may refuse to accept the valuation and ask for another one if he thinks the assets have been undervalued. And even if he does accept it, the matter can be reopened if some asset is sold at any time for more than the valuation price, unless a 'clearance certificate' has been issued.

Don't try to be too clever, however, particularly in dealing with an estate inherited by a married person. There is no capital transfer tax between married people, but what is saved in transfer tax may turn up again as a gains tax if an asset is sold for much more than the original valuation, and tax in the form of capital gains tax may have to be paid, if an asset is sold. Take advice, if you are not a professional, on whether a *higher* probate value may not be best.

At this stage, the affidavit is signed but not sworn. But this doesn't mean that you are not responsible for making a full disclosure. You may not be able to discover all the tax liabilities immediately, but allowance is made for that.

2 *Swear the executor's oath.* You go to a commissioner for oaths or a solicitor to swear the oath. This is vitally important.

3 After swearing the oath, *lodge the original will and probate papers at the Probate Registry*, together with two cheques, one for a fee based on the asset value and the other for any capital transfer tax required. Then, all being well, probate will be granted in a few weeks.

Many executors leave the probate process to their solicitors. If you decide to do it yourself, you will be charged an additional fee because of the extra work involved. About one in seven executors prove the will themselves through the personal application department of the Probate Registry. Local probate registry offices are in the telephone book. The principal office is in London and is now called the Principal Registry of the Family Division of the High Court.

There can be upsets. For example, the validity of a will may be challenged. You can avoid this to some extent by not touching the will once it is found. Don't remove any papers attached to it, but don't add any, either. You may have to swear that the will is in the same state as when you first received it.

Though delay is rare, executors should remember that the heirs cannot receive their legacies and that monies, insurance policies, etc., remain frozen until probate is granted. Delay can cause hardship, therefore, and should be avoided.

Dividing up the estate
With the granting of probate, you are ready to start on the next stage, supervising the execution of the wishes of the testator. Points to notice are:

- There is no reason why you should not benefit in any will where you are an executor. It is witnesses to wills who cannot benefit.
- If a will is simple and you are a friend, you may do the executor's work for nothing. But professionals will charge a fee.

The actual task of dividing up the estate varies enormously. It may be simple and just a matter of transferring a family house and money to the heirs, but it can be very complicated indeed. *Do not take the job on unless you are sure you can carry it out properly.*

Acting as a trustee

You may find, particularly where there are children, that you are not only executor but also *trustee*. This will prolong your involvement with the estate for many years. There are two common ways in which a trust may arise:

1 A husband or wife may not leave his or her estate outright to the widow or widower, but only the right to any income from capital for life, with the capital sum going to the children. It is more common when a man dies first. He may not trust his wife with total access to capital which he wants to go to his children eventually, or he may simply not want his widow to have the bother of managing the estate.
2 A trust may be set up for the benefit of children who have not yet grown up. The income, and sometimes part of the capital, is used for their upbringing and schooling, and the capital reverts to them either when they come of age, at eighteen, or sometimes later. Twenty-five is popular.

The trustee can find himself with a thankless task trying to balance the needs of the widow – the *tenant* of the trust – and the children – the *remaindermen*. The aim is to keep the money intact, or even make it grow, for the eventual benefit of the remaindermen, but at the same time to ensure that the tenant has adequate and increasing money to live on in a period of inflation. Friction can arise in cases where the trustee is allowed to give some capital to the tenant from time to time. This reduces what is left for the heirs and can upset even happy families. It can happen, of course, that the tenant and the remaindermen are not close, or even related; it is not rare for disputes to end up in court. The trustee will then need all the tact he can muster.

A will should state how wide the powers of the trustees are. It can stipulate that they can invest in whatever they like, but if it makes no stipulation the investments are covered by the Trustee Investments Act 1961.

Broadly, this Act allows up to half of the trust fund to be invested in the ordinary shares of companies quoted on the stock exchange. These are generally limited to the large companies and unit trusts and a certain dividend record is required. The rest has to go into fixed interest stocks, which are mainly government, local authority issues and some building societies.

You can give up your trusteeship, but only if you leave behind at least two other trustees, or a trust company. If you can't find anyone to take over from you, a solicitor or professional trustee will usually agree to act in your place. He will charge a fee, so make sure that the will allows you to pay him out of the estate.

As you can see, being a trustee or executor can be an enormous task. Think carefully before you agree to act. It is often a job for professionals.

Capital transfer tax

Once you have decided where you want your money to go after your death, and who your executors will be, the next most important thing is to look at the implications of capital transfer tax. Even in death we do not escape taxes, and anyone with more than £67,000 to leave, except to a spouse, needs to consider this tax. Here I will be looking at it only from the point of view of someone making a will, though CTT has to be paid on all transfers of capital, with certain exceptions, whether these take place before or after death.

Capital transfer tax, sometimes called the 'gift tax', replaced the old estate duty in 1975. If you have a will outstanding which is based on the old estate duty provisions, take professional advice. It is highly likely that it will have to be changed, or your heirs will suffer.

For the purposes of this tax, capital means all your assets, not just money. It means that when a business changes hands after death a transfer tax must be paid. It means that when agricultural land changes hands tax may have to be paid. Similarly with a work of art. The implications of this are clear. Where the asset is not actual cash, the person who inherits may have difficulty in finding the money. Estates may have to be broken up and other things sold to find the money.

This all means that you must try to leave your assets in such a way that the problems of raising the tax will be minimized. First of all, let's look at the rates of the tax as it is charged on death:

band from £	transfer tax on death % on slice
0–67,000	nil
67–89,000	30
89–122,000	35
122–155,000	40
155–194,000	45
194–243,000	50
243–299,000	55
Over 299,000	60

This table gives you an idea of the sort of amount of money which will have to be found for the taxman when you die. If you do not have the minimum amount of £67,000 you can ignore the tax, but if you are just a little above, consider the exemptions, which may well bring you back below the starting level again. The starting level is likely to rise as inflation continues. Here again I am looking only at what happens on death.

1 All your debts must be paid before the end value of your estate is assessed.

2 The first £67,000 is not subject to capital transfer tax.

3 All transfers between a husband or wife are exempt from the tax. This means that anything which one leaves to the other is liable for tax only when the surviving partner dies.

4 Unlimited gifts to charities or political parties are exempt if they are made more than one year before death, and similar gifts not exceeding £250,000 made on death or within one year of death are also exempt.

5 There is a formula to help businesses and also farmers. This basically allows relief from CTT on half the value of the business or farm. As far as farmers are concerned, the relief only covers working farmers who are wholly employed on the farm. Get your adviser to explain it to you. Deductions of CTT are 50 or 20 per cent, depending on the particular case.

6 If you have inherited a property less than four years after its previous owner received it and tax was paid the previous time, you will get 80

per cent relief from capital transfer tax in the first year, moving down to 20 per cent in the fourth year and nothing in the fifth year.

A lot of the sting was taken out of CTT at death by the 1982 Budget. From then on, the various bands were index-linked and so rise automatically if prices generally increase. You can also cut the amount of CTT which has to be paid at your death by making full use of life assurance and the £3,000 annual exemption on CTT by making gifts to your children or anyone else you would like to receive money. It is also worthwhile transferring some assets above that level while you are still alive, because the tax payable in each band is much lower than at death (see Section four, chapter 1). *It is simply foolish to leave your estate paying more CTT than necessary.*

Setting a will aside

Think carefully about what you are doing when you make your will, because it may be set aside by a court, even if it is perfectly valid and made in the proper manner. This can happen if someone who expected to inherit did not, or did not inherit as much as they felt they were entitled to. The most common case of this is when a man cuts his wife out of his will, or, less often, leaves nothing to his children.

Until 1939 there was nothing a family could do, in England and Wales at least, if a man died and it was found that he had left all his money to a cats' home, or perhaps a mistress his family knew nothing about. All that changed with the Inheritance (Family Provision) Acts 1939 and 1975. Under this, certain members of a person's family can apply to the executors and the court for a reasonable provision to be made for them from the deceased's estate. The relatives who are protected in this way are a husband or wife, a son under eighteen, an unmarried daughter of any age, and any children of the marriage who are not capable of taking care of themselves because of some physical or mental disability. The lesson, then, is to consider all the proper claims upon your money when you are making a will, and to be as fair as possible to all claimants.

If you live in Scotland, the position is different from that in England and Wales. You must check the situation with a solicitor. For example, you cannot cut your husband or wife out of your will. The spouse and dependant children have 'legal rights' over at least part of your estate. You cannot ignore these rights when making a will, and the matter will be set right by the courts if you fail to provide for your family. This means, of course, that people in Scotland have less freedom than in England and Wales in deciding what to do with their money.

A will can be revoked for other reasons as well, basically because it is held to be invalid. This can occur, for example, when:

1 It is claimed and subsequently proved in court that the person making the will – the testator – was of unsound mind at the time he or she made the will. Such claims will normally only be made when the testator was exceedingly old or seriously ill when making a final will, and probably when there had been several previous wills making very different bequests. Old people have been known to cut off their families suddenly and leave all their money to a charity. In such a case the family (in England and Wales) will probably be awarded something from the estate by the court. It has sometimes been claimed that the testator was under the influence of some person to such an extent that he or she left the estate to them. This has sometimes happened with family servants, or proprietors of nursing homes who may have come into the life of the testator when he or she was getting old.

2 A will fails to comply with the formal requirements. The most common reason for this is incorrect witnessing. This is yet another reason for using a solicitor.

3 It can be proved that a will has been forged.

When you should make a new will

It is clear that as your life changes, and your responsibilities along with it, you will need to make a new will. This happens if you have a new child, or children, if one of your legatees dies, or when your children grow up and become independent. All these are important reasons for making a new will, but overriding all is the need to make a new will if you marry. Marriage automatically revokes any previous will, so a new one must be made, except in the very rare circumstances when a new will has been made in the expectation of marriage. This is particularly important for anyone who is divorced and is contemplating remarriage. You may wish to make sure that you protect the children of an earlier marriage, and possibly even an ex-wife or husband. Unless you make a new will making this clear after your remarriage, your new spouse will inherit everything and your children will automatically be disinherited. A divorce, on the other hand, does not invalidate a will.

Anyone found guilty of murder or manslaughter cannot benefit under the will of the person killed.

This chapter has dealt only with making a will. An important part of looking after your dependants is making proper provision for them by means of a pension, part of which survives after your death. I have dealt with this in Section five, chapter 9.

6 The cost of dying

In the end, we all die, and a funeral has to be paid for. It is best, if possible, to make arrangements to meet the cost yourself beforehand, so that there is no problem for your relatives. The government assists by a death grant which is usually paid to the executor, who will be arranging the funeral.

The deceased's husband, wife, children or executors can claim the grant by signing the back of a special certificate which is received from the Registrar of Births, Marriages and Deaths, when the death is reported. This should be sent to the local social security office and they will send a claim form. Alternatively, one can call at the office. The grant varies according to the age of the person who has died. At present, the grant, which has remained unchanged for many years, is:

under 3	£ 9.00
3–5 inclusive	£15.00
6–17 inclusive	£22.50
man aged 18 or over (born after 5 July 1893)	£30.00
woman aged 18 or over (born after 5 July 1893)	£30.00
man born on or after 5 July 1883, but before 1893	£15.00
woman born on or before 5 July 1888, but before 1898	£15.00

Any man still alive who was born before 5 July 1883, or woman before 5 July 1888, does not qualify for the death grant. It is highly unlikely that the grant will cover the full cost of a funeral – though some local authorities do manage to dispose of unclaimed bodies for that price.

If you or your family have been receiving supplementary benefits, however, the Department of Health and Social Security will give considerable help towards the cost of a funeral – but not an elaborate one!

The National Association of Funeral Directors passed a resolution at its annual conference in 1976 that it would not set down recommended scales of fees for funerals, so it is very difficult to estimate exact costs.

In October 1982, the Old Fellows Manchester Unity Friendly Society published a survey on funeral costs. It revealed that the average cost of a funeral had reached £362 and that incidental costs, like gravestones, flowers, crematorium and cemetery fees, doctors and clergy, often double the total cost of a funeral. The average cost of flowers was £16, but occasionally people spent up to £125 on a single special order. Marble gravestones cost anything between £200 and £400.

The survey found that funeral costs were surprisingly uniform throughout the country, though there were, of course, great actual variations within the average: in London, the price ranged from £351 to £1,389. Church fees could vary from £16.50 to over £40. And all funeral expenses are subject to Value Added Tax at 15 per cent, an unnecessarily severe imposition in the view of many people. Its removal would reduce the average price of a funeral by between £50 and £60. It may sound a shocking thing to suggest, but if the costs of a funeral are estimated at a price the family simply cannot afford, they should try to get the undertaker to bring the bill down. The £30 grant does not cover even 10 per cent of the average cost.

Most funeral directors belong to the National Association of Funeral Directors, 57 Doughty Street, London WC1 (telephone 01-242 9388). Its members deal with about 420,000 of the half a million or so funerals in the United Kingdom each year. It has a code of conduct, and if you think you have been overcharged your complaint can be investigated by a committee, which can recommend, though not insist on, a cut in the bill.

When arranging a funeral, do not forget the optional extras which will bring the price up. Apart from those mentioned above, there is also a further fee for embalming, and death notices in newspapers must be paid for. No one wants to appear mean when arranging a funeral, but if you can bring yourself to do it, ring up two or three firms for estimates of the cost.

If you are making the arrangements yourself before you die, you can stipulate what sort of funeral you want. The cheapest way of disposing of your body is not to have a funeral at all, but to leave it to your local hospital. The only problem is that sometimes hospitals have a surplus of bodies and may refuse to take yours.

7 When a husband dies

The chances are that most women will spend their final years alone. If they are not single or divorced, the fact that women tend to live about five years longer than men, together with their tendency to marry men older than themselves, means that at any one time there are around three million widows in Britain. This is about four times as many as widowers. Put another way, it means that 15 out of every 100 women are widows. Most widows are over sixty with very limited earning power and, unless they have made sure that proper financial arrangements have been made for them, they are often in for a very thin time.

It's no use trying to run away from these facts, or thinking that it's ghoulish to discuss them with a husband before he dies. And it's no use thinking, 'It won't happen to me.' It usually does. Look around; you are bound to know several widows struggling to make ends meet. To avoid this, make your preparations early. It's too late when your husband is dead regretting that there is no proper widow's pension, no insurance to tide you over the inevitable expenses a death brings, or to pay off a mortgage on your house. Unless these arrangements are made well in advance, you will have financial worries added to your grief.

Preparing for widowhood
It is never too soon to prepare for your life as a widow. If you talk about the probability early on, you can get on with your married life and forget it. The sooner your husband is in a proper pension fund, the better will be your widow's pension if he dies. The sooner he takes out proper life insurance, the cheaper it will be and the greater will be the benefits. The sooner he makes a will, the more secure you will feel against any risks.

Although most widows are old, not all of them are, and at each stage in his life a husband should tailor his insurance to meet any situation which could arise on his death. If you have children, life insurance should cover their needs until they are earning. Make sure your husband has endowment insurance – as well as straight life cover – for the chances are that he will live until the children are grown up, so that you are building up a nest egg for you *both* to enjoy in later life. Look at the chapters on life assurance. What is available for women is also usually available for men, on slightly different terms, as a rule.

When your husband dies

1 First of all, you must register the death. You need a death certificate before you can claim national insurance benefits, make claims on life assurance policies, or settle your husband's estate. The death must be registered within five days in England and Wales and eight days in Scotland. These is a small charge for extra copies of the death certificate, and you can have as many copies as you wish.

2 Someone must make arrangements for the funeral. If you have decided on cremation, there are various forms which have to be filled in by doctors and they usually make a charge for completing each one. There is a small fee for the completion of the final form, which is done by the medical referee at the crematorium. Funerals cost money and most widows receive a death grant from the government of £30 (see the previous chapter). This grant has been fixed for many years now and certainly will not cover the cost of the funeral, which is likely to be around £300 – and it could be a lot more. If you cannot pay, you may

be able to get a loan or a further grant from the Department of Health and Social Security. The undertaker is quite likely to ask you for a deposit before going ahead with the arrangements.

3 You may be entitled to a widow's allowance (£50.10, plus £7.65 for each child, from November 1984) which is paid to you for twenty-six weeks to help you adjust to your new circumstances. The amount varies depending on whether you have children. Apply to the local office of the DHSS, if:

- you are under sixty, or
- your husband was not drawing a retirement pension, and
- your husband's national insurance contributions are sufficient for you to get the benefit

It may take a little time for the benefit to go through, while the records are checked, but the payment will be backdated. For this reason, it is a good idea always to have some money of your own in the bank to tide you over the first few weeks.

4 Your husband's estate should be settled. This is easy to do if he has made a will; if not, there may be problems. So try to make sure that your husband does make a will very early on and it is sensible to make one yourself at the same time. Every will names an executor – that is the person who sees that the wishes of the person making the will are carried out. You can be the sole executor of your husband's will, but it is a good idea to have a second person – maybe one of your children – to help you out. Before you can carry out your husband's wishes, you must settle all his debts and taxes and then seek what is called 'probate', unless your husband has left only a very small amount of money. After probate is granted, you can dispose of the assets he has left. You must make an appointment with the probate registry – there is one in most towns – or you can get a solicitor to do it for you. He will, of course, charge you for the work he does. Do not try to rush through winding up the estate. All the assets must be valued in case there is any capital transfer tax to be paid, which happens when the total value of the estate is more than £67,000. But, and it is a big but, if a husband leaves everything to his wife there is no tax to pay. The tax is only levied once on married couples when the surviving spouse dies (see Section four, chapter 1, and chapter 5 of this section).

If a husband has not left a will, a widow has the first claim on the estate and she must apply for 'letter of administration'. These are really the same as probate. Then there are rules about how the money and other items must be divided. Briefly, a widow gets everything if there are no children or close relatives, or if the estate is worth less than £40,000.

On estates worth more than £40,000, the widow gets all the

'personal effects' – things like the car, furniture, pictures, jewellery – the first £40,000 and a life interest in half of anything else which may be left. The other half goes to the children, if there are any. Where there are no children, but there are other close relatives, the widow gets up to £85,000 and half of anything else which is left. The rest is divided between the husband's relatives in quite a complicated way, though the widow gets a life interest on the money. Where there are children, the widow get the first £40,000, the children half of the rest immediately, and the other half when the widow dies, on which she has had a life interest. These are the levels at the moment. The government changes them from time to time. As you can see, there could be a lot of bother settling an estate without a will, so you can avoid that situation by persuading a reluctant husband to make one.

It is sensible for a widow to make a will, if she has not already done so, as soon as possible after a husband dies.

The long term

It comes as real shock to some women when they have to take financial responsibility for the first time. You can make it easier for yourself to adapt if you have worked jointly with your husband on all family financial matters. Don't let him put you off. Dealing with money is quite simple once you have a little experience and any husband who tells his wife not to worry about money matters is not doing her a favour in the long run.

The government recognizes the special problems of being a widow and on the whole is quite generous to them in comparison with other state benefits. Your local DHSS office will give you precise details at any one time of all the benefits available and their current levels.

When the widow's allowance stops, after twenty-six weeks, women become entitled to widowed mother's allowances, or widow's pensions. The widowed mother's allowance goes to women who:

1 have one or more children under the age of nineteen living with them, *or*
2 are pregnant by their late husband *and*
3 the usual national insurance contribution qualifications have been fulfilled by the husband.

Widows' pensions apply when the widow's allowance ends if:

1 You do not qualify for the widowed mother's allowance *and*
2 You are over 40 *and*
3 The usual national insurance contribution qualifications are fulfilled.

There are different levels of benefit, depending on your age when your husband dies – it goes up the older you are and, of course, there are the usual child benefits. Full details are given in the DHSS leaflet NI.13. You should find it at your local office. You may, if your husband dies because of an accident, or a disease brought on by his working conditions, be entitled to an extra payment. Details on this are in the DHSS leaflet NI.10.

Claiming your benefit

- If you are under sixty and wish to claim a widow's pension, fill in form BW1. Once again, go to your local DHSS office. The same applies for the widowed mother's allowance.
- If you are over sixty and your husband was already getting the married men's pension, all you have to do is tell the DHSS that he has died and they will make any adjustments necessary.
- War widows get extra pensions. If you think you are eligible, look at leaflet MPL.151, which will give you details and tell you how to claim.
- If you are very poor and for some reason do not qualify for a widowed mother's allowance or pension (your husband may have worked abroad, for instance, and not paid NI contributions) you may be able to get some supplementary grants, unless you are working. The government sets a scale of rates and these are usually adjusted upwards each year to allow for inflation. Some payments are made, too, for exceptional need. These are only given if you are not working, and small amounts of capital or savings are disregarded when a decision is made to give you a grant.

State benefits include cash payments to help you with your family expenses, free school meals for your children, rent and rates rebates, school uniform grants, fares to school, free prescriptions, free dental treatment, free fares to hospital. It is also possible to get education maintenance grants and even, though it is rare, help with boarding school fees. It is easier to get the last listed through the educational trusts mentioned in chapter 2 of this section.

Widows and earnings

As soon as your husband dies, you become a single person from the point of view of taxation. This means that instead of the wife's earned income allowance, for instance, you will get the single person's allowance (see Section 4, chapters 1 and 4). These are always at the same level, so you may not think that it makes much difference, but it does. The wife's earned income allowance can be set only against wages or salaries, whereas the single person's allowance, like the married man's allowance, can be set against any income you may have from savings or investments. If you are over sixty-five, you will also be able to claim the age allowance, and there are special allowances to cover you for the first financial year of your widowhood. Like any single parent, you will also be able to claim the additional personal allowance if you have any children still in full-time schooling and, naturally, if you are still making mortgage payments, they too will be allowed against your income. If you and your husband have worked your finances out properly, however, there should be an insurance policy which will automatically pay off any remaining mortgage if he dies.

As a single person, you will be liable for tax on any income you have once your allowances are taken into account. For tax purposes, your income will include:

1 The widow's allowance, the widowed mother's allowance or the widow's pension.
2 Any other pension or annuities, including any national insurance retirement pension or private pension from your husband's employment.
3 A few national insurance benefits, like mobility allowance or industrial death benefit.
4 Any wages or salary from your employment, or any earnings if you are self-employed.
5 Interest from any savings or dividends on shares.
6 Building society interest, if your total income puts you above the standard rate of tax levels.
7 Interest on any money which comes from your husband's estate.

This is a long list and you must take care that you do not miss anything out. It is also a good idea to make yourself familiar with tax matters while your husband is still alive, or dealing with all this when you are coping with your husband's death can be more upsetting than it would be if you understood exactly what you were doing.

There is, however, no tax to pay on national insurance or sickness benefits, supplementary benefits and family income supplement, invalidity pensions, war widow's pensions, child benefit (you will now also qualify for an extra £4.25 child benefit for your first child), child special allowances or guardian allowances.

Better still, try to ignore the fact that you are widowed and think of yourself simply as a single woman and, if you are young enough, get yourself a job. No qualifications? Well, that doesn't matter any more. There are plenty of training schemes available to help you make a new start in life – and you may even be able to get a grant to study, though, in these tough economic times, they are hard to come by. If you do apply for a grant and are turned down, do not give up. Try again. Only the widow herself can make her life acceptable and enjoyable. State benefits are rarely enough to live decently on and, if you go out to work, you will not only be helping to give yourself and your family a good standard of living, but also finding a new circle of friends and acquaintances. And of course, if you do go out to work, you will eventually qualify for some, if

303

not all, of a state pension in your own right to add to that from your husband's employment.

Remarriage

When you remarry, you lose your widow's pension or your widowed mother's allowance. Do not think that, by not marrying and living with someone instead, you will keep them. If the DHSS inspectors suspect that you are 'cohabiting', they may take away your allowances. They take the view that women and children are always dependants if there is a man around in the home, so, if you take in a lodger, make sure that you can prove that you are not living as man and wife, which is what cohabiting means. Should you lose the allowance, there is a complaints procedure. Ask at your local Citizens Advice Bureau.

If you are a widow in paid employment, you will probably find that you are paying more tax on your earnings than a single or married woman earning the same amount. This is because widows actually have higher taxable incomes, because of the various benefits they get from the state, and the taxman tries to take the tax payable on these directly from wages, rather than collecting the money after the end of the tax year. If the inspector cannot get any extra tax you should pay from your wages, he will work out the amount and ask you to pay in four instalments over the year. Since April 1982, the DHSS has taken tax directly from some National Insurance pensions. This has not affected the total amount of tax widows have had to pay, but it has lowered the tax they pay on earnings in compensation. *Check your total tax bill carefully to make sure that you are not paying too much.*

Coping with life alone

There is a tremendous temptation for widows to sit down and take the attitude that life is over. This is understandable, particularly for those recently bereaved. But life is not over, and many women have years of widowhood ahead of them. The best way to overcome grief and make your life better is to do something – anything. Voluntary work is fine, if you are not short of money: it gets you out of the house and distracts you from problems. If you can get some financial reward from what you do, if you are short of money, all the better. Start by finding out what benefits you are entitled to, and get them.

If you do take in lodgers or earn money in any way, you will probably lose your right to social security anyway, because your income will move above the levels below which it is paid. That is a small price to pay for a better, more varied life.

Getting help

Widows do have problems which they cannot always solve themselves. All is not lost. There are many organizations which can help. Write in the first place to the National Association of Widows, Chell Road, Stafford (telephone: 0785 45465), who will point you towards other groups who can assist you. The bodies which help single-parent families (listed in chapter 3 of this section) also help widows, as well as single or divorced parents.

Widowers

In some ways widows are better off than widowers. Families rarely insure mothers in the same way as fathers and it is unlikely that a mortgage will be paid off on the mother's death, or that there will be proceeds from an insurance policy to tide the family over the first few months. Men who are widowed after they are retired and their families have grown up are generally no too badly off financially, but there is very rarely any pensions provision for men, even widowed fathers with dependent children. If they choose to stay at home to look after very young children and the father has not independent means, the family will be forced to live on the very lowest supplementary levels. All the more reason to take out at least a small policy on the life of a wife. If an ordinary life assurance policy cannot be managed, term assurance to cover the years when the children are small is very cheap (see Section one, chapter 13).

Section four
Taxation

1 When we pay tax

Taxation is involved in many parts of our financial life. It is the prime means whereby the government raises money to run the country. The payment of tax is compulsory whenever it is assessed, whether on a company or an individual. Failure to pay your taxes can result in severe penalties.

Although the tax inspector and collector spread their tentacles into many parts of our daily lives, I will deal here only with the most common aspects of taxation which affect most people. You will need the help of an accountant who specializes in tax with the more complicated areas of taxation. I have indicated where these areas lie in chapter 5 of this section.

The government is planning a thorough review of the personal tax system. Discussions will begin in the autumn of 1985 and any changes are planned to be implemented by 1987.

Direct and indirect tax

The taxes individuals and companies pay are divided into direct and indirect:

Direct taxes are paid directly to the Inland Revenue by the tax payer. There are four kinds:

1 Unified income tax, which most of us pay through Pay As You Earn (PAYE) each week or month, or twice a year if you are self-employed.
2 Investment income, which comes from savings, dividends, rents and the like, is now added to earned income and taxed at the same rate. It has some significance for married people, because the investment income of a wife is always added to that of her husband; she cannot be taxed separately on it.
3 Capital gains tax, which you pay if you make a profit on the sale of

certain things, including shares, a second house, paintings and antiques.

4 Capital transfer tax, which is paid when you give your money or assets away either during your lifetime or after your death.

5 Corporation tax, which is paid by companies on their profis.

Indirect taxes are included in the price of many things that we buy and services that we use. These taxes are principally value added tax (VAT), customs and excise duties, which are paid on imports, and stamp duties, which apply on certain contracts like house purchase and buying shares. (I have dealt in more detail with VAT in chapter 3 of this section.)

The level at which we pay these taxes is announced for each financial year by the Chancellor of the Exchequer in his annual Budget. In this he sets out the rules for the country as a whole, just as every person should do for himself. Tax rates do not automatically change from year to year; they may be held at the same rate for several years – though it is unusual for there to be no change at all either in tax rates or personal allowances which are index-linked and can be set against income for tax purposes.

The tax year runs from 6 April to the following 5 April. Remember these dates, because they can affect the amount of tax you pay in some areas.

Unified income tax and the investment income surcharge

Unified income tax is the tax which affects most of us, as it applies to anyone at work and earning more than £2,205 (1985–6). It is called 'unified' because it combines what used to be two separate forms of tax, standard income tax and surtax. Collection has been simplified by putting them together and collecting both the standard (30 per cent) and higher rates of tax (40–60 per cent) mostly under PAYE for employees.

Tax allowances

If you look at your pay slip, you will see that you are not paying tax on your whole income. This is because we all have certain tax allowances, which we can set against our income before we reach the part which is taxed. At present (1985–6), these allowances are:

personal (which everyone except married women gets)	£2,205
married man's	£3,455
wife's earned income relief (if she is working)	£2,205
additional personal allowance (one-parent families)	£2,205
housekeeper (for widow or widower only)	£100
dependent relative – of man	£100
of woman	£145
person looking after children (for working widow or widower or divorcee only)	£100
additional personal allowance for children (only if housekeeper allowance not claimed)	£1,250

blind person's – if either husband or wife are blind	£360
if both are blind	£720
allowance for son or daughter who looks after you	£55
age allowance for 65s and over* – single	£2,690
married	£4,255

*On incomes over £8,800 the allowance is reduced by £2 for every
£3 by which income exceeds this limit.

mortgage interest	all interest on principal residence allowed up to mortgage limit of £30,000

You can see from this that the most highly taxed people are single people
with no dependants who have no mortgages. Those who get taxed least are
married men with a mortgage on their home and an aged relative or two to
support.

Additional reliefs are available under the Business Expansion Schemes.
These can range up to £40,000 a year. (See Section five, chapter eight.)

Earned and investment income
Income has been divided into two kinds for tax purposes – earned and
investment. Broadly, earned income is treated more favourably than
unearned, which includes anything which does not come directly from
employment.

Earned income is:

- Your wages or salary. This will include any 'fringe' benefits like a
  company car, which will be partly taxable.
- Any income from your business, profession, partnership or company.
- Any money you get from an invention. This would include income from
  books and songwriting.
- Any 'golden handshake' or redundancy you get when leaving your job –
  but you pay tax only on any excess over £25,000.
- Any state or private pension or the income portion of an annuity.

Investment income, on the other hand, is money which comes in without
your having to work for it – even though you may have worked to obtain
the investment in the first place (and paid tax on the money which you then
saved). It includes:

- National savings interest (in ordinary accounts, the first £70 interest is
  tax free).
- Building society interest, which is tax-paid if you are only paying standard rate tax. Clearing bank interest and other private-sector saving have
  has been treated in the same way since 6 April 1985.
- Interest on company dividends and government or local authority stock.

- Rents from any property you may let.
- Income from any trusts in your favour.

Some social security benefits are taxed; others are not. The taxable ones are:

- Industrial death benefit.
- Invalid care allowance.
- Invalidity allowance when paid with retirement pension.
- Old person's and retirement pension.
- Widowed mother's allowance.
- Widow's allowance.
- Widow's pension.
- Supplementary benefit.
- Sick pay (short but not long).

Non-taxable benefits include all those on behalf of children, industrial injury benefits, war disablement benefits and:
Maternity allowance.
Attendance allowance.
Death grant.
Family income supplement.
Invalidity allowance when paid with invalidity pension (also not taxed).
Mobility allowance.
Some supplementary benefits.
War orphan's pension and war widow's pension.

How much tax will you pay?
If you know the tax charged at various levels, you can work out how much tax you will pay after your allowances. The current rates of tax payable on taxable income are:

taxable income	rate of tax %	total tax paid in band	total tax payable
£0–£16,200	30	£4,860	£4,860
£16,201–19,200	40	£1,200	£6,060
£19,201–24,400	45	£2,340	£8,400
£24,401–32,300	50	£3,950	£12,350
£32,301–40,200	60	£4,345	£16,695
Over £40,200	60		

You may be wondering why earned and investment income are separated. This is because there used to be a *special investment surcharge* on anyone who has more than a certain level. This no longer applies, and income which comes from any source is simply added together and taxed.

Investment income does, however, have a relevance for married people, because, although a wife can be separately taxed on her earnings, her investment income cannot be separated from that of her husband. For people with a large investment income, or for some pensioners living largely on investment income, this can mean that a married couple reach the higher levels of tax sooner than two single people would do so. There is no way round this if it happens, except the extreme one of divorce.

Irregular incomes

Some people do not have a regular income. Actors, writers and composers, for example, get paid for the work they do as they go along. The Inland Revenue has devised a formula which enables them to spread out their earnings over a period, so that they avoid having to face massive tax bills in one year and then nothing another year. You will need expert advice on how to do this, so get an accountant. His fees will be allowed as an expense against your earnings.

Tax-free income

Certain kinds of income are generally not liable for tax. You will already know of some of these if you have read Section one, chapter 3, on savings. Here is a longer – though not complete – list:

- The first £70 interest on ordinary National Savings Bank accounts.
- Interest on national savings certificates.
- Bonuses on Save As You Earn schemes. (This scheme has been dropped, but existing contracts are still running.) Profits on index-linked savings.
- Interest on post-war credits (government stock issued to help the war effort).
- Prizes on Premium Bonds.
- Any gambling wins.
- Some social security benefits.
- Education grants or money which is a reward for passing an examination, if it comes from your employer.
- Severence payments (often called 'golden handshakes') or capital sums on retirement, if they are less than £25,000, and gratuities for extra service in the army, navy or air force.
- Wounds and disability pensions.
- The capital part of an annuity.
- Housing improvement grants from local authorities.

Capital gains tax

This tax is paid at the rate of 30 per cent (1985–6) on anything on which there is what is called a 'chargeable gain'. A gain of this sort arises when you buy something at one price and sell it at a higher one. It is not payable on all gains: as with all taxes, there are exemptions and any losses you make either in the same or a previous tax year can be set against the gains, though you cannot offset them against gains made in previous years.

The annual exemption from gains for the year 1985–6 is £5,900 and since April 1983 the annual exemption has been index-linked to the Retail Prices Index, so that CGT will be payable only on the *real* gain and not simply the inflationary gain which might come because of a fall in the value of the £ sterling. The 1985 budget introduced index-linking for losses. This means that what looks like a gain on paper may actually be a loss after allowing for inflation, which can be set against real gains.

To take a simple example. Say you buy shares worth £8,000 and sell them eighteen months later for £13,000. You would have a capital gain of £7,000. If you had no other gains or losses in that financial year, you deduct the £5,900 exemption (or whatever the current level is), leaving £1,100, less the costs of buying and selling as outlined in Section five, chapter 2, which will be taxed at the rate of 30 per cent. Gains tax, like income tax, is charged in years from 6 April to the following 5 April. Anyone is liable to it if they are resident in Britain or if they have a business here and make a profit on the assets of the business.

Exemptions
But capital gains is not chargeable on everything. There are certain exceptions:

1 The profit on the sale of your own home. If you have two houses, you will have to decide which is your principal private residence and you will pay capital gains on the other if you sell it.
2 The sale of your own car. If you are a dealer, however, you will have to pay tax on your profits in the normal way.
3 Bonuses on national saving certificates, Defence Bonds, Save As You Earn, National Development Bonds and index-linked savings certificates.
4 Any foreign currency which you take abroad for your personal use.
5 Gambling wins.
6 Compensation for damages.
7 Gilt-edged stock, but you must have held this for a year or inherited it.
8 Money gained when an assurance policy matures.
9 Gains in any one tax year up to a total of £5,900. If your total gain is £8,000 you can knock off £5,900, making £2,100 taxable.
10 Anything you give to the nation – paintings, sculptures, or your house if it is of historic interest, for example.

11 Charities and gifts to charities.
12 Any decoration for gallantry.
13 Anything sold for less than £3,000.
14 Any 'wasting asset' which is movable. This includes profits made on objects which do not have a life of more than fifty years, for instance boats or animals.
15 Sales by a closed company of assets on trust for the benefit of employees.
16 The sale of a debt is not liable to CGT as long as you are the original creditor and the debt is not a 'debt on security'. You will need professional advice about this.
17 Gains from gifts to individuals of no more than £100 in any financial year.

How much do you have to pay?
Gains of up to £5,900 a year for the financial year 1985–6 are free of tax and the sale of any chattels, if they are worth less than £3,000, are also tax-free. Before working out the taxable amount, you can deduct any expenses involved in acquiring or selling the asset – legal fees, stamp duty, any commission paid to professionals acting for you or advertising, for example. After that, the gain is taxed at 30 per cent (for the year 1985–6).

Points to remember
1 You may charge any losses against your gains. Losses can also be carried forward for relief in future, not backwards to past years. Both losses and gains are now index-linked
2 You cannot offset income tax allowances against capital gains. So even if you are living on a pension and paying no tax because your income is too low, you could still find yourself paying capital gains tax.
3 Gains are charged after all expenses are allowed.
4 You do not have a gain until the asset is actually disposed of.
5 Gains tax is payable three months after the end of the tax year in which the gain is made, or thirty days after the inspector has assessed the tax, if this is later.

Capital transfer tax
Capital transfer tax (CTT) is very complicated. If you have considerable capital you will need the advice of an accountant. Here I will set out only the aspects of the tax which may affect a lot of people.

Many people have not even heard of CTT – though they may have heard of estate duty, which used to be payable when a person died. CTT has replaced estate duty – with an important difference: it applies not only when people die, but also when they make gifts over a certain value during their lifetime. It does not mean that if you give a child pocket money you will have to pay CTT on it – even if the money is rather more, for example when you maintain a student at university away from home. It is charged only on a gift and comes within the £3,000 exemption as a rule.

CTT is payable on the cumulative total of all the lifetime transfers made after 26 March 1974 and on any assets which go to someone else on your death. I have already dealt with tax on transfers after death in Section three, chapter 5, so here we will look only at transfers made during your lifetime.

The rates chargeable on lifetime transfers are lower than those at death, and like CGT they have been index-linked since 6 April 1983. For 1985–6 the rates are:

each band of income £	rate %	tax payable at each band £	aggregate of CTT paid £
0– 67,000	nil	nil	nil
67– 89,000	15	3,300	3,300
89–122,000	17.5	5,775	9,075
122–155,000	20	6,600	15,675
155–194,000	22.5	8,775	24,450
194–243,000	25	12,250	36,700
243–299,000	27.5	15,400	52,100
Over 299,000	30		

This means that a person can now make gifts worth up to £67,000, in addition to the £3,000 annual exemption in any ten-year period without having to pay capital gains tax. After that level, the first £67,000 remains tax-free and the surplus carries tax at the rates shown in the table above.

CTT is usually payable by the donor, that is, the person making the gift, and it is his responsibility to declare any gifts and disposals he has made to the Inland Revenue. Donors may, however, make it a condition of a gift that the recipient must pay tax, so, if you receive a gift, check to see if the CTT is also being paid, or if you will be liable.

Exemptions
CTT is not payable on all lifetime transfers. The following are all exempt:

1 Any transfers between husband and wife in life and after death. This means that only one lot of CTT need be paid on the assets of a married couple. If a man gives all his money to his wife and then she happens to die first, it can all come back to him – if she has left it to him in her will – without being liable for CTT.
2 Total transfers in any one year of up to £3,000. You can carry any unused part forward for one year only.
3 Small gifts of up to £250 each to any recipient can be made in addition to this £3,000.

4 Gifts in consideration of marriage. A parent can give up to £5,000, a grandparent or great-grandparent £2,500, and anyone else £1,000.
5 Normal expenditure out of your income, including gifts.
6 Gifts to charities. There is no limit on these if they are made more than one year before death. After death, the limit is £250,000.
7 Gifts to the nation, such as pictures and sculptures, are exempt if they go to museums, art galleries or universities.
8 Gifts for public benefit. The donor cannot decide what comes under this exemption; it is up to the Treasury. In some cases they have refused gifts of historic homes, for example, because the upkeep is too expensive.
9 Gifts to political parties. The same rules apply as for charities. To qualify, a political party must have at least two members sitting in Parliament, or one member and a total vote for the party in the previous general election of at least 150,000. It is no use, therefore, thinking you can make CTT-exempt gifts to the small fringe parties which spring up from time to time, but whose total votes only number a few thousand.

Apart from these exemptions, there are certain other concessions. There are special concessions for agricultural land and woodlands, and when an asset is transferred upon a death very soon after it was transferred to the person who has died, there is some relief, up to a maximum qualifying period of four years.

Remember: you can reduce your liability for CTT by carefully disposing of your assets during your lifetime. And, if you use life assurance properly, the sum payable tax-free on your death may more than cover the tax payable on your personal or business assets. Briefly, what you do is to take out a life assurance policy for a sum assured that looks likely to cover your capital transfer tax liability when you die. You must make sure, however, that the premiums come within the annual exemption for lifetime CTT transfers, so that there is no complication there. A simple trust, then, takes care of the tax question. Take advice if you think such a move would help your family when you die.

How direct taxes are assessed and collected

When the Chancellor of the Exchequer sets out his tax proposals in the Budget in March or early April, long debates follow and there may be some amendments to his original proposals. When this process is finished, the Finance Act is passed, and it is then the business of the Board of the Inland Revenue to publish the new rates of tax. They then collect the new taxes, basing their assessments of how much we should pay on the details of income we send to them in our 'tax return'. New rates of tax become payable immediately after the new financial year starts on April 6, even though the Finance Act is usually not finally completed and passed until the end of June or July.

The Chief Inspector of Taxes

The 'assessment' of tax, as it is called, is the responsibility of the Chief Inspector of Taxes, who operates from Somerset House in the Strand in London. The detailed work is done by offices around the country. There are more than 700 local offices, each under the control of a district inspector and two or more tax inspectors.

If you live in London, you may have to send your return to Manchester. If you live in Manchester, it may be Newcastle-upon-Tyne. It has been a deliberate policy of the government to spread its offices around the country to lessen the concentration of government business in London.

Your local tax office will check your return and work out all your allowances, finally issuing you with a 'code', which is a number related to your allowances. This is also sent to your employer, who can then work out how much tax to deduct from your wages or salary each week or month. The inspectors will also deal with any enquiries you may make about your tax affairs.

These codings only relate to Pay As You Earn. If there are any discrepances at the end of the year, you will receive a rebate if you have overpaid and a bill if you have underpaid.

The Accountant and Comptroller General

The collection of taxes is dealt with by the office of the Accountant and Comptroller General. Its head office is Worthing, with offices around the country to send out the bills, and local offices to chivvy those who are dilatory in paying.

When the assessment is ready, the collector of taxes is notified. If you do not pay on time he will add interest, usually at the rate of 8 per cent a year, until the bill is paid, so it is a good idea to pay at once.

On the other hand, if the taxman owes you money and does not pay quickly, you are entitled to the same interest from him from the day the tax becomes due for repayment.

If you think your tax bill is wrong, it is no use writing or phoning to complain to the collector; his job is merely to collect. You must send any queries to the inspector at the office which deals with your tax. After agreement has been reached he will pass the details on to the collector, who will send you an amended bill.

The tax schedules

Taxation in this country is so complicated that the government has set out details of the various taxes in the Tax Acts, in six sections, known as 'Schedules'.

Schedule A deals with any kind of rent you get from property, which can be either buildings (unless it is furnished, when it comes under Schedule D) or land. You reach a net income figure after offsetting any expenses in maintaining the property. You cannot invent a figure for these: you will have to produce receipts for both materials and labour. Expenses may include repairs, any insurance premiums protecting the property; general rates and water rates, if you pay them; any services which you provide which are not paid for, for example the upkeep of gardens and private roads. There are also certain other permissible expenses, but these usually apply only to large property owners.

Schedule B deals with income from woodlands, but only when these are run as a business.

Schedule C deals with any income from local government stocks or gilt-edged, and foreign dividends on which interest is payable in the UK.

Schedule D covers all income from savings or investments in companies; income from the letting of furnished property (expenses are again allowed); income from any trade or profession or any freelance earnings; any income from abroad, unless it is earned income; and anything which is not covered in the other schedules.

Schedule E is the one we all know about. It deals with all income from employment, including, if you are a married man, your wife's income, unless you have chosen separate assessment or separate taxation (see chapter 4 in this section). It includes income from full-time and part-time work, tips, anything you get in kind (except luncheon vouchers worth 15p or less), and any pensions, including widow's benefits and some social security payments. Supplementary allowances, student grants, maternity grants and allowances, and the death grant are exempt from tax. Some pensions, like wounds and disability payments, are also exempt.

Schedule F deals with the distribution of dividends by companies.

An enormous number of items are dealt with in most of these schedules, far too many to enumerate here. But details of most of them are included in the tax return, which we all (apart from married women taxed with their husband) have to make if we have any income, earned or investment.

2 Your tax return

Filling in your tax return

There are a few general rules about filling in tax returns:

- All your income, including fringe benefits like company cars and private health insurance, must go in.
- Where you have no income from a particular source, like interest or dividends from shares, write 'none'.
- Claim all your expenses – though some, like travelling expenses to and from work, are not allowable against tax.
- When you have finished your return, check through it again to see that you have left nothing out.
- Then sign it with the date. You are signing a declaration which states: 'To the best of my knowledge and belief the particulars given on this form are correct and complete.' *This is most important. There are severe penalties if you lie to the inspector.* He will find out in the end, because anyone who pays you money will have to supply details to him. I have outlined the penalties later on.
- Always keep a copy of your return, because if there is something the inspector wants to query, you will then have it in front of you.

Here are some of the expenses you can claim:

1 The use of your car for business purposes. You will be allowed money for petrol and something towards wear and tear. You must tell the inspector how much you use the car on business and how much for your personal private use, giving mileages for each. He will then calculate your allowance.
2 Subscriptions to a professional organization, if it is essential to your work.
3 Superannuation contributions, unless they are to a trade union.
4 Special clothes or tools which are necessary to your trade and which you have to buy yourself if they are not supplied by your company.

Under the Taxes Management Act 1970 everyone, except married women, who has any income, earned or unearned, is required to make a 'return' of his or her income to the Inspector of Taxes.

The return is a form which asks for details of all your income. There is also space for you to set down what allowances you think you are entitled to. You do not put down the tax allowances set out in the Budget, but give details of your mortgage, dependent relatives, etc. If you have any expenses which are incurred in the course of your work, put these down, too, and the inspector will decide whether they are allowable or not.

From the details you give him, the inspector will work out your coding. If your circumstances change during the year – say, you get married – you must inform your tax inspector and he will change your coding accordingly.

There are three different types of return:

1 *P1*. This goes to people who are employed by someone else and have a very simple income. If you are single and have no dependants, you simply sign the form and give the name and address of your employer. It is not even necessary to give details of your income, because your employer will already have supplied them. Your allowance will simply be £2,205 (1985-6), the single person's allowance. Your employer will receive the appropriate coding and deduct tax from your wages accordingly. It is unlikely that you will receive a tax return form the following year or possibly even the year after that. Simple returns are only required every two or three years.

2 *11P*. This form is designed for those with more complicated incomes. A person who receives this form will quite likely have some income from employment and some freelance earnings, perhaps from the sale of his own paintings or writing or from private jobs which he does in his own time, and will be entitled to a variety of allowances. The form is basically the same as P1, but rather more detail is asked for. You will, for instance, have to show your income. This will be the gross amount which your employer will tell you each year on a form called a P60. If you are in a private pension scheme, the amount you pay in contributions will be deducted from your gross salary to show you the amount that is taxable before allowances.

3 *11*. This form is for the self-employed.

If you are married, and you and your wife are being taxed in the normal way – that is, all her income is 'deemed' to be her husband's for tax purposes – her income must be included on the husband's return. It is possible for husbands and wives to be taxed separately, and I will come to that in chapter 4 of this section. If you are taxed together, your wife will be able to earn up to £2,205 without her income attracting any tax. This figure is the same as the single person's allowance but, unlike that, it cannot be set against investment income.

To help you fill in your return, I have invented a family. Mr X is fifty and is a factory safety engineer earning £12,000 a year. He pays £900 a year into a company pension scheme. He uses his car for his trips to various factories. Mrs X is a schoolteacher working part-time for £5,000 a year and paying £375 into a pension fund. They have two children, one aged eighteen out at work and the other aged fifteen still at school. Mr X's widowed mother lives with them and has only her state pension, but

Mr X's father left him a house on which he made a profit of £9,000 when he sold it, in this tax year. Mrs X keeps some savings in an ordinary account in the National Savings Bank, which brings in £60 interest a year, and more in a building society, which earns £45 interest a year. Mr and Mrs X live in a house which they are buying on a mortgage on which interest payments amount to £700 a year. Mr X also has life insurance premiums which cost £40 a year on a policy taken out in 1981, and £30 a year on one taken out in early 1985, and bank borrowings of £300. He has been married before, has another child who is now twenty-seven, and pays £1,000 a year alimony to his ex-wife.

He now has to fill in his return, probably an 11P, because his affairs are quite complicated. He and his wife have decided to be taxed together, with his wife's income being considered his for tax purposes, because their joint incomes are below the level where it pays to be taxed separately.

The return covers six pages, providing space for all the details of his income, expenses and any allowances which may be set against it. A sample tax return is produced at the end of this chapter.

Page one is very important, because it is here that the tax payer signs his name declaring that the information on the other pages is true. There is also a space where you enter your date of birth and that of your wife, if you were born before 6 April 1926. If this is the case, make sure you fill this part in, because otherwise you will not get the extra personal allowance which is available to the elderly. This is £2,690 if you are a single person or a widow or widower, and £4,255 for a married couple. Mr and Mrs X in my example do not qualify, so they will leave this part empty. People who are retired fill in details of their pension here.

Income

The first section asks for details of your occupation and the name and address of your employer. Anything you pay into a private company pension scheme is deducted from your gross earnings to reach your taxable income. Mr X is in a pension fund, so his employer will already have told the inspector that he earned £11,000 (not £12,000, because the private pension contribution is sliced off the top of gross income. (National Insurance contributions are not).

When it comes to his wife's earnings, Mr X must put in all details of what she earns. He takes her gross salary and makes any deduction for pension contributions; the resulting figure is £4,625–£5,000 minus £375 pension contributions. Again, national insurance contributions are not deductable.

Now here is an interesting anomaly. Mr X must provide this figure, but there is no law which states that a wife must tell her husband what she earns. The inspector will eventually find out from her employer, but if she wishes not to tell her husband, the consequences are not particularly severe. The husband will just have to send an explanatory note and the Revenue will eventually track the money down.

Next come expenses which are necessarily required to follow one's occupation. There may be fixed deductions, which do not apply in the case of Mr X, but he does use his car for work, so he will be allowed something for that. The Inland Revenue will not allow all the maintenance and running costs of the car. It will make a deduction for his private use and will not make any allowance for travel between his home and principal workplace. In Mr X's case, this will be the headquarters of his company.

Suppose here that Mr X can claim that one sixth of the use of his car goes on travel from factory to factory, and that the car costs £24 a week to run and maintain. This is £1,248 and one sixth is £208.

The inspector will give you further details of any allowance you might be able to claim, if you write to him, though he may have further queries to make to substantiate your claim.

Expenses can also include any compulsory payment which you may have to make to a professional body in order to work. You must state the name of the body and the amount involved. Mr X does not have any unavoidable expenses like this. You cannot claim for any entertaining of clients, unless you are dealing with overseas clients, and even then the inspector will only accept what he regards as a 'reasonable' entertaining bill. The Inland Revenue has produced a booklet showing the flat rate expenses it is prepared to allow in different occupations. These are highest for carpenters working on passenger trains and lowest for electricity supply workers for their laundry. Write with a stamped, addressed envelope to Flat Rate Expenses, Public Enquiry Office, Inland Revenue, New Wing, Somerset House, London WC2R 1LB.

The next section deals with pensions and social security benefits. This does not affect Mr and Mrs X yet, but those who do have them should fill in details of their state and company pensions. If the wife has paid full national insurance contributions and is therefore entitled to a pension in her own right (see Section five, chapter 9), an X is entered in a square provided.

Check back on page 287 to see if you receive any of the taxable benefits.

We then come to private pensions, which will include any company pension you receive and, if you are self-employed, any pension you have bought for yourself. If for any reason you have a pension from abroad, that should also be entered.

The following section deals with trades and professions. It is here that any relief is claimed for absence or business abroad. This relief is being phased out and will no longer apply after 6 April, 1986.

The next section deals with rents from any property you may let out. This is divided into furnished and unfurnished property. You should also enter any income you may get from ground rents or land. Provide a separate list if there is not enough room on the form. You will need to indicate which properties belong to the husband and which to the wife.

You can set your expenses against any income you receive from property. These will include any rent or rates you yourself have to pay on the premises; upkeep of furniture; maintenance and repairs; the cost of providing services for tenants; insurance premiums; any fees you pay an agent for letting the premises, and management expenses. You must remember to keep all your bills, and if you have made a loss, which is not all that unusual, you will be entitled to relief.

The return now goes on to any interest you may have which is not taxed before you get it. You must include here any interest which is free of tax, like the first £70 in the National Savings ordinary account, and any bank interest, dividends on government securities and on the now defunct British Savings Bonds. In this section you should also note any interest you might get from any private loan you have made to anyone. For Mr X, it is necessary to include Mrs X's £60 interest from her National Savings Bank ordinary account, even though it will not be taxed.

The following section deals with any dividends from British companies and any tax credits from unit trusts. You must give a full description of each holding – the number of shares you hold, the name of the company or unit trust, and the amount of the dividend or tax credit. Again, there are separate sections for husband or wife. As far as unit trusts are concerned, you must include details of any reinvestment in new units of the income you receive. There then follows a section for any other dividends, interest, income from trusts and annuity income which has already been taxed. There may be additional taxes to pay for very high earners.

Next we come to any interest received from a building society, and here Mr X must enter Mrs X's £45 a year. As he is not paying tax above the 30 per cent standard rate, there will be no more tax to pay, but the interest must nevertheless be included on the return.

Next come payments from settlements, including gifts, then any payments you have received from the estate of anyone who has died in the past financial year.

We come finally to any profits made from any trade or business. You must fill in the type and address of the business and give details of the profits. If you have any expenses, set these out, too, if necessary on a separate piece of paper. This section could include things like commission which you might get on sales. Nothing for Mr X here.

Any money from maintenance or alimony and people who are separated or divorced and receive money under court orders must be entered here. The divorced or separated husband will have deducted tax at the standard rate of 30 per cent before sending the payments but the wife should write in the gross amount and the Inland Revenue will make any adjustment necessary. It is most important that women in this position fill in the return, particularly if they have no other income: they often qualify for a rebate.

Outgoings

The income section of the return is now completed and we turn to outgoings.

Mr X is involved in the first section, which deals with interest on loans for the purchase or improvement of property. He has a mortgage on which he pays £700 in *interest*, in addition to the capital repayments, and he has a bank borrowing of £300. From April 1983, the government changed the method of allowing tax relief on mortgages. The building society or other lender will deduct the standard rate of tax relief from the monthly payments. Anyone paying the higher rates of tax will have the difference between that and the standard rate included in his tax coding.

Mr X's bank borrowing is divided into two parts. He has an overdraft of £100 towards new furniture and a loan of £200 to build a garage. The first £100 is not tax-deductible, because only loans for houses or house improvements are, but the £200 for the garage is allowed against his tax. The bank will furnish him with the details of the interest, which he can then relay to the inspector. Improvement means more than just decoration.

You can only claim tax relief on a mortgage or mortgages attached to your 'main residence', and the limit on that mortgage is £30,000 (see Section one, chapter 8). Once again, husband and wife are treated as one person and cannot have two main residences.

There are exceptions, however. You are also allowed tax relief on mortgage interest on a house occupied by a relative who is incapacitated by old age or infirmity, as longs as he or she does not pay you any rent. There is an exception, too, for divorced or separated husbands. They are allowed tax relief on two mortgages, one on their own home and the other on that of their divorced or separated wife, as long as the total is not more than £30,000. Mr X has been divorced, but the mortgage on his first wife's house has been paid off.

If you have sold your house and have a bridging loan for a period, you will be allowed tax relief on that interest, but you must consult the inspector. Bridging loan relief does not go on for ever. The Inland Revenue usually feels that twelve months is long enough for you to sell your house. After that time, you will probably have to carry the full amount of the interest, without the benefit of tax relief.

The last section on outgoings asks for details of other outgoings and includes any covenants and settlements you may have made. You must give details of the covenant, stating the name of the charity or person who will be benefiting from it. You should enter the gross amount, although you have paid it out net. If it is for £900 a year for the seven-year period, write in £900, but pay the recipient only £630, that is, £900 net of income tax at the standard rate. The recipient will later be able to reclaim the tax deducted, as long as he is not liable for tax.

This section also includes alimony payments, and here Mr X inserts the £1,000 he pays to his ex-wife under a court order. It is important, for, if the agreement is voluntary, no tax relief will be allowed on it. Again, the gross amount has been entered, although Mr X will actually have paid out £700, that is, the amount of the order less 30 per cent standard rate tax. He will later have to make good the 30 per cent to the Inland Revenue, and the Inland Revenue has a formula for adjusting his coding. If for any reason the payment is made gross, this should be stated on the form.

You may also pay rents to someone abroad. If you do, write these down gross, but deduct standard rate tax before making the payments.

Capital gains

We now come to capital gains, which I have already discussed earlier, in chapter 1 of this section. Basically, you pay at a maximum rate of 30 per cent, on all your net gains over £5,900 (1985–6).

Mr X made a gain this year on the sale of the house his mother lived in and which his father signed over to him many years ago. He must give details of the disposal of the house and of the amount of the gain, compared with the value of the house when it was given to him, and allow for the index-linking. So he puts down £8,200. This is the £9,000 profit he made less his selling expenses of, say, £800.

Husbands' and wives' gains are aggregated as if they were one person. Gains can arise in all sorts of ways, the most common being sales of property, shares, unit trusts and land.

If you have made total gains of £5,900 or less in any one year, you will not be taxed, so write 'gains not exceeding £5,900'. Write 'none' if you have made no gains. Remember to charge all your expenses against your gains. That includes any losses you may have made. You must separate out each gain, including development gains you may make from land.

The person making the tax return must also set down any 'chargeable' assets he has acquired. If you have acquired a valuable painting or a second home, for example, you should put down details of it and its value, so that the gains tax – if any – can be calculated should you ever sell it.

Allowances

In the final section of the return you set out what allowances you think you are entitled to. The inspector will automatically deal with the single person's allowance. But if you are married, and either living with your wife or wholly maintaining her on a voluntary basis, you must put that down. You give her Christian or other forename, followed by the date of your marriage if you got married after 5 April 1984, and then her maiden name.

If you are maintaining a separated or divorced wife (or husband) under a court order, you can ignore these first sections, as you will already have entered your alimony payments as one of your outgoings. So Mr X here puts only the name of his second wife.

Next, if you and/or your wife were born before 6 April 1921, there is a space for an 'X'. Do not forget this or you will not get the extra age allowance to which those over sixty-five may be entitled. There is a leaflet available from your tax office, 'Income Tax and the Elderly', which you may find helpful.

Now we come to children. Mr and Mrs X cannot claim any allowances for their children. Child benefit will go to Mrs X for the younger still at school. The older one is now working and filling in his own tax return.

Anyone claiming for a child but only themselves getting the single person's allowance may also be entitled to an additional personal allowance. The same applies to a married man whose wife is totally incapacitated throughout the financial year. In the latter case the additional allowance is to provide for someone to come in and take care of the incapacitated wife.

The opposite does not apply. A wife with a totally incapacitated husband cannot apply for this relief, even if she goes out to work and maintains the family and is therefore unable to be at home to look after him. The Inland Revenue is concerned only that there is a woman in the house who could look after her husband. In cases like this, some women who would prefer to work are forced to claim social security, or have to pay someone to look after their husbands but get no corresponding tax relief.

The return now goes on to the housekeeper allowance; you cannot get this as well as the additional personal allowance. If you are making this claim, details of the person for whom the claim is made, her marital status, her residence, her relationship to you, if any, and how, whether and how much she contributes herself to her keep.

Next, dependent relatives. You may claim if a relative (or one of your wife's if you are married) is unable to work because of incapacity or old age. Similarly, you may claim if your mother (or your wife's) is a widow, separated or divorced, and dependent on you. So here Mr X can claim for his mother, who is living with him on a state pension and nothing else.

You must fill in the name and address of any dependants, their relationship to you, details of any pension they receive, how much you give them and whether they live with you. You must also state whether another relative helps to maintain the person and give the dependant's date of birth and the nature of the infirmity if there is one. You are not limited to helping to maintain only one relative, though Mr X will claim only for his mother.

Next comes the allowance which is permitted if you have to depend on a son or daughter's services. This applies if he/she lives with you to take care of you, or your wife, because you are old or infirm. But you must be maintaining her, and the allowance is the smallest that is available. Similar details must be given as with other dependent relatives.

You qualify for the blind person's allowance only if you (or your wife) are registered as blind. It is not enough, for example, to be extremely short-sighted. The allowance is reduced if you get any other tax free allowances for your disability. You cannot get this allowance and the son's or daughter's services allowance, so if you qualify for both claim the blind person's: it is more than three times as much as the daughter's services.

Next come death and superannuation benefits. If you are simply in a private pension scheme, you will normally put nothing here, because your employer will already have deducted your contributions from the total earnings he sent to the Inland Revenue.

But two kinds of schemes are not included. First, superannuation schemes which provide benefits for a widow or orphans, when relief is given as if it were a life insurance policy.

And second, superannuation or death benefit schemes run by trade unions, in which a proportion of the contribution goes towards a superannuation payment after retirement. Again, relief is given as if it were a life policy. The proportion of the contribution has been agreed with many trade unions. If you are a member of a union, ask them about any schemes they may have.

The usual details are required: the name of the scheme, the full contribution, and the proportion which goes towards death or superannuation benefits.

In the life assurance section, you simply have to write down the amount of premiums, if they are more than £1,275, or any deferred annuity payments over £85. Life assurance tax relief is now normally deducted by the company before you pay your premium. It is at half the standard rate of tax. Any policy taken out since 13 March 1984 does not qualify for any relief, so our Mr X will be paying premiums net of 15 per cent on the £40 premium on his 1981 policy, but will pay the full £30 a year on the 1985 policy.

You must finally include any retirement annuity payments. Give details of employer or insurance company as appropriate, the number of the scheme, and the amount you will pay in the tax year.

That's it. Check through your form, sign it and send it off. It is not as

District

Tax
Return
1985-1986

Date of issue

IN ANY ENQUIRY PLEASE QUOTE

▶ /

Income and Capital Gains
for year ended 5 April 1985

Allowances for year ending
5 April 1986

You are required to complete pages 2–6 of this form, sign the Declaration below and send it back to me within 30 days. It will help if you will also give the information requested at the bottom of this page.

Please read the introduction to the enclosed notes before you start to fill in the form; the notes are there to help you. If you need further help or information please ask me.

H.M. Inspector of Taxes

Declaration

False statements can result in prosecution

To the best of my knowledge and belief the particulars given on this form are correct and complete.

Signature .... Date .... 19 ....
A woman should state after her signature whether she is single, married, widowed, separated or divorced

Private address
Use CAPITAL letters

....

.... Postcode ....

If you make the return as Executor,
Trustee, Receiver, etc., state in what
capacity and for whom made: ....

Pensions information —these details will help me to give you the right PAYE code

		Nature of pension	Self	Wife	State "Weekly" "Monthly" etc.
If you and/or your wife were born before 6 April 1926 please enter date(s) of birth ▼	*Please state here the current weekly/ monthly/four weekly/ quarterly rate of each Social Security or other pension you receive*		£	£	
			£	£	
			£	£	

Self		*If you or your wife are likely to begin receiving a pension before 6 April 1986 please state* ▶	Nature of pension ....
Wife			Starting on *(date)* ....
			Rate of pension ....per week/month/four weeks/quarter
			Payable to *(self or wife)* ....

11P (1985)

INCOME: Year 6 April 1984 to 5 April 1985

	See Note	Details		Amount for year Self £	Wife £
Employments or offices	1	Occupation	Employer's name and address		
	5–7	Earnings, (including fees, bonus, commission)			
		Tips etc.			
		Wife's earnings (including fees bonus, commission)			
		Tips etc.			
	8–9	Benefits, expense allowances			
	10	Leaving payments and compensation			
	11	If you or your wife received a taxed sum from the trustees of an approved profit sharing scheme enter "X" here (See also Note 7b)		▶ ☐	▶ ☐
		If the sum is included with other income above also enter "X" here		▶ ☐	▶ ☐
	12	Duties performed abroad Employment concerned		▶ ☐	▶ ☐
		Dates of absence enclose statement if necessary	Deduction claimed enter "X" { 12½% 100%	▶ ☐	▶ ☐

		Expenses in employment		Amount for year Self £	Wife £
	15	Details of expenses			
	16	Fees or subscriptions to professional bodies	Name of professional body		

Social Security pensions and benefits	20	Retirement pension or old person's pension	If the pension, or any part of the pension your wife receives or is entitled ▶ ☐ to, arises by virtue of her own contributions enter "X" here		
	20A	Unemployment/Supplementary benefit	Enter the full taxable amount ▶		
		If part or all of the taxable benefit is included at 5 above, also enter here the amount so included ▶			
	21	Widow's and other benefits	Nature of benefit .... see identity page of Order Book		

| **Other pensions** | 22–23 | Pension from former employer and other pensions | Payer's name   Address | | |

Trade, profession or vocation	1 25–27	Nature	Business name and address		
	29	Balancing charges and stock relief recovery charges		Dates of absence enclose statement where necessary	
	28	Relief for absence on business abroad			
	29	Deduction for capital allowances	Self £ Wife £		
		Stock relief	£ £		
	30	If exceptionally your profits for Class 4 National Insurance Contributions purposes are affected by interest paid, certain capital allowances or losses not given in the assessment, give details on a separate sheet and enter "X" here ▶ ☐			

INCOME: Year 6 April 1984 to 5 April 1985

	See Note	Details				Amount for year	
Property			Address	Gross income including premiums £	Expenses *enclose statement* £	Self £	Wife £
	35	Unfurnished lettings					
	35	Furnished lettings					
	35	Furnished holiday lettings					
	36	Ground rents or feu duties					
	37	Land					
Interest not taxed before receipt		*Enter ALL the interest from each account*					
	38	National Savings Bank } *Including any exempt amount see Note 38*	Ordinary account ... ... ▶				
			Investment account ... ... ▶				
	39	Other banks *enter name of bank*					
	40	Other sources (including War Loan, British Savings Bonds and loans to private individuals)					
Untaxed income from abroad	41						

	See Note	Name of United Kingdom company		Amount for year	
Dividends from United Kingdom companies and tax credits	42			Amount of dividend £	Amount of tax credit £
		Self			
		....			
		Wife			

	See Note	Source *show each separately. Enter the gross amount for each holding, trust, etc.*	Self £	Wife £
Other dividends, interest, trust income annuities etc., already taxed	43–46			
Interest from United Kingdom building societies	47	Name of society		

Attach a separate sheet if there is not enough space in a section

INCOME: Year 6 April 1984 to 5 April 1985

	See Note	Details	Amount for year Self £	Wife £
Settlements	48	*Include income and capital from settlements, parental gifts etc. and transfers to be treated as your income*		
Payments from estates	49	*Include receipts from estates of deceased persons in Administration*		
Any other profits or income	50–58	*Enter the gross amount* Source *show each separately*		
	58	Maintenance, alimony or aliment received		
	58	Taxable gains on life assurance policies, etc.		

OUTGOINGS: Year 6 April 1984 to 5 April 1985

	See Note	Details	Amount for year Self £	Wife £
Interest on loans *excluding bank overdrafts* **for purchase or improvement of property**	60–62	Only or main residence a. Building Societies Society Account No. Loan at 5 April 1985:– .... Loan paid off in year to 5 April 1985:– .... Please tick if you did not pay under the net interest arrangements (MIRAS) ☐ b. All other lenders: Name of lender Account No. Enclose an interest certificate if — you paid interest without deducting tax or — you claim higher rate tax relief.	*The society will advise me of the amount*	
	63	Let property — no. of weeks let ▶ ☐ — address	*Enclose certificates*	
Interest on other loans *excluding bank overdrafts*	60, 65	Qualifying loans	*Enclose certificates*	
Other outgoings	67	Covenants, bonds of annuity and settlements Covenanted payments to charities	*Enter Gross amount before deduction of tax*	
	68	Alimony, aliment or maintenance		
	69	U.K. property rents or yearly interest paid to persons abroad		

Alterations in untaxed income or outgoings since 5 April 1984

	75			

CAPITAL GAINS and Development Gains: Year 6 April 1984 to 5 April 1985

	See Note	Details		Self	Wife
Chargeable assets disposed of	76–85	Date of disposal	Description	Amount of gain for year *Distinguish Development Gains* £	£
	83				
Chargeable assets acquired	86	Date of acquisition	Description	Cost or acquisition value £	£

CAPITAL TRANSFER TAX

If you have made a gift or other transfer of value you may be liable to Capital Transfer Tax. In some cases transferors are required to deliver to the Capital Taxes Office (not the Income Tax Office) an account of transfers they have made (see Note 88) and there are penalties for failure to do so.

ALLOWANCES: Claim for Year 6 April 1985 to 5 April 1986

See Note	*Before making any claim read the appropriate note*				
90	**Married man living with wife or wholly maintaining her** Wife's Christian or other forenames .... If you married after 5 April 1984 please state (a) date of marriage .... (b) wife's former surname				
93	**Additional personal allowance** Details of child in respect of whom your claim is made— Full names of child *surname first*	Child's date of birth Day : Month : Year	Child 16 or over on 6 April 1985, name of university, college or school or nature of training	Does the child live with you?	Is any other person claiming the allowance for the child?
	If your wife is unable to look after herself— What is the nature of her illness or disablement? .... Is this likely to continue throughout the year ending 5 April 1986? If so *enter "X" in the box* ▶ [ ]				
91	**Age allowance for persons born before 6 April 1921** If you or your wife were born before 6 April 1921, *enter "X" here* ... ... ▶ [ ]				

ALLOWANCES (continued)

See Note		Before making any claim read the appropriate note					
94	**Housekeeper** Full names of housekeeper surname first	Status of housekeeper single, married, separated, divorced, widow or widower	Is the housekeeper living with you?	Relationship if any	If the housekeeper is not your relative, is he or she employed by you for that purpose?		

See Note		Relationship to you (or to your wife). If "mother" state whether widowed, separated or divorced	Dependant's annual income excluding voluntary contributions			If not living with you enter the weekly amount you contribute	1. Does any other relative contribute? "YES" or "NO" 2. If "YES" enter the weekly amount	Dependant's date of birth	Nature of illness or disablement if any
95	**Dependent relative** Name and address of dependant		State pension or benefit	Other pension	Other income				
			£	£	£	£	1. 2. £		

See Note		Status of son/ daughter single, married, separated, divorced, widow or widower	1. Is he/she living with you? 2. Do you maintain him/her?	Which of you is aged, or ill or disabled, yourself or your wife?	If aged enter date of birth Day / Month / Year	Nature of illness or disablement if any
96	**Son or daughter on whose services you have to depend** Full names of son or daughter surname first		1. 2.			

See Note				Date of registration
97	**Blind person's allowance** Self or wife	Local Authority with which registered		

See Note		Name of society, union or scheme	Full contribution for year to 5 April 1986	Portion for death or superannuation benefits
98	**Death and superannuation benefits**			
	Friendly Society— combined contribution for sickness and death benefits		£	£
	Trade union subscription		£	£
	Compulsory payments to provide annuities for widows and orphans		£	

99 Life assurance – limits to relief

If in the year ended 5 April 1985 you and/or your wife paid more than

(a) £1,275 in life assurance premiums (including deferred annuity premiums) *enter the total amount paid* ... ... ▶ £ ....

(b) £85 in deferred annuity premiums and compulsory payments to provide annuities for widows and orphans *enter the total amount paid* ... ... ▶ £ ....

See Note			Contract number or scheme membership number	Amount paid in year to 5 April 1985	Amount to be paid in year to 5 April 1986	Enter year of birth	If a special form is required enter "X"
100	**Retirement annuity payments** Enter the nature of the trade, profession or vocation or the name of the employer if earnings arise from a non-pensionable employment or office	Name of insurance company etc. or trust scheme					
				£	£		

Printed in the UK for HMSO Dd.8400339 4,250,000 10/84 9530.   **Do not forget to sign the declaration on page 1** difficult as it sounds. You will be entitled to some allowances but not all of them. Take the form slowly. If you make a mistake, the tax office will query it, but no action will be taken against you if it is a genuine mistake – though if you deliberately mislead the inspector you may find yourself suffering quite stringent penalties (see chapter 5 of this section). All being well – and it usually is – you will eventually get a detailed coding sent to you from the office. A copy of the code will also go to your employer.

Check the coding: the inspector can make mistakes as well. Your coding will have a number, and an H after it if you are a married man; otherwise it will be L. If, however, you do not wish your employer to know whether you are married or not, ask the tax office to designate your code with a T.

A last point for women: if you are filling in a tax return on your own account, because you have elected to be taxed separately from your husband on your earnings, use the column marked 'self', not 'wife', even if you are married. If you are a married woman being taxed with your husband, only he fills in a return. If you do not like the idea of him dealing with this, turn to chapter 4 of this section.

A sample tax return is reproduced on the previous pages. The form is Crown Copyright and is reproduced with the permission of the Controller of Her Majesty's Stationery Office.

3 Value added tax

Value added tax, or VAT, as it is called for short, was introduced in Britain on 1 April 1973 to replace the old purchase and selective employment taxes. It was brought in to bring our indirect taxes into line with other members of the EEC, as they all have some kind of VAT, though it differs in detail from country to country. In Britain, it is levied on a wide range of goods and services at the rate of 15 per cent.

VAT is a new departure in taxation policy in Britain and has caused a lot of headaches. This is not because it is particularly complicated – it isn't – but because the Customs and Excise language of the instructions has confused many people and – most unusual in Britain – those responsible for paying the tax have to act as their own tax assessors to some extent, rather than having that side of the work done for them completely by tax inspectors.

Fortunately, though we all pay VAT in some form or another, we don't all have the bother of working it out. If you are buying something, you can forget about VAT. The trader will have worked it out and incorporated it in his price to you. Prices usually include VAT, though some traders prefer to show it separately so that you know exactly what you are paying in tax. It can also fool you into thinking the price is lower than it is, so watch out for this.

Who is liable for VAT?

The operative factor here is whether you have a 'business'. If you have, you may be liable for VAT. The Inland Revenue defines a business as any trade, profession or vocation. Clubs and associations, such as sports clubs and members' clubs, are also included, but not trade unions.

All businesses under this definition which have supplies coming in worth more than £19,500 a year must register themselves for VAT with the Customs and Excise department. Supplies in this case can be in the form of money (an author's earnings or a restaurant's takings, for example), or specific goods.

If you don't have this amount coming in, you can register, voluntarily. If you are not registered you will not have to charge VAT to any of your customers but you will not get any allowance on any VAT you have paid to someone else in the course of your business.

If you have not registered, but then find your supplies are more than £6,500 in any one quarter of the tax year, you must tell the Customs and Excise. They will then register you, unless you can prove that your total supplies will not be more than £19,500 for the full year. This can happen quite often – for example, with authors or seasonal businesses.

Take advice if you are not sure. If you do the wrong thing, your problems with the 'Vatman' may go on for years.

What is liable for VAT?

VAT is levied on all imported goods and on a wide variety of products made and services rendered in the United Kingdom itself. Another whole range of goods and services is *zero-rated*, as opposed to exempt. This means the VAT rate is nil per cent, but this could be changed at any time.

It is important to know the difference between exempt and zero-rated goods, because if you are selling zero-rated articles you can claim a refund for any VAT which you have paid to other people, whereas if you sell things which are exempt you cannot.

Here is a list of zero-rated and exempt items. You will notice that they are quite different in character.

zero-rated

food – but not pet food, alcohol, soft drinks, ice cream or potato crisps

water – but not distilled and bottled water

books – but not stationery and diaries

talking books and wireless for the blind

heating fuel and power – but not petrol and derv

construction of buildings – but not repairs, sales by a builders' merchant, or architects' and surveyors' fees

transport – but not taxis and hired cars, or pleasure boats

large caravans – but only caravans longer than 22.9 feet or 7.5 feet wide

bank notes

drugs, medicines, medical and surgical appliances –but only if purchased on a prescription from a registered pharmacist

charities – but only donated goods sold for the relief of distress. Other business supplies are treated normally.

clothing and footwear – but only young children's protective clothing and crash helmets

exports

exempt

land – leasing and hiring out of land, but not hotels, holiday accommodation, camping sites, parking space, timber, mooring and sporting rights

insurance – all types

postal services – except telegrams, telephones and telex

betting, gaming and lotteries – but not admission charges or club subscriptions

finance – but not brokers' commissions or unit trust management fees or consultancy fees
education – but not correspondence schools or secretarial colleges
health – but not health farms, beauty clinics, etc.
burial and cremation

All other sales of goods and services are taxed at 15 per cent.

How VAT works

If you are registered for VAT, you will have to make returns every three months. The account you return for any three months must be made within one month of the end of the period, and the tax must be paid at the same time.

This is what you have to do:

1 Total all the tax invoices you have received.
2 Total all vouchers for tax on imports.
3 Total all outputs.

The sum will then look like this:

total outputs	£20,000	
VAT allotted		£3,000
total invoices and vouchers	£8,000	
VAT paid out		£1,200
balance to be paid to the Customs and Excise		£1,800

You can see that if you keep all your receipts and bills the process is quite simple, but you must keep your records in order.

To show how the tax is added on a single item, let's look at a product which the retailer finally sells to the customer for a price of £200, excluding VAT.

	price	VAT	Customs and Excise receives
Raw materials imported by the manufacturer	£10	£1.50	
Manufacturer sends tax on import to Customs and Excise			£1.50
Manufacturer sells product to wholesaler	£50	£7.50	
Manufacturer sends VAT			£6.00
Wholesaler sells product to retailer	£100	£15.00	
Wholesaler sends VAT			£7.50
Retailer sells to customer	£200	£30.00	
Retailer sends VAT			£15.00
Customer pays VAT			£30.00

The total price to the customer, then, is £230, of which the Customs and Excise gets £30. You will see that the amount of VAT sent to the Customs and Excise at each stage is adjusted according to the amount already paid.

Points to notice
1 A group of companies can opt to be treated as a single business and inter-company trading is then ignored for VAT purposes. Alternatively, divisions can be registered separately.
2 VAT must be paid on the purchase of second-hand goods, but in some cases – antiques, works of art, cars, boats and a few other things – it is only chargeable on the dealers' mark-up. There are other special rules which apply to cars.
3 If you are buying on HP the VAT is payable when the contract is signed.
4 You cannot recoup VAT on business entertaining, unless it is for overseas visitors.

If you want more details, there are a series of Notices on every aspect issued by the Customs and Excise department. These are free from any Customs and Excise office, as listed in the phone book.

4 Marriage and taxation

Separate assessment

In most of the major decisions affecting our lives, the taxman is involved. Marriage is no exception. Contrary to rumour, two cannot live as cheaply as one. The costs of marriage and a family, which I discussed in Section three, chapter 2, can be formidable. For once, the tax system does something to help, and the married man is given extra allowances for his wife and children.

Briefly, the law says that, financially, husband and wife are to be treated as one person – that one being the husband. This means that only he makes a tax return to the Inland Revenue, and he includes his wife's income along with his own. This is known as aggregation of income. He gets all the relief which is available. He pays any tax underpaid by his wife as well as himself, and gets any rebate, even if it applies to his wife's income only.

This law has been relaxed over the years, giving women more control over their money. Some couples, when both are working, opt for what is known as separate assessment of earnings. This does not change the amount of tax paid, but divides the allowances in such a way that husband and wife pay their share of tax according to their income. Doing this can stop a good many family rows about money, but there is no tax advantage. All that happens is that the total tax is calculated and divided between husband and wife in proportion to their incomes. Reliefs are divided like this:

- Life insurance relief goes to the one who pays the premiums on policies taken out on or before 13 March 1984: after that date, the relief was abolished, but not retrospectively.
- Relief for dependent relatives goes to the one who supports them.
- Other allowances are split in proportion to their incomes.
- The tax allowance to the wife must not be less than the single person's allowance.

How separate assessment works

Example: a couple earning £30,000 jointly, each earning £15,000, with £3,000 investment income each.

	Mr X £	Mr X £	Mrs X £
earnings	30,000	15,000	15,000
investment income	6,000	3,000	3,000
total income	36,000	18,000	18,000
tax:			
16,200 at 30%	4,860		
2,000 at 40%	1,200		
5,200 at 45%	2,340		
7,900 at 50%	3,450		
rest (4,700) at 55%	2,585		
total tax before allowances	14,435	7,217.50	7,217.50
allowances:			
married man's	3,455	3,455	—
wife's earned income	2,205	—	2,205
total allowances:	5,600	3,455	2,205
tax relief value of allowances	1,698	1,036.50	661.50
total tax payable	12,737	6,181.00	6,556.00
		12,737	

337

In the table on p.337, the left-hand column shows what happens in a simple situation, if husband and wife are taxed together. The other two columns on the right show the same couple separately assessed. They earn £130,000 between them and have a total investment income of £6,000, both divided equally. This is unlikely in real life, but it shows how the system works. The table shows how the total tax paid is the same, whether they are assessed as one person or two. You will note that at the same income levels the wife pays rather more tax than the husband. This is because his married man's allowance is higher by £1,250 than her earned income allowance. As it is still more usual for wives to earn less than husbands, this discrepancy is not normally so noticeable.

Separate assessment solves some problems, but not those of higher earning couples who find themselves penalized in the tax they pay in comparison with two single people on the same salary. Two wages added together reach the higher levels of tax far sooner than two separate incomes.

Separate taxation

In the Finance Act 1971 the government went some but not all the way to solving their problems when it allowed separate taxation (not separate assessment) for married women on their *earned* income only. They realized that many women found it was simply not worth their while going out to work. After paying someone to replace themselves at home, and paying tax, they were out of pocket, and many valuable workers were lost.

When you have a progressive tax system as we do in Britain, if you aggregate married couples' incomes you eventually penalize people for being married. The way the system works makes a jointly taxed (aggregated) couple better off until their total income reaches £25,361, depending on individual circumstances, because the husband gets an extra allowance for his wife in addition to her own personal earned income allowance.

After £25,361 being married actually costs money in tax terms, unless a couple elect for separate taxation. And joint incomes at that level are not exceptional these days. Working husbands and wives should consider each financial year whether they are in effect paying a 'morality tax', and if they are to do something about it.

A couple must 'elect' for separate taxation. The request must be made by both husband and wife not earlier than twelve months before the start of the financial year in question and not later than twelve months after the end of the financial year.

Inland Revenue leaflet no. 13, 'Taxation of Wife's Earnings', explains the whole process in detail and updates the figures each year to show where separate taxation starts to be favourable.

If a couple elect for separate taxation they, are treated as single people as far as their *earned* income is concerned. (Unearned income from rents, savings, dividends, etc., is still regarded as the husband's income, even if the wife owns the property, shares, or whatever.) Each then makes their own tax return, the husband including in his any unearned income of his wife's.

'Earnings' for the wife include everything she gets from paid employment, but not:

• Child benefit.
• Any national insurance benefits she may get which do not result from her own insurance.
• Any pension or other allowances given in respect of her husband's past employment.

Tax reliefs are then allocated like this:

• The husband loses the allowance he gets for his wife and receives – as she does – the single person's allowance.
• The husband gets all the child relief for his own children, but not, for instance, for those of his wife from a previous marriage.
• The individual can only offset such items as trading losses, deeds of covenant and interest against his or her own income and not that of the other.
• Some allowances are lost, including age allowance.

Other reliefs are allocated as if the couple were not married. This means, for instance, that husbands and wives would each get relief on the premiums insuring their own lives. If a husband has been getting relief for premiums paid on his wife's policy, he will lose it if the couple decide to be taxed separately. Mortgage relief can be divided.

Here are two simple examples of how separate taxation works. In the first example, the couple earn £30,000, divided equally between them.

How separate taxation of earnings works
Example (a) (below): couple earning £30,000, each earning £15,000; no investment income.

In this case, there would be a tax saving of £696 a year. In contrast – example (b) (below): a couple earning £20,000 a year equally divided between them; no investment income.

If they were taxed separately, they would lose £375 a year.

Where the benefit from separate taxation starts and its precise level work out differently in different circumstances. The closer together the two incomes, the greater the saving. Again, the smaller proportion of unearned income in the total, the greater the saving. Where a dependent relative is supported by the wife (for revenue purposes, she cannot support her husband's relatives while he is alive and working), the allowance rises from £100 to £145. This increased allowance is only permitted in cases of separate taxation, *not* separate assessment, and it is one of the few ways in which women have an advantage in the tax system.

| | taxed together | taxed separately | |
	Mr Y £	Mr Y £	Mrs Y £
earnings	30,000	15,000	15,000
allowances:			
married man's	3,455	—	—
wife's earned income	2,205	—	2,205
single person's	—	2,205	—
total allowances	5,660	2,205	2,205
taxable income:	24,340	12,795	12,795
16,200 at 30%	4,860	(all) 3,838.50	3,838.50
3,000 at 40%	1,200	—	—
5,140 at 45%	2,313	—	—
total tax payable	8,373		7,677

(b)

	Mr Z £	Mr Y £	Mrs Z £
earnings	15,000	7,500	7,500
allowances:			
married man's	3,455	—	—
wife's earned income	2,205	—	2,205
single person's	—	2,205	—
total allowances	5,660	2,205	2,205
total taxable income	9,340	5,295	5,295
all at 30% tax	2,802	1,588.50	1,588.50
			3,177

If you are close to the level where you will benefit from being taxed separately, particularly if you are recently married, it may be best if you opt for separate taxation from the word go. This breeds an attitude of self-reliance and independence early on, and means, particularly if you are a woman, that you will always be able to cope with your financial affairs. It would be foolish, however, to throw money away just for the sake of being independent.

When a couple are taxed together, the husband is liable for all tax, and although it's nice when you get a rebate, it's sometimes difficult to persuade a wife who may feel she's already paid enough tax on PAYE to hand the extra money over if she has underpaid.

Remember, all this only applies to earned income. A husband must give details of their joint dividends and interest on his tax return. There is, however, no law which says that a wife must tell her husband about her income, earned or unearned – though the Inland Revenue will always catch up with you in time.

The whole system of taxing married people is under review, but sweeping changes are not expected until at least 1987. Meantime, there is nothing to stop a married couple from being separately taxed on their earnings and separately assessed on the whole of their income, but for a couple to do it without an accountant (see below) requires a good working knowledge of the tax system.

Living together

For high income earners, there is certainly a lot in financial terms to be said for living together, rather than marrying. Such couples are always taxed separately and there is no adding together of their investment income. They also both get the full £30,000 allowed for mortgage relief, which can substantially reduce the new cost of a home for them, or they can have two homes with full tax relief. One way or another, they are able to increase their net income in comparison with a married couple.

It is also possible today for a non-married spouse to benefit under the other partner's pension scheme after death, so even that gives marriage no advantage over living together.

It is, however, sensible for such couples to marry, if possible, after retirement. Incomes generally drop to levels where there is no advantage from separate taxation and mortgages have usually been paid off. Death is nearer and capital transfer taxes can be avoided, because there is no CTT between husband and wife.

Marriage for the high income earner has advantages only in the matter of lifetime CTT and Capital Gains Tax, neither of which apply between husband and wife.

Unemployed husbands

Working wives with unemployed husbands have the edge, taxwise, on those husbands with unemployed wives. This is because a working wife's income will be counted as the total income of both and receive the benefit of her earned income allowance and his married man's allowance. In contrast, if she does not work, he does not get the benefit of her allowance, which, unlike other personal allowances, can be applied only to her earnings. The difference can be quite substantial. For the year 1985–6, a married man with a non-working wife and no other allowances would pay £2,563.50 tax on a £12,000 income. In contrast, if he were not working, the wife's tax bill would be only £1,902 on the same salary.

Employing a wife

Men who are sole traders or partners can cut their tax bills by employing their wives, rather than raising their own salaries and so putting themselves into a higher tax bracket. Similarly, company directors can save corporation tax in the same way, though the savings are usually rather less.

The Inland Revenue will require to know that the wife is doing a genuine job: you cannot simply switch your income from yourself to a wife and expect the tax authorities to accept that she is working. Preparing the books, acting as secretary, working in the business or in, say, a shop, or answering the telephone in business hours would all be legitimate activities justifying a salary.

As long as one keeps below the level of the single person's allowance (£2,205 for the year 1985–6), there is no National Insurance or tax to pay on the whole amount. After that level, National Insurance is payable on the whole amount, so it is better to keep the level below the allowance. the saving may not seem much over the year, but it does add up over the years to something quite substantial and, of course, there is extra benefit if, by paying a wife, a husband is able to cut his own tax bill in the higher rate bands.

There are other possible benefits, too. By taking careful advice, a man can build up a pension for his wife. Contributions towards this pension can be fully allowed for tax. This is because she is an employee and as such entitled to a pension and also to a tax-free sum on retirement. It is important to take advice, so that you are sure of remaining within the rules, which change from time to time. Quite large amounts can be invested with full tax relief and the benefit is continued in retirement, because any money paid in pension is treated as earned income and a wife can therefore set her earned income allowance against it.

5 When you need an accountant

Most people can fill in their own tax return without using an accountant to help. You cannot charge your accountant's fees against your income tax as an outgoing if all he does for you is fill in the return. It is for the more complicated business accounting that an accountant does that fees are allowed against tax. Most people who are employed by someone else and do not have family complications should be able to manage their return themselves. If there is any inaccuracy, the inspector will probably spot it and query the matter with you.

But once you get into the realms of, for example, separate taxation and assessment, covenants, divorce, property leases, fringe benefits, golden handshakes, your domicile and residence, overseas income and double tax relief agreements, or tax due from a company you own or a partnership of which you are a member, you should seek the advice of an accountant.

It is not simply a matter of filling in the return, but of knowing when and what allowances can be set against your tax and the most efficient way to do it. Accountants are, or should be, highly skilled in making sure that you pay the minimum tax without infringing the law (see the last chapter in this section).

To discourage you from trying to deal with these matters yourself, I will set out here just the briefest details of the tax implications of the following:

Covenants

These (and gifts and settlements) can help you and the recipient save tax. A covenant must cover at least four years, and cannot be made by you to your dependent children. You can make one to other people's children, however. Many people make them to grandchildren or god-children, to charities, and to old people on low incomes. The money is paid by the donor after standard rate tax, but if the recipient is not liable for tax it can be reclaimed. Remember, though, if you make a covenant to a child which is more than £2,205 a year (the current single person's allowance) a year, the child or its parents will have to pay tax on the surplus. (For covenants by parents to student children over eighteen, see Section three, chapter 2).

Divorce and separation

It pays everyone involved to have a court settlement. This means that the husband (or nowadays it could be the wife) will be able to deduct any alimony paid from his taxable income, and in turn the wife or husband (though this is much rarer) may be able to reclaim some of the tax paid. It is always foolish to delay coming to a legal agreement, for as a rule everyone is better off, and there are means of saving money on both sides in the way that the payment is divided between the separated or divorced spouse and any children of the marriage.

Property leases

If you have any major dealings in the leasing of property, you must discuss these with an accountant, or you may lose money, in addition to losing any right to repossession of your premises.

Fringe benefits

There are many fringe benefits which must by law be declared. They include:

- Rent-free accommodation close to your work.
- The use at home of a television set paid for by your company. This will be taxed at 10 per cent of its annual value.
- Cash vouchers.
- Season tickets supplied by the employer.
- Company cars. The value upon which you will be taxed varies with the size, price and age of the car. The rates are changed in each Budget, with the level depending on the engine capacity of the car in question.
- Employer payments into private medical schemes.
- If you get a loan for any purpose other than to buy your home, either interest-free or at a much lower rate than most people have to pay, you will be taxed on the 'benefit' you receive between that and the official rate, which is fixed by the Treasury. There are some rules about this, and some exceptions, so you will need the advice of an accountant.

Golden handshakes

These are payments made to people either as compensation for loss of their job before their contract or notice expires or as a reward for so many years' service with a company. They are called 'golden' because they used to be completely tax-free, but today they are partly liable for tax. The first £25,000 is ignored, then tax relief is withdrawn on a sliding scale until a level of £75,000 is reached. Any excess over that is taxed in full as income for the particular tax year in which you receive the golden handshake. An accountant can help you get the best deal.

Domicile and residence

You may not actually live in this country, but you will be liable for full tax here unless you take certain steps to make sure that the Inland Revenue knows you are no longer resident. This has an effect on the UK income, capital gains and capital transfer tax that you will have to pay.

Your domicile is the place you regard as your natural home. You can only have one domicile, unlike nationality, where you can sometimes have two. Most people are domiciled in the country where they were born. But you can have a domicile of origin, of choice, or of dependency.

Residence is different, and is fixed from year to year, depending on where you are, and you can be regarded as being resident in two countries at the same time. This depends mainly on where you spend most of the year, or where your 'place of abode' is. Residency applies not only to individuals but also to companies.

All these questions are very complicated, so if you contemplate living abroad or keeping one home here and one abroad consult an accountant to ensure that you do not pay too much tax. If you wish to live abroad permanently, here are some of the ways of proving that you are doing so:

- Live there.
- Buy a house there, or rent one on a lease.
- Start a business there.
- Marry someone from there.
- Change your will to fit in with the law of the country to which you have moved.
- Arrange for your family to live with you.
- Buy yourself a burial plot there.

There are many other things you could do. For instance, you could change your nationality, which would fix it once and for all – but that is not necessary. What you must do is prove to the satisfaction of the Inland Revenue that you live in your new country for all practical purposes.

Tax on foreign income and double tax relief

This is an arrangement which the UK has with many other countries to try to ensure that people do not pay tax twice over. For instance, you may get a dividend from one country which is already taxed, then have to pay tax all over again in the UK.

Various arrangements have been devised, and before you even think of investing overseas you should explore the situation with an accountant.

Quite apart from anything else, there are certain rules for assessing what overseas remittances (income) actually are, what allowances you can deduct, and how much you can leave abroad. All these questions need special knowledge which is rarely available to the ordinary person who suddenly finds that he has some income from overseas, perhaps from a long-lost uncle.

Below is a list of the countries which currently have double tax relief arrangements with the UK. These agreements are rarely cancelled, but they are altered slightly from time to time, so ask your accountant precisely what the particular agreement is with the country in which you are interested.

In addition to these, there are many more limited agreements which apply only to certain businesses. These mostly just cover profits on shipping and air transport and include Argentina, Brazil, Lebanon, the USSR and Portugal. Agreements with Iceland only cover shipping profits and those with Iran and Spain only cover air transport profits.

Double tax relief arrangements exist with the following countries:

Antigua	Grenada	Norway
Australia	Guernsey	Pakistan
Austria	Indonesia	Portugal
Barbados	Irish Republic	St Christopher and Nevis
Belgium	Isle of Man	St Lucia
Belize	Israel	St Vincent
Botswana	Italy	Seychelles
British Solomon Is.	Jamaica	Sierra Leone
Brunei	Japan	Singapore
Burma	Jersey	South Africa
Canada	Kenya	SWA (Namibia)
Cyprus	Lesotho	Swaziland
Denmark	Luxembourg	Sweden
Dominica	Malawi	Switzerland
Falkland Is.	Malaysia	Tanzania
Faroe Is.	Malta	Trinidad and Tobago
Fiji	Mauritius	Uganda
Finland	Montserrat	USA
France	Netherlands	West Germany
Gambia	Netherlands Antilles	Zambia
Ghana	New Zealand	Zimbabwe
Greece	Nigeria	

Corporation tax

Corporation tax is paid by companies not individuals. Most companies have their own accountant, and rightly so. If you have just set up a company, you may feel that doing without an accountant is an economy you can make. This is always a mistake.

Companies do not keep to the country's financial year ending 5 April; they can at present choose any date on which to end their accountancy year – though all new companies are being encouraged to choose 31 March, for the sake of uniformity.

The system of corporation tax is called the 'imputation system'. What happens is that the company pays dividends to its shareholders and then pays tax to the Inland Revenue of 35/65ths of these dividends. This is called 'Advance Corporation Tax' (ACT), which is then deducted from the final corporation tax bill, so that in fact the full 50 per cent is not paid at the end of the year. Small companies pay at a reduced rate of 30 per cent (the same as the standard rate of tax) on profits which do not exceed a certain amount. An accountant is needed to work out at what level of profit the company will pay what tax. In the 1984 Budget, the Chancellor of the Exchequer announced that Corporation Tax might be reduced to 35 per cent by the financial year 1986–7. In that case, the net rate, balanced by ACT, will be very low indeed.

If a company makes losses for some years, these can be offset against profits that are made later. Such a situation is quite common among new companies, and later on the relief can be useful. Losses can also be offset against corporation tax already paid; the result is then a tax repayment.

If you are a 'close' company, that is, a company which is controlled by five or fewer people and what are called their 'associates', which broadly means close relatives, there are special tax provisions. You are *not* a close company, however, if your shares are quoted on the stock exchange and at least 35 per cent of the shares are owned by outsiders. Check to see what your situation is.

Partnership taxes

Partnerships (see Section two, chapter 5) are not taxed in the same way as individuals, either. How do you know that you are in partnership – because there need not necessarily be a written agreement? To find out, you must ask yourself a lot of questions. Here are just a few of them:

- Is there a written agreement?
- Are the partners responsible for all debts?
- Has a business name been registered?
- How are the profits divided?

The senior partner, who is known in law as the 'precedent partner', must make the return of the income and the outgoings of the partnership as a whole. The gross income is split between the various partners, sometimes in equal shares, sometimes not, and they are then responsible for income tax in the usual way, each making their own individual return.

If they show a loss, that is shared out in just the same way as a profit, and each partner can use this loss in several ways to offset his profits from other years. When partnerships are simple, the partners may be able to manage without an accountant, but in more complicated ones they would be well advised to call one in to help assess their income and outgoings in a satisfactory manner.

New rules brought in by the Chancellor of the Exchequer in the 1985 Budget aim to cut down on tax avoidance which was previously possible in partnerships when the membership changed. The rules affect only the early years of new partnerships and not the final years of old partnerships.

6 Keeping your taxes to a minimum

Tax evasion

Only the very poor escape taxes in this country, and to many people the amount they pay seems excessive. But taxes are compulsory. There is no way out of paying taxes which are levied by law, and anyone who does not pay tax for which he is liable is breaking the law. This is called *tax evasion*, and it carries quite severe penalties. This is not just a matter of not paying your tax bill, but extends to not telling the Inland Revenue the truth and the whole truth about your income. If you don't tell the Inland Revenue that you have a bit of money tucked away in a bank account earning taxable interest, for example, you could find yourself paying a fine of £100 *when* – not *if* – they catch up with you, as they always do in the end. Even a failure to fill in and send back your annual tax return can land you with a fine of £50.

Here are a few of the penalties which the Inland Revenue has thought up for us, though they will accept less sometimes if they think there are extenuating circumstances and you have made a genuine mistake:

if you	you may be fined
send an incorrect return	£50 plus any additional tax, or in the case of fraud, £50 plus *twice* the additional tax.
help someone to prepare an incorrect return	£500
give wrong information to the Inland Revenue	£500 if you are convicted of fraud; otherwise £250.
do not tell the Inland Revenue that you are liable for tax	£100

Tax avoidance

This is quite another matter. There is no law which says you must not arrange your financial affairs in such a way that you pay as little tax as is legally possible. That is just part of sensible money management. There are some rules about tax avoidance as well, but these are mainly to do with overseas income and investments and don't affect the majority of us.

Remember, a tax accountant is a tax payer's best friend. Go to a proper one – don't take advice from just anyone. As with so many things, many people think they know more than they do. Your accountant knows the rules and regulations and where savings can be made. You will have to pay him according to the amount of work he does for you, but if your affairs are at all complicated the Inland Revenue will probably let you charge his fees as an expense against your tax – though, as I have already said (chapter 5 in this section), they won't if all the accountant does for you is fill in a simple tax return.

Tax savings

Since income tax affects more of us than any other form of tax, let's look at that first to see where you can make savings, or at least to make sure you are getting all the allowances and reliefs you are entitled to. But there are also ways of avoiding paying unnecessary capital gains or capital transfer tax.

Personal reliefs and allowances. It goes almost without saying that you should claim all your allowances as soon as you are entitled to them, for example when you marry.

Married people's earnings. Ask yourself whether you wouldn't be better off taxed separately, or if you are already taxed separately whether aggregation wouldn't suit you better. Many couples find that as their circumstances change old patterns of payment no longer keep the joint tax bill to a minimum, so think about this every new tax year.

Wife's earnings. If you are in business and it's at all possible, pay your wife a wage. She can then claim her earned income allowance. But don't try to pay her more than the job is worth; the Inland Revenue will not allow it.

Employees' fringe benefits. Get as much as you can in a tax-free form. Governments constantly cut down on the tax-free element of these, but they are still worth having. The tax charged on a company, for instance, is very little compared to the value of the full use of the car to the recipient. Make severance payments in the form of 'golden handshakes', which save tax for the employee.

Business expenses can be offset against income tax. There's a wide variety of these, from the normal costs of business to the use of a car for business or even fees to a professional body. If in any doubt, check with an accountant.

New businesses. Time the start of your business to keep down your tax bill for the first few years. You'll need an accountant's advice on this.

Overseas income. If you have money abroad, take the advice of an accountant. He may be able to save you a lot of tax.

House purchase. I've been over the rent-or-buy debate earlier. If you decide to buy, take advice as to which kind of mortgage will save you most tax. Pay close attention to the life of the mortgage, and try to get the most relief at the time of your maximum earnings.

Make sure that you also get tax relief, where appropriate, on home improvement loans. For this, you must – together with your mortgage – keep within the £30,000 limit for home loan relief.

Business expansion schemes. These can save tax to quite high levels. (See Section five, chapter eight.)

Self-employed annuity contracts. These provide an excellent way of saving tax if you work for yourself, and relief ranges up to 75 per cent for high incomes (see Section five, chapter 9).

Deeds of covenant. These can save money over a four or more year period. Payments are made by the covenanter after deducting tax at the basic rate, which can then be reclaimed by the beneficiary if he is not a tax payer (see chapter 5 of this section).

Capital gains tax. No tax is paid if you keep your gains below £5,900 each year. Towards the end of the tax year, look carefully at any investments you have, in case you can set some losses against gains. Work out the most favourable way for you to be treated for gains tax.

Capital transfer tax. Give away as much as you can, within the limits, while you are alive. The amount you are allowed to give varies each tax year. If you are married, leave as much as you can to your spouse when you die.

Repayment of tax. The Inland Revenue is notoriously slow at paying back overpaid tax, so get your claim in as quickly as possible.

Here are four rules for tax planning:

1 Never make yourself miserable trying to save tax. Probably the ultimate in this is emigrating when you know it would make you and your family unhappy.
2 Never cut off your nose to spite your face. There is no point in losing money in a business just to save tax – though if you did, you wouldn't be the first to do so.
3 Never impoverish yourself. Don't give away all your money to save capital transfer tax. The law may change anyway, and it is the law on the date of your death which counts.
4 Never go in for long-term tax saving schemes. The law may change and you may be stuck with them. Always be flexible and review your planning from time to time.

Your tax inspector
Cordial relations with your tax inspector can do much to make your affairs straightforward and easy to deal with. He is not an ogre and does not want

you to pay more tax than you should. He will always help if you ask him about any possible allowances to which you might be entitled. It is simple financial sense to cooperate with him.

If you want to make yourself better informed in the areas which affect you, get hold of one of the many useful booklets which the Inland Revenue produces on various aspects of the tax system. They are easy to understand and will give you more detail than I am able to do here and are updated more often than this book. The leaflets are all numbered and the ones which most commonly affect the individual are:

IR22	Personal allowances
IR34	PAYE
IR4	Income tax and pensioners
IR4A	Age allowance
IR32	Separate assessment
IR13	Wife's earning election
IR31	Income tax and married couples
IR30	Separation and divorce
IR23	Income tax and widows
IR29	Income tax and one-parent families
IR28	Starting a business
IR45	What happens when someone dies
CGT8	Capital gains tax
CTT1	Capital transfer tax

Section five
Investing

1 Investing in the stock market

Taking a risk

If you have pursued a sensible financial policy, you may eventually find
that you have as much money as you want in reserve for a rainy day, that
you have a reasonable income coming in from your savings, and that you
still have some capital left over.

Even if you have not reached this desirable state, if you are young and
without responsibilities you may feel that you can afford to do something
a little more exciting than saving in a bank or building society with your
spare cash.

In either case, this is the time for you to turn to investing rather than
saving. Basically, both amount to the same thing; the aim in each is to
increase your wealth. But while regular saving should mean that your
capital is secure and growing and that you are gaining the maximum
income from it, investing can give rather more. The aim of investment is
to increase the value of your capital and your income rather more than
you would do by saving. To do this, you must take a risk.

You can invest in many different ways – by buying shares in the
country's biggest companies; by buying properties to rent out, or to
improve and sell; by buying antiques, silver, precious stones and the like,
which you hope will eventually increase in value; or by putting some
money by in a pension fund to secure a better income in your old age.

All these ways of trying to increase your wealth have one thing in
common: they all involve some risk. The degree of the risk varies,
depending on what sort of investment you choose, but it is always there
to some extent. The company in which you invest could double its profits
and thus the value of your investment; alternatively it could go bankrupt
and you could lose all your money. The value of the painting or antique
you brought could increase sharply, or it could become unfashionable. In
the latter case, if you try to sell, you would be lucky to get back the price ·

you paid for it originally. Changes in the law relating to renting and security of tenure for tenants could depress the value of the property you bought, or, in contrast, a sudden change in renting policy on the part of the government could dramatically increase the value of your property. All your pension plans could come to nothing, because you are taking a risk on how long you will live and you may not reach pensionable age before you die. On the other hand, you could live so long that you get far more in pension than you ever put into the fund.

In any one of these areas you can make a profit and increase your wealth, stay exactly where you are, or lose some, if not all, of your money. This is the essence of investment – *you take a risk when you start out for the chance of making a better than average profit*. The purpose of this section is to help you minimize the risk of loss and maximize your chances of profit.

Only the individual can decide whether he is ready to take a risk. You must look at your total financial situation. How secure are your sources of money? Is there any danger of losing your job? Have you responsibilities towards others which will not allow you to take risks? Have you the temperament to take a risk?

This last is rather important. All the preconditions for investment may be there, but if worry over them is going to ruin your life, stick to things which are safe and secure. Go back to section one, chapter 3, and look for secure havens for your savings.

Now, assuming that you fully appreciate the risk you are taking, let's start with the stock exchange and investment in shares.

Why stocks and shares?

Buying stocks and shares is a favoured way of investing for several reasons. First, if you have shares in a company you are one of the owners with certain rights to its profits and assets – though unless you are actually running the company these rights may be somewhat remote.

Second, many people believe that if the economy generally expands the profits of individual companies will also grow and that dividends will rise with them. As a result share prices will rise, bringing a profit to shareholders.

Third, dividends are now usually declared and paid twice a year. The first payment is called the interim dividend and the second the final, or second interim, making a particular total for a company's financial year, so the investor can be assured of an income which will offer a certain return at the price he paid for the shares, regardless of how the share price moves up and down.

There are disadvantages in buying stocks and shares, however. Companies have liabilities as well as assets and they are therefore not so clear-cut an inflation hedge as are objects and articles. At certain times, the liabilities of a company may assume greater weight and depress the share value. However, in sound companies at least, such setbacks are followed by a recovery in values, as the profits of most companies will rise with inflation; this must eventually work through to shareholders. But you may buy shares in a company which does badly no matter how much the economy generally expands.

The Stock Exchange

The Stock Exchange is the market place used by the public to buy shares in British industry and commerce. Many of Britain's larger companies have only grown to the size they have by issuing some of their shares on the open market to raise money for expansion. As well as the official market, a new unlisted securities market has been set up for smaller companies which do not quite meet the stock exchange rules for quotation (see page 355).

The 1980s have seen great changes in the Stock Exchange, changes which are by no means over. Not only have the basic rules been affected, but new companies, particularly foreign-owned ones, are buying into the old share-dealing firms and the chances are that the whole system will change in the next few years. Precisely what those changes will be is impossible to forecast at the moment. It remains to be seen whether the small investor, who has largely been squeezed out of the market recently, will find that the new arrangements cater better for his needs.

It seems clear, however, that the unique British system of share dealing is set for some modifications. Already, the number of firms operating in London has dropped by two-thirds in the past twenty years, as stockbroking companies have got together to survive. At present, the Stock Exchange is discussing new forms of dealing, which will bring to an end the distinction between jobbers and brokers (see below) by 1986.

There are several branches of the Stock Exchange around the country, the London one being easily the biggest. Until 1973, these were all separate, with their own rules, and the exchanges outside London concentrated mainly on local shares and the very large countrywide British companies – though of course they could always get a share for you which was quoted only in London. Then, in 1973, the exchanges amalgamated themselves to form one body, which is simply called the Stock Exchange. The regional centres have stayed open and the local stockbroking firms in those areas have also remained. Its operations are scrutinized by the Stock Exchange Council, which is made up of elected partners from broking and jobbing offices.

If you want to buy shares, you will have to operate through one of these stockbroking firms. You cannot go to the Exchange like going to a shop, or write up for shares. You must use a stockbroker, and he in turn buys shares from a (stock) jobber, who makes a market by different buying and selling prices. If you do not have a stockbroker, you can buy shares through your bank, which will have its own stockbroker who deals for the bank. On the whole it is better to have your own stockbroker and to try to build up a relationship with him. He should be highly knowledgeable and able to advise you about the best times for buying and selling, or whether to buy and sell at all.

If you are new to investing, it is probable that you do not know a stockbroker. At one time, the only way to find one was by introduction. Today, however, the Stock Exchange issues a list of brokers who are prepared to act for small and unknown investors. You may also see an advertisement, but not many stockbrokers do much advertising, except occasionally for prestige purposes. In fact, they have only been allowed to advertise for the past few years, and not many have taken the opportunity. Here are the addresses of the various stock exchanges round the country that you can write to for advice.

Birmingham: The Secretary, The Stock Exchange, Birmingham B3 3JL
Liverpool: The Secretary, The Stock Exchange, Exchange Street East, Liverpool L2 3PB
London: The Public Relations Officer, The Stock Exchange, London EC2N 1HP
Northern Ireland: The Secretary, The Stock Exchange, 10 High Street, Belfast BT1 2BP
Scotland: The Public Relations Officer, The Stock Exchange, 227 Ingram Street, Glasgow G2 1BU
York: The Secretary, The Stock Exchange, 3 St Sampson's Square, York YO1 2RL.

The Unlisted Securities Market
Until the 1980s, share dealings in Britain were confined to a single listing on the London Stock Exchange and its provincial offices. It gradually became clear in the early 1980s that this market was simply not catering for all the companies which wished to have a share quote. Its rules for accepting a company's shares were too onerous for some and too complex for others.

The problem was solved by the setting up of an Unlisted Securities Market, with far less strict rules. Such a division of the market has been common in the United States of America for many years. In the new market, companies need not be of a minimum size, only 10 per cent of the shares need be marketed instead of 25 per cent, the cost of a listing is much cheaper than in the main market, only very brief details must be advertised rather than a full prospectus and, finally, although a three-year record is liked, it is not essential (and need not show profits). A company could actually come forward with a blueprint for development with no trading behind it. The USM is, therefore, a much more direct way for (particularly) smaller companies to raise limited amounts of capital.

Of course, the relatively slack rules for a share quotation imply that shares quoted on the USM carry more risk than those on the main listing. Nevertheless, the USM has been rather successful in its first couple of years, although the total value of the shares quoted does not amount to that of a single one of Britain's major industrial giants which are quoted on the main board.

It is important for would-be investors in the USM to recognize the risk. At the same time, it has to be said that many of these companies may carry the seeds of higher-than-average growth in coming years and produce huge profits.

The over-the-counter markets

Another market has emerged in recent years, which provides companies which are not quoted on any stock exchange with a market for their shares and a means of raising finance. It is called the over-the-counter (OTC) market. Anyone dealing in this market should recognize that there is no one supervising it and that there is no investor protection. The OTC works in two ways. One is simply by agents, who match buyers and sellers and charge them a commission for the service. No other parties are usually involved in this sort of deal. Other dealers actually act as principals, buying and selling on their own account. They have bid and offer prices, just as in the Stock Exchange, and their profit is the difference between the two. This is not yet a market for the small investor to get involved in, but it is wise to be aware of it, as its influence may grow in coming years.

Before you think about investing, start to read the financial pages of your newspaper. As you get more interested, try reading one of the many excellent books on investing. Buy the latest book or the latest edition. The investing world changes rapidly, and you need to keep up to date with the best opportunities. Learn as much as you can, but until you really feel confident always take the advice of your stockbroker or bank manager. Try James Rowlatt's *A Guide to Saving and Investment* (Pan Books, 1984 edition).

All the advice and all the reading in the world will not make you an investment expert immediately. That will only come with experience.

Shares

A share is just what it says. When you buy one – or, rather, usually a fair number – you are buying a share in the company and become one of the owners of the company.

Each company has what is called an authorized capital. This is the total value of the shares it can issue at any one time to the public. The shares which have actually been issued make up the issued capital. The issued capital may be as much as the authorized capital or it may be less.

This capital can all be divided into the same kind of shares or into different kinds. However it is done, every share will have what is called a par value. This is the nominal value and can be any amount, 10p, 25p, 50p and £1 being the most common – though it can be higher or lower, as low, say, as 1p. It is highly unlikely that the price the investor pays – the market price – will be the same as the par value. This is used only for the purpose of declaring a dividend – the name used to describe the interest paid on each share. Dividends are announced today both in percentages and in cash. A 10 per cent dividend on a £1 share will be 10p; on a 25p share it will be 2.5p, and so on.

The Stock Exchange does not only sell shares in companies, it also sells government stock. These are debts which the British Government owes to the private investors who buy the stock. They have their uses, which I will come to later. It also buys and sells the shares of some of the major foreign companies and some foreign government stock, but these are only suitable for the professional or very knowledgeable investor, so we can ignore them at this point.

Loans and debentures
You are not likely to come into much contact with these in the early stages of investing, unless perhaps you inherit some. Strictly speaking, they are not shares; they are given the name 'stock', and are the debts of the company. In the event of liquidation (the term used to describe a firm going bust), stockholders have the first claim on any money which is to be shared out. They carry a fixed rate of dividend, which is normally paid twice a year, and are usually issued in £100 lots.

They may be simply a general loan to the company, or they may be what is called 'secured' on a particular piece of the company's property, just as a house mortgage is secured to the house itself. They are then called debentures. Where there is no security they are called loans. Debentures come first in the money shareout if a company is liquidated.

Debentures and loans may have a date attached to them. This is the date at which the company must pay off the loan (we will see this again with government stocks). In the case of debentures, it may mean that the holder can exchange them at a future date, or dates, for shares in the company.

The prices of loans and debentures vary depending on demand, and the return rises and falls with interest rates. An offer for sale may be at a fixed price, or investors may be asked to tender for the shares at whatever price they choose. The shares then go first to the highest bidders. Tenders are not very frequent. Some debentures can be exchanged for ordinary shares in the company, on certain ratios and dates. They are then called *convertible debentures*.

Preference shares

These are part of the true share capital of the company. The preference share, sometimes still called stock, is a special class which comes before ordinary shares (see next section) when the company goes into liquidation. They are what is known as 'fixed interest' stock. No matter how well the company does, you will never get more than this fixed interest, though of course if the company does badly you are safer with your fixed interest than you would be had you bought ordinary shares where the dividend rate varies.

Prices may go up and down, their level being influenced almost as much by interest rates generally as by how the particular company is faring. When interest rates are rising, prices fall, so that the return on shares is equal to general interest rates; conversely, when rates are falling, share prices rise. Obviously with the interest fixed it is not possible to make great profits on preference shares, but they have a useful place in an investment 'portfolio' – all the shares that you may hold at any one time.

Many older preference shares have a low fixed return, and their prices have fallen below the par value, which is always possible for any type of share. Say interest rates generally are around 10 per cent, and your preference shares carry a 6 per cent dividend. If the par value is £1, it is highly likely that the price will be around 59p, which gives you a 10.2 per cent yield (this is the return you get on every £100 invested). This formula can be set out as follows:

$$\frac{\text{par value} \times \text{dividend}}{\text{market price}} \quad \frac{100 \times 10}{59} = 10.2 \text{ per cent.}$$

If you want to be doubly sure of your dividend, you can always buy cumulative preference shares. With these, if a company has done so badly that it has not even been able to pay a dividend on its preference shares, all arrears will be paid up as it recovers.

If a company goes bust, the preference shareholders will be paid back before equity holders, but not until after any holders of debentures and loan stock. Preference shares do not constitute a 'debt' in the same way, and holders have no legal status as debtors.

Since corporation tax was introduced (see Section four, chapter 5), the dividends of preference shares have had to be declared *net* of tax. This means that the old designation of dividend entitlement, such as 10 per cent Preference, where this implied the gross payment, would now be 7 per cent *net* (after 30 per cent standard-rate tax).

358

Equity shares

This is where the real risk comes in investing and also where the real profits can be made. Ordinary shares, or equities, are at the end of the line as far as security goes; holders of equity take the most risks, so their rewards and their downfalls will be the greatest. They may be called ordinary shares, or stock units. It does not matter; there is no real difference.

Again, equity shares all have a par value, but it is their market price which matters. The holders of ordinary shares are part-owners of the company and are entitled to a share in its assets and profits, after all the fixed charges have been paid.

Voting and non-voting shares. Equity holders are usually entitled to vote on matters affecting the company. If you do not like the way a company is run, you can tell the directors at the annual general meeting, and if you are really displeased you can vote against the acceptance of the annual report, which must be made and presented to the shareholders once a year.

There are also non-voting shares, which carry all the rights of the voting shares, apart from the vote. The dividend will be the same on both types of share. The non-voting shares are often called the '*A*' *shares*, and in some very large companies they are more often quoted than the ordinary shares. In a large company, it often does not matter whether you have a vote or not.

The issuing of non-voting shares has been very useful for some companies, especially those where the original family is still running the business. They have offered a means of raising money to expand without losing any control over the business.

The non-voting are often a few pence cheaper than the voting shares, so you get an effectively higher yield on them. But – and it is a big but – you have no control over the company's affairs at all. In a takeover situation, for example, the bidder need not make an offer at all for non-voting shares. It is power he is after, not just quantity of shares, and there is no power in non-voting stock. Occasionally – though it is more frequent in America than in the UK – groups of small voting shareholders have gathered together enough support to change the course of a company or, say, sack one of the directors, or the entire board.

In general, the Stock Exchange disapproves of non-voting shares and would not permit the issue of new ones. It seems probable that they will eventually disappear. When 'A' shares are given a vote, holders of the ordinary shares are usually compensated by the issue of a few extra shares.

Ordinary and 'A' ordinary are the most common varieties of equities, but there are others, as well. Some shares are called *deferred* or *deferred ordinary*. These are quite rare, and usually have some sort of restriction on them. Holders may not get a dividend until after the holders of ordinary shares, for example, or may not be entitled to a full share in the assets of the company.

The market price. If you look on the financial pages of most newspapers, you will see that each day they give the market price of the different shares. The market price is the amount people are prepared to buy or sell shares for. If a company is doing well and investors expect that it will pay a bigger dividend soon, the price of the shares will probably rise – unless everyone is very depressed and prices generally are falling. Similarly, if a company is thought to be doing badly, its price will fall, unless the setback is thought to be only very temporary.

The price of the shares is different depending on whether you want to buy or sell. You pay more if you are buying and get less if you are selling. The difference between the two prices is called the 'jobber's turn', and is the profit he makes for the service he provides. The price given in the newspapers is usually a 'middle price'. Depending on how 'active' the shares are – that is, how many people want to buy or sell them – you will have to take a few pence or more off if you are selling and add a few on if you are buying. The more active the shares, the nearer the actual price will be to the quoted 'middle' one. This difference between buying and selling prices will *not* disappear when the distinction between jobbers and brokers is abolished.

Your true interest. It is the market value of the share which is important to you, not its par value, because it is that which tells you what return you will get on your investment. If your £1 shares carry a dividend of 20 per cent, but the price you pay – the market price – is £2, your true interest – this is called the *yield* – is 10 per cent, not 20 per cent, because you have paid twice the par value for the shares. You can work out the true yield on any share at any price by using a simple formula:

$$\frac{\text{par value} \times \text{dividend}}{\text{market price}}$$

Take a 50p share standing at a market price of 89p, paying a 12 per cent dividend:

$$\frac{50 \times 12}{89} = 6.74$$

Your yield will then be £6.74 for every £100 you have invested, not 12 per cent, which is the dividend. Work out a few more examples until you understand the principle properly.

Dividends must now be declared in cash amounts, and *net* of income tax. You always need to know whether a dividend is being spoken of in gross or net terms.

New issues

When a completely new share comes on to the market, it may be issued in a variety of ways:

1 *A public issue.* This invites investors to apply for stated amounts of shares or fixed interest stock.

2 *An offer for sale.* This is broadly the same as a public issue, but it will have been 'underwritten' by an issuing house. This means that the issuing house will already have bought all the shares at a lower price than the one asked from the public. If the shares are all sold, the issuing house makes a profit; if not, they have to keep them and perhaps sell at a loss. When this happens, it is called 'leaving the shares with the underwriters'. Whatever happens, the company selling the shares is assured of its money. When times are good, offers for sale are often 'oversubscribed', and those lucky enough to get the shares may be able to sell at an immediate profit as soon as dealings start on the stock market.

3 *An introduction.* This is not often used for equities. It is a means of establishing an official open market in shares where there are enough investors already existing to justify a market. It does not work in the same way as an offer for sale – though some of the shareholders may say that they are prepared to sell some or all of their holdings at stated prices.

4 *A placing.* This is just what it sounds like. Shares are placed at a fixed price with financial institutions and price investors. A quotation will only be granted by the Stock Exchange if enough shares will be made available to create a reasonably free market in the shares when dealing starts.

5 *A tender.* This is basically the same as an offer for sale, but the price is not fixed in advance. A minimum level is stated, then those who want the shares put in a bid, just like at an auction, except that it is in writing. Everyone who gets the shares eventually pays the lowest price that is accepted. The bids are counted off from the highest price down until the total number of shares on offer has been sold. Many investors do not like this kind of new issue and it is not often used, though the Government has sometimes used it in its privatization programme, notably when it sold shares in Britoil. That offer did not go well, to put it mildly, and the shares sold well below their original price on the first day – not at all what people were hoping for when they took up the tender!

6 *A rights issue.* Sometimes a company may need money for expansion and decide not to do it through borrowing, but by raising it from the shareholders, who are then given the right to subscribe to new shares in a certain proportion to their shareholding.

This is how it works. Suppose a company's shares are standing in the market at £2.60 and the directors decide to offer rights in the proportion of one new share for every two already held at price of £1.40. After the issue, if the shareholder takes up the rights, for each two shares he held previously he will have three shares worth a total of £6.60, or £2.20 each.

This is the price that all the shares would be quoted at immediately the new shares are released on to the stock market. The new share will be selling at 80p above the price offered to shareholders. This is called the premium. Of course, theoretically the price of the existing shares will come down, but there is rarely a complete adjustment, because most companies use the capital they raise sensibly and so add to the profits and assets of the company.

If you are offered a rights issue I believe you should take it up, though not everyone would agree with me. If you do not, you will effectively have a smaller share in the company than you had before, as well as foregoing the possible profit. This is called 'watering your equity'. If you really do not want to put up extra money, you can always sell your 'rights' to the shares at the premium before the money is due to be paid. If you ignore the offer altogether, you may lose money, as the price of your existing shares may come down, though the company will usually sell your rights and send you the proceeds.

7 *Scrip issues*. A lot of fuss is made about these issues, because they are a 'free' issue of shares, but in fact they mean nothing. A scrip issue is made when a company thinks that its reserves are getting out of line with its issued capital, so it makes an issue of shares to make them more equal. The scrip may come in any ratio, one-for-one, one-for-three, one-for-ten or even two-for-one. Say it is a one-for-one issue. After you have received the new shares, the share price will fall by half, so the value of your total investment is unchanged. Dividends, too, will be adjusted to take account of the increase in the number of shares.

You may make a profit after a scrip issue, however, when investors think the company is doing well – and companies rarely make scrip issues if they are on the verge of bankruptcy. As a result, the market price may not adjust totally and the new shares in, say, a one-for-one issue will be quoted at a little more than half the old price. The price will soon come into line again if the company fails to produce higher profits and an effectively higher dividend.

8 *Share splits*. Like scrip issues, they mean nothing as far as the value of your investment goes. A company may decide that the price of its shares is so high that it puts investors off and limits the market in them. If a £1 share is standing at £8.40, the company may consider that, by splitting the shares into four 25p units at £2.10 each, a better market might be created in them. Alternatively, the opposite process can take place and shares can be consolidated.

9 *Takeover bids*. When there is a successful takeover of one company by another the deal may be done in cash or in shares. Bids may be a straight cash sum, or shares in the bidder company may be offered to shareholders in place of their old ones, or sometimes a combination of the two, or an option. Takeovers are governed by a code of conduct which is

administered by the Panel on Takeovers and Mergers, which sees that all bidders behave properly, especially when two or more are in competition with one another for the same firm. Do not accept a takeover bid for your shares until the last minute, in case a better offer comes along, though then of course you are taking a chance that so many investors do this that the offer is withdrawn and the share price falls back to its original level.

New shares are also created when convertible debenture stockholders exercise their option to change the stock into ordinary shares, and sometimes when executives and directors exercise stock options which they have been offered by their companies.

2 Buying and selling stocks and shares

The costs

Broker's commission

You already know that a stockbroker will buy and sell shares for you. For this service, he will charge a commission, and this will be the biggest item in your costs, apart from the cost of the shares themselves, if you are buying. Like everything else, commission charges have risen in recent years. The smaller the deal, which is called 'the bargain', the less profitable it is to the stockbroker, so the charge for bargains up to £300 is at the discretion of the broker. This means that he can charge what he likes, but the minimum will be £10 if you are buying, and £7 if selling. Then the following rates apply:

size of bargain equities	% rate
Up to £7,000	1.65
on the next £8,000	0.55
on the next £15,000	0.5
Then at a reducing rate.	

Brokers are free to charge more than these minimum rates if they wish and the minimums are expected to be abandoned by 1986, anyway.

Remember that commission is also payable when you sell, so if a broker charged you the minimum each time on £200-worth of shares, you would have to make a profit of £17 or 8½ per cent, to cover his commission alone. It is not always easy to make such a large profit, at least in the short term.

Transfer stamp duty
In addition to the broker's commission, you will have to pay what is called transfer stamp duty when you buy – though not when you sell. This is levied at the rate of one per cent for residents of the United Kingdom. You do not have to pay it on gilt-edged stocks, or on new issues which are being quoted in the stock market for the first time. Nor do you have to pay it on most company fixed-interest issues, including convertibles.

The contract stamp
This was a very small charge and was abolished in the 1985 Budget.

The process
You can see that the bigger the deal, or 'bargain', as it is called, the relatively less the cost. Many small investors find today's charges prohibitive and have turned instead to unit trusts rather than buying individual stocks. (See chapter five of this section.)

A new charge has been levied in recent years, but it is not heavy. Contracts where the basic value of the shares is over £5,000 carry a 60p Council for the Securities Industry levy.

What you do
Assume a stockbroker has accepted you as a client, or that you are happy for your bank to make the order for you. You can then give your instructions by telephone. You must be very clear what you want to do, for the stockbroker will do exactly as you tell him – though, of course, he may advise you to wait before buying or selling, or not to buy or sell those particular shares at all. You can ignore that advice and he will then put the bargain through for you, but think carefully before you do.

You should tell him exactly how many shares you wish to buy or sell. If you are sensible, you will also say what price you are prepared to pay or accept. You may, for instance, have read in your paper that morning that Bloggs and Company have got a tremendous new order from the Middle East, and you may then think that at the price they are quoted the shares look cheap. Say they are 135p each to buy. What you have to remember is that other people can read too, and that particularly includes stockbrokers and jobbers when it comes to share prices.

The jobber may have gone to the Exchange that morning thinking that at last night's price the shares are too cheap and that he must set a price of 138p to begin with, to see what the demand is like. If it is heavy and he wants to encourage people to sell so that he can meet the demand, he may put the price up even further.

By the time you ring with your instructions, the price could have reached 145p. At this level, the shares may not be such a bargain, so tell the broker what your price limits are. The same goes for selling; you must tell the broker the lowest price you are prepared to accept.

The broker will carry through your instructions, as will the bank through its broker, even though they are not written down. The Stock Exchange motto is 'my word is my bond', and that is how both jobbers and brokers operate. Only leave open the price at which you will buy or sell if you are convinced that the price of the shares you are buying will go on rising or the shares you are selling will go on falling. You can never be sure of either of these things, and that is where the risk comes in.

The next day you should receive the 'contract note' through the post. This will give you details of your bargain. If you wish, your stockbroker will always telephone you to confirm after he has done the deal. The contract will tell you the price at which you have bought or sold and the total value of the deal, transfer stamp duty, commission and the VAT which must be paid on the commission. The contract note will look like this:

1 To buy
   800 Jones and Company Stores Ltd at 89p   £712.00
   Add
     Transfer stamp   £7.12
     Commission at 1.65%   £11.75
     VAT at 15 per cent*   1.76
                       ———
Net cost   £732.63
2 To sell [in a later account]
   800 Jones and Company shares at 96p   £768.00
   Less
     Commission at 1.65%   £12.67
     VAT at 15 per cent   £1.90
                       ———
Net proceeds   £753.43

*Value Added Tax is payable on commission only.

You can see from these two examples that, although there was profit of £56 if you take only the buying and the selling prices of the shares, the true profit after all charges is a mere £20.80 on this transaction.

The stock exchanges are officially open from 9.30 in the morning until 3.30 in the afternoon, but if you are anxious to complete a deal on one particular day your broker can always deal 'after hours' until about 5.30. After hours, dealing is done on the telephone.

What the broker does

You telephone the broker. He then gets in touch – either himself or through one of his partners, who may be 'dealing' on the 'floor' of the Stock Exchange – with the jobber, to try to buy the shares within the limits you have stated. The 'jobber' will be holding supplies of the shares and is constantly trying to balance supply and demand.

The dealer will not say whether he is buying or selling and the jobber will quote two prices, the 'offer' and the 'bid'. The former is the price at which he will sell to you as the buyer, the latter the one he will buy from you as the seller. If the price is within the limits ordered, the dealer will then clinch the bargain. If it is not, he will come back for further instructions.

He may think the price of the shares you were going to buy will go on rising and that you may want to think again about your price limit, or if you are selling he may think the price is going to fall further and that you should get out at whatever price you can. On the other hand, he may advise you not to buy or sell at all on that particular day. *Listen to the advice your broker gives you, even if in the end you decide not to take it. After all, you are paying for it.*

Paying for your shares

You do not have to pay immediately the broker sends you details of the transaction. The Stock Exchange works on a series of what are called 'accounts'. Each account is usually of two weeks' duration, starting on a Monday and finishing on a Friday – though sometimes, when it covers a bank holiday, it may be longer.

You will get a bill covering whatever purchases or sales you have made during the period of the account. The bill will tell you your balance. You will get a cheque for the balance if you have made an overall profit; if you have lost, you will be asked for a cheque. If you buy and sell the same shares within one account, there is only one lot of commission, not two, to pay, so you need less apparent profit to make a real one than if the transactions take place in two different accounts.

The bill will come to you a few days before the 'account day', which is the day on which either you must settle your bill or you must receive a cheque. Account day is always the second Monday after the end of the 'accounts'. The length of time before account day leaves time for the broker to do the paper work. You must pay by then, because it is also the day that the broker and the jobber settle their books and all Stock Exchange companies balance up with one another.

To show you how it works, here is the account calendar for November and December 1985. You will notice that, as well as showing all the accounts and account days, it shows what are called 'new time dealings'.

These are usually (bank holidays excepted) the Thursday and the Friday before an account begins, when you can deal as if it were the new account. You have to pay something extra for this privilege.

November 1982						December 1982					
Sunday		3	10	17	24	Sunday	1	8	15	22	29
Monday		4§	11*	18§	25*	Monday	2	9*	16	23*	30
Tuesday		5	12	19	26	Tuesday	3	10	17	24	31
Wednesday		6	13	20	27	Wednesday	4	11	18	25	
Thursday		7‡	14	21‡	28	Thursday	5‡	12	19‡	26	
Friday	1	8†	15	22†	29	Friday	6†	13	20†	27	
Saturday	2	9	16	23	30	Saturday	7	14	21	28	

* Dealings start. † Dealings end. § Account days. ‡ New time dealings.

You do not own the shares from the time you pay for them, but from the moment the broker has done the deal for you. This means that you are entitled to any dividends or new issues which are declared, and that, in the event of a takeover bid, the offer will be to you. It takes some time, however, for all the formalities to be gone through, and it can happen that these things are sent initially to the former shareholder. The two brokers involved will make sure that you eventually get them, wherever they have gone in the first place.

It may not be convenient for you to have dividends sent to you, and if you wish you can have them sent to your bank. You simply inform the registrar of the company. This is useful in some circumstances. You may move and forget to tell the company of your new address. If dividends go to your bank, this will not matter for some time.

Taxation on dividends

When you receive your dividend, it will not be the amount which has been declared by the company. Before it pays you, the company is directed by the government to deduct tax at the standard rate (30 per cent at present).

Say you were expecting £100 – a 10p dividend on 1,000 shares of £1 par value – this will arrive as £70 – that is, £100 less 30 per cent. This does not apply to all stocks; some gilt-edged are different (see next chapter).

If you do not pay tax, as may happen when you are retired or unemployed, you must then reclaim the tax which has been paid. If, on the other hand, you pay tax at a higher rate than 30 per cent, as many investors do, you will have to eventually pay the extra. It is clearly easier for the government to collect tax in this way rather than having to chase each shareholder for it.

367

Capital gains tax

You will be taxed on any gains you may make on your stocks and shares. At the moment, it is levied at 30 per cent. Paying this is a matter between you and your tax inspector. You will be expected to declare your gains – and, of course, your broker will have a record of your transactions. The inspector can go to him if he wishes, so it is not a good idea not to declare your gains.

You balance up any losses you may have had against any gains – you only make a loss or a gain if you have actually sold, not if the price of the shares has simply gone up or down – and you are taxed on the net gain you have made, if any. Net gains are calculated not on the actual profit, but after all the charges like commission, transfer stamp duty and contract stamp have been deducted.

By carefully weeding out your investments at the end of the financial year, you can minimize the amount of capital gains tax you have to pay. If you have a net loss one year, you can carry it forward to offset any gains you may make in the future, but you cannot carry losses backwards to offset earlier gains.

If the total value of your gains – all chargeable gains, including those on stocks and shares – is £5,900 or less in any one financial year, there is no gains tax to pay. The calculation of the gain can be quite complicated, depending on when the shares were bought, whether the holding was purchased in several lots and whether all the holding is sold. Since April 1983, gains have been index-linked (see Section four, chapter 1) and since April 1985, losses, too, have been index-linked. The latter move can change an apparent profit into a loss. Indexation of the annual exemption will continue in future. This means that as long as there is inflation in the country, its annual level will rise. Either get advice from an accountant or explain the transaction in detail to the inspector, if it is a complicated one.

The timing of your investments is as important as the shares you choose. Even the prices of the best shares fluctuate. If you buy at the wrong time, you can lose money even on the shares with the best market performance.

Employee shareholdings

Some employers offer shares in their company free to employees. Normally these go only to senior employees and there is a time gap before they are able to take possession of the shares. The theory is that, by giving or selling employees shares on a favourable basis, you build up the loyalty to the firm of employees you do not want to lose. The rules about employee shareholdings change all the time and there have been times when such schemes have been illegal.

Check to see if your company has a scheme. It may be open to all employees and there may be a means of buying shares at a certain price and date and then paying for them over the longer term on a kind of hire purchase arrangement at nominal interest. You would, of course, not be able to sell the shares until they were paid for.

If you are fortunate enough to be given stock, this will be taxed as a fringe benefit at the price on the day you received the stock. Limits are set on this by the government.

Bonuses, which are a means whereby employees share in the profits of the company, are also taxed as income in the hands of those who receive them. There are various approved schemes for share options, which enable employees to take up a shareholding, which are tax-exempt. In his 1985 Budget, the Chancellor of the Exchequer announced that any shares held for at least five years in an approved scheme would be free of capital gains tax when sold. If an employee or a director gets shares in other than a Treasury-approved scheme, tax must be paid, but it can be paid in instalments.

3 Investing in gilt-edged

The government owes the public a lot of money. Some of this comes from the money deposited in the various government-controlled savings schemes and some from what are called *gilt-edged stocks*. These are the debts of the government to the private investors who buy the stock.

Stock, which carries a fixed rate of interest, which varies from stock to stock and is determined by the level of interest rates generally when the government issues the stock, is always dealt in £100 units. There are over 100 kinds of stock available – including straight loans to the government, stocks issued when industries were nationalized, corporation and county stocks, and some Commonwealth and Colonial loans.

The gilt-edged market is one of the means used by the government to run the economy. The various forms of taxation provide the other major source of revenue. The government buys and sells in the market and whatever it does can influence interest rates. It operates through its own broker, but the broker's actions are always stealthy, so that no one ever knows whether it is buying or selling at any one time. If the government buys, it tends to put market prices up; if it sells, the reverse happens.

Private investors are interested in the gilt-edged market because its price levels reflect the levels of interest rates. If a member of the public thinks, for example, that interest rates will fall, he may be tempted into gilt-edged because prices will rise. If interest rates are very high, however, the price of gilt-edged will be very depressed. As prices rise, the government can get rid of some of its holdings and control, to some extent, the amount of the rise.

Gilt-edged stock is very easy to buy and sell. Stockbrokers charge less commission on it than they do on other deals. There is also no transfer stamp duty on transactions in gilt-edged, nor any capital gains tax, unless you buy and sell within a year.

At present, commission on any gilt-edged bargain of less than £300 is 'at discretion', or whatever the broker decides. On the first £2,500 it is 0.8 per cent and after that at reducing rates, depending on whether the stock is short-, medium- or long-term.

Different kinds of stock

It can be very important to understand the difference between the various kinds of stock:

Short-dated stock. These stocks are due to be redeemed within five years of your purchase. They are unlikely to change much in value and are 'safe' because their value will move slowly towards the level of the repayment price.

Medium-dated stock. These have a life of between five and fifteen years when you purchase them. They will fluctuate rather more than 'shorts', but may have better tax-free redemption profits, especially if they carry a low rate of interest.

Long-dated stock. These have a life of more than fifteen years and their prices will be influenced by the general level of interest rates. When interest rates are rising, their prices will be falling, and vice versa.

Irredeemable or undated stock. These stocks need not and probably will not ever be redeemed. Their prices are totally geared to interest rates. There are not many of these and they will either have no redemption dates stated at all, or they may be said to be redeemable after a certain date. The most well known are War Loan 3½ per cent, which date from the 1914–18 war, and Consols 2½ per cent.

These should be bought for income, and at certain times they have very high yields indeed. War Loan has been down to £18, at which price the yield was 19.4 per cent. Do not buy them thinking there will be change of heart by the government and the stock will be repaid. This is such a long shot as to be virtually out of the question, though groups get together from time to time to pressure the authorities. The price will move with interest rates, so it is possible to make an untaxed profit when these are falling.

Gilt-edged can be very useful to those on low incomes. Interest on some of the stocks is paid gross without the deduction of income tax; so there is no bother of reclaiming. It is also easy to buy. You can use a stockbroker in the ordinary way, but some of the stocks can be bought through the National Savings Stock Register.

The following list shows the securities which be bought in this way at the end of 1984.

Stock	*Interest payable*	
15% Treasury Stock 1985	**22 February**	22 August
3% Treasury Stock 1985	**21 May**	21 November
8½% Treasury Stock 1984–6	10 January	**10 July**
13¼% Exchequer Stock 1987	**22 January**	22 July
6½% Funding Stock 1985–7	**1 May**	1 November
7¾% Treasury Stock 1985–8	**26 January**	26 July
2% Index-linked Treasury Stock 1988	**30 March**	30 September
3% British Transport Stock 1978–8	1 January	**1 July**
10½% Treasury Stock 1989	**14 June**	14 December
5% Treasury Stock 1986–9	15 April	**15 October**
13% Treasury Stock 1990	**15 January**	15 July
2% Index-linked Treasury Stock 1990	**25 January**	25 July
8¼% Treasury Stock 1987–90	**15 June**	15 December
11¾% Treasury Stock 1991	**10 January**	10 July
5¾% Funding Stock 1987–91	**5 April**	5 October
12¼% Exchequer Stock 1992	25 February	**25 August**
13½% Exchequer Stock 1992	22 March	**22 September**
6% Funding Stock 1993	15 March	**15 September**
13¾% Treasury Stock 1993	23 May	**23 November**
14½% Treasury Stock 1994	**1 March**	1 September
9% Treasury Stock 1994	17 May	**17 November**
12% Treasury Stock 1995	**25 January**	25 July
12¾% Treasury Stock 1995	15 May	**15 November**
9% Treasury Stock 1992–96	**15 March**	15 September
15¼% Treasury Stock 1996	**3 May**	3 November
13¼% Exchequer Stock 1996	**15 May**	15 November
3% Redemption Stock 1986–96	1 April	**1 October**
13¼% Treasury Stock 1997	**22 January**	22 July
8¾% Treasury Stock 1997	1 March	**1 September**
6¾% Treasury Stock 1995–8	**1 May**	1 November
15½% Treasury Stock 1998	30 March	**30 September**
9½% Treasury Stock 1999	**15 January**	15 July
12¼% Exchequer Stock 1999	**26 March**	26 September
13% Treasury Stock 2000	14 January	**14 July**
9% Conversion Stock 2000	**3 March**	3 September
14% Treasury Stock 1998–2001	**22 May**	22 November
13¾% Treasury Stock 2000–3	25 January	**25 July**
3½% Funding Stock 1999–2004	14 January	**14 July**
12½% Treasury Stock 2003–5	21 May	**21 November**
2% Index-linked Treasury Stock 2006	19 January	**19 July**

Stock	Interest payable	
8% Treasury Stock 2002–6	5 April	**5 October**
2½% Index-linked Treasury Stock 2011	23 February	**23 August**
5½% Treasury Stock 2008–12	10 March	**10 September**
7¾% Treasury Stock 2012–15	**26 January**	26 July
2½% Index-linked Treasury Stock 2016	26 January	**26 July**
4% Consols	1 February	1 August
3½% War Stock	1 June	1 December
3½% Conversion Stock	1 April	1 October
2½% Treasury Stock 1975 or after	1 April	1 October
2½% Consols		
2½% Annuities	5 January	5 April
2¾% Annuities	5 July	5 October

The heavy type indicates the repayment date in the relevant year when the stock is repaid.

The list is subject to variation from time to time, as securities are repaid or new securities included. An up-to-date list may be obtained on application to The Director, Bonds and Stock Office, Lytham St Annes, Lancs FY0 1YN.

The charges you pay are only £1 for every nominal amount of stock of £250, then 50p for every further £125 of nominal stock. The National Debt Commissioners do the dealing for you and the price is based upon the one ruling in the stock market at the time when you apply.

Redemption yields

If you are interested in gilt-edged stock, you will hear a lot about redemption yields. With all stock, except the undated, you have a guarantee that you will get your money back as long as you hold the stock until the redemption date, when it will be paid back at par, £100.

The nearer you are to redemption, of course, the smaller will be the guaranteed profit. It does not follow, however, that the further away the redemption date, the less you will have to pay. The price will depend on the interest the stock carries, which is also known as the 'coupon', and the general rates of interest currently prevailing. At times of low interest rates, for instance, a high-coupon stock would be standing well above its redemption price and would fall as interest rates rose. Redemption yields are complicated to work out and not the same as the simple yield on each £100 invested. The *Financial Times* gives both the straight and the redemption yield every day. If you want the formula, the Stock Exchange will send it to you. Here is how some flat and redemption yields compare:

stock	redemption date	market price	flat yield %	redemption yield %
Exchequer 10%	1987	£96	10.42	1109
Treasury 12%	1995	£108⅞	11.38	11.07
Treasury 9½%	1999	£95¼	10.29	10.55
War Loan 3½%	undated	£35⅞	9.69	—

From this you can see how redemption yields and flat yields vary. In these examples, the redemption yields higher than flat yields for the shortest dated stock, Exchequer 10 per cent, 1987, and lower for the longer-dated. War Loan 3½%, of course, has no redemption yield, as it has no date for repayment.

Index-linked gilts

Since the 1982 Budget, it has been possible for everyone to buy index-linked gilt-edged stock. Before that, the stocks were limited to pension fund purchases. The first issue was 2 per cent index-linked Treasury stock, due for redemption in 1988. Both the principal and the interest on the stock are index-linked to the retail prices index. This means that anyone who bought the stock at the beginning and holds it to maturity will get back the value of the holding, increased by the rate of inflation during that time, having received 2 per cent interest throughout, also index-linked.

For the government to issue such stock shows that it feels that it has inflation beaten – a bold claim. Whether they are right or wrong, however, there is no way the purchaser can lose the value of his initial investment over the medium term (the stock has only a six-year life altogether) and, if the rate of inflation increases again, stock looks better than index-linked saving certificates for those who simply want to maintain the value of their money, rather than make a profit.

Anyone who does not hold the stock to redemption can sell it at any time, but only on the open market, so there is no price guarantee. There is no capital gains tax to pay on the stock if it has been held for more than one year.

By the end of 1984, there were ten such stocks quoted, with some redemption dates running past the year 2000.

4 Working out your investment policy

Understanding the stock market

Once you know the mechanics of investing, you will be eager to go on to learn how to invest wisely with the minimal risk.

It will take a long time for you to understand how the market works, however. First of all, you must appreciate that share prices can go up or down. The following table shows how the *Financial Times* industrial share index of thirty shares has moved in the past ten years. (The index is produced by averaging out the prices of active shares from (usually) large companies whose share price movements are thought to reflect the general movement in the market as a whole.)

year	index high	date	index low	date
1975	377.8	19 November	146.0	6 January
1976	400.8	4 May	265.3	27 October
1977	477.4	18 May	357.6	1 January
1978	535.5	14 September	433.3	2 February
1979	558.6	4 May	406.3	15 November
1980	515.9	21 November	406.9	3 January
1981	597.3	30 April	446.0	14 January
1982	637.5	11 December	518.1	5 January
1983	776.2	22 December	598.4	12 January
1984–5*	1024.6	22 January 1985	755.3	23 July 1984

*To 22 March 1985

You can see from this table that stock market prices can fluctuate widely. In 1975, for example, they dropped back close to the levels of twenty years previously.

The picture given by the *Financial Times* ordinary share index alone is somewhat misleading, however, since many investors will have portfolios of shares which have grown much more over the last ten years than is shown by just this one indicator.

Moreover, growth in income, when added to the capital sums involved, alters the 'total return' on investment considerably. It produced, very roughly, a doubling in the value of a representative fund between 1967 and 1977. Even so, the crash on the stock markets in 1974 and 1975 was a frightening phenomenon, and the fluctuations since then still illustrate the importance of timing. Share prices do not automatically rise with inflation, like other prices. The factor which affects stock market prices uniquely is sentiment. This is the view that investors take not only of a company's prospects but also of the country's. As a rule, market specialists are looking nine months to a year ahead. Everything may look rosy in the economy, but if the forecasts are not good share prices will begin to fall. On the other hand, they are likely to start recovering before real evidence of economic recovery shows up in the official figures.

It is most important to learn to understand stock market 'sentiment'. Without it, you can buy or sell just at the wrong time. Even if you have made a very sound investment in a company that is doing well, it cannot fail to be affected to some degree by general market sentiment.

Interest rates also affect share prices. If they are high, then investors will be looking for higher yields on their stocks and prices will come down. If interest rates start falling, then prices will begin to rise and yields to fall.

There are many other factors which affect stock market prices, but you can only learn these by experience. You can best begin the process of learning by reading and using your own experience to help you work out what may be good investments.

Picking out promising companies
Choosing good investments is not simply a matter of working out what industries seem likely to grow and become more profitable. That would be comparatively easy.

We have all seen the growth in electronics in recent years, and the enormous orders for supplying equipment to bring North Sea gas and oil ashore. Then there are the companies with interests in the gas and oil resources. Does this make all of them a good investment? In contrast, there are companies which operate in countries overseas where there is some risk that they might lose all their assets for political reasons. Does this make all of them a bad investment?

The answer to both these questions is, not necessarily. There is far more to investing than choosing a home-based, expanding industry. Some will do better than others; some, even in the most flourishing trade, go bankrupt.

How do you sort the good from the bad? After a while you will begin to pick out companies which seem more promising than others. If you read the papers – and read the industrial as well as the financial news – you will slowly gather information about companies which will stick in your mind. But this takes a long time and to begin with you will have to rely on certain indicators, like the yield or the company's prospects. The newspapers can be a great help here. Some of those which take investing seriously will tell you not only the price of shares but also their yields.

Yields can be important for the beginner. If one company's shares offer a rather higher yield than similar shares of other companies, there must be a reason for it. The company may be doing badly, its shares may be tightly controlled, or it may – and this does happen – not have been noticed. If this is the case, it will eventually come to the fore and its price will move to the correct level. If you are one of those who spotted it first, you could make a good profit eventually.

On the other hand, the yield on a certain company's shares may be lower than with similar companies. Again, there could be several reasons. The company may be doing, and may be known to be doing, much better than its competitors (of course, it may not be, in which case, when the results of the year's trading are announced, the price will come sharply back into line). Investors may be expecting a bid for the company and the price will already have risen to around the level of the expected bid price. Or it may just be one of the 'glamour stocks', where a great growth is forecast for the future, without any basis in current trading.

Sometimes investment in these sorts of companies comes off, sometimes it does not, but they are dangerous for the new, inexperienced investor, especially if he does not have much capital.

Just looking at the prices in the newspapers can therefore suggest a lot. You can take your investigations from there. The *Financial Times* has the best share prices service. Here is an extract from one of its lists to show you what it looks like:

high	low	company	price	change on day	net dividend	times covered	yield	price/ earnings ratio
74	52	Longton Inds.	58	—	2.0	2.4	4.9	9.7
236	138	Low & Bonar 50p	216	—	†7.5	3.6	5.0	4.4
88	45	MCD Group	88	+1	†1.5	3.9	2.4	14.9
37½	13	MJI Corp 10p	14½	—	1.25	2.8	12.3	(3.3)
27½	21	MY Dart 10p	24xd	+½	0.75	1.6	4.5	(17.1)
156	134	M'c'rthy Ph. 20p	143	—	7.5	2.7	7.5	6.2
169	134	Macfarlane Gp	164	—	†3.87	2.9	3.4	11.8
45	37	Maclellan 20p	41	−1	t1.7	2.1	5.9	(9.7)
64	45	Magnolia Group	45	—	2.5	3.2	7.9	4.4
64	28	Mainmet Hldgs 10p	33	—	—	—	—	—
270	157	Man. Ship Can. £1	227	—	5.5	3.5	3.5	11.7
95	65	Marley	89	+4	†3.2	2.5	5.1	10.0
58½	40	Marling Ind. 10p	55½	—	d3.0	5.6	3.3	6.5
46	29	Marshall L'xy 'A'	33	+1	†1.2	3.6	5.2	(5.9)
55	77	Marshall's Univ	50xd	—	H1.75	—	5.0	15.0
89	77	Do. 7½pc Cn Red Pf £1	81xd	—	7½%	—	13.2	—

†Interim since increased. Many other footnotes are also given in the *Financial Times* each day.

Where no par values are given, the shares are always in £1 units.

All these figures will tell you something:

1 *Highs and lows.* This shows you how much the price has moved about this year and how close to either extreme the current price is.

2 *The middle price.* This is neither the buying nor the selling price but lies midway between them. If there is 'xd' by the price this means that account has been taken of a recently declared dividend in the quoted price.

3 *Changes on the day.* This tells you whether the price has moved and how far up or down, and is also some indication of whether the shares are active. But you can only get a true indication of this from the *Stock Exchange Daily* official list, which shows numbers of 'bargains' and tells you what prices shares have been bought and sold at during the day. It comes out each evening.

4 *The dividend.* This is usually given in pence per share.

5 *Times covered.* This tells you how safe your dividend is. Total earnings (another name for after-tax profits) are divided by the total amount of the dividend to all shareholders. If the total dividend is £100,000 and earnings are £450,000, the sum is £450,000÷£100,000=4.5, so the dividend is 'covered' four and a half times by profits. In such a case, a company can stand a quite sharp fall in profits without having to cut its dividend. In contrast, say the dividend costs £100,000 and earnings are only £120,000, the dividend is only covered 1.2 times. This does not give much leeway, so quite a small fall in profits could mean a cut in the dividend. Not all companies cut their dividends even if profits fall below the cost of the dividend. They may have built up reserves for a rainy day, or judge that the setback is only temporary.

6 *Dividend yield.* This tells you in percentage terms what income you can expect for every £100 you have invested in the shares. It is expressed gross before tax, so if you are a tax payer you must net it down to allow for tax at your personal rate.

7 *Net price/earnings ratio.* It is very useful to understand this, as it shows you how many years of profits are reflected in the current market price. Say net earnings (profits) are 10p a share and the share price is 60p, you are buying six years' profits at that price. The P/E ratio indicates what investors generally are thinking about the company.

If investors expect profits to be static or to move only slowly upwards, they will not be prepared to buy at a price which shows a high P/E ratio. If, on the other hand, they think profits are going to rise sharply, they will be prepared to buy on a high P/E ratio, because increasing profits will bring that level down at their own particular purchase price. For example, if you buy on a P/E ratio of twelve and profits rise by one third in the following year, the ratio will drop to eight at your purchase price.

These lists appear in the *Financial Times* every day but Monday, as the market is closed on Saturday and Sunday. On Monday, the months in which the dividends on each share are due are given in place of the highs and lows and the change on the day.

The financial pages of newpapers

If you are a real beginner, you will probably start by reading the news-papers. Let's see what you can expect them to do for you.

Newspapers gear their writing to their readership. This means that, in the case of financial news or comment, they differ greatly. It does not mean that one is better than the other; it simply means that what you will read in a particular paper is pitched to the general level of the reader. It would be no use a complete beginner with no knowledge of finance starting off with the *Financial Times*. Most newspapers are very success-ful at finding their right market.

No preferences, so here are the daily papers in alphabetical order to help you find the best one for your needs:

The *Daily Express* has a financial page every day. It covers the main events of the news and is written in a way which can be easily understood by the layman. There is now also a midweek financial pull-out. The main shares prices are quoted daily.

The *Daily Mail* also has a daily page, which is well liked by people who work in the financial business. It also has 'Money Mail' each Wednesday. This covers a variety of financial subjects in a simple straightforward way, which is helpful even for those who are quite advanced. Rather more share prices are quoted daily.

The *Daily Mirror* sticks to things which effect everyone, like savings and mortgages. It also deals with industrial and financial events which may effect us all in a broad way.

The *Daily Telegraph* is the paper of the middle classes, and it caters for them. Its financial pages are substantial, and each Saturday it carries a family finance section, which is of great help in planning your savings and investment.

The *Financial Times* is really for the professionals, those involved in the business of money. It has the most extensive list of stock market prices and the most detail on them. It also has various indexes which show the movement of share prices generally, commodity prices, foreign exchange rates, and major share prices in foreign countries, as well as many articles on investment and news from different companies. Each Saturday it has advice for investors and gives general financial and legal advice. Once you have grasped the basics, you can find much to interest you in the paper.

The *Guardian* has a daily financial page in a business and industrial section and a Saturday family finance section. It serves people who are less affluent than the *Telegraph* readers and its articles are easy to follow, with sound advice. It sometimes takes a 'social' rather than a financial approach to money matters.

The Times covers business, industrial and financial news and produces a full page of the main share prices every day. Its articles are less specialized than in the past, when it aimed more to interest the professional investors. Today, the appeal is more to the affluent, but non-professional, investor.

So much for the dailies. Then there are the Sundays. Of these, the *Sunday Telegraph* is most concerned with the needs of the private investor, the *Sunday Express* gives share tips, and the *Observer*, which has been expanding its business coverage, combines news stories from the business world with share tips and easy-to-follow financial advice. The *Sunday Times* has a complete business section, the 'Business News'; this covers industry, commerce and the economy, but rarely gives straight investment advice. The rest of the Sundays cover finance when it is news, rather than having regular columns of advice each week.

There are also several financial weeklies, the most important of these being the *Investors' Chronicle*, which, as its name suggests, exists for the private investor and the professionals. You will need to understand financial terms to read it, but when you do, if you are serious about investing, it is almost a must. Monthly magazines like *Planned Savings* and *Money Management* can be very useful, once you have grasped the basics.

Company accounts

Understanding company accounts is important to the investor. They can tell him a lot about the company and, as two years' figures are always given, the investor will also know whether the company has done well or badly compared with the previous year. This, together with the chairman's report, which may come with the accounts or may be saved until the annual general meeting, can help him decide whether to keep the shares or not.

Section three, chapter 7, shows you how company accounts are drawn up. It gives a very simple form of accounts, but no matter how big the company the principles remain the same.

You will be able to see some things about a company just by glancing at the two sets of figures – the balance sheet and the profit and loss account. You can also work out more complicated ratios, which will help you see how the company has done in comparison with recent years.

Even if you do not work out these figures yourself, newspapers and investment magazines will refer to them, so it is a good idea to understand what they mean. Here are the definitions of a few of the more usual ones. I have not included any we have already talked about:

Profits. These may be gross profits – that is, sales less costs. Mostly, however, pre-tax profits are chosen as the main indicator of how a company is faring. These are total profits less costs and any items which may be exceptional to particular year's trading, except for tax. Tax is not included, as it is a charge which is outside the control of the company, a variable item depending on government policy.

Net earnings. These are net profits, after all charges such as tax, minority interests and any preference dividends have been subtracted. Surplus Advance Corporation Tax is regarded as part of the tax charge. This is what is theoretically available to be paid on equities, but the directors usually put part of it to reserve for future development.

Net assets per share. This is the value of the company assets which correspond to each ordinary share in the company. The figure is worked out by taking the book value of all the assets of the company, minus things which are difficult to measure like goodwill, and dividing the result by the number of shares.

Asset value may matter or it may not. It shows the underlying value of the shares, but this is of more significance in some industries than others. Oil and heavy engineering companies, for example, tend to produce high asset values for their shares because they are industries which need a lot of assets in order to operate. Shares in service industries like retailing, on the other hand, tend not to have very high asset values.

Return on assets. This shows how much money is made on the company's assets. It is worked out by taking pre-tax profit figures plus loan stock interest and expressing it as a percentage of issued capital, loan capital (but not intangible assets) and reserves. It is one measure of efficiency in a company: the higher the return, the more efficient the company seems to be.

But, again, this is not always the case. Companies with few assets – again, the service companies – often produce what looks like an amazingly high return-on-assets figure. This cannot be compared with the return on assets in the heavier industries, however, as these require enormous assets to operate at all. This calculation is sometimes called return on capital employed.

Profit margin. This is pre-tax profit expressed as a percentage of turnover. It is less important than return on assets, because certain industries work on a large profit margin whilst others are forced to operate on low margins and make their profits by massive turnover.

Cash flow. These are profits which are kept back in the business for further development (retained profits) plus depreciation.

Current ratio. Current assets divided by current liabilities.

Many other ratios can be worked out, but these are mainly of interest only to professionals. They include such items as stock turnover, debtor turnover, profits per employee and total wages turnover. But if you manage to understand the above, you have quite enough to enable you to make the most of your investment opportunities.

Getting investment advice
Be quite ruthless in seeking out investment advice; it is, after all, your money which you are laying on the line when you invest.

You can get advice from *newspapers*. Some of them run regular features answering investment queries and problems. This is somewhat hit and miss, however, as most newspapers do not deal with personal enquiries. It is just a matter of luck whether the question you send in will be answered in the feature – and then, of course, the answer will be available to every investor. If it is not, your letter will most likely go unanswered.

This may seem unfair, but it costs money to run an investment advisory service and it is just not a newspaper's basic job. Some of them will answer your letter for a fee. On the whole, writing to newspapers is not the best way of getting advice. Newspapers are primarily useful in telling you what is going on in the market; they may suggest that some shares are worth buying and what they have to say will influence your overall investment policy.

Ask your *stockbroker*. He should know what is going on in the market and will anyway have a good idea what shares are being favoured by investors generally. As with any profession, the quality of stockbrokers varies, but you will soon find out just how good your broker is at investment advice, or whether he is really only useful for putting your order through. All the training and expertise in the world cannot make up for 'flair'. Try to make sure that you have a stockbroker with that vital quality.

Ask your *bank manager*. He is likely to go to the bank's broker to seek the advice you are needing, so do not expect him to come up with advice immediately. His specialization is banking, not broking, but he has sources of information not always available to the ordinary investor.

Consult a *merchant bank*. These organizations have developed enormously in the post-war era. They not only carry on their traditional banking and acceptance business, but have also widened out into the field of company management and investment advice.

They are not for the small shareholder as a rule, however, because they will insist on a minimum total value of your investments before working for you. This may be £20,000 or it may be much higher – though they will sometimes make exceptions for favoured customers who put other business their way.

They will charge a fee for their services, but this may be worked out in many different ways. It may be a percentage of the total value of your investments, or an initial fee plus a proportion of any profit they may make for you.

There are some *specialized companies* which have grown up in the last twenty years which do nothing but manage investor's portfolios. They are not interested in the very small investor, either, but they do not usually set their sights as high as the merchant banks. They like to deal with a minimum of £30,000 to £40,000, but will occasionally take on people with £10,000. After all, if they are successful the small investor may become quite a big one. Their fees are similar to those of the merchant banks, and they may insist that you follow their advice. If you do not, they may well not wish to act for you.

There are several more *technical publications* which may help you. The *Stock Exchange Daily* official list is the source for dealings in shares and jobbers produce daily lists and a variety of other information. Most stockbroking firms today issue a monthly newsletter, and some of them are very good indeed. There are also monthly Stock Exchange lists published by Matheison's and by Straker. These give information on prices, highs and lows, details of dividends and dates when they are payable.

One excellent source of information about individual companies is *Extel Statistical Services*, 37/45 Paul Street, London EC2A 4PB. They produce cards on every public company whose shares are quoted and also on some which are not. They have cards covering a variety of foreign companies, some private companies, and various kinds of information on new issues.

Every time there is information from the company, a new news card is issued. There is also a card which shows the position looking back over several years. This is brought up to date at the end of the company's financial year. You can take the whole British companies service for £1,590 (end 1984), but this is unlikely to be needed by the ordinary investor; or you can buy one card in the company in which you are interested. It costs £2.60 for a basic company card, which gives a range of financial information going back some years, plus the current news card, which gives more detailed information on what has been happening in the past year. Extel also has a similar service for the Unlisted Securities Market and for the over-the-counter markets. Individual cards cost £7.80 in those services.

Rules for investing

In investing, you will only learn by trial and error. The more advice you take, the less error there is likely to be and the less the overall risk. Compare the progress of shares you would have bought, had it not been for the advice of your broker or bank manager, against the shares they have recommended. It can be a chastening experience.

Even if you are a beginner, however, you can follow your own counsel and guard against loss by following twelve basic rules of building up a balanced 'portfolio', made up of a variety of investments:

1 Do not put all your eggs in one basket. This means never start off with shares in just one company. Spread your risk. You may not

make quite as much money on shares in a range of companies as you would with an investment in a single one if that one does well, but the risk is much smaller. The greater the spread through industries, as well as particular companies, the safer for the beginner.

2 If you are really investing for income to live on, spread your investments over different types of shares. Decide how much you should put into fixed-interest stocks to give you a basic income before you go into riskier things.

3 Study all the aspects of every investment before you make it. Avoid declining industries and stick to those which in general will grow. Use your eyes. Many women have made good investments by backing their choice of retailers with an investment.

4 Always be ready to sell if you have made a mistake. Treat your portfolio as a constantly changing thing. If a really good opportunity comes along, take it, even if it means selling some of your existing shares at a loss.

5 Keep some cash available all the time to take up opportunities which come along. These may be new issues, perhaps rights issues. Put this money on short-term deposit somewhere where you can get hold of it quickly, but where it will earn interest meanwhile. Never invest all your money, in case you suddenly need some cash for an emergency, otherwise you may have to sell at an unnecessary loss.

6 If shares in a particular company have increased substantially in value and you would like to make sure of the profit, but not give up your interest entirely, sell some of the shares, perhaps enough to bring your remaining holding down to the cost of the original purchase. This is a good idea, because even if prospects still look good, there can be a danger in overloading your portfolio with shares in one company.

7 There are times when it is worth selling any particular share you have. No shares stay at peak levels, or go on rising without any setback – even if their fall is only in sympathy with a general setback in the market. There have been times when not to sell even the best shares was foolish.

8 Keep a careful watch on your portfolio and value it from time to time. Do not assume because shares generally are rising that the value of your portfolio is moving with them. Do not do this every day, or even every week or month, but try to do quarterly valuations and decide what, if anything, should be sold.

9 In an ideal portfolio, dividends will come in at fairly regular intervals throughout the year. But you cannot always achieve this. The vast majority of companies' financial years end on 31 December. The dividend announcement will come any time in the next four months and the payment some time after that. So some bunching of your

dividends may be unavoidable. When the dividend is paid is a point to bear in mind if you are looking at two possible investments which seem equal in all other respects.

10 There is an old adage in the stock market which urges you to let profits run and cut losses. There is certainly some sense in this when it comes to losses. Recovery always takes some time. It may be better to accept a loss and transfer your money to some other investment where you can recoup much sooner.

11 Taking a loss can also help you with your capital gains tax. Net gains are calculated to the end of the financial year, 5 April. It might help you to take a loss around this date to bring your gains tax bill down or eliminate it altogether, and to reinvest it after the new financial year has started.

12 Finally, decide what your investment policy is and follow it through. Are you looking for income now or for capital gain in the future, with little regard to present yields on the shares? How much risk are you prepared to take? Do you see yourself as a long-term investor, or a speculator? Decide what proportions of your capital you want to put into the more risky investments. Perhaps you will want to put half your money into stocks and shares which will provide you with a good or fixed income, and to take a bit of a gamble with the rest.

Speculation

Speculating is fun. It is basically a gamble, but a gamble in which you may well not lose your original stake. It's fun to see your purchases rise in price and beat the general trend in the market. But it's dangerous, too. If you do not have the instincts of a gambler, do not start to speculate. You can lose as much as you gain. But if you want to speculate and still safeguard your money to some extent, here are a few rules to follow:

1 Many speculators buy and sell in the same account. This means that they do not actually have to put any money up: they just pay the difference if the price goes down and get a cheque if it goes up. Try to have sufficient funds so that if your speculation goes wrong you can actually take up the shares, pay for them, and sell later without a loss.

2 Do not fall for any inside information you may be given. Sometimes people do have inside information. When they do, they should not tell anyone or take advantage of it themselves by dealing. 'Insider' dealing is against the law. Even if the tip is an accurate one, it may turn out to be allowed for in the current price.

3 Check on any company yourself. Even if a tip turns out to be a bad one, is it a good investment anyway?

4 Do not speculate in any shares where the market is not active. You can get locked in and see all your profit slip away if there are no buyers around and you have to lower your selling price accordingly.

5 Do not be too greedy. Get out when you have made a reasonable profit.
6 If a speculation goes wrong, get out before the price crashes.
7 Know as much as you can about the area in which you choose to speculate. If you know a great deal about the retailing industry, for example, follow your hunches there, rather than buying shares in an area you know nothing about.

Insider dealing

Generally you can buy and sell whatever shares you want, but there is one exception to this. It is when you take advantage of some information about a company which is not generally available to the investing public. This is known as insider dealing and could happen, say, when an employee bought shares in his company before profit figures, which he or she knew would be good, were announced. Of course, insider dealing is not always in front of good news. Shares could be sold before the price fell on a dividend cut or the loss of a contract.

Insider dealing can happen, too, when an employee or a director passes on information to a third party. A new law imposes penalties on anyone found guilty of insider dealing. It can involve a fine, or a prison sentence of up to two years. It is not insider dealing, however, when you work out for yourself that a company might be coming in with good results. This could happen when, say, publicly available official figures showed that retail sales were rising steeply and you bought stores companies' shares in anticipation of higher dividends and profits.

Forming an investment club

An investment club can be profitable and fun. It is also a good way of learning more about investment. A group of people get together and each agree to put up a weekly or monthly amount which will go into the purchase of shares. They will need to be people with a reasonable amount of spare cash available which they are willing to put at risk by investing in shares which are chosen collectively. As the costs of investing are so high, it is sensible to get together a minimum of over £300 (to avoid the discretionary charges of the broker) for each investment. For ten people – which is a manageable size – this would mean an investment of £7.50–£8.00 a week each, to produce £30 each a month.

The decision on which shares to buy is taken after a general discussion with majority approval. Obviously, if you are a person who likes his own way when investing, do not join a club.

You may, of course, have any number of people you wish in an investment club. The more there are, the more important it is to draw up proper rules and appoint a treasurer and secretary.

Whatever the size, however, there are a number of basics to be decided upon:

1 The share each person will have in the club, the terms on which he or she can leave, and the notice required. You could, for instance, decide that anyone who left in money for less than a year was entitled only to the money they had put in, or an exact share of the current total assets, whichever is the lower. If the club has lost money overall on its investments, it will be the latter.

2 Proper accounts must be kept, including details of all investments and the time and the price at which they were bought.

3 Decisions must be made on how to deal with taxation and dividends – whether, for example, dividends will be shared out once or twice a year, or reinvested for a period.

4 If you decide that all members need not put in the same amount of money, you must divide their voting rights accordingly.

5 You should put some limit on the life of the club. If you wish to extend it you can always do so, but there should be a definite period after which people have the option of taking their original stake and their profits out without penalty.

Investment clubs can work well, but obviously there can be difficulties. Think carefully before you form or join one. The National Association of Investment Clubs, Halifax House, Fenwick Street, Liverpool 2 (051 236 6262), issues a helpful free leaflet explaining how to set up a club.

5 Unit and other trusts

Unit trusts

You may feel, if you are an absolute beginner, that the whole process of investing is far too daunting: you have no stockbroker, your cash is limited, and you do not like the idea of the high risk involved. Yet you would like to share in the growth of the eonomy and of the companies in that economy. Well, there is a way you can do that. It is by investing in unit trusts.

When you invest in a unit trust, you are putting your faith in professional advisers who make the investment decisions for you. Look at their track record and you can decide whether to back them or not. There are frequent articles about them in the financial press. A unit trust is a means whereby a large number of individuals are able to pool their money into a single fund which is taken care of by professional investment managers. To be set up, a trust must be authorized by the Department of Trade and it must have a properly constituted trust deed. The trustees are always banks or insurance companies. Their job is to look after the cash and stock in the trust: in other words, to make sure that investors' money is kept safe. They have nothing to do with the choice of investments, however: this is the sole responsibility of the investment managers. Share prices and, it follows, the individual holder's investment will fluctuate, depending on the skill of the managers of the trust.

These managers buy a number of shares, split the total into units of equal value, and offer these units to anyone who wants them. Every unit will have in it a little bit of each share bought. The units are quoted just like shares, with a buying and selling price, but usually they are not actually quoted on the Stock Exchange. The unit trust managers issue a price each day and most of the newspapers carry some, if not all, of them. This price is worked out according to a formula fixed by the Department of Trade and is a direct reflection of the price of each share in the fund.

Unit trusts first developed in the USA, and came to Britain in the early 1930s. It is only in the post-war years that they have really caught on here, however, but they have proved a great help to people who want to build up their capital slowly and without the risk involved in investing in just a few stocks.

Each unit trust is completely separate from any other trusts, but several different ones are run by each management company. They are subject to all the same rules as any other trust. They have a trustee – usually a bank – to see that the trust is properly managed. The managers who run the fund are accountable to the trustees and must show that all the money they receive for the fund is used correctly. In the past twenty years, unit trusts have grown a great deal, and there are now well over 500 trusts in which British investors can put their money.

You can buy almost any number of units – some minimum amount is usually stated, but it is not large – or you can buy units on a monthly plan, whereby you can add to your investment steadily by investing a few pounds each month. You can withdraw your money at any time at the current sale price. Building up your capital in this way has several advantages.

You do not need a lot of money to start off with. Unit trust managers are content to deal with far lower investments than stockbrokers, because when small orders are added together they make one single big purchase (or sale). This means that each unit trust holder is getting all the advantages available to a big investor.

You spread your risk. The average unit trust will have shares from at least twenty companies in it – that is a rule for trusts – and some of them many more. This means that, if one investment goes wrong, the others are still there to maintain the value of the units. This spread of investment means that the prices of unit trusts should not fall as much as an investment in any single company might. Conversely, they are unlikely to rise as much, either.

It is important to realize, though, that even in a unit trust you can lose money. If the market goes down like it did in 1974, no one escapes the trend.

But when prices rise, the prices of unit trusts tend to rise slowly and you may feel that this is an unexciting way to invest and that you would rather trust your own judgement and have a go at making a 'killing'. Of course, not all trusts and not all managers are equally successful. It is partly a matter of luck at the beginning which trust and which management group you choose.

The trusts are run by expert managers. When you invest in a unit trust, it is like having your own professional investment adviser. Of course, the advice you get is going to hundreds of others, too, and there will not be the personal touch. And you will have to follow your own counsel at the beginning. Do you want a trust that overall has a high income, one which is aiming mainly at capital gain, or one which specializes in commodities, North Sea oil, or EEC investment, or companies in other countries?

Whatever you want there will be a trust – indeed many trusts – to suit you. How do you choose your managers? This is a matter of luck to some extent, but you can get some idea, though it is by no means an absolute guide to the future, by looking to see how individual trusts have fared in recent years.

Most newspapers, *The Times*, the *Financial Times* and the *Daily Telegraph* in particular, run regular features, usually on a Saturday, with tables showing which trusts have done what over various periods of time. Every so often the *Investors' Chronicle* does a major survey, and there are also specialist magazines – *Money Management* is one – which can provide useful advice.

Beware, however, of the high fliers of the past. They may not continue to do well. Commodity shares may have exhausted themselves for the time being; maybe there has been a setback in a foreign market which has previously been showing a rise. If you have satisfied yourself that one group of managers seems to have done well – it may even be simply that the price of the units has fallen less than in other trusts in a market setback – then check on the type you have chosen. If interest rates are falling, for instance, a purchase of a high yielding trust now could provide you with some capital gain as well as a good income at the price you paid.

There is a tax advantage. Trusts pay income tax on their dividends like anyone else. But the companies in which the trust has invested will already have paid what is called advance corporation tax and so the dividend is subject to a tax credit, which will be equal to the amount of ACT which has been paid. The dividends from the companies in which the trust has invested are passed on to the shareholder twice a year. Of course, not all dividends are payable at the same time, but it would be administratively very expensive to keep dishing dividends out to unit holders as soon as they come in. The tax credit covers your income tax liability, so there is no tax for the standard rate tax payer to pay. If you do not pay tax at all, you can reclaim this credit. If, on the other hand, you pay tax at the higher rates, you may have more to pay.

Since the March 1985 Budget, you will normally pay capital gains tax on any gains you make over £5,900 a year, including unit trusts in the total.

Do not confuse unit trusts with *investment trusts*. The latter are limited companies, whose business is to invest in a number of companies. They have the same purpose as unit trusts, which is to spread the risk of investment by employing expert management, but they are not 'open-ended' like unit trusts. Unit trusts simply buy more shares the more money they get in, whereas investment trusts are ordinary limited companies and as such are quoted on the Stock Exchange. If they want to raise more money to invest, they must do it with a 'rights issue' in the ordinary way.

The prices of investment trust shares fluctuate far more widely than those of unit trusts. A price of a unit is always the total value of the trust's shares divided by the number of units. Investment trust shares, on the other hand, may be bought or sold below, or above, their asset value – though, of course, if the trust is broken up, the assets will be divided among shareholders at the asset value. In recent years, investment trust shares have often tended to be below their asset value; this is known as 'selling at a discount'. It could not happen with a unit trust.

Buying and selling unit trusts is very easy. You simply fill in a form or write a letter to the fund involved and enclose your cheque. If you are going for one of the monthly plans, you either send a cheque each month or arrange a banker's order.

Where to get information

There are well over 500 unit trusts operating in this country, run by around 100 management groups. If you want to find out the range of trusts offered by each group, you will have to write to or phone them. The *Financial Times* publishes a full list of unit trusts, their prices and changes on the day, each day. Its list also includes the names, addresses and telephone numbers of the various management groups. Even if you do not want to buy the paper every day, it is worth buying occasionally when you are thinking of unit trust investment. Choose a Saturday, when there are interesting general savings and investment articles as well.

How to buy

If you have decided that you like the idea of investing in unit trusts, take your time about deciding which one. Day-to-day fluctuations in the price of unit trusts are small and you are likely to lose very little by delaying your purchase until you are sure which trust you want. Read your newspapers and magazines and base your decision on the following criteria:

1 Is it the kind of trust you want? Does it offer the right sort of income, and good prospects of growth? Is it specialized enough?
2 Is the management record generally good? Is it particularly good in the unit trust you are considering? Do the shares in the portfolio meet with your approval as investments?
3 How big is the trust? It may be bigger than £100 million or it may be quite small, £1 million or less. The bigger it is, the more 'average' its performance is likely to be. The smaller it is, the more chance of gain or loss.
4 How little may you invest, either in a savings plan or in a lump sum? A few trusts will not allow you to invest less than £1,000 (and management costs are lower as a result), and a £100 minimum is quite common. Some trusts may not have regular savings schemes.
5 What other services does the trust offer? These can be many and varied. Apart from savings schemes and unit-linked policies (see next section), they may also have share exchange schemes, whereby you can swop individual shares you hold for the equivalent value in units. Children's gift plans are quite common, too. These differ to some extent from trust to trust, but basically they allow you to invest on behalf of minors.

Now you have chosen your trust. The next step is to apply for the units. You simply write to the fund you have chosen and enclose your cheque. The price to you will be the offer price ruling on the day your cheque arrives. Like shares, unit trusts have bid and offer prices – the former is the one you sell at, the latter the one you buy at. The gap between them is usually higher than that for individual shares. This is because a purchase carries all the normal charges of share dealing, plus the unit trust managers' fee. A spread of about six per cent is usual, but it can go rather higher than that. We have already gone into the reasons for this gap. If you are making an outright purchase, you will buy an exact number of units and the managers will return the balance. If you are starting a savings plan, you buy in units and fractions of units each month.

to trusts about the level of charges. An initial charge of 5 per cent or ¾ per cent a year is quite usual.

3 The unit trust must have an absolutely independent trustee. This trustee, which must also be a large concern, is there to look after the shareholders' interests, as laid down in the 'trust deed'.

4 Every unit trust must have its own trust deed, which lays down the rules as to how the trust is to be run. Trust deeds do not vary much, however, and all must follow certain guidelines issued by the Department of Industry. A trust deed will include the formula according to which the unit prices are calculated, details of the management charges, and some rules for the investment policy of the fund. It may say, for instance, that the trust may not invest more than a certain proportion of its funds in one company. The figure is usually 5 per cent, but it can be higher. Nor is a unit trust allowed to hold more than 10 per cent of the equity of a single company, and it must limit its investments to the securities quoted on the Stock Exchange. Unless a trust obeys the rules of its trust deed, the Department of Industry will not authorize it and it cannot advertise its units to the public.

5 No unit trust is allowed to operate door-to-door selling techniques.

All this means that investors are fairly well protected when it comes to the running of the trust. The only thing they are not protected against is fluctuations in share prices. That is where management skill comes in. The unit trust manager has to try to do better than average when share prices are falling, and at least as well when they are rising.

Insurance, property bonds and other funds

Alongside unit trusts, you may see the prices of insurance and property bonds quoted. These operate in more or less the same way as unit trusts, except that property bond companies invest in property and not shares. They are not authorized, however, as the Department of Industry authorization only goes to trusts which invest in companies quoted in the Stock Exchange. This means that property bonds cannot be advertised to the public in the same way as unit trusts.

The managers of these funds have got round this advertising difficulty by linking the bonds to a life insurance policy, which can be advertised. If you invest in one of these bonds, you pay a premium for a single-premium life assurance policy, or an insurance bond – hence the name property bond.

The operations of property bond companies are not governed by the same rules as unit trusts, and the rules are a little less stringent. It is still possible for rather unscrupulous people to set themselves up in this field, so if you are interested in property bonds stick to companies which have a wide spread of interests.

Property bonds are useful for people who like the idea of an interest in property but cannot afford to buy actual properties, but there are snags. With unit trusts, you know the exact price of your units every day, but with property it's anybody's guess. Professional valuers make estimates of the value of property, but they cannot possibly estimate precisely what the property would fetch if it were sold. Again, it is far easier to sell shares than property. If people rushed out of property bonds to such an extent that properties actually had to be sold, they might realize less money than they would if the selling process was more leisurely and simply part of the continuing activity of the fund.

To avoid such disasters, the fund will keep a certain amount of money in case of emergencies, but if it gets into a really bad way it might still have to delay repayment for some time.

If you think you may need your money suddenly, property bonds are not for you. These bonds do not have the special tax concessions available to the holders of unit trusts, either.

Details of the bonds and the names, addresses and telephone numbers of the companies managing bonds and funds are given each day in the *Financial Times*, which also shows the previous days's price changes.

Managed funds

Recently, a new type of fund, called a managed fund, has appeared. This is a combination of a unit trust and a property bond. You make your payment and the managers invest in property, in equities or sometimes in fixed interest stocks.

The money is moved around from one place to another, depending where the managers think the best opportunities lie at any one time.

The idea is to provide holders with more regular growth than you can expect in a unit trust.

You can also invest in these funds by means of a regular savings plan linked to an assurance policy. Your premium buys shares which are valued regularly and the value of the policy depends on the value of your total units, so that you always know what your policy is worth.

Funds for foreign investment

There are two other kinds of funds which are organized in the same way as unit trusts but which specialize in foreign investments.

The first of these is quite straightforward. The fund is based in the United Kingdom. Anyone living in Britain can buy a stake in these funds.

There are also what are known as 'offshore' funds, which are legally based outside the United Kingdom and are not subject to any UK taxes or currency restrictions. As result, they can most advantageously be used by non-residents. Although their base is offshore, they are actually managed by many of the same companies which operate unit trusts and property bonds. They are often based in places like the Channel Islands and the Isle of Man, which are not subject to UK tax laws, but many of them are much further afield, in places like the Bahamas and the Cayman Islands, where taxes are non-existent or very low.

It is unlikely that the permanent UK resident will have much interest in these funds, but the prices of both kinds of funds are quoted daily in the leading national press, the 'offshore' funds under that specific heading. Again, the *Financial Times* gives daily details.

6 Investing in metals, commodities and currencies

The commodity markets

It is possible to invest money outside the stock market in various other metal, commodity and currency markets. You can, of course, acquire an interest in these markets by investing in the companies who specialize in them, but you can also invest in the actual commodities themselves.

Few small investors go in for this kind of investment. It requires a lot of cash and quite a lot of nerve. It is not advisable to think about these markets unless you have at least £10,000 to invest – and that should not be your entire capital. Despite all the risks, however, the number of investors in these markets has risen over the years; it increased ten times between 1970 and 1975 alone and has gone on rising since.

The risk is a straightforward one. The prices of these goods vary. They can go up and down with remarkable rapidity. Let's look at some of the reasons for this:

- A commodity may be superseded by another and its price may fall.
- A new source of, for example, a metal may be found, making its production more widespread and bringing down its price.
- Strikes at a major supply point may hold up supplies. The price will then go up.
- A bumper crop may bring prices down.
- A bad harvest may put prices up.

- Political developments can influence supply in both directions. A war will almost certainly cut off the source for some time and bring prices up. A coup can affect a commodity either way. A country can pursue a policy of not selling to customers abroad and bring prices up that way.
- A recession can cut demand – and prices.
- Economic conditions in a country can change quite sharply and quickly, resulting in a change in the value of a currency in relation to other currencies.

And these are only *some* of the reasons.

For many years, fourteen different commodities have been traded in London, which is one of the world's bigget market places for them. Here is an alphabetical list, including the countries which are the main source of supply. You can assess the risk yourself.

1 Barley – British needs are basically supplied from within the UK.
2 Cocoa – 30 per cent of the world's supply comes from Ghana, the rest from Nigeria, the Ivory Coast, Brazil and the Cameroons.
3 Coffee – from South America, Africa, the East Indies, the West Indies and India.
4 Copper – from the USA, Chile, Canada, Zambia, Zaire, the Soviet bloc and China.
5 Gold – South Africa, the Soviet bloc and China are the main producers, but there are many small ones as well.
6 Lead – from Canada, the USA and Australia.
7 Platinum – from the USA and South Africa.
8 Rubber – 90 per cent of natural rubber comes from South-east Asia.
9 Silver – from Canada, the USA and Australia.
10 Sugar – from Cuba, Brazil, Australia, India, the EEC, the Soviet bloc and China.
11 Tin – from Malaya, Indonesia, Bolivia, Thailand, the Soviet bloc and China.
12 Wheat – the surpluses available come mainly from Canada, the USA, Australia and New Zealand.
13 Wool – from South Africa, Australia, Argentina, New Zealand and the USA.
14 Zinc – from Canada, the USA and Australia.

New commodities have been added to this list. They include gas oil futures, crude oil, soyabean meal and aluminium, and cotton (in Liverpool).

No one knows exactly how much of these commodities the Soviet bloc and China could or do produce, but the way these countries deal can be an important influence on commodity prices.

It is important to understand how the commodity markets operate. They are based on what are called 'futures'. First of all, the commodity is offered for sale locally, then the rest is offered in the world market at a price to suit both sides. By the time the commodity reaches its destination, the price may have fallen or risen.

This is where the dealer comes in. He buys or sells a commodity for delivery in the future. He agrees to buy or sell the commodity in the future in accordance with a standard contract under the guidance of an organized commodity futures market. No one is actually going to come and deliver fifty tons of zinc to you – unless you are a manufacturer and need it for production. The futures price is *not* what you estimate the price will be in one, two or three months' time. It is today's price, plus hypothetical transport and storage costs, something for inflation and an interest charge. The price of the actual commodity, metal or currency fluctuates quite separately from futures dealing. Companies use futures to protect themselves from fluctuations in the day-to-day or 'spot' price, as it is called. It is very difficult to run your business at a guaranteed profit if you cannot have any control over the price of the raw materials or money you might need to pay for imports. This activity on the part of companies is called 'hedging'.

The private investor also promises to buy or sell at a certain price on a certain future date. If you think the price of the commodity is going to rise, then you would buy today in order to sell in the future at the new price. If the price moves up meanwhile, the difference between the two prices is your profit. Unlike the company, the private dealer is not hedging. This is pure speculation.

If, on the other hand, you think prices will fall, you contract to sell at today's price on a specified future date. If the price duly falls, you can buy at the lower price and sell at the original price and make a profit.

You can buy and sell these options at any time through a commodity dealer, who, like a stockbroker, will charge for his services. The commission is usually lower than for buying shares, however, because the amounts involved are much larger; it should average out at about half a per cent.

If you do not have large sums of money available, you may be able to join a 'syndicate', whereby a number of small investors pool their resources and share out the eventual profit or loss according to the proportion invested in the syndicate. The commodity brokers themselves often organize such syndicates, and the agreements are carefully drawn up to protect investors, so that their liability is limited to the amount of their original investment.

There are some snags in this form of investing. The gains are not usually allowed by the Inland Revenue to be capital gains; they are counted as income and taxed accordingly – that is, usually at a much higher rate than capital gains tax.

Probably the best way for someone with limited capital who wants to get into commodities is to invest in one of the specialist unit trusts which holds shares in the companies which produce or mine commodities.

Dealings in commodities and metals are done in Britain at London's metal exchange and there are also smaller exchanges around the country. Currency deals, or financial futures, as they are called, take place in London at the London International Financial Futures Exchange (LIFFE), which opened in September 1982. Other countries have their own exchanges, the biggest and the most active in the United States. After a slow start, business at LIFFE has been growing and, as well as dealing in sterling, the exchange also deals in Eurodollars, the Swiss franc, the German deutschmark and the Japanese yen. The last three are all traded against the American dollar. In 1984, two new 'contracts' have been offered by the exchange. They are in the new *Financial Times* 100 index and the UST-bond, which is based upon a theoretical 20-year 8 per cent US Treasury Bill. Dealing in these helps to iron out fluctuations in the share prices and fixed-interest stocks. They are not for the private investor, unless he is extremely wealthy.

Do not think you can 'hedge' your holiday spending money against a fall in its value while you are away – £25,000 is the value of a typical contract.

Commodities offshore
Various unauthorized unit trusts have been set up as offshore funds to deal in commodities. They are scrutinized by the offshore authority where they are based and also by the British government's Department of Industry. Sometimes you can invest as little as £500 to £1,000 in them, but, as with any ordinary unit trust, the investor has no say in the investment policy of the trust.

Like unit trusts, they lower the risk of commodity investment, and as no dividends are paid it is possible that the investor may only be liable for gains tax and not for income tax when he sells his holding, as he can do at any time.

Investing in commodities can be very profitable, but it is not really for the small investor or anyone who is not fully aware of the risk involved.

7 Investing in property

Renting out property

You may decide that shares are not for you. Having seen the prices of property rise steadily over the years, you perhaps think that would make a more secure investment. In many ways this is true, but the owning and renting of property for income has become much less attractive in recent years. There are several reasons for this:

1 You can no longer get tax relief on a mortgage on a second home.

Landlords used to be able to have several mortgages that were all eligible for tax relief, so they made money in two ways, in tax relief and in rents.

2 The mortgage ceiling for tax relief is now £30,000 and there is no guarantee that it will be increased or even remain this high.

3 When you sell any house or flat which is *not* your principal house, you must pay capital gains tax on any real profit you make (see Section four, chapter 1).

4 Rents are taxed as investment income, which has implications for married women who rent out property (see Section four, chapter 1).

5 In periods of inflation, the costs of upkeep and maintenance have risen sharply, far more sharply than rents, as a rule.

6 It is sometimes impossible to get rid of your tenants.

Slowly rising rents and tenants' security of tenure have come about through a series of Rent Acts, starting in 1919. The last one was enacted in 1977. All the Acts have had the same purpose: to give security to tenants and to see that they pay a fair rent. The landlord has come in for little consideration in most of these Acts. For instance, rents stayed frozen from 1939 until almost twenty years later. Landlords were sometimes paying out more on maintenance than they got in rents, unless they were prepared to let their properties fall into a bad state of repair.

The Housing Act 1980
A new Act, the Housing Act, came into force in 1980. This introduced some changes in renting and included a 'tenants' charter' for those in local authority housing, New Towns, or in housing associations. It defined more clearly than before a tenant's right to stay in their house or flat, set out the conditions under which it became possible for tenants to buy their homes, and allowed them to sub-let or take in lodgers.

A court order is now required before a secure tenant can be made to move. Rowdy behaviour or a failure to pay rent are two of the circumstances in which a landlord might get possession, though there is a long list of occasions when it becomes theoretically possible. A landlord can, for instance, get possession on the grounds that the good management of the property requires that you move. In this case, however, alternative accommodation must be provided and the court will decide if it is suitable if you turn it down.

Other clauses in the Act permit tenants to pass a tenancy on to a wife or husband on death, or to a close relative who has been living in the property for more than twelve months, the right to make home improvements, and a guarantee that there will be no increases in rent as a result. Tenants can sometimes even get a home improvement grant and, where a tenant moves, he or she can sometimes get some of the money back from the landlord. If you have been a tenant for some time and made improvements, these must be allowed for in calculating the purchase price should you eventually buy your home.

In certain cases, landlords must consult their tenants about housing management which affects them. Repair and improvement programmes, caretaking systems and changes in rent-collecting methods are just three things which come under the consultation clause.

The Housing Act did not only deal with those in local authority or semi-public housing; it also introduced a new form of letting for private tenancies signed after 28 November 1980. It is known as a 'shorthold' and differs from other tenancies in that there is no security of tenure after the end of the lease. It must be for a fixed period between one and five years and, during the term of the lease, the tenant is fully protected, as long as the conditions of the tenancy are not broken.

In addition to security during the term of the tenancy, there are other requirements for landlords before the tenancy can be registered as a shorthold:

- The letting must be to a new tenant.
- The landlord must give the tenant a notice *in the form laid down by law*, so that the tenant is absolutely clear that this is what is being offered and not some other form of lease. Failure to do this could give a tenant the right to stay on after the term of the lease ends.
- A *fair rent* must be registered with the rent officer, *or* the landlord must obtain a certificate of fair rent before granting the tenancy *and* an application for the registration of a fair rent should be made not later than twenty-eight days after the start of the tenancy.

Most lettings by non-resident private landlords, however, come into the category of *regulated tenancies*. It does not matter whether the premises are furnished or unfurnished and the tenant has rights concerning the amount of rent he can be charged and security of tenure. Regulated tenants:

- Cannot be evicted without a possession order from the court.
- Can pass on the tenancy to a member of the family on death.
- Can apply for a *fair rent*, if they think the rent is too high, as can the landlord if he thinks it is too low.
- Can be sure that once a registered rent is charged, it cannot be altered until there is a review or cancellation.
- Can insist that any rent increases up to the registered rent are phased in.
- May be eligible for a rent allowance.
- May be eligible for a home improvement grant.

Getting possession

If you are a landlord, you will find it very difficult to get rid of a tenant who is clean and quiet, pays rent on time and does not damage your property. These rules apply whether the accommodation is furnished or unfurnished.

If the only way of getting rid of a regulated tenant is to offer him money, you are allowed to do this.

You can get possession on several grounds, however:
- If you can prove a tenant has been a bad tenant and caused a nuisance to neighbours, or used the accommodation for immoral purposes.
- If the tenant has damaged the property.
- If the premises have been sub-let without the landlord's permission.
- If the tenant has given notice to quit and withdrawn it after the landlord has re-let or sold the premises.
- If the tenancy is a condition of employment and the tenant leaves the landlord's employ.
- If the landlord needs the house for himself or his family to live in. The court will not grant possession if the hardship to the tenant would be greater than that to the landlord.

And certain forms of letting do not give the tenant security of tenure:

1 If you let a bedsitter in the house you yourself live in, you can be fairly sure of getting repossession when you want it – as long as you continue to live in the house. Even in these cases, however, the tenant has some rights. He can go to the rent tribunal for a fair rent to be assessed, or he can ask for notice to quit to be extended by up to six months while he looks for somewhere else, and a tribunal will usually grant this, unless the landlord can prove that the tenant is a bad one – not paying rent, damaging the room, etc.

2 If your work takes you abroad for a period and you wish to let your house while you are away, you must tell the tenant in writing that you are the owner-occupier of the house and will be requiring occupancy at the end of the tenancy. Make sure that you get a written acknowledgement that he has received the information.

3 If you have a cottage ready for your retirement and you want to let it meanwhile, you should also give the tenant notice of this before he moves in. Alternatively, you can let it to different people for short periods.

4 Holiday lettings are outside the Rent and Housing Acts.

5 Some lettings to students are also outside the Rent and Housing Acts.

6 Where you provide cleaning, meals or other services.

Fair rents
Getting possession is not the only problem for the landlord. Ensuring that you get a proper rent is another. To help both landlords and tenants who cannot agree on a rent, the concept of the *fair rent* has been developed for most rented property in Britain, apart from the most expensive. Under the rules, either the landlord or the tenant – or both jointly – can apply to the local rent officer or rent assessment committee to ask for a rent to be set under the terms of the 1977 Rent Act. Once the rent is registered, it remains in force, even if there is a change of tenant, until a new registration is made, or the registration is cancelled.

Rents are a very thorny area. It is not always easy to balance the interest of the tenant with that of the landlord, who does not wish to see his income effectively lowered because of inflation.

Rents are usually constant throughout a lease. When a fixed term ends, a landlord may renew it at a higher rent, but if the tenant thinks it is too high he can go to the officer or assessment committee and ask for it to be lowered. Fair rents are not market rents and can be very different from them, because no attention is paid to the scarcity of the property in question. The rent officer takes into account any circumstance of the letting, *except the personal ones of the landlord or tenant*. So he will look at the state of repair of the letting (not any damage which might have been done by the tenant), its location, character and age. He will also take account of the quantity and quality of any furniture provided and he must assume that demand for homes in a particular area does not greatly exceed supply. Before deciding, the rent officer discusses the case with the tenant or landlord if they wish.

If a landlord and tenant cannot agree about a rent, they can make a joint application. Once made, an application can be withdrawn, if the other side agrees. *You cannot get rid of or harass in any way a tenant who has had his rent lowered by a tribunal.*

When rent is not paid

If rent is not paid, the landlord has the right to take, known as 'distrain', the tenant's goods, and either hold them as security until the rent is paid or sell them to pay it. He cannot, however, take certain personal items, such as loose money, clothing or bedding under the value of £50. He must give back to the tenant any proceeds from selling over and above the rent. The consent of a court is required before any goods can be distrained. If the rent remains unpaid, the landlord can eventually terminate the lease, but this is a fairly long process.

The landlord must write to the tenant, setting out the reason why he has broken the lease. Then either the tenant pays or the landlord can go to court. The court has discretion over whether or not to order that the tenant forfeits the lease. Even if it does, the tenant still has twenty-eight days in which to pay the rent. If he pays, he can stay where he is.

The position from the tenant's point of view

If you are a tenant, the laws mostly work in your favour. As long as you are a good tenant – pay your rent, do not damage the premises or upset your neighbours – you can stay for as long as you want provided that:

- The landlord does not live on the premises.
- You get no other services, like breakfast or general board, or services like cleaning and changing of sheets.
- You do not live in a student's hostel, or holiday accommodation.

You have certain entitlements and obligations under a lease. The landlord cannot, for instance, interfere with your 'quiet enjoyment of the premises'. This has nothing to do with noise, but would apply if your landlord cut your gas or electricity off, or threatened you in any way.

The landlord may or may not be required to do repairs. If you have a full repairing lease you will have to do them all – inside and out. Sometimes the landlord will do outside repairs but not inside ones. Where the premises are let for less than seven years and the tenancy was granted after 24 October 1961, the landlord is by law responsible for maintaining the structure of the building and some essential repairs, like those to sanitary installations, for example. You cannot, of course, expect him to do repairs he does not know about, so it is up to you to tell him.

In return, you must pay the rent and treat the premises with reasonable care. Any damage which is done by the tenant or his family must be repaired by them.

Check your lease on all these points. *Repairs can cost a lot of money if you are responsible for them.*

Your lease may allow you to assign it to someone else, or it may not. Generally, even if it does, you will have to have the landlord's agreement that the assigned tenant is acceptable. Leases less than three years long generally do not allow assignment. Normally it is illegal to charge anyone money for a lease, or when assigning a lease, though a 'premium', as it is called, is permitted in some cases – when a lease is for 21 years or more; when a tenancy was not regulated at the time it was granted and a premium was lawfully charged; or when tenancies are granted by the Crown Estate Commissioners, the Duchy of Lancaster or the Duchy of Cornwall. You can, however, sell your furniture or fittings. *Take care when you do this not to sell them at an inflated price, because the new tenant can sue and get the excess money back from you.*

Summing up

In view of all these rules and regulations, you may well decide that investing in property is not for you. You can always buy property bonds instead (see chapter 5 of this section). That way, you will not have any day-to-day problems.

If, on the other hand, you do decide to go ahead and you want your properties free from time to time, you can gear your letting policy to people who are not likely to stay long.

These include foreign diplomats, executives of overseas companies and students. None of these is absolutely guaranteed to move, but they are much more likely to than most. Of course, you may have to put up with no tenants from time to time if you cannot find the kind you want immediately.

If you decide to go ahead, take legal advice and read one of the various books which spell out the implications of the Rent and Housing Acts in full. The Department of the Environment produces two clear booklets which can help you, whether you are a landlord or a tenant. They are 'Regulated Tenancies' and 'Leasehold Reform'.

Buying property abroad

If you are thinking of buying a second home, you may feel you would like something overseas, to use for holidays now and retirement later.

This can be a good idea, but there are many pitfalls. Property markets abroad are not always so well organized as in the UK, and do not forget that locals can see a foreigner coming so you may be asked a totally unreasonable price for what you are buying.

If you are thinking of buying abroad, however, the sooner you do it the better. A house is always an asset, wherever it is, and can be sold if you decide later that you do not wish to retire there, or even to use it for holidays, but check to make sure there are no legal problems in getting your money back home. Prices everywhere have been rising in recent years.

The first thing to do is to decide upon the area you are interested in and then take professional advice.

Never buy in a development which is not yet completed, unless you are sure the project is secure, and *never* under any circumstances buy when only the plans are available. Too many people have lost money this way. Don't be caught out. Don't buy anything you haven't seen. If you buy something which needs renovation, check on building costs in the area. Nowhere is cheap anymore.

You can buy property anywhere, and places like Fiji, the Seychelles and the Caribbean are becoming more and more popular. For the moment, however, most British people will buy in Europe, so let's take a look at that.

Buying in Europe

You will find, first of all, that the costs of buying and selling tend to be higher in continental Europe than in the UK. An estate agent may charge both buyer and seller, the former about 3 per cent and the latter about 5 per cent. On top of that come legal costs and various government charges, which will generally include VAT on the total cost of the property.

The legal process will be conducted through a notary, and transactions are not valid unless carried out in front of one. The purchase is achieved through a formal agreement settled between the parties beforehand, which is then endorsed in front of the notary. Make sure that the seller has full title to the property you are buying, or later on you may find that you have not bought it at all.

You may be able to get a mortgage to help with the payment, but if you do you will find interest rates far higher than in the UK. Few countries have a mortgage system as good as that of the United Kingdom; it is rare to get an advance abroad for more than 50 per cent of the price of the property. Not only that, you are unlikely to get tax relief on a local mortgage, even if you live there, and you won't, generally, if you are still resident in the UK.

For this reason, most people who buy property abroad pay cash, unless some kind of individual or group mortgage scheme is available for a large-scale modern development – though it is sometimes possible to get a mortgage in Britain for a purchase overseas and then qualify for tax relief on the interest paid.

There are various overseas mortgage schemes offered in Britain, but these do not qualify for tax relief.

Since the ending of exchange control, there are no problems about getting the money out of this country: it can be done simply by bank transfer. But beware: the country in which you buy may still have exchange controls or some other restrictions, which may make it difficult to get your money out, if you sell.

Living abroad

Before you even think of living abroad, check on the rules and regulations governing your residence there, and consider the following points:

1 How much time will you want to spend abroad? Any money you get from letting your property while you are not actually living there must be declared as income to the taxman in the UK.
2 Is your income sufficient? Some countries insist that you have a minimum regular income before allowing you to become resident. Try the embassy of the country for information on this.
3 What is the tax position? Britain has a double tax relief agreement with some countries. This means that overall you may pay less tax. In some places, there are no taxes at all. Detailed information is available from Overseas Territories Income Tax Office, 26 Grosvenor Gardens, London SW1.
4 What will your personal living costs be in the country of your choice? Will you want many trips back home? Can you grow your own produce? What things can you not do without? Think about this very seriously, because all your plans will come to nothing and you may lose a great deal of money if you find you cannot manage.
5 What about insurance? The cost of medical treatment outside the UK can be very high. Do you need insurance to cover it? Remember that the older you get, the more likely you are to need medical treatment. Have you got your house and its fittings properly insured?
6 Will you need a car, or will local transport do? If you have to have a car, check the tax situation if you take a car from the UK.

7 Do you need a permit if you want to be a permanent resident?
8 Have you insured yourself against a change in the political climate?
   There can be changes wherever you go to live and foreign residents may
   not always be welcome. You can insure yourself against this, but it is
   likely to cost you money, about £1.50 for every £100-worth of assets you
   insure. It's probably cheaper to cut your losses and run if the worst
   happens. Remember that there are a lot of 'cowboys' in the property
   world. Be absolutely certain that you are not dealing with crooks when
   you buy property abroad, especially if you do not speak the language.
   Make sure you deal only with reputable people – and that includes
   lawyers.

8 Other investments

You may decide that you do not want to invest in property or shares or
anything else where money is exchanged for a piece of paper which
guarantees rights or benefits, or both, to its holders. Yet you may still want
to invest in something.

   There are many other fields in which sound investments can be made,
ranging from stamps to antiques and paintings. Whatever you decide to
buy, there will be a number of excellent books to help you. This chapter is
intended simply to put forward general advice in just some of the possible
areas. No recommendations will be made: for these you must go to an
expert in your chosen field.

   You can collect almost anything and there is a chance that it will
appreciate in value – though of course it may not. If this happens with, say,
your antiques, you will just have to use them as furniture in your home. If
you are a beginner with not much money, try to spot the next vogue.
Always buy things you think are attractive. Beautifully made objects in
almost any field can go out of fashion, but they always return after a few
years. Meanwhile, you can buy at low prices. The year 1977, for example,
saw a great number of jugs, plates, ornaments and general bric-à-brac to
mark the Queen's Silver Jubilee. Then, in 1981, there was a vast range of
products celebrating the wedding of Prince Charles to Lady Diana
Spencer. If past experience of such occasions is any guide, in a few years
these ornaments will be selling at high premiums on their purchase prices.

   Royal occasions of all kinds have been celebrated in this way in the past,
and almost all the souvenirs produced have turned out to be good

investments – if fairly modest ones. This is because they are usually produced in limited editions – that is, a fixed number only. Inevitably, many get lost and broken; then the souvenirs become rare, and their prices rise.

Limited editions of all kinds are produced for these occasions – books, medallions, pots, plaques, lithographs, almost anything in the ornamental line. Not all of them become worth a great deal of money, but some do. They are rarely a profitable short-term investment. If you buy something new today, think in terms of your grandchildren benefiting.

But there are all kinds of frauds. A limited edition might not be as limited as is claimed. Beware of the claims made by glossy advertisements. Check before buying if you possibly can.

The best investments

What are the best investments, then? The most reliable guide is to see what auctioneers think. Here is how Phillips of London viewed what would be sound hedges against inflation, bought at 1984 prices:

Under £500
Furniture – George IV to Victorian chest of drawers.
Paintings – portraits.
Watercolours – topography by mid-rank artists.
Prints – modern British etchings.
Objects of art, clocks, etc. – 19th-century mahogany bracket clocks.
Carpets and rugs – Shiraz, Afshar.
Silver and plate – modern tea-sets and candlesticks.
Jewellery – 18th-century gold rings. All gold pieces. Aquamarines; Roman.
Ceramics and glass – attractive small shapes in English porcelain.
Oriental – Chinese decorative paintings.
Art Nouveau and Deco – lesser-known cameo glass.
Other collectors' items – signed first editions; toys; dolls; golf items; good cameras; pocket globes.

£500–£3,000
Furniture – Georgian 'brown furniture'.
Paintings – portraits, mainly Dutch; English landscapes.
Watercolours – mid-Victorian decorative (to £200 only); 19th/20th-century Scottish.
Prints – fine 18th/19th-century decorative, O.M. and modern.
Objects of art, clocks, etc. – longcase clocks.
Carpets and rugs – tribal Persian of best quality.
Silver and plate – chambersticks and coaster pairs.

Jewellery – as under £500, depending on piece.
Ceramics and glass – early English porcelain and pottery.
Oriental – K'ang Hsi and late Ming; lacquer furniture.
Art Nouveau and Deco – furniture; bronzes, carpets.
Other collectors' items – Victorian illustrated travel books; garden books; Georgian swords; 18th-century microscopes.

Over £3,000
Furniture – Fine English; good Victorian; Edwardian.
Paintings – Italian and French 17th-century. Topographical records.
Carpets and rugs – Herez, Mahal.
Silver and plate – Georgian candelabra.
Ceramics and glass – 19th-century and English ironstone dinner services.
Oriental – as £500–£3,000.
Art Nouveau and Deco – Galle lamps; bronzes; top jewellery.

Buying antiques

There is such a wide choice when it comes to buying antiques that it is difficult to know where to start. If you are serious about collecting, it is best to stick to one particular kind of piece, or period. That way you will build up your knowledge and have a better chance of picking up something really good than if you dabble about here and there. Here are some useful tips for you to follow.

Start off by trying to *find a kind of antique that appeals to you personally*. One of the nice things about antiques, as opposed to bank notes or share certificates, is that they can be put on show in your home while they make money for you. It seems a pity to collect Spode china, for example, if you don't like it yourself.

In choosing an area, you should also try to *find one that has not been overexploited before*. For example, 1890s posters, blue and white printed earthenware, and English literary autographs are still, in some experts' opinions, undervalued. You then have the chance of pioneering a collection with a relatively low outlay.

If possible, approach your collecting in an orderly and professional way. *Keep a book as a 'catalogue'*, entering for each item everything you can find out about it – where bought, for how much, previous owners, previous appearances in sales, etc. This catalogue will be invaluable when you come to sell the collection. It can be handed over to the auctioneer and will help him in making *his* catalogue.

You should also have each major piece photographed. These photos can then be used in the eventual sale catalogue; they will also, like the catalogue, be of immense use if by an unhappy chance your collection is stolen. In that case, the catalogue and pictures can be given to the police immediately.

Never buy damaged pieces. If you do, you will soon find that what to the seller is an 'honourable scar' or 'hairline crack' becomes magnified into a 'bloody great piece broken off', or simply 'AF' ('all faults') in the auctioneer's catalogue.

If you are not used to buying antiques, and have no great knowledge of them, it will save you money in the long run to *operate through a reliable dealer*, accepting his advice on which pieces to buy and letting him bid for you in the auction rooms.

Whatever the dealers' associations say, the 'ring' still operates in many sales, and, while in no way wanting to encourage this nefarious practice, you will come to grief if you run counter to it and antagonize the dealers. Let the wily professional take the strain. The commission you pay him will be justified.

Nevertheless, the best way of collecting antiques is to *make yourself an expert in what you are collecting*. Do your homework: read books on the subject, visit museums and attend sales. It could become a delightful hobby which will not only make you money but also stop you dying of boredom after you retire.

Buying and selling at auctions

You can buy your pieces from a shop or a dealer, but you may like to try your hand at buying in an auction. Anything can be auctioned, even property; some auctioneers specialize in one particular range of goods.

If you do want to try buying at an auction, first go to several simply to study the techniques. Buying at auctions involves skill, if you are not going to lose what you want or find yourself paying a ridiculous price for it.

When you are beginning, you can always ask a dealer to buy for you. Put a price limit on what you want to buy and watch how he goes about it.

When you buy at an auction, you compete with other prospective buyers and the object goes to the person who names the highest price. You do not usually have to pay anything to buy, but recently some auctioneers have raised the commission they expect for auctioning an item and split it between the buyer and the seller. Previously only the seller paid.

One problem with buying at an auction is that the quality of the goods purchased is not guaranteed under the Supply of Goods (Implied Terms) Act 1973. But you might be able to claim under the Misrepresentation Act 1967 if you feel you were told a deliberate lie about the item you have bought. Supposing a chair is described as a genuine Chippendale and when you get it home it is clearly a fake. In that case, you may be able to claim your money back. (For more about auction law, turn to Section six, chapter 3.)

If you are selling, you must get the item to the auctioneers in time for it to go into the catalogue. If you wish, you can set a reserve, price below which you do not wish to sell. If the item does not reach the reserve it is withdrawn from the sale and either sent back to you or put in another time – when you can change the reserve, if you wish.

Collecting silver

One of the most pleasant aspects of collecting silver is that you can use and enjoy your investment at the same time as it is growing in value for you. Some pieces of antique silver, especially when they are of particular historical interest, fetch very high prices and are just for the wealthy collector, but silver is also good for the beginner, because there is a wide range of items to be had at prices from a few pounds up.

Silver is not as valuable as gold, but it has proved a good investment for many people. What makes it especially attractive is that, with British silver at any rate, you know what you are buying because of the hallmark. Gold, of course, is also hallmarked.

Rule number one, then, is know what you are buying. Is it silver, and if so, what kind? If it is British silver (or gold) it will carry a hallmark. This is a measure of the standard of the precious metal and was introduced in London in 1238 (in 1975, hallmarking was extended to include platinum). Silver which passed the Goldsmiths' Guild test was marked with a leopard's head. The marks developed, and today there are four Assay Offices in the United Kingdom – in London, Birmingham, Sheffield and Edinburgh (there is one in Dublin too) – which authenticate silver, gold and platinum. Formerly there were a number of other Assay Offices.

The hallmark is a row of small letters and pictures stamped into the metal. Together, these tell you how old the silver is and who made it. It also includes the Assay Office mark, which identifies the particular office at which the article was tested and marked, and the standard mark, which denotes that the precious metal content is not less than the standard indicated. A 'lion passant', for instance, appears on every piece of sterling silver. It faces left, holding a paw in the air (when it faces right, it means it came from Newcastle and was made in the years from 1721 to 1727 only). Sterling silver is 92.5 per cent pure silver; the rest is metal alloy. There are also marks which commemorate special events. The illustration above is an example of a complete hallmark, including the 1977 Silver Jubilee commemorative mark. It shows the sponsor's mark, followed by the mark for sterling silver, the London Assay Office mark, the date letter for 1977, and the 1977 Silver Jubilee mark. The illustrations on pp. 414–5, reproduced by courtesy of the Assay Offices of Great Britain, give the pre- and post-1975 standard marks and Assay Office marks for silver, gold and platinum.

Continental silver is less easy to identify. It often has a lower silver content than sterling silver, perhaps as little as 80 per cent. This cannot legally be sold as silver in Britain, but it may be worth buying as an antique or collector's piece. Any silver which came into the country after 1842 had to be assayed and hallmarked so that people knew what they were buying. The best bargains in continental silver are from Spain or Portugal, though Dutch is popular with buyers.

There are many books on silver and its hallmarks. If you use one, you can easily tell whether the piece you are thinking of buying is one of those prized by collectors.

Get your silver valued for insurance purposes. There is no laid-down fee for valuation, but as a general guide you will pay something like £2 basic fee, plus 1 per cent of the valuation up to £20,000, plus 20p an article after the first item.

Don't go wandering into a shop asking a dealer to make an offer to get an idea of the value. He will give you a price which will allow for a profit for him on resale, so you may be very disappointed at how low he rates your treasure, which may well have a higher insurance value.

Silver plate
Silver isn't always what it seems to be. Very often it is silver plate. This consists of a coating of silver on copper, and the process has been used for over 200 years. Even though its worth in silver is small, pieces of silver plate *can* be valuable as collector's items. Like silver, it is hallmarked, often including the letters EPNS, which simply means electroplated nickel silver.

Collecting bank notes and coins

Your money may well be worth more than its face value, and collecting bank notes can prove quite a profitable hobby. Dealers will buy pre-decimilization 10/- notes, for instance, which are in 'very fine' or mint condition – that is, showing no signs of wear – for £1.50 to £6. Dealers will sell for about 25 per cent more than they buy for notes which are regularly bought and sold.

Obviously, this sort of profit is only worthwhile if you deal in large amounts. There are some quite recent notes, however, which fetch much better prices, particularly where there are oddities in the water-marking or the serial numbers or where only a small number of those particular notes were issued. Some £1 notes issued in 1967, for instance, are fetching up to £40 when they are in 'extremely fine' condition.

Assay Office Mark
British Articles

Prior to 1975	Assay Office	From 1975
gold & Sterling silver Britannia silver	**London**	gold, silver & platinum
gold silver	**Birmingham**	gold & platinum silver
gold silver	**Sheffield**	gold, silver & platinum
gold & silver	**Edinburgh**	gold & silver

Notes · (ı) Some variations in the surrounding shields are found before 1975 (ıı) All Assay Offices mark Britannia silver, but only London (prior to 1975) had a special Assay Office mark for this standard.

Imported Articles

Prior to 1975		Assay Office	From 1975	
gold	silver		gold & silver	platinum
		London	unchanged	
		Birmingham	unchanged	
		Sheffield	unchanged	
		Edinburgh	unchanged	—

Standard Mark
British Articles

Prior to 1975	Standard	From 1975
	22 carat gold Marked in England Marked in Scotland	916
	18 carat gold Marked in England Marked in Scotland	750
14 585	14 carat gold	585
9 375	9 carat gold	375
	Sterling silver Marked in England Marked in Scotland	
	Britannia silver	
—	Platinum	

Imported Articles

22 916	22 carat gold	916
18 750	18 carat gold	750
585	14 carat gold	585
375	9 carat gold	375
925	Sterling silver	925
9584	Britannia silver	958
—	Platinum	950

Any Bank of England notes issued before 1900 are valuable. They are fairly rare and may be worth more than £1,000 each. When you get this far back, the actual denomination of the note ceases to have any impact on the price; it is the rarity value which is important. If you go back as far as the eighteenth century, notes are so rare that no catalogue prices are given.

Some of the Treasury notes issued in the 1914–18 war, and known as 'Bradburys', sell at between fifty and a hundred times their face value. Other Treasury notes, which were withdrawn in 1928 when the Bank of England took over the issue of notes, command good prices. Specimens signed by C. P. Mahon or B. G. Catterns are worth buying.

Some of the £1 notes which ceased to be issued after 1948 are valuable. They are signed by J. B. Page and carry the serial letter 'M'. This 'M' note indicates that the note was a replacement for a faulty note, which had already been checked and destroyed by the Bank of England. Errors themselves are rare, so the 'M' notes are rare as well. You might be able to get £12 for one in good condition.

Old coins can similarly be valuable. Gold prices have been depressed in the past few years and any purchase now should be a good long-term investment. A relatively new hobby is collecting old bank cheques.

Collecting stamps

Unlike collecting gems, antiques or silver, which can be very expensive, we can all have a go at stamp collecting. There can be few people who do not try this hobby as a child, but for adult collectors it is a very serious business. Like collecting gems and antiques, stamp collecting has been more rewarding for the investor in recent years than either the stock market or bank deposits.

But, as with all collecting, you have to know what you are doing. Stanley Gibbons – the best known British dealers, who produce annual catalogues – say that little after 1930 is worth the serious collector's attention, apart from a few exceptions which for one reason or another have become scarce. *Rarity and condition is all in stamp collecting.* Here are a few examples of selling prices at late 1984 levels:

1840 Queen Victoria 1d black: £2,750 mint, £240 used.
1946 Victory, 1st day cover: £275.
1964 Shakespeare 1s 6d: £22 phosphor mint.
1973 Royal Wedding – traffic gutter pairs mint: £120.
1974 Churchill Centenary set mint: £3.50.
1980 80th birthday Queen Mother 12p: 30p mint or used.

If you find you have some of these stamps tucked away and want to sell, you must knock at least 25 per cent off these prices. Remember that catalogue prices are dealers' *selling*, not buying, prices. If you have a few hundred pounds to spend, Stanley Gibbons runs a general investment advisory service. Experience shows, however, that major discoveries by amateurs have always been rare and are virtually non-existent today.

First-day covers have been popular with serious stamp collectors for years. Until recently, these were simply stamps with a postmark showing the date they were issued. They were often good investments.

Today, they have become an industry, and the post office sells the stamps on fancy envelopes with a special postmark. As more and more people have begun buying first-day covers, they have become devalued, and it is more difficult to make a profit on them. First-day covers can be provided by the post office for a few pence above the face value of the stamps, but some dealers have recently started providing elaborate covers for clients, which can cost a considerable amount of money and – more important – may be a doubtful investment. If you buy first-day covers:

- Either use the post office or buy and post the stamps yourself, or use a recognized stamp dealer.
- Buy a complete set.
- Make sure you are not paying for an envelope rather than the stamps themselves.

Stamps have not been a particularly good investment in the past few years. British stamps are the finest, but not such a good investment as when fewer were printed.

Investing in gems

Many people have been badly caught investing in gems. For example, people who bought those little packages of diamonds which the buyer is not supposed to open for a period after purchase, otherwise he cannot get his money back later on sale, even if the price of diamonds has gone up in the meantime. If you see one of these schemes – now fortunately rare – ignore it.

You really need a great deal of money to invest in gems. The small stones in most rings are not worth very much. These should be bought just for pleasure, because retail mark-ups are very high (sometimes 100 per cent) and it is difficult to get your money back for many years, until perhaps a ring acquires an antique or fashion value.

Even the prices of diamonds have fallen recently, but they should recover in the long term. The prices of fine sapphires, emeralds and rubies have kept their prices better, but are not such big business. If you have the few thousand pounds needed for a really good one-carat gem (a carat weighs 0.2 grams), you can expect to make a profit of around 50 per cent a year, because good-quality gems are in short supply and more people are keeping their best stones rather than selling them for currency, which is falling in value.

Take expert advice before you buy. A bad stone may be worth only about a tenth as much as a good one. Carat, colour, clarity and cut are the keys, and only the very skilled can judge.

Size, which is what matters if you are investing, is of no significance until you reach half a carat for diamonds. two carats for rubies, four for sapphires and one for emeralds.

In Britain, most dealing is done through London's Hatton Garden, where about fifty merchants operate. If you are sensible, you will buy through them and not through advertisements from private people.

This is a very conservative trade, but new dealers have been emerging recently who will buy for you at trade price plus commission. Look out for them.

The London Diamond Bourse and the London Diamond Club are two places where you will find reputable gem 'brokers'. They do not normally deal with the general public, but individual brokers will sometimes advise. There is little possibility of a properly supervised and managed diamond 'fund' for smaller investors because of the problems of grading diamonds. There are a number of different assessment scales in the world, and much depends on the experts' view. If such a fund could be set up, it would also assist in selling and would cut down the excessive profit margins to which small investors, are subjected.

Do not buy a diamond unless you know what sort of stone you are buying and make sure that it has an internationally recognized grading certificate, which should be sealed in a plastic bag with your diamond. Watch out, there are a lot of sharks about.

Investing in wine

There can be few wine drinkers who do not think at some time of 'laying down' some bottles of wine as an investment.

First, you must think about where to store it. In some cases, the merchant or shippers will be prepared to do that for you, and that has the advantage that you will then have no temptation to nip down and deplete your investment by drinking the occasional bottle.

You may prefer to keep it at home, however, if you have suitable space available. Wines like to be kept in dark, cool places, but modern houses are rarely built with the cellars which suit wines so well. In fact, the actual temperature is not that important, as long as it does not go over 70°F or below 40°F. What is important is that the temperature should not vary much. All wine will go off if the temperature keeps changing sharply. Lie the bottles on their sides. This prevents the cork from shrinking and letting in air.

If you do start a cellar, whether in your own home or at the shippers, always keep a book of your purchases. This should record the name of the wine, the name of the shipper, the year, the price, the quantity bought, any comments on it, and the earliest and latest maturity dates. You do not have to keep your wine till maturity, however. It is saleable at any stage along the way.

Wine buying can be fun. It is not too expensive, if you buy the wine young and then leave it to mature. But it does have its risks, and these should not be under-rated.

The logic behind investing in wine seems sound. Some wines are ready for drinking very soon after they are made. Others go on improving if they are kept – sometimes for up to fifty years. And, as they improve, they rise in price. In theory, then, you only have to pick the right wine and your profit will follow automatically.

In practice, it does not always work out like that. Wine prices do not always rise as expected. Perhaps there turns out to be too much of a particular kind at a particular time, or, as it matures, its taste does not fulfil its early promise. So wine buying is as much a risk as any other kind of investment – though, if the worst comes to the worst, you can always drink it.

Only the best wines are worth laying down. On the whole, these are French wines, with a few from Germany and a very few from Austria and Italy.

Vintages vary from year to year, from superb to bad and any graduation in between. You will need a wine shipper's advice as to what is worth buying in any particular year.

Champagne also comes in vintages. In some years, when quality is poor, no vintage is declared, but there are also non-vintage champagnes produced every year. Even good non-vintage champagne will improve for some time after it has been shipped. Vintage champagnes are not sold until they are five years old.

Port also comes in vintage and non-vintage years, each individual shipper deciding for himself whether a particular year will be a vintage one for him. The quality varies enormously from year to year, and the length of time it takes to reach maturity also varies. The 1963 vintage, for instance, which was regarded as very good, was not really ready for drinking until 1980. Anyone who bought in the early years can expect a good profit.

Most people are mainly interested in quite straightforward wines, however. Here, by area rather than by year, are some examples of the average length of time it takes wines to mature. All cheaper wines may improve with time, but most can be drunk at once.

France
• Alsace: the better reserves and 'grand vins' will improve for up to about six years.

- Loire: there is a great variety and no 'average' maturing period. Some sweeter wines will last fifty years, and others deteriorate quite quickly.
- Red Bordeaux: five years is a minimum, but some wines last for fifty years or more. Middle quality wines improve for about twenty years.
- White Bordeaux: ten to fifteen years.
- Red Burgundy: there is a great variety here, some wines are for early drinking, some later. Take the advice of a wine merchant or shipper.
- White Burgundy: well-balanced vintages improve for up to ten years. Most vintages also have light wines which are ready for drinking almost immediately.
- Red Rhone: vintages from the north keep longer than those from the south. Best ones keep for twenty years or more.

Germany
- Mosel: these wines are often drunk young, but improve if kept for a year. Some will keep up to fifteen years.
- Rhine: almost all of these wines are good to drink after two or three years. Some improve for ten years, but bottles more than seven years old are unusual.

You can see from this brief list that there are many varieties within each region. Add to that the differing qualities and quantities each year, and it is easy to see that buying as an investment is not always as easy as it might appear. *You must get expert advice*.

If you think wine is a good investment and have the skill to get the best vintages, but nowhere to store them, you can now invest linked to life assurance. At the end of 1981, Lloyd's Life linked with wine merchants Lay and Wheeler to offer a five per cent discount on list prices, free credit, free storage and insurance, plus tax relief for a minimum of £30 a month. More schemes are sure to follow. For grandparents, Justerini and Brooks have a covenanting scheme – the wine will mature about the same time as the child.

Business Expansion Schemes

The Business Expansion Scheme was introduced on 6 April 1983, replacing the Business Start-up Scheme, which had not proved popular with the investing public. The idea behind it is to encourage people to provide money for businesses by giving them tax relief.

Individuals can get the tax relief by investing their money with the managers of approved funds, who apply these funds for the subscription of shares issued by companies which qualify under the scheme. The tax relief comes in when the shares are issued in return for subscription, and not when the money is put with the approved fund manager.

This is how it works. First of all, there are individuals who qualify.

These must be resident in the United Kingdom for a period of two years before the issue date of the shares and for five years after it. The individual must not be an employee of the company involved; a director, unless unpaid; have an associate (close family member) who is an employee or paid director; nor own more than 30 per cent of the issued capital or voting power in the company.

Secondly, there are qualifying companies. These must also be resident in the United Kingdom and for a period of three years after the issue of the shares, or the start of trading, if that is later, they must not be quoted on the Stock Market or the Unlisted Securities Market; remain resident in the United Kingdom; exist wholly or mainly for the purpose of carrying on a qualifying trade; have no unpaid share capital; and be independent and not controlled by another company. There are rules about what is a qualifying trade. Basically, they are manufacturing companies.

Tax relief is available just like any other allowance and sliced off income before liability for tax is calculated. It is available for shares issued in 1983–4 and each of the following three years. The maximum relief is £40,000 in each year of assessment. Any relief not used up can be carried forward and used in the next year. Individuals can participate in one or more schemes, but no relief is available unless at least £500 is invested in shares in each particular company. Relief applies when shares are issued, not when the money is placed with the fund managers. If investors break the rules, they may lose some or all of the relief.

Claims for relief should be made as soon as the issue of shares takes place. You do not have to wait for your return before submitting your claim. Participation in a scheme can cut sharply into tax bills. An individual paying tax at the standard rate and putting £2,000 into a scheme could save £600 in tax in the year the investment took place and £1,200 for anyone paying tax at the highest rate of 60 per cent. The schemes are not suitable, however, for people who cannot afford to leave their money where it is for five years at least.

Details of the expansion schemes on offer and the fund managers are printed regularly in investment magazines, such as the *Investors' Chronicle*.

9 Providing for your retirement

The pensions situation in the United Kingdom has never been satisfactory. It is highly confusing and pensions have been used as something of a political football by governments of all parties. New schemes, when introduced by one administration. have barely had time to settle down before a new government changes everything.

This chapter sets out the situation as it held at the end of 1984. It is never too soon to think about providing for your old age. Start in your early twenties if possible; the longer you leave it, the more it will cost. If you think that twenty is too soon, think of how we pay our national insurance contributions from the moment we go out to work, and that is for the barest minimum pension at retirement age.

If you are going to augment the state pension with schemes of your own, the longer the period you do it over, the greater your chances of achieving a pension somewhere near your old salary levels.

Suppose you are a married man and you want to retire on an income of about two thirds of your pre-retirement salary; you want that income to be inflation-proof, and you want your wife to have a continuing income should you die before her. To achieve this you will have to have to hand at the end of your working life between seven and ten years' pay. Yet it is impossible to say what that sum will actually be, because no one knows what the rate of inflation will be. All we know is that between 5 and 10 plus per cent has been normal in the past few years.

In this chapter, we are going to see how these very reasonable aims can be achieved. Let's start with the state pension, which we all get if we have been working.

The state pension scheme

A new state pension scheme started in April 1978. It is commonly called the Castle scheme, because it was introduced by Mrs Barbara Castle when she was Minister of Social Security; it was part of the Social Security Pensions Act 1975.

The scheme provides a new formula for state pensions (though a similar one proposed by Sir Keith Joseph when the Conservatives were in power (1971–4) died when Labour was returned to office). What is new about the scheme is that it provides not only a basic pension for everyone who has contributed but on top of that a further, varying, slice of pension. This slice depends on extra contributions, which are related to the size of your income, and is known as 'the flexible tier' or the earnings-related part of the pension. This relates only to contributions made since April 1978.

Today there are very few people, except women who have never worked or those few older married women who have never paid the full national insurance contributions, who do not qualify for a state pension. The basic pension has gone to the employed, the self-employed and even the unemployed, if the necessary national insurance contributions have been paid. Payment has been compulsory since 1948, so there are very few people still working who have not paid enough.

The state scheme divides the state pension into four parts:

The flat-rate pension. At present this goes up a little most years. From November 1984–5, it is £35.80 for a single person and £57.30 for a married couple. This adds up to £1,861.60 and £2,979.60 a year, clearly a rock-bottom income. Unless you have no fixed outgoings except food and fuel, you are likely to be poor, if this is absolutely all you have. There has been a £10 Christmas bonus for the past few years as well.

To qualify for the flat-rate pension, you must have paid contributions from the age of eighteen to retiring age. Students are exempt, and anyone who was over eighteen when the national insurance scheme started in 1948 is exempt as far as the period before 1948 is concerned, provided they kept up their payments until they retired. There is a three-year qualifying period, but there can be few people alive who retired before 1951. If you have been sick or registered unemployed, you will have been credited at the time with your national insurance contributions. If you have failed to pay for any part of the time, your pension will be scaled down accordingly. If you are going abroad for any considerable time, you should take steps to see that you are covered if you want the full pension when you retire.

If you continue working after the retirement ages of 65 for men and 60 for women, your pension may be reduced while you are still under 70 (men) or 65 (women). The level of reduction depends on the amount you earn.

The Earnings Related Castle scheme only applies to those who have retired since April 1978. And is only for those employed by other people; if you are self-employed, you will have to make other arrangements, or you will find yourself with only the basic pension when you retire.

Employers have the option of contracting out of this scheme, if they already have a suitable company pension scheme. But even where there is a company scheme, some employers have decided to contract in so as to give their employees the benefit of both schemes. In this case, the employer may scale down the employee's contributions to the company scheme, and also his benefits.

The flexible tier formula is complicated, and it is difficult to tell how much you will get when you retire. Here is an example. To make it clear it has been necessary to keep it very simple, so it is probably an over-simplification in comparison with most real-life cases.

The man who is twenty-five in 1985 pays into the Castle scheme for forty years, until he is sixty-five. At the end of this period he will be entitled to a pension of 25 per cent of that part of his earnings between one and seven times the single person's flat-rate state pension. This means that he gets 1/160th of that part of his income for each year he contributes. However, a man of forty-five or over with twenty years or less to work to retirement would get 1/80th for each year he contributes. This is because the scheme is related to a quarter of 'average' weekly earnings. At the start of the scheme, maturity is put at twenty years; after that, it will be the average of the best twenty years.

This kind of scheme differs from a normal company's final salary pension scheme (see later in the chapter) because the Castle scheme is not based on final salary. A company scheme might give you 40/60ths or 66.7 per cent of *final* pay for forty years of service, whereas the Castle scheme will only produce 40/160ths or 25 per cent of revalued earnings between one and seven times the flat-rate state pension.

Assume the 25-year-old man earning £140 a week joins the scheme in 1984–5 and that the flat-rate state pension for a single person is then £35.80 a week. The pension earned during the year 1984–5 (assuming regular weekly earnings throughout) is 1/60th×£104.20 (£140−£35.80), which is 65.1p. This 65.1p will be revalued each year in line with an earnings factor, which will be announced by the minister each year and which is supposed to enable the 65.1p to keep pace with inflation.

If the man had no further pay increases and there was no inflation over the next forty years – both highly unlikely – the employee would get 40×65.1, or £26.04 a week, when he was sixty-five.

But although the annual revaluation provides protection against inflation, it makes no allowance for a higher salary through promotion. In contrast, as I have already said, most company schemes are now based on *final* salary. An employee might start with half the national average earnings but finish up with earnings of four times the national average. The 1/160th or 1/80th which he earned in his first year of service still provides 1/20th of his pension when he retires at the end of his career.

Unlike the majority of private schemes, no money is invested to underwrite future demands under the Castle scheme. The scheme is financed on a pay-as-you-go basis from the flexible national insurance contribution, which means that your future pension rights are vulnerable to changes in the ratio between the numbers of people who have retired to the numbers still at work. This is one of the reasons why the present Conservative government is trying to reduce the cost of pensions to the state.

An employee who is contracted out of the Castle flexible tier must get better benefits from a private scheme (the contracting-out rules stipulate this). Further, employees' contributions to a company scheme will normally qualify for tax relief, whereas no such relief is available on contributions to Castle. It is therefore likely that most employees will prefer to be contracted out of Castle. However, the contracting-out terms are complicated.

Some employers have decided that the whole contracting-out exercise is not worth the time and trouble and run their own pension schemes entirely on top of Castle. Others have decided to cut back their own company schemes to compensate for benefits being provided under Castle and also to compensate to some extent for the increased contributions which Castle would require both from employers and employees. Care should be taken to make sure that employees are not totally overburdened by pension contributions.

The state graduated scheme. This applies to relatively few people. It was introduced in 1961 and discontinued in 1975. When you retire you will be entitled to any pension which you earned during this period. Not everyone was involved in the scheme. Some companies, for example, only contracted women employees in, as they were often not eligible for the company pension. (This no longer applies; company pension schemes must now be open to women.)

The amount you will eventually get – or are getting, if you have already retired – depends on your weekly or monthly earnings during the period and whether you were 'contracted out' of the scheme for any part of the period. In any case, you are unlikely to get much from the scheme. The Department of Health and Social Security issued certificates telling you how many 'units' you had standing to your credit. Each unit was worth 2½p a week, £1.30 a year, revalued for inflation. No one is going to get rich on that.

Supplementary benefits. These only go to the very poor and are designed to bring the money they have available to spend above the poverty level. Basically, it has been recognized that the flat-rate pension is not enough to live on, and those who do not have money from any other source are entitled to supplementary benefit plus an allowance for rent and rates. Supplementary benefits are never enough to live comfortably on, so do not think that the fact that they are available – and are a right for those on low incomes – is an excuse for not making a proper pensions arrangement for yourself.

National Insurance Contributions

Until 1975, pensions were paid for partly out of the flat-rate national insurance stamp and partly by graduated contributions. From April 1975, national insurance stamps were done away with, except for the self-employed. Social security contributions are now expressed as a percentage of earnings – again with the exception of the self-employed, who still have to stamp cards.

The 1985 Budget brought a fundamental change in National Insurance contributions, designed to encourage employers to take on low-paid workers. At the same time, those on higher salaries and wages have become much more expensive for their employers, in terms of NI contributions. Previously, employees had to pay the full rate of contributions (9 per cent) on their salary, if they were earning more than £35.50 a week, with a notional maximum of £265 a week. That maximum remains for the employee, but the employer now has to pay 10.45 per cent on all earnings over £130 a week with no theoretical maximum. Instead of a single rate, there is now a sliding scale as follows for both employee and employer:

Earnings per week	Contributions	
	Employees	Employers
£1–£35.50	nil	nil
£35.50–£54.50	5%	5%
£55–£89.50	7%	7%
£90–£129.50	9%	9%
£130 plus	9% up to £265 a week	10.45% on all earnings

The new rates mean that, as far as the low-paid are concerned, both the employee and employer pay lower NI contributions. At the same time, contributions for the self-employed were reduced from £4.75 to £3.50 and the additional voluntary contributions by the self-employed towards the basic pension were lowered to £3.40 a week, from £4.65, without affecting benefits.

These changes take effect from 6 October 1985.

It is not compulsory in law to retire at sixty or sixty-five, but your company may insist that you do and it is at these ages that you become eligible for a state pension. If you are able to defer your retirement, and you want, and are capable, of going on earning, you will get a bigger pension when you eventually do retire.

You can draw your pension if you wish, however, even though you are still working – though if you are a woman aged between sixty and sixty-five or a man between sixty-five and seventy your pension will be reduced if you are earning more than £70 a week (1984–5). If this is the case, it is probably best to defer taking up the pension until you actually retire.

How to claim your pension
As you near sixty (woman) or sixty-five (man), you should take steps to register your claim to a pension, so that it begins to be paid the moment you retire. As a rule, the Department of Health and Social Security writes to everyone entitled to a pension, enclosing a claim form. *If you have not received this three months before you retire, make enquiries at your local social security office.*

If you are a married woman and are entitled to a pension in your own right, you must make a separate application. If, on the other hand, you are claiming a pension on your husband's contributions you must still make a separate claim and give notice of your retirement, even if you do not work outside the home. You cannot claim on your husband's contributions before he is sixty-five and retired. Fill in the form immediately and send it back. If you do not claim your pension, or notify the Ministry of your retirement, your pension will be delayed and you may lose benefit.

The form will ask you to state the date of your retirement. It will be either the day you stop working, if you are over sixty or sixty-five, or your actual birthday if you are retiring on that date. Give the day on which you wish to be treated as if you had retired, assuming that you will be taking up the pension, even though you are still working when you fill in the form.

Your pension will normally be paid in advance weekly at any post office. If this is inconvenient, however, you can arrange for it to be paid in arrears four-weekly or quarterly, by a crossed order which you must pay into a bank account. If you prefer this way, ask the local social security office for form NI.105, which gives all the details.

The Ministry of Health and Social Security has issued a leaflet, NI.15, which explains all your pension rights in detail. It is free from any local social security office and can be found in many post offices as well.

A final point: do claim your pension. You may feel you do not need it and that you do not want to live on the charity of the state. This is foolish: *you are entitled to your pension and you have been paying for it – or your husband has – over many years.*

More changes ahead?

There have been many different schemes since state pensions were first introduced by Lloyd George in 1908. Then, the rate for men was 25p a week, and 50p for a married couple. This was the first time the state had recognized the need for some government assistance to the aged.

There was no change in principle until 1948. Then the Beveridge pension scheme arrived, along with a package of other benefits which were the foundation of the welfare state as we know it today. These included unemployment and sickness benefits, death grants and widows' and maternity allowances. All were incorporated in the National Insurance Act 1946. In 1948, the pension was £1.30 for a single person and £2.10 for a married couple. Ten years later, these had increased to £2.50 and £4.00 respectively.

The next big change came in 1959, when the Conservative government set up the graduated scheme, which came into effect in 1961. This was ended in 1975. Then, in the late sixties, came the Crossman scheme – the first earnings-related plan. This never came into operation and died with the Labour government in 1970.

Then it was Sir Keith Joseph's turn. In 1973, he introduced a State Reserve Scheme in the Social Security Act of that year. It was similar to the later Castle scheme, with the very important difference that the money raised in contributions would be 'funded' – that is, put into investments to pay for future pensions.

That scheme was dismantled by the next Labour government, and the Castle scheme, which relies on current contributions to pay for pensions, was introduced. This means that each working generation must pay for the pensions of the retired generation. As the birth rate falls and the proportion of old people becomes greater, the burden on those still at work could become quite heavy.

This brief history of pensions raises the question of how long the Castle scheme will last. The present Conservative administration could bring it to an end before long. Pensions have been bedeviled by politics since they were first brought in and a period of tranquility for pension holders seems desirable. At the moment, some retired people have a flat-rate pension, a graduated pension, a little bit of the flexible tier and an occupational scheme.

Private pension schemes

Contracting out of the Castle scheme

If an employer is contracted out of the earnings-related part of the Castle scheme, he must have a pension scheme of his own which fulfils the following conditions. They are not onerous:

1 He must provide minimum pensions of 1/80th of employees' earnings for each year they are contracted out of the state flexible tier scheme. The actual amount may be geared to final earnings, or to contributions paid year by year.
2 The amount of the pension must be at least equal to the state earnings-related pension.
3 There must be a widow's benefit in the scheme for death in service. Widow's post-retirement benefits must be at least half the guaranteed minimum pension of the employee.
4 Employees must be able to claim their pension at the state retirement ages of sixty and sixty-five. If they go on working to sixty-five and seventy for women and men respectively, the pension must be increased by a minimum of 8½ per cent a year. After sixty-five and seventy, no further increases are permitted.
5 Some guaranteed pension must be assured if the employee leaves before the retirement age. This pension must be revalued in line with the national increase in pensions as time goes on.
6 Men and women must be treated alike in terms of eligibility for schemes. Higher entry age and less good benefits for women have had to go under the Sex Discrimination Act – though this has not changed the retirement ages. There is a great deal of argument about whether men's retirement age should come down, or women's go up.

If your pension scheme fulfils all these conditions, your company can be contracted out of the flexible tier scheme – though you still have to go on paying for the flat-rate pension.

In deciding to start a scheme, the employer will have the following points in mind:

● The preservation of a good employer–employee relationship.

- The total cost of the scheme, and how much he can afford to pay in contributions to balance those of the employee.
- How difficult it would be to run. Most large employers have had to set up special departments to operate their schemes. This could be prohibitive for a small employer.

If an employer does decide to contract out of the earnings-related scheme, there is some saving for both employee and employer in terms of the National Insurance contributions paid.

Eligibility for company schemes
Just because you work for a company does not mean you can automatically join their pension scheme. Most schemes insist that you have a minimum of one year's service, or they do not allow you to join until you are twenty-one, twenty-five or even thirty. This is to weed out those who do not stay for a reasonable length of time with a company. Some schemes used to be for men only, but that is now illegal; other companies have different schemes for executives and factory workers.

If you are a partner in the firm or run your own business, you are not allowed to participate yourself in any scheme you may set up for your employees – unless you become a limited company, in which case you can be treated as an employee, with all the national insurance benefits and company pensions. This applies even if you are a director and own almost all the shares.

Should you join a company scheme?
The first step when considering joining the pension fund, if you are given the option, is to read the rules and ask questions on any aspect that bothers you. These are some of the questions you could consider:

- How will the pension be calculated? Will it be inflation-proof both before and after retirement?
- Is the scheme approved by the Inland Revenue? This has tax implications (see later in chapter).
- What are the widow's and orphans' benefits?
- How is the period of employment calculated? Is there any lump sum of money if death occurs before retirement? Are there any provisions for early or late retirement? What happens if you leave before retiring?
- How much do you pay and how much does the employer pay? How are these contributions invested?

Most people pay between 5 and 7½ per cent of their income in private pension contributions, but about a third of those in private schemes are in pension funds where they pay nothing and only the employer contributes.

How much should you pay? It is difficult to say, because it is important to be in a good scheme and pay, rather than in a bad scheme and not pay. If you pay 5 per cent and your employer 10 per cent, you will get a better pension in the end than in any scheme where only your employer pays and he pays less than 15 per cent.

If you do not have to pay, you must make as many enquiries about the scheme as if you were paying. You may find that you will have to supplement your company pension with some other form of regular saving.

Very few schemes are identical. All will have some element which refers only to the particular needs of the employees in a particular company. Remember that if you are an employee it is only by joining a pension scheme that you have any hope of raising the seven to ten years' salary that you will require on your retirement to maintain a reasonable standard of living.

The Castle scheme may be good for those with low earnings, but anyone earning more than the maximum of £265 a week to which the scheme applies will lose out with every extra £1 he earns. Remember, too, that for every pound you put into a company scheme your employer (on average) will put in twice as much, and you will get the benefit from the total contributions. So if you are paying 7½ per cent of your salary into the pension fund and your employer pays 15 per cent (though this would be very high), you are getting the equivalent of an extra £30 a week if you earn, say, £200 a week.

There are some tax advantages, too. Anything you pay into a private pension fund is sliced off your income completely. And, of course, you pay no tax on the contributions your employer puts in. Allowing for tax at a standard rate of 30 per cent, the £6 a week you put in and the £12 from your employer (in the example above) are worth £23.40 a week in salary terms. Put another way, if you had to pay tax on the £18, it would be worth only £12.60 to you.

A further advantage is that the money you pay and the money your employer pays on your behalf is invested. The money which is invested may – it depends on the skill of the fund's investment managers – grow in capital value and will certainly earn dividends, which are *free of tax*. Some of this money may be paid out in bonuses to pensioners or be used to raise the level of pensions.

Things to watch
How much of your salary is your pension based on? It may be all your pay or only a part of it. Schemes may include or exclude overtime, bonuses and any other extras in calculating your pensionable pay. As a rule, the Inland Revenue will insist that fluctuating items in your pay are averaged out over the last three years and included in a pensionable pay. If the 'floating' items in your salary are substantial, they can affect your pension.

For a pension contribution to be eligible for tax relief, the scheme must be approved by the Inland Revenue. If it is not, the amount you pay in contributions will not be taken off your taxable income and you will also have to pay tax on your employer's contributions.

The maximum pension that the Inland Revenue allows anyone in a private scheme is two-thirds of final pay. This means that the company may have to limit your eligibility to forty years (that is 40/60ths, or two thirds). When this is the case, there is no point in men joining a scheme until they are twenty-five and women twenty.

When you retire, your pension is treated as earned income and taxed under normal PAYE. You will also be taxed on your state pension, even though there is no tax relief attached to your national insurance contributions while you are working.

How will your pension be calculated?
The pension you are entitled to can be calculated in a variety of ways:

1 The most common way is to pay 1/60th or 1/80th or some other fraction of your final pay for each year you contribute to the scheme. This type of scheme favours men, when their pensions finally arrive, because they will have five extra years in which to contribute. The total benefit over the entire pension period is about the same for men and women, however, because women tend to die later than men. It just means living longer on less. Another disadvantage for women and single men, except in a few schemes, is that there is no widower's or children's pensions should they die, even though they pay the same contributions as married men.

2 Instead of being based on final pay, the pension may be the same fraction of your average pay for each year of service. If this is the method chosen, salaries are usually treated in bands and the company should have a table showing you the pension at various salary levels.

3 Where companies are small, the employer and the employee may pay in a fixed amount of contributions, which are invested and then used at the time of retirement for whatever pension the money will buy. These are known as 'money purchase schemes' and are not very common, because the employee is at the mercy of the financial situation when he retires.

4 You may get a fixed amount of pension, whatever you earn. This is usually at a very low level and is of little use to the higher-paid. It may also be at such a low level that the employer cannot contract out of the earnings-related scheme. In these cases the earnings-related element may bring the total pension up to a reasonable amount.

5 You may be offered what is called an 'integrated' scheme. This will give you a pension which is a certain proportion of your final earnings, often two-thirds, less any state pension you may get. Say you are earning £300 a week when you retire; two thirds of that would be £200, but you must take off the married man's state pension of £57.30, leaving you with a

private pension worth £142.70, not £200. These schemes have become complicated with the advent of earnings-related pensions. They are not attractive, but you will be stuck with it if that is the method chosen by your employer. It is scarcely worth changing jobs just to get into a good pension scheme – though for a man in his fifties, it could be. A job giving maximum pension rights for the rest of his life could be worth more than a big increase in salary for the few years left to retirement.

Of all these alternatives, the one based on final salary is most preferable.

A capital sum

Some schemes allow you to receive a tax-free capital sum when you retire, deducting an appropriate amount from your monthly pension. The standard formula approved by the Inland Revenue is 3/80ths of final pay for each year of service.

Some schemes offer the pension of 1/80th plus 3/80ths of final pay as a capital sum. Put together, this is considered to be about the same as a pension only, with no capital sum of 1/60th.

A lump sum can be useful, because you may then be able to finish paying off your mortgage if it is not cleared and so not have to worry about that when you retire. Or you can buy an annuity (see Section one, chapter 13), which will boost your post-retirement income and bring tax advantages as well. By doing both, you can sometimes increase your net income after tax by 30 per cent.

Will your pension be enough?

In a period of inflation, you may well think that your pension will not be enough for you to live on when it arrives. You can increase the amount you have by taking specialist advice, or you could consider some of the saving and assurance schemes discussed in chapters 3 and 13 of Section one or regular saving in unit trusts, discussed in chapter 5 of this section.

AVCs

Only about a quarter of those in a private pension scheme actually receive the full amount permitted by law. For such people, some companies run what are called AVC schemes. This stands for 'additional voluntary contributions' and they can help improve pension levels considerably. At the moment (late 1984), however, only about seven per cent of those eligible make the contributions. The reason for this is that they can only be made through the company one works for, and not all companies operate the scheme.

If you are worried about the level of your ultimate pension, check with your company. If it does not have one, it is worthwhile persuading it to become involved, because the benefits can be substantial, even for those who do not join such schemes until their mid-fifties. This is yet another area where there may be changes if portable pensions are introduced. The government may then allow the individual to make contributions, even if his employer does not run a scheme.

If you change your job
Very few of us stay with the same employer for forty years, so when you join a scheme you must find out what happens if you leave.

The Social Security Act 1973, which came into operation in April 1975, requires all company schemes to preserve pensions rights for employees who leave if they are aged twenty-six or over and have completed five years' service; some schemes give you the option of taking your money out when you leave. The latest proposals will make transfer to a new employer a right in law. Some pension schemes provide for preservation as from year one. Others provide for transfer payments. Yet others inflation-proof preserved pensions. From 1 January 1986, the new rule about increases in preserved pensions of the rate of inflation or 5 per cent a year comes in.

For example, if you joined the Civil Service scheme at twenty-five and left at thirty-five and were entitled to £5,000 a year preserved pension at the date of leaving, this £5,000 would increase each year in line with the Retail Price Index until you reach the age of sixty (the Civil Service retiring age), when it would become payable. After this, the pension would be increased each year in line with prices, in order to maintain its real value.

If you are contracted out of the Castle scheme, your 'preserved pension' will be 'dynamized' in a similar way. This is again a difficult technical area. It will pay you to examine the provisions of your own pension scheme carefully before making any final decision to change jobs.

If you have the option of taking your money out when you leave and you decided to do so, remember that you will lose all the benefits deriving from the employer's part of the total contribution. This is an Inland Revenue rule.

A tidier alternative is to transfer your pension rights, though this can mean that you lose some years' benefits. Transferability can operate in two ways:

1 A lump sum can be sent to the pension scheme of your new employer.
2 A pension can be paid based on your final salary and the number of years you had worked for the company at the time you left. This is kept by your new employer and paid to you on your retirement. Not all schemes permit transferability, so you could well end up with several small pensions from a variety of companies when you retire. But this is preferable to taking a refund at any time.

If you are self-employed
The self-employed always come off worst when it comes to any benefits,

and pensions are no exception. Under the new Castle scheme, for example, they only get the flat-rate pension and are not eligible for the earnings-related part. Yet they are the section of the population most exposed to risk. They may have no capital when they retire and a very limited pension. This means that they have to look after their pensions themselves.

At present, the flat-rate contribution for the self-employed is £3.50, plus a further £3.40 voluntary payment towards the basic pension (and additional payments in some cases).

In recent years, the government has become increasingly generous towards the self-employed in allowing them tax relief on money they put towards their pensions. At present, anyone born in 1934 or later is allowed to put by 17½ per cent of their total income in this way before tax relief stops. This is known as 'retirement tax relief' and is at even better levels for older people. For 1985–6 the relief is shown in the table below.

The insurance companies have developed many schemes to help the self-employed and these go under the general title of 'deferred annuities', though they may be called something fancy which does not make this immediately apparent. Consult an insurance broker to find the best deal for you.

To make sure you get the best scheme possible, get the advice of a pensions expert. There are many possible combinations and you will be able to choose whatever suits you best. This is a very complicated area and you are unlikely to make the best decision without some assistance.

birth	%
1934 or after	17.5
1916–33	20.0
1914–15	21.0
1912–13	24.0
1910–11	26.5
1908–09	29.5
1907	32.5

If you wish to retire early
You cannot get a state pension until you reach the state retirement age, unless you get a disability allowance. But some people who are quite fit would like to retire early. If you only contribute to the state scheme, the only way you can do this is to have some form of capital to live on until you reach retirement age. But remember, if you do not continue to pay full national insurance contributions, that pension will be scaled down.

Those in private company schemes usually do better, but not always. Some private schemes allow for pensions on early retirement on certain terms; others will not pay out until retirement age. In the former case, if the terms are not punitive, you could do better drawing your pension early, because the extra years' benefit from, say, retiring five years earlier, will more than make up for the cut in the rate of pension.

Some schemes might allow you to retire early but take, say, 5 per cent off your pension for every year early that you retired. So if you retired five years early, your pension would be cut by a quarter. You might get more total benefit over the total period you are pensioned for, but you would be a lot poorer while it lasted.

Some schemes offer the best of both worlds and let your maximum pension under your particular scheme run from sixty (in these cases, women may or may not be able to go at fifty-five).

For most people, however, early retirement will probably have to remain a dream, for this is how the average private pension works.

Let's take a man of fifty-five who would like to retire. We'll assume he is earning £200 a week, which if he stayed at work until sixty-five would rise to £300. His pension is worked out at 1/60th for every year of service, and he has been with the company for thirty years. If he wants to take an early pension, this is likely to be no more than half the amount he would get retiring at sixty-five. Even this may not be allowed, and he may have to wait until he is sixty-five before getting the money. There are two sums he must work out:

1 If he continued working until he was sixty-five, his weekly pension would be based on forty years with the firm and a final salary of £300 a week. He would then get 40/60ths of £300, or £199 a week. Add on the state pension and his total pension would be over 80 per cent of his final salary.
2 If he retires at fifty-five and his pension is calculated on the same formula, he may only get 30/60ths (for thirty years' service) of his final salary of £200 a week, reduced by an early-retirement factor of 50 per cent, giving him £50 a week. Even if his salary remained unchanged for the period to retirement, the difference in working to sixty-five rather than fifty-five could be as much as £83 a week – £133 instead of £50 a week.

You can of course make up these differences by regular saving, but it will mean that throughout your working life you will have to put away much more of your capital towards your retirement than would otherwise be the case.

Remember, retiring early might be fun and give you a better life, but you must consider all its aspects before deciding to do it.

If you wish to retire abroad

There can be problems if you wish to retire abroad, as far as your pension is concerned. Retiring abroad is far more common than you would think, and is not simply confined to the very rich. More than 150,000 people are drawing British state benefits abroad. Almost 100,000 of these live in America or the Commonwealth countries of Canada, Australia and New Zealand, many having gone out on retirement to join their children who have emigrated.

There is no problem in taking your pension abroad when you retire, but what happens to that pension afterwards can be. Often, no increases in pensions are payable abroad. This means that, despite inflation – and inflation happens everywhere – those who retired in, say, 1965 on a basic pension of £4, or £6.50 for a married couple, will still be getting that amount rather than the £35.80 or the £57.30 which is paid to anyone who has stayed in the UK.

This does not apply everywhere; there are, for example, reasonable social security agreements between Britain and the other EEC countries. And some countries – Australia is one – will pay retired people a pension even if they have not paid the relevant contributions there. This is done in an attempt to keep families together in the new country, for there is a tendency for emigrants to return home when their parents get old.

The situation is different for every country, and you should study all the methods of adjusting pensions before you retire. Write to the Department of Health and Social Security (Overseas Group), Newcastle-upon-Tyne NE98 1YX, and ask them what your position will be in the country to which you plan to emigrate.

If you are a woman
Although you will get the same flat-rate pension, you are likely to get less than a man on the earnings-related part of the state scheme because despite the Equal Pay Act, the gap between women's and men's wages is still very wide.

This has implications, too, if you are in a private scheme. Women are allowed to retire at sixty. This means they get less pension each week whatever kind of scheme they have been in – though by the time they die they will probably have had as much in total as most men, if not more. For the moment, at least, the government has turned its back on any proposals for equal retirement age.

There have been a number of improvements in recent years as far as women's pension rights are concerned. They now have to have equal access to private pension schemes, on the same terms as men as far as their own, but not dependants' pensions are concerned. But many women, particularly the older ones, may have been excluded from pension schemes in the past and only recently have been able to join. Inevitably, this also means that they will end up with a lower pension than a man.

All this may not matter so much for the married woman, who gets a pension on her husband's contribution, but it means that the single woman can often find her income sharply reduced after retirement.

It is just as important for a woman to be in a pension scheme as a man, whether married or not. Married people who have been used to living on two salaries will find it difficult living on one pension.

Some married women who opted out of the NI scheme before 11 May 1977 are covered by their husband's contributions. If they did not opt out, or have started working since that date, they must pay full contributions.

Women no longer have their pension curtailed if they stop working to bring up a family. A married woman can now spend up to twenty years looking after her children and, provided that she has a full contribution record over the rest of her working life, she will get a full pension.

Women have advantages in comparison with men in their rights as widows. Any widow over fifty inherits the whole of her husband's pension rights under the earnings-related scheme. This privilege is not similarly extended to men.

Because women live longer and are generally younger than their husbands – only 35 per cent of women are older than their husbands – the widow's element can be a valuable addition to pension rights.

Some older schemes have no widow's right (these cannot be contracted out of the Castle scheme), but in most schemes the employer will give a 50 per cent pension to a wife in return for the employee taking a slightly lower pension while he is alive.

In some schemes, the employer gives a guarantee of a minimum pension for a number of years. If the husband then dies suddenly soon after retirement his family will continue to receive this pension until the time is up. Five years is normal, but it is sometimes ten.

If a woman is in a private pension scheme in her own right and has dependents she may find that she is not so well treated as a man and may have no benefits for them written into the scheme. Some older funds allow dependants' pensions to women on the same terms as men, but most do not. This is changing now under EEC rules.

If you are in a private pension scheme yourself and have dependents fight for the right. If you cannot get these benefits, consult an insurance broker, or get your firm to do it for you. You can get single, premium insurance policies which, in the event of your death, will give your children a guaranteed income until they are able to earn their own living. In similar circumstances, a man should of course take out a policy of this kind. They are not expensive.

10 Gambling

The government makes money out of gambling, so do the bookmakers; the punters – the people who actually do the gambling – do not. Of course, a few people win large sums of money on the football pools or the horses, or on some other kind of bet, but on the whole the odds are weighted very much in favour of the people who organize the business, and the government, which collects tax on the various forms of betting.

Gambling is big business for the government and a valuable source of revenue. Because it is impossible for gamblers to win overall, gambling cannot really be considered part of an investment policy. But many people spend money on it, partly for pleasure and partly as a serious business.

You can bet on anything – the weight of your baby when it is born, the colour of its eyes, its sex, which party will win the next general election, or how many runs a particular batsman will score in a game of cricket.

The average person is more likely to stick to the football pools and the occasional bet on a horse in one of the big races, like the Derby or the Grand National, or who will win the Miss World competition.

The football pools

Football pool forms are as familiar in many families as the daily newspaper; half the adult population bet around £500 million a year. A £1 bet is average for individuals, though syndicates bet much more. They may have many members, who contribute an equal amount each week and share any proceeds.

Really big wins on the pools are few and far between, but there are many smaller prizes to tempt the punter and keep him hoping for the big one. The pools companies reckon that the chance of winning a prize of £100,000 or more is about the same as the chance of being murdered.

The big prizes go on the Treble Chance pool, where the punter selects eight draws each week from the list on his form, and 95 per cent of the stake money goes on this.

The publicity which results from a big win of £750,000 or more is extremely important for the pools companies, as it brings an upsurge of business each time. The pools companies offer the big winners an investment advisory service. It may seem impossible, if you have not had a big win, but some past winners have managed to get through hundreds of thousands of pounds and end up as poor as they were before they won.

The pools company has to pay tax on all the money they receive, but any win is tax-free to the punter. When all the administration is done and taxes are paid, the promoter makes less than 3 per cent profit. Tax and prizes together take up over 75 per cent of their total income, and the distribution and running of the pools is costly administratively. About 20 per cent of the money which comes in on the pools goes out in prizes. This means that punters *overall* must lose over 80 per cent of their money.

This is how the wins are paid out. The promoters call them 'dividends'.

The Treble Chance pool. The first prize takes 60 per cent of the prize money, with a limit of £900,000, the second prize 10 per cent, and the third 9 per cent. The fourth to sixth prizes are 8, 7 and 6 per cent, respectively. Any surplus money is equally divided among the lower dividends in the same pool. To win the Treble Chance, you have to select eight draws on any one Saturday. The more draws there are, the more people get high points, and the smaller the individual dividends.

Some people study form each week in selecting their draws; others put them anywhere, perhaps in the same positions each week, as the order of the teams varies. Most people do several lines. This is known as a 'permutation'. You can if you wish pay all your money at the start of the season and give the company your regular permutation; they will then check it every week.

Ten homes, four aways and four draws pools. These are less popular but they are the ones where punters believe that skills come in. It is easier to win on one's home ground, but some clubs have a good away record.

If you invest enough in these on a system, it is alleged that you can get through the season in balance, or losing very little. But your wins are unlikely to be great, either. Anyone who gets a one-column forecast correct gets all the money available for prizes. If no one gets it right, then the money is divided or given to the person nearest an all-correct forecast.

Easier six. In this, the results of all six matches selected must be forecast, and the marks are 3 for a draw, 2 for a no-score draw, 1½ for an away win, or a void or postponed game, and 1 for a home win. The punter who forecasts most accurately wins the whole of the prize money.

If you are making a claim, your coupon must be sent off with a postmark showing that it was posted *before the match took place*. Moreover, it will not be accepted by the promoter if it arrives after 3 p.m. on the day the matches are taking place.

If you think you have won the Treble Chance, you must claim as soon as possible after the matches end, and certainly not later than the Monday following. You claim via registered letter, enclosing a complete copy of the winning entry and stating:

- The name and address on the coupon.
- The number of points claimed.
- The reference number.
- How the coupon was submitted (whether the promoter had a collector who took the coupon from you at home, for example).

If you win on other pools, you should automatically get the money by the following Saturday. If you do not, you then claim.

Your claim will not be allowed if:

- You have not sent any money with the coupon.
- You have not signed it, or it comes from the address of a school or college, or is sent in on behalf of an employee or spouse, rather than yourself.
- If you are under eighteen.
- If it is illegible in any way and not absolutely clear.
- If it gets lost in the post, or does not reach the promoter for any reason, or is damaged. For this reason, you may be safer with a collection, if there is one near you.

There are further rules for abandoned or unplayed matches, and more 'small print' in the rules, which the company will send you. Study them carefully.

I have no advice on how to win. If I had, I would have taken it myself. Some people swear by skill and study, but it is interesting to see how many winners pick randomly or win after the first few tries. You will have to have your own philosophy.

The horses

Most people, unless they are firmly against gambling on moral grounds, have a flutter at least once in their lives, even if it is only on a horse whose name they fancy or a jockey who has a long list of wins.

Though this type of gambling is not nearly so widespread as doing the football pools, the stakes (the money you put up) are much higher. The amount of money the industry is taking in is thought now to be reaching £1,500 million a year – four and a half times as much as the pools companies.

Most of this money goes on the big races, but there are professional gamblers whose lives are spent at the racecourses. As long as you are eighteen years old, you will have plenty of opportunities for betting.

All bets are made on 'odds' – that is, you win a stated amount for every pound you stake. The less chance a horse has of winning, the 'longer' the odds; the more chance, the 'shorter' they are. A horse with a string of failures may be quoted at long odds of 100–1. This means that, if it wins, you will get £100 for every £1 you have staked. The favourite could be at 2–1 only, or 'evens' – when you only win £1 for every £1 bet.

If you bet 'each way', this means your stake is split between a win and a place if the horse comes in the first three (or four for classic races) where the field is over a certain number. Say you put down £2 at 5–1 and the horse wins. You will then collect £5 on your first £1, a quarter of the odds on your second £1, and your £2 stake. If it comes second or third, you only collect on the other £1, at about a quarter of the odds. Place bets are not allowed when there are five horses or less, and the third is not permitted when there are only between five and seven horses in the race.

There are a variety of very complicated bets whereby you can increase your winnings. I will describe these later on. First, the places where you can bet:

Bookmakers. They can take bets on the course or off the course in a betting shop. There are some differences, depending on which you choose. Let's say you bet £1 at 10–1 to win on course and the horse wins. Theoretically, you should get back your £1 and your £10 win, but bookmakers today expect the punter to help towards the tax they have to pay, so they deduct 4 per cent from the £11 total due to you. That means your net winnings are £10.56; the tax amounts to 44p.

If you bet off-track in a bookmaker's office, you do a little worse. On the same bet, usually 10 per cent is taken off for tax, betting levy and bookmaker charges. This means that your net win would be £11 minus £1.10, or £9.90.

You can also place a bet with a bookmaker by phone. To do this, you will have to have a certain amount of credit permitted by the book-maker; he will check on this before allowing the bet.

In one way or another, over 90 per cent of British punters bet via bookmakers.

The totalizator. This was set up by the government in 1929, when off-course cash betting was still illegal. Its aim was to provide another form of betting and raise money for the improvement of racing. You can bet in either cash or credit on the course or in one of the totalizator betting shops. The money you get is worked out by dividing the total money placed on the race by the number of winning tickets. There is no fixed deduction, but it usually averages about 18 per cent. This would then bring your net winnings, on the above bet, down to £9.02.

Form is far more carefully studied in horse racing than in the football pools, and there is no doubt that favourites are favourites because they are outstanding horses with a good record. But all kinds of things can go wrong, and favourites don't always win. If they did, racing would be far duller. Some jockeys have a good record, too – though it is doubtful whether you would win much overall by following one particular horse or jockey through the season.

If you want to study form, there are always the newspapers. All the dailies, except the *Financial Times*, which specializes in speculation of another sort, give daily racing cards, and most of them have a number of staff tipsters. Tipsters' records vary and are by no means consistent, so do not follow them if you fancy another horse. There are also two racing dailies, the *Sporting Life* and the *Sporting Chronicle*. They give an enormous amount of detail about each race. It will take you some time to work your way round the terminology.

If you have a win, you may still not be satisfied with it. There are various ways of increasing your winnings, if you happen to be lucky a second time or more.

A double: links two horses in one bet. The horses are in two different races, and if the first one wins the whole of the stake money and the winnings are automatically transferred to the second horse.

A treble is similar, but there are three horses. The chances of making a treble are obviously less than on a double.

The accumulator works on the same principle, but with four horses or more. There have been cases of people winning on seven or more horses, but you need pretty strong nerves for this and a relaxed attitude if you lose in the end.

Forecasting usually entails betting on the first and second in a race and, depending on the size of the field, can sometimes be linked to take in the two horses who will come first and second in any order for one stake.

These are the most common sorts of bets, but there are others. They come with such names as *Any-to-come* (ATC), where winnings from one race are reinvested as the punter thinks fit in other races, and *Up and down*, where two horses are backed singly, each with an ATC bet on the other. A *Rounder* is when three horses are backed singly, and if one wins the other two are backed on a double. And a *Roundabout* is a Rounder with double stakes.

Then come the really complicated bets. A *Round Robin* involves ten bets – three horses are linked up and down on each pair, plus three doubles and a treble. A *Patent* is three horses backed in three single bets, three doubles and a treble. The gamble involving the most separate bets is a *Heinz*, so-called because it involves fifty-seven bets on six different horses. In between it and the Round Robin come a *Canadian* (twenty-six bets and five horses), a *Flag* (twenty-three bets and four horses) and a *Yankee* (eleven bets and four horses).

Owning a horse

Perhaps you would like to be on the other side of the racing business and own a horse yourself. Anyone can be lucky and buy a good horse, which turns out to win large prizes and can later be sold for stud, but the chances are that these horses will go to the big names in racing. The fact that the average horse wins around £1,000 a year and can cost more than £3,000 in training and other expenses is a sobering thought. Most owners run at a loss and hope to make it up eventually with big prizes or wins on other horses. Some people go into a syndicate with a horse, and you can then get your original investment in it returned with a profit when it is sold for stud. Racehorse-owning is still very much the preserve of the rich, however. For the ordinary person, it is simply out of range.

Gaming

It is well known that casinos and gaming clubs make vast profits, though no one is certain of the actual figures. They are kept a well-guarded secret. One thing seems certain: if gamblers knew what the levels of these profits were, many of them would be deterred from gambling with the odds so stacked against them. On average, there is a 6 per cent bias in favour of the 'house', the gaming club. This is called the percentage.

You must remember, if you gamble, that in most cases it is luck and not skill when you win. Most gamblers work on systems and will swear that their particular one works. This is simply not true; no technique or system can be guaranteed to beat the draw. Never lose sight of this fact, and if you can only afford to lose very little, limit your stake firmly. Above all, once you have reached your limit never try to recoup your losses by staking further money.

Games vary enormously, however, and some do involve a considerable degree of skill. Poker is the obvious example. Bridge also requires skill, but it is not counted by habitués of gaming clubs and casinos as gambling in the same sense as the others. Others involve not so much skill as prodigious memory, to remember exactly what cards have already been drawn. Blackjack is the leader among these. And some games are all risk; roulette is an outstanding example.

Gambling games can be divided, then, into *games of chance* – games in which there is no element of skill, called by gamblers 'mechanical games', such as lotteries, raffles, bingo, 'one-armed bandits', most dice games, and some card games, like faro, baccarat and roulette – and *games of skill and chance*, which give the skilled operator a better chance. There is still an element of luck, but the player can bend it to his advantage to some extent. These include most card games – poker, gin rummy, bridge, blackjack and pinochle – and also backgammon.

If you wish to join a gaming club, the entry fees are expensive; such clubs are only for the relatively rich. Entry to casinos is often free, and there are few limits on what you can win – or more frequently lose.

There are several excellent books you can study if you are interested. Cuthbertson's *Card Games* is a complete encyclopedia. Unfortunately, it is out of print, but you may be able to get a copy second-hand. *Challenge to Chance* by E. Lennox Figgis, also out of print, discusses gambling systems most entertainingly. *But remember, no system can win.*

Bingo

Bingo, which is simply a form of the children's game Housey-Housey, has become a very popular part-time betting activity with housewives. A much smaller proportion of the takings goes in tax than on the football pools; and there is no tax on winners.

Each player sits at a board marked with squares with numbers in them. Numbers are called out at random, and if the player has that number on her board she – it is usually a she – covers that number with a piece of plastic. When all the squares are covered it's Bingo! and the first player to do this is the winner.

To play Bingo, you will have to become a member of a club. This has now become a mere formality and costs nothing. Then there is an admission charge, which in the bigger clubs will be between 30p and 50p. Around 15–20 games are played each session, and there will be a charge for each 'chance' (stake). Prizes vary from club to club and from night to night. Most people who are regular Bingo players spend about £5 a week on it, but there are some who bet up to £50. Prize money varies, but in the bigger clubs it may be as much as £1,200 a game, and sometimes linked games offer even higher prizes.

A final word

Some people condemn gambling, but I believe this can be a mistake. For most people it is a source of relaxation and pleasure and costs them very little. A bet of 60p a week on the football pools is not going to break anyone's budget; nor is an occasional flutter on the St Leger. All forms of recreation and entertainment cost money, and if you are sensible you will regard betting in that light. For most of us, gambling is just building castles in the air, and there is no harm in that.

Some people, however, find gambling compulsive, and whether it is bingo, the pools or the horses you start becoming addicted to, you should stop if this happens to you. Once it gets out of hand, gambling is just as family- and soul-destroying as too much alcohol or drugs. Those who find their gambling has got out of control can go to Gamblers Anonymous, 19 Abbey House, Victoria Street, London SW1 (01-222 4252), which will try to help cure them of their addiction – because that is what it is.

Section six
Your money and the law

1 Going to law

Litigation can be very expensive. You will have to pay a solicitor, and possibly a barrister, to represent you. Getting any legal advice is also expensive. But if you do not have any spare money over and above your daily necessities, do not despair: this does not mean that you cannot get legal advice or take action in court. In this chapter, I will look at three ways of taking legal action which need not result in any cost to yourself.

Legal advice

This is a relatively new service, introduced in 1973. The procedure is far more informal than that for legal aid. You simply go to a solicitor who is party to the scheme (not all of them are, and some will not consider legal aid cases, either) and give him details of your financial situation. He will know whether you are eligible or not. Your local Law Society branch or Citizens Advice Bureau will give you a list of solicitors who are in the scheme.

Whether you are eligible or not depends on your disposable capital and your disposable income. From November 1984, the upper disposal limit for both income and capital was set at £4,710 for civil cases and £44 a week for criminal cases. 'Disposable income' is worked out after deductions like tax, national insurance, rent and rates, mortgage payments and allowances for dependants.

'Disposable capital' is any money which you actually have available, leaving aside personal and household effects. It would, for instance, include any savings or investments you have and any income from them. The latter is your total income from all sources, taking off any liability for tax and national insurance contributions and anything you may need for your dependants.

The levels of disposable income and capital change all the time. Only a solicitor can tell you if you are eligible at any one time.

If you are eligible, there are a variety of things the solicitor can do for you.

They include:

1 Giving general advice, and writing letters and conducting negotiations on behalf of clients.
2 Drawing up legal documents such as wills.
3 Sometimes – but not usually – conveyancing.
4 Advising on what action should be taken in court – though the solicitor cannot take this action himself. Suppose you have to appear before an industrial tribunal over a redundancy payment. The solicitor can prepare the papers for you, but the scheme does not cover his appearance before the tribunal on your behalf.

This legal advice service is known as the 'green form scheme'. Applicants may be referred to the local supplementary benefits office for a financial assessment rather than the solicitor taking it upon himself. Sometimes the service may be totally free; at other times the applicant may have to make a contribution.

Legal advice and assistance can be transformed into full legal aid, if that becomes necessary.

Legal aid

The legal aid system began in 1949 under the first Legal Aid and Advice Act. Before that, going to law really was the prerogative of the rich, unless a barrister felt charitable towards a particular case. Legal aid is designed to give everyone equal rights before the law, and you should not hesitate to seek it should the occasion arise. The financial qualifications are the same as for legal advice and assistance. You are expected to pay only what you can afford, and there is no stigma involved. It is the right of every citizen to be adequately represented in court, whether he or she has the means to pay or not. The richer you are, therefore, the more likely it is you will be turned down. Check to see if aid is available for what you want. Legal aid is divided into two parts:

Aid in civil cases
If you do not have a solicitor, get a form from your local Citizens Advice Bureau, the court office, or the committee of the local branch of the Law Society which runs the scheme in your area. Ask them to issue a certificate. If this is refused and you think you have got a good case, you have the right of appeal to the area committee of the Law Society, but you can take it that you will be granted a certificate if you have any case at all.

The chances are that you will be applying for aid in a divorce case; nearly half the total applications are for divorces. But the law is being tightened up, and certificates will not be granted so freely in divorce cases in the future as in the past, for it is felt that the system has been abused and, if you find you have some money later from, say, the sale of your house, you may find that you have to pay the money back. Your certificate may apply to action in any court, from the House of Lords down, but not for an action before a tribunal.

Aid in criminal cases

Getting legal aid for criminal cases is generally much faster than for civil cases. If you are accused of a criminal offence, you simply fill in an application form after you are charged. The request is considered by the clerk to the justices, who may grant it unconditionally or may ask for a down payment to be made to the court. If he does the latter, or turns down the request altogether, then the application form is put before the magistrate.

The same attention is not paid to the accused's assets in a criminal case as in civil matters. The magistrate only considers whether the accused has the money *readily available* to pay. Only after the case is finished is consideration given to the applicant's ability to pay the whole or part of his costs, in instalments if necessary.

Legal aid must be granted regardless of assets in murder cases. It is generally expected that it will also be granted in trials by a judge and jury and in certain other circumstances: when a case raises a difficult point of law; when the accused is in danger of suffering damage to his reputation or livelihood or of losing his liberty; or when the accused is unable to follow the proceedings or defend himself because of a lack of understanding of English or mental incapacity.

Well over 99 per cent of applications for legal aid in criminal cases are granted.

Small claims

It may well be that you do not want to pay for advice from a solicitor, and would not be granted legal aid on such a trivial matter, yet you do wish to make a claim upon someone. This is where the so-called small claims court comes in. It is actually not a court at all, but part of the arbitration procedure of the county court. The court itself deals with claims up to £5,000, but for claims under £500 it has instituted an informal, flexible and cheap way of settling claims. It need cost you nothing, if you represent yourself. Of course, the opposing side may well choose to be represented by a solicitor or a barrister, who might be able to put your opponent's case better than you put your own. It deals with matters such as:

- Failure to pay for work done, goods delivered or money lent.
- Failure to supply goods ordered, or delivering the wrong or defective ones.
- Damages caused by negligence. This could arise following a road accident, if you feel the accident was the other driver's fault and you do not want to risk losing your no-claims bonus.
- Salary in lieu of notice, or any salary owed.

- Rent arrears, possession of property.

If the amount you are claiming is £500 or less, it is advisable to use the small claims court, because costs in ordinary courts are not allowed for small claims, even if you win your case. For claims over that, go to a solicitor for advice.

This book is not the place to go into the details of how to make a claim (there are many helpful books on the subject), but broadly you can take steps to recover the money once you have made a formal complaint or demand in writing and have followed it up with a reminder, which states that you will be applying to the court for restitution.

Next, you must supply the court with details of what you are claiming. These 'particulars of claim' can be quite short, but should be enough to let the defendant know why you are making the claim and how much you think is owed.

To start the action, you must fill in a form called a 'request'. When this is filed at the court, a small fee for the issue of summons must be paid. The court bailiff will then serve the summons and this involves an additional small fee. You can serve the summons yourself, but this may not be a good idea – though you can always try to find the defendant if the court fails to do so.

If the defendant then decides it is not worth the bother of arguing in court, he may well pay up, or he may decide to ignore the summons. If he does not turn up to defend the claim, the plaintiff (the person making the claim) will get judgement. If he does turn up, the court will decide whether he is liable and to what extent.

If the claim is accepted by the court, the plaintiff can ask for any expenses he has incurred to be paid by the defendant. These may include court fees and witness fees. If your claim is not allowed in full, you may be able to recover only a certain proportion of your costs.

If the judgement does not go the way you want, you can appeal, but think carefully before you do this. It will cost money, and if you have lost the first round, the chances are, unless you have new evidence, that you may end up losing more than your original claim.

The Lord Chancellor's Office has produced an excellent booklet to help both plaintiffs and defendants, called *Small Claims in the County Court*. It is by Michael Birks and is available from all branches of HMSO.

2 Consumer protection

Standards of consumer protection are high in Britain and many official bodies exist to help consumers. The Office of Fair Trading watches over the whole retail area on behalf of the shopper, and has published a variety of leaflets of codes of practice in different forms of selling goods and services. You can get them at the Citizens Advice Bureau.

As a result, most shopkeepers and providers of services today recognize their responsibilities to their customers. But not all do. There are still some, for instance, who are well aware of their customers' rights but nevertheless try to avoid their own responsibilities. A few even go so far as to try to persuade the customer that he has no legal rights at all against the shop.

Two instances of flouting the law are particularly common. The first is refusing to give cash refunds and trying to persuade customers to take a credit note instead. The second is trying to persuade customers that they should return defective items to the manufacturer rather than, as one is entitled in law, returning them to the shop where they were bought, and leaving the shopkeeper to deal with the manufacturer. *Watch out for these dodges and do not stand any nonsense.*

It is important for you as a consumer to know your rights, at least in outline, because if you wish to complain about something you have bought or some service you have used, you must be sure that you actually have the right in law to complain.

Your rights as a consumer

Britain has a long history of consumer protection. The first-ever government Act to help the consumer was introduced as long ago as 1893. It was the Sale of Goods Act, and it is still the basic law in the area, though it was amended in 1973 to close a variety of loopholes which some manufacturers had managed to find in the original law. A common example was putting special clauses into order forms and guarantees which limited the buyer's rights. In the case of cars, for instance, you used to find that you could not buy a car at all unless you signed such an agreement. The Supply of Goods and Services Act in 1982 further extended consumer protection.

In 1967, the Misrepresentation Act was passed. Under this the customer can claim compensation if he has been deceived by the seller. This Act applies not only to everyday goods which are bought in the shops, but also to houses and anything bought at auctions.

Next came the Trade Descriptions Act 1968, which punishes traders who make false or misleading statements about the goods or services they offer. If the description turns out to be false, a customer is entitled to return the goods and get the correct ones or his money back.

Customers may have to rely on descriptions of goods on the outsides of packets and tins which they cannot open until they get home. If something turns out not to be what is described on the packet, take it back. The law will support you, and anyone who deliberately misdescribes anything which is on sale is liable to a fine. Remember, though, that genuine mistakes can happen, so do not be over-hasty in demanding your rights. Listen to what the shopkeeper has to say first of all. In some cases, if it regards the case as a serious one the court may order financial compensation to the complainant.

When you buy something, it does not matter whether you pay in cash or in instalments. You have the same legal rights. If you buy on credit, of course, you can always take matters into your own hands and refuse to make further payments until an article is replaced or repaired. But take care if you do this. You may not be able to prove your case and could end up with a court ordering you to pay.

The Fair Trading Act 1973 provided for the appointment of the Director General of Fair Trading and a Consumer Protection Advisory Committee. This checks on all consumer matters and sees that the law is obeyed. It deals with consumer credit, monopolies and mergers, and restrictive practices, and any trade practices which it thinks might be harmful to the consumer.

There are three rules which must be followed in law. They lay down that:

1 Goods are of *merchantable quality*.
2 They must be *fit for the purpose* for which they were bought.
3 They must be *as described* on a package, display sign or by the seller.

Merchantable quality

This requirement basically means that a customer must know the true condition of any product when he buys it. It does not mean, therefore, that whatever you buy must be perfect, only that you must know when it is not. Goods clearly marked 'seconds' or 'imperfect' cannot be returned on the grounds that you did not know of this when you bought them.

Nevertheless, even something imperfect can be expected to function. If bits are broken and parts are missing (and this is not stated on the goods when you buy them) you will be entitled to your money back. If you buy a fridge, for instance, which is badly scratched on the outside, and you can see this before you buy, you will be unable to get your money back after delivery, but if it does not function when you get it home you can send it back and get a replacement or your money back.

Remember, 'merchantable' does not automatically mean 'perfect'. It simply means 'fair' or 'reasonable'.

This is what the Act says: 'An article must be fit for the purpose for which articles of that kind are commonly bought, as is reasonable to expect, having regard to the description applied to it, and the price paid (if this is relevant) and any other factors.'

Fit for the purpose
For a product to be fit for the purpose for which it was bought, it must function satisfactorily and be properly designed. If an electric kettle gives you a shock every time you switch it on, it is obviously not fit for its purpose, which is boiling water safely. Anyone who had known of its condition at the time of purchase would not have bought it.

But you could not, for instance, automatically get your money back if you bought a face cream which brought you out in spots. It would have to bring everyone out in spots before that was the case. Manufacturers and shopkeepers cannot be expected to know of and cater for any particular allergy you might have.

You may buy something with a particular use in mind. If you make that use clear when you buy, and if when you get it home the article, though merchantable in some other circumstances, is unsuitable for the purposes you have described, then you are entitled to take the article back and reclaim your money. But you must have a cast-iron case. If you are at all doubtful about the article, try to get down in writing the purpose for which it is being bought. Otherwise you may have difficulty in proving your case.

As described
This is very simple. A handbag which is plastic should not be described as leather, or an acrylic jersey as wool, for example.

Buying from samples
The law here is very clear. If you make an order after studying samples, the goods ordered must be identical in colour, shape, quality and any other characteristic with the sample from which they were chosen.

Buying by mail order
Many people buy through mail order after seeing an advertisement in a catalogue or a newspaper. In such cases, you cannot examine the goods before taking them away, so you are forced to rely on the supplier's description. If there is any difference at all between the description of the goods and those which you receive, you are entitled to your money back. But you cannot, in law, return something just because you do not like it when you see it, although most mail-order firms allow you to do this. It is simply a matter of whether the description tallies with the actual article.

Newspapers, which rely for the bulk of their revenue on advertising, are very anxious to maintain high standards in advertising, particularly in the mail order sphere. If you have any complaints, do not complain only to the advertiser, but also to the editor and advertising manager of the newspaper. They can put pressure on any recalcitrant advertiser who does not immediately offer a replacement for the faulty item or give you your money back. *Do not think that you are being a nuisance by complaining. It is a neighbourly act.*

Guarantees

Should you or should you not sign a guarantee when you purchase goods? You will very probably have heard people say that a guarantee is not worth the paper it is written on, that you sign away some of your consumer rights or that the article must be covered by the 'merchantable quality' and 'fit for the purpose' rulings, anyway, so why bother with a guarantee at all?

Some of the comments used to be true in certain cases. If you did not sign a guarantee, you did not place yourself within the limits of the conditions in the guarantee. But all that has now changed.

Shopkeepers and dealers are no longer allowed to put limiting clauses in any guarantee they may offer. If they do, these clauses can be disregarded. *It is now in your interest to sign guarantees. Unless you do so, you may find that you have rights only against the person who sold you the goods and not against the manufacturer.*

Nevertheless, read the guarantee carefully to see just what it covers. Are parts and labour costs included, or is it just parts? What is the status of the company providing the guarantee? Is it covered by insurance? If the company offering the guarantee goes out of business, you will have no redress. This is very important, particularly when you have home improvements done. A lot of companies vanish from the scene, leaving behind disappointed customers and shoddy work.

Services

The Unfair Contract Terms Act 1977 and the 1982 Supply of Goods and Services Act brought the law on services into line with sales. Disclaimers for liability for personal injuries, death or damage to property which result from negligence have no legal standing. If, for instance, your coat is ruined at the dry-cleaners, the cleaner can no longer disclaim liability simply because he exhibits a notice saying so. But, if you are warned beforehand that it might be damaged and you accept the risk, you have no redress if something goes wrong. You may still see disclaimers. Remember they are not legally valid. The Act also puts the hiring of goods under the Sale of Goods Act 1973, and hirers must now guarantee that the goods they offer are fit for use. Similarly, contractors can no longer disclaim responsibility for working materials.

Since 4 July 1983, if you have no express agreement with someone who does a service for you, the law requires that the supplier must carry out the work with *reasonable* care and skill, and within a *reasonable* time. In return, you must pay a *reasonable* price.

When you lose your rights
In certain circumstances you may lose your rights under the law. We have already seen, for example, that when a defect is pointed out before you buy, you cannot get your money back.

The same applies when you are known to have examined something carefully yourself before buying and the flaw is such that your examination would have revealed it. You would have better protection in law if you had made only a very superficial examination.

If you are buying a car, for instance, it might be better to rely on the seller's word that it works properly rather than test it yourself. If you have tested it, you will have no case against the dealer. So, if you know nothing about cars, either get in an experienced person to test it, or take the dealer's word for it. If you have a car tested by the AA or RAC, they will accept responsibility for any faults they do not discover.

This is particularly important with cars, but the same principle applies to everything you buy, even though the purchase may not be particularly important in your overall budget.

If you buy privately from someone who is not in the business of selling that particular item, it is assumed that you have examined whatever you are buying and are satisfied with its condition. You will have no redress under the law.

The law does not allow you simply to change your mind after buying something, nor if you damage the goods yourself, or got the item as a present – the purchaser must always make the claim.

How the law is enforced
Below the Office of Fair Trading, which supervises all consumer law, are the trading standards officers (who used to be the weights and measures inspectors). They are employed by local authorities and are responsible for seeing that the various laws protecting the consumer are not flouted. If you have a problem and cannot get satisfaction from the retailer, go first to them. They do not deal with all aspects of consumer law themselves, however.

Local authorities employ environmental health officers (previously public health inspectors and before that sanitary inspectors) who are responsible for the cleanliness of restaurants and foods shops and for the quality of food. And many councils now have consumer advice centres, which offer a wide variety of advice. Check in your area. These centres exist not only to help you if something goes wrong, but also to help you make the right choice in the first place.

There is also a second tier of government-sponsored organizations. The best known of these are the National Consumer Council, the Scottish, Welsh and Northern Ireland consumer councils and the councils for the various nationalized industries. These organizations are not responsible for enforcing the law, but advise the government on general policy matters. They do not normally deal with individual cases.

Next come a wide variety of voluntary organizations. These do not have anything to do with law enforcement, either, but they have plenty to say for themselves and put a lot of pressure on official bodies for action. The Consumers' Association is the best known of these. It publishes the various *Which?* magazines, which are almost essential reading for sensible consumers. Among these publications is *Money Which?*. This can help you with your money problems, but even more useful is the general monthly publication *Which?*, which sets out the pros and cons of a wide variety of products. *Which?* will always suggest a 'best buy', but you can easily work out your own individual choice from the range of information offered.

3 Buying second-hand goods

Buying from a shop or dealer

We saw in the last chapter how the customer is protected by the law when he buys anything, and how the law also protects you when you buy imperfect goods – or 'seconds'.

These laws for the protection of shoppers also protect people buying second-hand, as long as they buy from a shop or a dealer rather than from a private seller or at an auction (see below). Anything you buy from a shop or dealer must be of 'merchantable quality' and 'fit for the purpose' and 'as described', as I set out in the last chapter, even if it is second-hand.

The problem is whether the goods are 'saleable', and this will depend to a large extent on the price being asked. Almost everything which is sold is worth *something*, so it is a matter of getting the price right for the condition of the article in question. The wise buyer will look particularly carefully at anything second-hand before buying – though he will actually be in a less strong position legally than the person who makes no such examination, as the latter cannot be presumed to have known what the defects were at the time of buying, whereas the careful buyer can.

Cars are a notorious example of this. If you are sensible, you will get a qualified engineer to examine a car before you buy it. But if a fault then develops, the dealer can argue that you ought to have known about it, as the engineer should have discovered any fault that was there at the time. *If the AA or RAC check a car for you before buying, they now accept responsibility for any defects they overlooked.*

Even if you do not have a proper inspection of a car – or indeed any other purchase – before buying, anyone who deals fraudulently with you can be prosecuted under the Trade Descriptions Act. A dealer who puts a car mileometer back to persuade the buyer that the car has been less used than it has been, can be fined and the customer compensated. If you complain to them, the local trading standards officers will carry out an inspection for you. Estate agents, however, are one group exempt from the Act, which accounts for the fanciful way many of them describe the premises they sell. They have their own Act, which is far less comprehensive.

Under the Supply of Goods (Implied Terms) Act 1973, a garage cannot put anything in the 'small print' of a sale contract which takes away the buyer's right to a car which is serviceable, even though it is second-hand.

Buying at auctions

If you become a collector of any of the things discussed in Section five, chapter 8, you will probably at some time try your hand at buying at an auction. Remember that special rules apply when you buy at auctions.

Most important of all, you will have no protection as far as 'merchantable quality' goes – though you can sometimes claim under the Misrepresentation Act 1967 if what you buy turns out to be a fake (if it was claimed to be genuine) or is not what the catalogue said it was.

There are certain regulations regarding the proper conduct of auctions, however:

- The highest bidder always gets the goods, unless there is a 'reserve' price which the bidding does not reach. If you have made a bid and want to change your mind, you must do it before the auctioneer's hammer falls. After that, you are the owner whether you want to be or not.
- The auctioneer is usually the agent of the seller, but he can sign the purchase agreement on behalf of the buyer once it has actually been bought.
- An auctioneer is not allowed to buy articles from a seller without the latter's permission. If he does buy with permission, he cannot deduct any commission from the selling price. Anyone can claim against an auctioneer, if he thinks the auctioneer has cheated by buying himself. Such a claim can be made even quite a long time after the event, and it

is then up to the auctioneer to prove that he had the consent of the seller to buy.

- If you set a reserve price, the auctioneer must know what it is, but bidders are not told. If the highest bid is below the reserve, then the person who made it cannot insist on buying whatever is under offer.

  In a house auction, the printed conditions must state whether the seller has the right to bid and if there is a reserve below which the seller will not sell.

- It is illegal for two or more professionals to get together and agree not to bid against one another – which means that one of them can get something at a lower price than if the bidding was open. This activity is known as 'the ring'. The penalty can be from six months' to two years' imprisonment.

  If you think this is happening, you may have trouble proving it. But if you can do so, you are entitled to get the object back from the dealer, and, if he has already sold it, you are entitled to damages from all the dealers who were involved in the ring.

- No seller can take part in the bidding himself in an attempt to push up prices, or employ what is called a 'puffer' to bid for him. Any seller who wants to take part in the bidding will have to give this information in the catalogue, or it will be announced by the auctioneer when the 'lot' – as each item or set of items is called – is called by the auctioneer.

  If a buyer is tricked by this ploy, he can make the seller take the object back or claim damages from him. If two people engage in fake bidding, they can be sued for criminal conspiracy.

- Auctioneers must not pretend to accept bids which have not been made. This is known as 'taking bids out of the air' and can result in a prosecution for deception.

Unsolicited goods

In the past, many people used to receive an enormous variety of goods through the post, accompanied by an invoice, so that if the recipient liked them he could simply send back a payment. This is called 'inertia selling', and can be very annoying. Some companies even went so far as to threaten people who ignored their offers, and did not return them, with court action. All this has now been outlawed under the Unsolicited Goods and Services Act 1971. Should you receive anything through the post in this way you can just ignore it, and you need not spend any money on postage to send it back to the company involved. You can become the legal owner of anything which comes to you in this way by:

1 Doing nothing. If the firm does not come to collect the item within six months, it belongs to the person to whom it was sent. Take care, however, not to stop anyone collecting it.

2 Writing to the company concerned and telling them to come and collect the goods, giving a name and address for collection. On receipt of such a letter, they must act within thirty days or the goods belong to the person to whom they were sent.

4 The law on credit purchases

It's all very well to appreciate why borrowing to buy the things you need is a sensible thing to do in a period of inflation when the value of money is falling, but it is also very necessary to understand the law as it relates to the various methods of financing any purchases whereby you defer payment over a period. The aim of the law here is to protect both the purchaser of the goods and the seller, or lender of the money.

All agreements, whether they are hire purchase, credit sales, leasing or rentals, which are for £15,000 or less, come under the Consumer Credit Act, which protects the customer. *Remember, it is the amount you actually borrow which determines whether you are covered by the Act.*

The regulations under the Consumer Credit Act 1974 were phased in gradually. Since May 1977, those who operate in the business of giving credit must have a licence to do so if they make credit agreements of more than £30, and since November 1977 credit reference agencies who amend their files on a consumer's credit-worthiness have been required by law to send the revised information to any traders to whom they had supplied earlier information on a particular customer. Potential customers who are refused credit must now be told the reason why.

The Consumer Credit Act 1974 finally became fully operative ten years later when the 1964 Hire Purchase Act was repealed. This left us with just one law regulating the whole business of consumer credit.

First of all, you must understand the difference between the two forms of credit purchase – *hire purchase* and *credit sale*. In general, a hire purchase agreement is complicated and a credit sale simple. This is because with hire purchase you do not own whatever you may think you have 'bought' until you have made the last payment under the agreement. You literally 'hire' it until that point.

What happens is that the finance company buys the goods from the retailer and then hires them out to the buyer, signing them over when the last payment has been made. There are about 1,000 companies in this business, but a few big ones dominate. If you arrange for a credit sale, on the other hand, you own the article from the moment you take delivery.

This basic difference of ownership at the point of the agreement means that there are important differences in the two contracts – differences which can have important legal implications. Let's look at some of them:

Defaulting on payments. With hire purchase, the lender has the right to take the goods back if the 'hirer' defaults on the payments. With a credit sale, he cannot. This further means that you cannot sell something that you are buying on hire purchase, because you are not the legal owner. There is no such prohibition with a credit sale – though if you do sell you may find that you are liable to make the whole remaining payment immediately. So check the contract.

The hirer – for that is what you are until you finish paying – is protected by the law in some ways. If less than one-third of what is owed has been paid and payments stop, the finance company has the legal right to send someone round to take the goods back. If more than a third has been paid, however, the company must get a court order before it can retrieve its property. If you have defaulted because you are in financial difficulties, a court may allow you to keep the goods. In that case it will fix a new scale of payments. In contrast, if you miss one payment under a credit sale deal, you become liable to pay the rest immediately.

The golden rule is, *if you get into difficulties over keeping up your payments, tell the company*. It will not want to go to court any more than you do and will often modify the agreement so that you can pay off over a longer period.

Returning the goods. Under a hire purchase deal, you can insist at any time that the company takes the goods back. When this happens you will not have to pay more than half the total hire purchase price, if the article has been kept in good condition. The court may rule that the payment is even less. If you have bought under a credit sale, you cannot cancel the agreement and send the stuff back, unless it is defective.

When there is a court order against you. If the bailiffs come to take away your furniture and other effects, they cannot take anything which is currently being bought on hire purchase, because it does not, legally speaking, belong to you until you have paid off the loan. The bailiffs can take anything away that you may be buying on a credit sale, because in that case you are the rightful owner.

Maintenance of the goods bought. Hire purchase agreements are complicated and often very long with a great deal of small print. Very few people bother to read the small print, but whether you read it or not you are bound by all the conditions of the contract. These will vary, but you will usually find that you are required to keep the goods in a sound condition and insure them against all risks until you are the real owner. If you buy something on credit sale, you can knock it about as much as you wish.

Under the Act, you can claim that you were misled when signing any